D0983755

JSOT/ASOR MONOGRAPH SERIES
5

**JOURNAL FOR THE STUDY OF THE OLD TESTAMENT
SUPPLEMENT SERIES**
115

JSOT Press
Sheffield

I HAVE BUILT
YOU AN
EXALTED HOUSE

Temple Building in the Bible in Light of Mesopotamian and Northwest Semitic Writings

Victor (Avigdor) Hurowitz

Journal for the Study of the Old Testament
Supplement Series 115
JSOT/ASOR Monograph Series 5

Published by JSOT Press
JSOT Press is an imprint of
Sheffield Academic Press Ltd
The University of Sheffield
343 Fulwood Road
Sheffield S10 3BP
England

Typeset by Sheffield Academic Press
and
Printed on acid-free paper in Great Britain
by Billing & Sons Ltd
Worcester

British Library Cataloguing in Publication Data

Hurowitz, Victor (Avigdor)
    I have built you an exalted house: temple building in
    the Bible in light of Mesopotamian and Northwest
    Semitic writings.—(JSOT/ASOR monograph; no. 5)
    I. Title II. Series
    III. JSOT supplement, ISSN 0309-0787; 115
    299.1

ISBN 1-85075-282-6

מנחת תודה להורי
דב בער (ברטרם) בן אבינדור שליט״א
שרה (סיידי) בת אהרון ז״ל נ״ע
כי מידכם הכל ומידכם נתתי לכם

CONTENTS

Part II

THE ACCOUNT OF BUILDING THE TEMPLE IN JERUSALEM (1 KINGS
5.15–9.25) IN LIGHT OF MESOPOTAMIAN AND NORTHWEST SEMITIC
WRITINGS

PREFACE

It is with great pleasure that, nearly twenty years after embarking on an investigation of temple dedication ceremonies in the Bible, I can present to the interested reader this study of temple building in the ancient Near East. This work has gone through a long and arduous gestation—growing from seminar papers and a master's thesis, into a doctoral dissertation, and then journal articles, papers at conferences and classroom lectures. It has benefited from countless discussions with teachers, colleagues, students, friends and relatives. In its present form, it is a substantially revised, expanded and updated English version of my Hebrew University PhD dissertation.

Due to circumstances beyond my control, the publication of this book has taken somewhat longer than anticipated. In order to keep the work as up-to-date as possible, several relevant new studies which have appeared since February 1988 have been added to the bibliography and have been referred to briefly in the footnotes, but no major revisions have been introduced.

From among the numerous people who have assisted me through their advice, criticism, friendship and support, I would like to thank above all my doctoral advisors at the Hebrew University, Professors Menahem Haran and Aaron Shaffer; Professor Hayim Tadmor, with whom I had the great privilege to study Mesopotamian royal inscriptions and discuss many aspects of the present work; and Professor Donald J. Wiseman, who directed my studies during my year as a student at the School of Oriental and African Studies, University of London. I am most grateful to the Lady Davis Fellowship Trust for their generous support of my doctoral studies from 1977 to 1979. I would also like to thank Mrs Nirah Naveh, Mr Curt Arnson, Dr Philip Miller and Mr Peter Salinger, the librarians of (respectively) the Hebrew University Library of Archaeology and Assyriology, Hebrew Union College, Jerusalem, Hebrew Union College, New York, and the School of Oriental and African Studies,

University of London. I am grateful for their patience, assistance and innumerable special favors. Final work on the proofs and indexes was done during a Sabbatical year, 1991–92, spent as a fellow at the Annenberg Research Institute for Judaic and Near Eastern Studies in Philadelphia. I am most appreciative of the time, ideal working conditions and generous stipend provided by the Institute. Lastly I would like to express my love and deep gratitude to my wife Channie and my son Daniel, for helping me understand what Qoheleth learned from Siduri.

Philadelphia
23 Addaru I, 5752
24 February, 1992

ABBREVIATIONS

AAA	*Annals of Archaeology and Anthropology* (Institute of Archaeology, Liverpool)
AB	Anchor Bible
AbB	F.R. Kraus, *Altbabylonische Briefe in Umschrift und Übersetzung, Heft 1: Briefe aus dem British Museum (CT 43, 44)*
ABL	*Assyrian and Babylonian Letters*
AfO	*Archiv für Orientforschung*
AfOB	*Archiv für Orientforschung*, Beiheft
AHw	W. von Soden, *Akkadisches Handwörterbuch*
AJA	*American Journal of Archaeology*
AJSL	*American Journal of Semitic Languages and Literatures*
AKA	E.A. Wallis Budge and L.W. King (eds.), *Annals of the Kings of Assyria*
AnBib	Analecta biblica
ANEP	J.B. Pritchard (ed.), *Ancient Near East in Pictures, Relating to the Old Testament*
ANET	J.B. Pritchard (ed.), *Ancient Near Eastern Texts*
AnOr	Analecta orientalia
AnSt	*Anatolian Studies*
AOAT	Alter Orient und Altes Testament
AOS	American Oriental Series
ARAB	D.D. Luckenbill, *Ancient Records of Assyria and Babylonia*
ARI	A.K. Grayson, *Assyrian Royal Inscriptions*
ARM	Archives royales de Mari
ArOr	*Archív orientální*
ARRIM	*Annual Review of the Royal Inscriptions of Mesopotamia Project*
AS	Assyriological Studies
ATD	Das Alte Testament Deutsch
BA	*Biblical Archaeologist*
BARev	*Biblical Archaeology Review*
BASOR	*Bulletin of the American Schools of Oriental Research*
BB	A. Ungnad, *Babylonische Briefe aus der Zeit der Hammurapi-Dynastie*
BHK	R. Kittel (ed.), *Biblia Hebraica*
Bib	*Biblica*
BO	*Bibliotheca Orientalis*
BKAT	Biblischer Kommentar: Altes Testament

BZAW	Beiheft zur *Zeitschrift für die alttestamentliche Wissenschaft*
CBQ	*Catholic Biblical Quarterly*
ConBOT	Coniectanea biblica, Old Testament
CT	Cuneiform Texts from the British Museum
EA	J.A. Knudtzon, *Die El-Amarna-Tafeln, mit Einleitung und Erläuterungen*
EM	*Encyclopaedia Miqra' it* (Hebrew)
FRLANT	Forschungen zur Religion und Literatur des Alten und Neuen Testaments
GKC	*Gesenius' Hebrew Grammar*, ed. E. Kautzsch, trans. A.E. Cowley
HAR	*Hebrew Annual Review*
HP	M.J. Seux, *Hymnes et prieres aux dieux de babylonie et d'assyrie* (Paris: Cerf, 1976)
HSM	Harvard Semitic Monographs
HSS	Harvard Semitic Studies
HUCA	*Hebrew Union College Annual*
IAK	*Die Inschriften der altassyrischen Könige* (Ebeling, Meissner and Weidner 1926)
IB	*Interpreter's Bible*
ICC	International Critical Commentary
IDBSup	*Interpreter's Dictionary of the Bible: Supplementary Volume*
IEJ	*Israel Exploration Journal*
IRSA	E. Sollberger and J.-R. Kupper, *Inscriptions royales sumériennes et akkadiennes*
JANESCU	*Journal of the Ancient Near Eastern Society of Columbia University*
JAOS	*Journal of the American Oriental Society*
JBL	*Journal of Biblical Literature*
JCS	*Journal of Cuneiform Studies*
JEOL	*Jaarbericht. . . ex oriente lux*
JESHO	*Journal of Economic and Social History of the Orient*
JNES	*Journal of Near Eastern Studies*
JPOS	*Journal of the Palestine Oriental Society*
JQR	*Jewish Quarterly Review*
JRAS	*Journal of the Royal Asiatic Society*
JSOT	*Journal for the Study of the Old Testament*
JSOTSup	*Journal for the Study of the Old Testament*, Supplement Series
JSS	*Journal of Semitic Studies*
JTS	*Journal of Theological Studies*
KAH	L. Messerschmidt, *Keilschrifttexte aus Assur historischen Inhalts*
KAI	H. Donner and W. Röllig, *Kanaanäische und aramäische Inschriften*
KAR	*Keilschrifttexte aus Assurs religiösen Inhalts*
KB	*Keilinschriftliche Bibliothek*
KTU	M. Dietrich *et al.*, *Die keilalphabetischen Texte aus Ugarit, einschliesslich der keilalphabetischen Texte ausserhalb Ugarits*

LAS	S. Parpola, *Letters from Assyrian Scholars to the Kings Esarhaddon and Assurbanipal*
Leš	*Lešonénu*
LFM	A.L. Oppenheim, *Letters from Mesopotamia—Official, Business and Private Letters of Clay Tablets from Two Millennia*
LKA	E. Ebeling, *Literarische Keilschrifttexte aus Assur*
MAOG	Mitteilungen der altorientalischen Gesellschaft
MARI	*Mari: Annales de recherches interdisciplinaires*
MRS IX	J. Nougayrol, *Le palais royal d'Ugarit IV: Textes accadiens des archives sud* (Mission de Ras Shamra, 9)
MRS XI	C. Virolleaud, *Le palais royal d'Ugarit V: Textes en cunéiformes alphabétiques des archives sud sud-ouest et du petit palais* (Mission de Ras Shamra, 11)
MVAG	Mitteilungen der vorderasiatisch-ägyptischen Gesellschaft
NAB	*New American Bible*
NBU I	E. Ebeling, *Neubabylonische Briefe aus Uruk*, I
NCB	New Century Bible
NEB	*The New English Bible*
NJPSV	*TANAKH: A New Translation of the Holy Scriptures according to the Traditional Hebrew Text*
OIP	Oriental Institute Publications
OLZ	*Orientalistische Literaturzeitung*
Or	*Orientalia*
OTL	Old Testament Library
OTS	*Oudtestamentische Studiën*
PAPS	*Proceedings of the American Philosophical Society*
PEQ	*Palestine Exploration Quarterly*
PTMS	Pittsburgh Theological Monograph Series
RA	*Revue d'assyriologie et d'archéologie orientale*
RB	*Revue biblique*
RCAE	L. Waterman, *Royal Correspondence of the Assyrian Empire*
RHPR	*Revue d'historie et de philosophie religieuses*
RIMA	*Royal Inscriptions of Mesopotamia*
RLA	E. Ebeling, B. Meissner *et al.*, *Reallexicon der Assyriologie*
RSP	L.R. Fisher and S. Hummel (eds.), *Ras Shamra Parallels*
SAHG	A. Falkenstein and W. von Soden, *Sumerische und akkadische Hymnen und Gebete*
SANT	Studien zum Alten und Neuen Testament
SBLDS	SBL Dissertation Series
SBLSBS	SBL Sources for Biblical Study
SBLMS	SBL Monograph Series
SBT	Studies in Biblical Theology
StudOr	Studia orientalia
SSI	J.C.L. Gibson, *Textbook of Syrian Semitic Inscriptions*
TCL	Textes cunéiformes du Louvre
TCS	*Texts from Cuneiform Sources*

TDNT	G. Kittel and G. Friedrich (eds.), *Theological Dictionary of the New Testament*
ThWAT	G.J. Botterweck and H. Ringgren (eds.), *Theologisches Wörterbuch zum Alten Testament*
UET	*Ur Excavation Texts*
UF	*Ugarit-Forschungen*
UT	C.H. Gordon, *Ugaritic Textbook*
VAB	Vorderasiatische Bibliothek
VT	*Vetus Testamentun*
VTSup	*Vetus Testamentum*, Supplements
WMANT	Wissenschaftliche Monographien zum Alten und Neuen Testament
WO	*Die Welt des Orients*
WVDOG	*Wissenschaftliche Veröffentlichungen der Deutschen Orient-Gesellschaft*
YNER	Yale Near Eastern Researches
YOS	Yale Oriental Series
ZA	*Zeitschrift für Assyriologie*
ZAW	*Zeitschrift für die alttestamentliche Wissenschaft*
ZDMG	*Zeitschrift der deutschen morgenländischen Gesellschaft*

INTRODUCTION

The Problem

> Is this not great Babylon, which I have built by my vast power to be a
> royal residence for the glory of my majesty? (Dan. 4.27).

For nearly two millennia, Nebuchadnezzar's arrogant boast was, for
the Western observer, one of the rare and precious memories of how
the ancient monarchs of Mesopotamia viewed their own construction
projects. The accuracy of this recollection may be indicated by the
words of James A. Montgomery, who, commenting on this verse,
remarks: 'Every student of Babylonia recalls these proud words in
reading Nebuchadnezzar's own records of his creation of the new
Babylon'.[1] Another biblical allusion to the role of the ancient Near

---

1. See Montgomery 1927: 243, and note Wiseman 1983: 42. Nebuchadnezzar's
'tour' of Babylon from atop his palace, mentioned in the previous verse, is
reminiscent of the advice given to the reader of the Gilgamesh epic (col. I 9-16 and
cf. XI 302-303; see Tigay 1982: 141-42, 261ff.): *ušēpiš dūra ša Uruk supūri ša
É.AN.NA qudduši šutummi ellim amur dūršu. . .ittaplas samētāšu . . .elīma ina
muḫḫi dūri ša Uruk itallak*, 'He had built the wall of Uruk the sheepfold, of hallowed
Eanna, the holy storehouse. Behold its outer wall. . .peer at its inner wall. . . Go up
onto the wall of Uruk and walk about.' In both cases, the tour is meant to impress
the reader/sightseer with the great works of the royal builder, thus giving the great
builder eternal life through fame. This idea, which, in the case of Nebuchadnezzar, is
immediately refuted by a voice from heaven, becomes a butt of satire in the 'Dialogue
of Pessimism' (W.G. Lambert 1967: 148 ll. 76-78), where the obliging servant tells
his master: *ilīma ina muḫḫi tillāni labīrūtu itallak amur gulgullē ša arkûti u pānûti ajû
bēl limuttimma ajû bēl usāti*, 'Go up onto the ancient rubble heaps and walk about.
See the skulls of recent and ancient (men). Which is the malefactor and which is the
benefactor?' The same theme is played upon, apparently, in Ps. 48.13-15 as well.
There, the pilgrim to Zion is invited to '*Walk around Zion, circle it, count* its towers,
take note of its ramparts; *go through* its citadels, that you may recount it to a future
age. For God—he is our God forever; he will lead us over death.' Zion is God's
city, founded by him forever (v. 9), and eternal life is offered to the pilgrim who
takes pride in God's city.

Eastern king as builder, this one of an ancient 'wise man', appears in Job's desperate wish:

> For now would I be lying in repose, asleep and at rest, with the world's kings and counselors who rebuild ruins for themselves (Job 3.13-14).[1]

This appraisal too is quite realistic, according well with the self-estimation of ancient Near Eastern sovereigns themselves.[2] Over a century of discovery, decipherment and publication of monuments and documents from the 'Lands of the Bible' shows that royal (and divine) building activities served as a prevalent and respected theme for the styluses and chisels of court and temple scribes from all over ancient West Asia. This is readily seen from the testimony of hundreds of building inscriptions,[3] and from literary, poetic and mythic works originating in Egypt, Mesopotamia, Aram, Canaan, and even Israel.[4]

---

1. See Pope 1965 *ad loc.*; Gordis 1978: 37 *ad loc.* Note as well Eccl. 2.4-6, where Qoheleth, in a feint of kingship, asserts, 'I multiplied my possessions, I built myself houses and I planted vineyards. I laid out gardens and groves, in which I planted every kind of fruit tree. I constructed pools of water, enough to irrigate a forest shooting up with trees.' These items are no more and no less than the accomplishments proclaimed by Assyrian kings such as Assurnasirpal II, Sargon II and Sennacherib, all of whom tell in their building accounts of royal palaces, gardens and parks, and canals to irrigate them.

2. For the role of building temples in the image of the Mesopotamian king, see Labat 1939: 177-240; Frankfort 1948: 267-74; Lackenbacher 1982. For the place of building in the characterization of the Israelite king, see Ahlström 1982: 1-6, 10-43.

3. The importance of building in the self-depiction of the kings is expressed not only in building stories in which the king plays the dominant, central role, but also in the kings' titularies. For these royal titles, see Seux 1967 under the Akkadian entries *banû, edēšu, epēšu, ḫerû, kânu (mukīn māḫāzi), petû, šuklulu, šuršudu* and the Sumerian entries *dím, dù, gibil* and the derivative terms. According to Mesopotamian mythology, humanity was created to relieve the gods of carrying brick baskets. See *Atra-ḫasīs* (Lambert and Millard 1969), and the newly published myth concerning the creation of man, Mayer 1987: 55-68. Note as well Gadd 1948: 7 n. 1.

4. The Bible is not the only repository for descriptions of royal building projects. According to the testimony of the editor of the book of Kings, royal building activities were reported in even greater detail in the sources which he had at his disposal, such as the Chronicles of the Kings of Judah and Israel. See, for example, 1 Kgs 15.23, 22.39, and 2 Kgs 20.20. Similar references occur throughout the biblical book of Chronicles. Unfortunately, such original records did not survive, nor are there any extant Israelite royal building inscriptions. It is also unclear whether the building reports said to be contained in the 'Chronicles' were based on

In light of the numerous documents which are concerned either partially or completely with building, and considering the well-known connections between ancient Israelite literature and the writings of its neighbors in so many areas, the question poses itself whether in the accounts of building projects there is something to be learned from one corpus about the other. Is it possible to uncover, in the many biblical and extra-biblical writings dealing with building activities, certain points of similarity, literary or ideological parallels, and even genetic links? Furthermore, if such parallels and similarities do in fact exist—a matter of no small importance and interest unto itself—what is their significance, how can they enlighten us about the development of biblical literature, and what can they teach us about the beliefs, ideas and customs of biblical Israel?

Previous Studies

The possibility that the building stories found in the Bible are in fact comparable with the accounts of building projects which have reached us from the writings of the peoples surrounding Israel has, to be sure, not been beyond the thoughts of several scholars of the Bible and the ancient Orient, and occasional suggestions to this effect are encountered in a number of studies and scientific commentaries.

A small part of the extra-biblical writings bearing on 1 Kgs 5.15–9.25 (the unit which will occupy center stage in the present study) has been presented (albeit unsystematically) by Montgomery and Gehman in their commentary on the book of Kings.[1] Nonetheless, because of methodological considerations, comparison between this biblical account and foreign literary sources was not exploited or further developed by Martin Noth in his subsequent monumental commentary.[2] On the contrary: Noth almost entirely ignored the pertinent extra-biblical building accounts, and it may well be assumed that he

---

or in any way related to inscriptions placed within the buildings. The famous Siloam inscription (*KAI* 189) is most likely not an official, royal account of the project, but is probably more of a 'graffito' prepared by the workmen engaged in hewing out the tunnel. The lack of any of the elements typical of the building stories to be discussed below, as well as the emphasis the inscription places on the activities of the workmen themselves, would seem to lend support to this evaluation. See Sasson 1982–83.

1. Montgomery and Gehman 1951.
2. Noth 1968.

considered them irrelevant to solving the problems of the book of
Kings and its literary growth. Extra-biblical texts are stressed once
again in B. Long's recent form-critical introduction and overview of
the book of Kings.[1]

The ancient Near Eastern material relating to building projects
likewise has only slightly influenced commentaries on other biblical
books containing either major building stories or matter otherwise
relevant to temple buildings, such as Exodus–Numbers, Ezekiel 40–
48, Zechariah, Haggai, Ezra–Nehemiah and Chronicles. Notable
exceptions are S. Mowinckel's studies of Ezra–Nehemiah which relate
Nehemiah's memoirs to Mesopotamian royal inscriptions,[2] several
recent articles and commentaries on the books of Zechariah and
Haggai,[3] and my own inquiry into the Priestly account of building the
Tabernacle.[4]

Of particular significance for the present study are the two ground-
breaking contributions of A.S. Kapelrud[5] and M. Weinfeld.[6] These
scholars, each in his own way, compared more than half a dozen
biblical and extra-biblical building stories so as to demonstrate that
they were all written according to the same literary pattern. They
identified the component elements of this literary pattern, and, on the
basis of the overall similarity between the stories investigated, tried to
reach certain conclusions about the literary history of the account of
Solomon's temple building project. In particular, it was proposed that
Solomon's dream at Gibeon, in which God granted him wisdom with
which to judge the people of Israel (1 Kgs 3), is actually a substitute
for an original dream in which God commanded him to build a temple.

1.   Long 1984: 78-115.
2.   Mowinckel 1964. For the extra-biblical evidence relating to Cyrus's decree
permitting the restoration of the Temple, see Bickerman 1946; de Vaux 1971; and
Tadmor 1964. The Aramaic letters in Ezra 4–6, and especially their similarities to the
papyri dealing with the restoration of the Jewish temple in Elephantine have been
recently discussed by Porten (1978). Rebuilding the temple in Jerusalem is also mentioned as an event of the not too distant past in a prayer of Ezra in Ezra 9.9. On the
language used, see Avishur 1982. Echoes of rebuilding the Temple are heard as well
in Isa. 44.24-28; 60.
3.   See the commentary of E. and C. Meyers 1987 and Halpern 1978 with
bibliography.
4.   Hurowitz 1985.
5.   Kapelrud 1963.
6.   Weinfeld 1972: 244-54.

It must be admitted that some individual aspects of these suggestions have not been received with universal approval.[1] Nonetheless, the weaknesses in several details of the proposals, as well as the fact that only a small portion of the extant extra-biblical material has been exploited, do not detract from the overall validity of the assertions that certain biblical and extra-biblical building stories are written according to a common, well-defined literary pattern and that they contain various shared ideas. Furthermore, one can only welcome the attempt to exploit this basic insight as an instrument for advancing the solution to several problems which have arisen in the course of routine literary criticism of the biblical stories. In my opinion, recognition of the structural and ideological similarity between certain biblical and extra-biblical accounts of building projects is both correct and illuminating, and may serve as a seminal point of departure for a more detailed investigation of the biblical stories about building temples.

Goals

The present work is a detailed comparative and contrastive[2] study of biblical and other ancient Near Eastern accounts of temple building. For reasons of convenience it will be presented as an inquiry into a single biblical story—the account of Solomon's construction of the Jerusalem Temple that appears in 1 Kgs 5.15–9.25. It will investigate the points of similarity and difference as well as the nature of the relationship between this biblical pericope and several descriptions of building projects collected in the course of a sweeping survey of royal building inscriptions and literary works of various genres which have been recovered from the writings of Mesopotamia and the Levant.[3]

---

1. See, for example, Rofé 1973; Zalevsky 1972–73; Rummel 1981: 277-84; Brekelmans 1982: 53-59; Kenik 1983: 34-38, 181-82 n. 11. The suggestion made by Kapelrud and Weinfeld concerning the original content of Solomon's dream will be discussed below at the end of Chapter 8.

2. For the importance of contrast in comparative studies, see the programmatic remarks of Hallo 1977, 1980.

3. See below for the sources upon which this study is based. I am incapable of dealing first hand with Egyptian writings, and have had to rely solely on investigation of standard collections of translated texts. I should state, however, that, in perusing corpora such as Breasted 1906 and Lichtheim 1973, 1976 and 1980, I was left

Despite concentration on the story found in the book of Kings, the other building accounts found in the Bible will not be ignored, and such material as can be illuminated by the available extra-bibilical material will be discussed.

The first part of this book will examine the building reports as complete literary units. The thematic structures of a selection of building accounts will be analysed, the accounts will be compared with one another, and an attempt will be made to point out the similarity between the thematic structures of the extra-biblical stories and the structure of the story of building the Temple in Jerusalem which appears in 1 Kings. It will also be shown that the same literary pattern found in these accounts also underlies the Priestly story of building the Tabernacle in Exodus 25–Numbers 7, the story of rebuilding the (Second) Temple in Ezra 1–6, Nehemiah's account of repairing the Walls of Jerusalem, and perhaps even Josephus's account of the Herodian rebuilding and aggrandizement of the Temple. This section will continue, in essence, along the way set out by Kapelrud and Weinfeld, but it will bolster considerably their basic conclusion concerning the existence of a common type of building account in the literatures of several neighboring cultures. At the same time, however, the analysis and comparison will be much more comprehensive. Many more texts will be considered, and they will be examined in far greater detail than before. Expanding the textual basis for the investigation from slightly more than a handful of texts to several dozen compositions will make it possible to reach conclusions somewhat different from those reached by previous scholars, pertaining to the characteristics shared by the various stories and the ultimate description of the literary topos.

In the second part of this work, several individual aspects of the building stories will be investigated, following the order of their appearance in the texts examined in Part I. In what might be called a 'comparative–contrastive close reading', the chapters in Part II will compare the account in 1 Kings not only with the stories which were presented in the first part of the work, but with many more extra-

with the impression that building accounts similar to those known from Mesopotamia and Israel were not common in Egyptian writings. Hittite texts provide us with several detailed building rituals (see Kellerman 1980; Unal 1988), but there seem to be no examples of the type of building accounts which will be the topic of discussion here.

biblical building stories and with documents representing several other literary genres.

In all sections of the discussion considerable attention will be directed towards literary and form-critical questions, utilizing structural, linguistic and stylistic similarities and differences as a tool in defining the literary 'forms' or genres composing the biblical passage. Nonetheless, interest will not be restricted to literary issues. The chapters dealing with the decision to build, the acquisition of building materials, dedication ceremonies and building prayers will contain lengthy discussions of matters relating to religious beliefs and ideas, cult, and material culture. The concluding section will address briefly the 'higher-critical' problem of the literary history and development of the Temple building account in 1 Kings, applying the results of the previous chapters.

Limits

The present work will not touch at all upon questions of the architecture of the temples and the physical aspects of their appurtenances. The material and architectural facets of Israelite and other ancient Near Eastern temples have been discussed frequently and in great detail by biblical scholars, Assyriologists, archaeologists and art historians. On the basis of scriptural testimony together with external evidence of all sorts, frequent attempts have been made to conjure up a clear image of the Solomonic Temple and place it in its proper position in relationship to other ancient Near Eastern temples.[1] I hope eventually to make my own modest contribution in this area, but this is beyond the scope of the present work.[2]

Similarly, even though the finds of this study may have certain historical implications, no attempt will be made here to confront directly the questions which arise occasionally concerning the historical accuracy of the biblical account, and in particular the biblical tradition

1. See the modern commentaries and the appropriate articles in the various Bible dictionaries and encyclopaedias as well as several more detailed comparative studies such as Albright 1946: 142-45; Busink 1970; Ouellette 1966. For a recent popular synopsis of the archaeological finds relevant to the architecture of Solomon's Temple, see Fritz 1987. For a complete survey of Mesopotamian temples, see Heinrich 1982.

2. See Hurowitz, forthcoming 1, forthcoming 2 and forthcoming 3.

which attributes the building of the Temple to King Solomon.[1]

This study will make use of scores of extra-biblical documents, including numerous Mesopotamian sources. The mass of Akkadian and Sumerian material utilized here may give the mistaken impression that this work is intended primarily for the Assyriologist. The reader should rest assured, however, that the primary focus of this study is the Bible. For this reason, certain topics which occupy a prominent place in Mesopotamian building accounts—such as foundation rites or brick molding ceremonies—will not be discussed here at all, and this is because their importance for the Bible seems to be at most marginal.[2]

On the other hand, it is hoped that this study will not be without interest to the Assyriologist. Some topics which will be treated in the present framework at great length (precisely because of their importance in the Bible) have hitherto not been dealt with systematically in assyriological literature. Certain other topics have already been

1.   For the question of the existence of monumental architecture in Israel during the time of Solomon, see Albright 1958; Wightman 1990; and Dever 1990. Cf. the literary-critical studies of Waterman (1943, 1947, 1948), Wright 1948, and, most recently, the tradition-critical study of Rupprecht 1977. Waterman and Rupprecht, each in his own unique and independent way, attempt to demonstrate that the information transmitted in the Bible relating to the building of the Temple and the architecture of the Temple is not firmly rooted in traditions dating from the reign of Solomon. In Waterman's opinion, Solomon constructed nothing more than store-rooms for his treasures, and these structures, over the course of time, were converted into a sacred building. Rupprecht, for his part, suggests that in fact the building of the Temple predated Solomon. This king, according to Rupprecht, merely adapted a pre-existing Jebusite sanctuary to the needs of a new religion.

2.   Mesopotamian building rites, and in particular foundation ceremonies which could be expected to leave archaeologically detectable remains, have been discussed in detail by Ellis 1968. For an overall survey and synthetic look at temple building in Mesopotamia, see Frankfort 1948: 262-74; Labat 1939: 177-201. For the terminology and formulae of the Assyrian *Bauberichte* down to the time of Shalmaneser V (722 BCE), see Borger 1961 and Schramm 1973, *passim*. A fine detailed study of the Assyrian royal building accounts from the earliest inscriptions down to those of Tiglath-pileser III is now available in Lackenbacher 1982. For Sumerian and Akkadian building terminology and the practices reflected therein, see the dictionaries and specific studies such as Dunham 1982; Dunham 1986; Baumgartner 1925; Falkenstein 1966. Possible echoes of Israelite customs resembling Mesopotamian foundation rites may be heard in biblical passages such as Isa. 28.16; Ps. 118.22; Job 38.4-11; Ezra 3.8-13. For these see the commentaries and cf. Halpern 1978 and the previous literature cited there, as well as Roberts 1987.

studied by Assyriologists but in ways somewhat different from the way they will be investigated here. These topics include various literary aspects of the Gudea Cylinders, the thematic structure of the building stories, divine approval for building projects, acquisition of wood for building projects, and dedication ceremonies.

Finally, it should be pointed out that the subject of building comes up in the Bible dozens of times—both in brief references to building projects and in extended building accounts which are no shorter or less detailed than the story in 1 Kgs 5.15–9.25. This story itself has a parallel version occupying most of 1 Chronicles 17–2 Chronicles 8. The Chronicler's temple building account is demonstrably a tendentious reworking and expansion of an earlier story. Most of the additional material is clearly aimed at answering questions such as why did David not build the Temple, and how did Solomon become aware of David's desire to do so. It also serves tendentious purposes such as forging literary and ideological links between the Tabernacle and the Temple, depicting Solomon as the divinely sanctioned heir and temple builder, and, especially, enhancing David's personal contribution to the building project.[1] It perhaps even makes the Temple building story more relevant to an audience of the early Second Temple period by emphasizing the role of popular contributions to the building fund, and by introducing certain changes in the description of the temple itself. The building of the Tabernacle is described in the Priestly Source in the Pentateuch in Exodus 25–31, 35–40, Leviticus 8–10 and Numbers 7. Rebuilding the destroyed Jerusalem Temple is reported in Ezra 1–6, and this building project forms the background to and is addressed by the prophecies of Zechariah and Haggai. The long vision concluding the book of Ezekiel (chs. 40–48) begins with a detailed divine command concerning the rebuilding of the Temple and restoration of the cult at that time in the future when the Children of Israel will be ashamed of their sins. The bulk and literary backbone of Nehemiah's memoirs deals with the restoration of Jerusalem's breached walls and burnt gates (Neh. 1–6, 12). The books of Kings and Chronicles

1. See the commentaries as well as Braun 1973; Braun 1976; Williamson 1976; Seeligman 1979–80; Abramsky 1982; DeVries 1988. For an innovative look at David's role in building the temple, see Meyers 1987. Although reservations may be expressed about the soundness of reconstructing history solely from inference based on sociological models, it should be said to the author's credit that her case for David as temple builder is not based on the testimony of the book of Chronicles.

frequently refer to royal building projects including repairs carried
out in the Temple itself (2 Kgs 12, 14; 22, see 2 Chron. 24, 34).

It goes without saying that all these stories are subject to clarification with the help of comparison to extra-biblical building accounts,
and much of the material which will be presented below to illuminate
1 Kgs 5.15–9.25 is relevant to them as well. However, each story
presents its own particular problems and peculiarities, and in the
present framework there is room for a detailed comparative analysis
of only a single story. For this reason, it is fitting that discussion
should center around the biblical story which most resembles the
building stories known from outside the Bible, both in its overall structure and in numerous linguistic and ideological details. Furthermore,
the building story contained in the book of Kings developed and
approached its present 'canonical' form contemporaneously with the
Assyrian and neo-Babylonian building accounts which comprise the
most significant part of the extra-biblical corpus. In contrast, the
prophecies of Haggai and Zechariah (as well as the building reports
contained in the books of Ezra and Nehemiah) were composed after
the last of the major Mesopotamian building accounts known to us,[1]
and if there is any connection between them, it is in all probability
indirect. As for the Tabernacle story, its date of composition is still
questionable since it is inextricably tied up in the yet undecided
questions of the historical background and literary character of the
Priestly material in the Pentateuch. It may be from as early as the
time of Hezekiah, as claimed by Menahem Haran,[2] in which case it is
coeval with some of the major Assyrian building accounts to be discussed below. On the other hand, it may have reached its present form
in the Persian period, as is commonly held, in which case it is contemporary with only a diluted Mesopotamian tradition of building
accounts. Whether the present story is dated early or late, it may yet
be based on oral or written prototypes of much greater antiquity. Let
it be briefly stated, however, that comparison with extra-biblical
building accounts contributes, among other things, to clarifying the
complex problem of the evolution of the story and the relationship

---

1.   But cf. the inscription of Antiochus Soter (trans. A.L. Oppenheim in *ANET*,
p. 317; note Ellis 1968: 184 para. 42), dated 280–262 BCE, which still contains
echoes of classic Mesopotamian traditions and language.
2.   Haran 1978.

between the command and the implementation chapters, but these matters merit an independent inquiry.[1]

A Note about Terminology

In this work frequent use will be made of three basic expressions: royal inscription, building inscription and building story (account or report). These terms are similar but are not synonymous. They will be employed here in the following manner:[2]

a. *Royal Inscriptions*

These are inscriptions which report the deeds of a king (or occasionally a high official, a noble, or member of the royal family) at whose command, or in whose honor, the inscription was composed. The royal inscriptions had the purpose of eternalizing the name and fame of the kings by describing in varying degrees of detail their noteworthy accomplishments, with emphasis on warfare, hunting, legal, social and religious reforms, and, above all, public works such as building projects.[3]

b. *Building Inscriptions*

These are (royal) inscriptions composed on the occasion of constructing or repairing a given edifice and intended to perpetuate the name of the builder. Building inscriptions were usually placed somewhere within the building itself. A substantial portion of the known royal inscriptions are in fact building inscriptions. A building inscription frequently

1. See my articles, Hurowitz 1985, 1984.

2. For the native designations of the various types of inscriptions deposited or displayed in buildings, see Ellis 1968: 142-52. The literary and formal characteristics of the Mesopotamian royal inscriptions have been studied by Mowinckel 1923, and more recently Grayson 1980 with bibliography. For literary and formal discussions of individual royal inscriptions see Hallo 1961; Hallo 1962; Borger 1961; Schramm 1973; Langdon 1912; Berger 1973.

3. For the function of the royal inscriptions and their literary origins, see Speiser 1967: 270-312, and Oppenheim 1960. As for the reasons for composing royal inscriptions according to the native scribes, see the inscriptions of Nebuchadnezzar in Langdon 1912: 74 no. 1, col. II ll. 44-53; pp. 110ff. no. 13, col. II ll. 72–col. III l. 6: 'All my exalted deeds. . . I wrote upon a tablet and set it up for future times. All my deeds which I wrote on the tablet, may the informed see/read (them) and remember the glory of the gods *(tanitti ilāni liḫtasas)*.'

describes more of the king's memorable deeds than just the one particular building project, and the accounts of these deeds often occupy the vast majority of the inscription. But even in such cases, the building report remains primary. It is emphasized literarily by being placed at the end of the inscription or by being used as a literary framework for the rest of the inscription.

c. *Building Stories (Accounts or Reports)*

These are long or short prose or poetic narratives describing a building project. Most extant building stories appear within the context or serve as the literary framework of the royal building inscriptions, yet they may be found not infrequently in literary and historical works of varying 'genres' such as hymns, myths, epics and chronographic works. The building story is an extended, composite literary topos which can make up part or all of any composition.

Sources Used in this Study

Because of the nature of the extra-biblical sources concerning building projects, this investigation is based in large part on information gathered by surveying building inscriptions, royal inscriptions and various literary compositions. A full list of cuneiform royal inscriptions published before 1975 may be found in Borger 1965–75: III, 2-36. New material—some innovative and significant for this study—some merely repeating motives already known—is being published constantly, and naturally supplements the material listed in Borger's catalogue. An attempt has been made to keep abreast of this material and to include it where appropriate. New editions and translations of Sumerian and Akkadian royal inscriptions are presently in preparation under the auspices of the Royal Inscriptions of Mesopotamia Project at the University of Toronto, and the American Oriental Society Translation Series. The initial volumes of each series have recently appeared[1] and the reworking of the well-known material, as well as a modest amount of new material, is most welcome. Independently, H. Steible, I. Gelb and B. Kienast, and I. Kärki have produced corpora, respectively, of Sumerian royal inscriptions from Lagash and Akkadian royal inscriptions from the Sargonic and Old Babylonian

---

1.   See Grayson 1987; Cooper 1986; Frayne 1991.

periods.[1] Although these collections were examined in my quest for significant new material, it was impossible, unfortunately, to make full use of these publications, so that references are made to older, standard editions. Texts of all types which have been mentioned explicitly in this study have been listed in the bibliography. The bibliography also contains all the text catalogues and text collections (of editions and translations) which were reviewed in the course of my research. I am certain that I did not manage to uncover and become familiar with every known building account from the ancient Near East, but I am cautiously confident that the material upon which the present study is based is representative of what actually exists.

1. See Steible 1982; Gelb and Kienast 1990; Kärki 1983.

PART I

ANCIENT NEAR EASTERN BUILDING ACCOUNTS FROM GUDEA TO
HEROD: THE THEMATIC STRUCTURES OF SELECTED EXTRA-BIBLICAL
AND BIBLICAL BUILDING ACCOUNTS

Chapter 1

BUILDING STORIES IN SUMERIAN AND OLD BABYLONIAN LITERATURE

Temple building is a well-attested subject in Sumerian literature. Building accounts and references to building projects of various sorts appear in a variety of Sumerian writings.[1] There are also liturgical compositions of several types which mention building projects and which were apparently recited in the course of building rituals.[2] A thorough discussion of all of these interesting works would be well beyond the scope of this study. The analysis in the present chapter will be limited, therefore, to five compositions which have similar thematic

   1.   The Tummal Inscription, the legends concerning Amar-Suen, the Curse of Agade, Enmerkar and the Lord of Aratta, the pseudepigraphic inscription of Lugalannemundu, Enki's Journey to Nippur, Enki and the World Order, and Inanna and Ebiḫ are some of the important historiographic, epic and mythological works in which the building of temples plays a prominent role. Construction projects are also recorded in numerous date formulae or year names. The principal evidence concerning such projects is found, of course, in the building inscriptions themselves. It is common that a single building project will be recorded simultaneously in various literary genres, especially year names, royal hymns and building inscriptions (see e.g. Hallo 1970, esp. 118-19). There are also cases where the building inscriptions have incorporated the language of date formulae (see Frayne 1982).
   2.   Certain of the hymns in honor of or addressed to temples, gods and kings (the so-called 'temple hymns', 'divine hymns' and 'royal hymns') are related in their subject matter, and (in my opinion), in their cultic use, to building rituals, and in particular to dedication ceremonies in which the god would enter and take up residence in his new dwelling (the god's sitting in the temple is mentioned in the closing refrains of numerous hymns). The public laments over cities which have been destroyed mention the devastation of the cities as well as their restoration, and, according to a suggestion made by Thorkild Jacobsen and accepted by many other Sumerologists, these laments were recited during foundation ceremonies (see Jacobsen 1941; Hallo 1970: 119; Kutscher 1975: 1-8; M.E. Cohen 1981: 1-6, 40-50).

structures and which resemble in structure the biblical account of building the Temple by Solomon.

1. *The Cylinder Inscriptions of Gudea of Lagash*

The two cylinders of Gudea,[1] upon which are inscribed the longest and best known of his many inscriptions,[2] tell about the rebuilding of Eninnu, the temple of Ningirsu. Even without the third cylinder (the suggested existence and possible content of which will be discussed below), the two extant cylinders constitute a marvellous literary work which was, perhaps, one of the longest in the Sumerian language.

a. *The Third Cylinder (Cylinder X)*
Scholars have questioned whether the two extant complete cylinders

1.   Since their discovery by M.E. de Sarzec, the cylinder inscriptions have been published numerous times in the form of photographs, copies, transliterations and translations into European languages. Some of these are outdated and need not be mentioned. The standard hand copy of the text is that of Thureau-Dangin 1925. He also produced a complete transliteration and translation in *SAKI*, 88-141. A subsequent edition of the text, noteworthy mostly for the useful concordance which it provides, was prepared by Price 1927. For recent complete translations, see Lambert and Tournay 1948a and 1948b; Falkenstein in *SAHG*, 137-82; Castellino 1977: 215-64; Jacobsen 1987b (this masterful and inspiring rendition was, unfortunately, published too late to be fully utilized here). Summaries of the texts and translations of individual passages prepared by Jacobsen and Kramer (on the basis of transliterations prepared by A. Poebel) may be found scattered throughout various books addressed to both specialist and general audiences. All the inscriptions of Gudea have been studied in detail by Falkenstein (1966 and 1949-50). Another translation is being prepared presently by Edzard. There has yet been no attempt to publish a comprehensive commentary on the Gudea cylinders which would include photographs, copies, transliteration, translation, and philological, exegetical and literary notes. Jacobsen is preparing detailed notes to accompany his translation. Unavailable to me is the recently completed Dropsie College PhD dissertation of Richard Averbeck. A long summary of the contents of the cylinders is presented by Kramer (1963: 137-40 and 1988). An outline of the cylinders is found in Falkenstein 1966: 179-80. An interesting (but unconvincing) attempt to interpret the cylinders as a script or libretto for a cultic pageant was made several years ago by Sauren (1975). Discussions of individual passages will be mentioned in the following notes.

2.   For a list of the rest of Gudea's inscriptions and bibliography, see Falkenstein, s.v. Gudea *RLA*, III, 676-79; Falkenstein 1966: 171ff.; Edzard 1978: 57-70; Borger 1965-75: III, 4-5; Steible 1991.

represent the entire work, and opinions have been expressed in both directions.

The major consideration favoring the completeness of the work in only two cylinders is a literary one. The opening passage of Cylinder A tells about determining destinies in the heavens and on earth, and is reminiscent of the opening passages of various other compositions (especially Sumerian and Old Babylonian royal inscriptions) the completeness of which is beyond doubt. In addition, the story in its present two cylinder scope has a well balanced literary structure. The first cylinder opens with determining destinies in the divine realm and concludes in the earthly Eninnu, while the second cylinder begins in the earthly Eninnu temple and ends with destinies being determined in the divine sphere. Furthermore, the internal continuity of the story, as well as its similarity to other building stories, indicates that nothing is missing.

Additional evidence for the integrity of the work in two cylinders seems to be provided by the lines concluding the two cylinders. Cylinder A concludes, *é ^{d}nin-gir-su-ka dù-a zà-mí mu-ru-bi-im,* which Falkenstein translated (erroneously), '(Mitte des Preisliedes für den Bau des Hauses Ningirsus)', implying that the line marks the middle of the work.

Were it not for external evidence, it is questionable whether anyone would consider doubting the completeness of the work as it stands. Nonetheless, important external evidence does seem to exist, indicating that there was indeed a third cylinder which stood at the beginning of the composition.

First of all, along with the two complete cylinders, an additional twelve fragments were found belonging to a Gudea composition, not all of which can be joined to the two surviving cylinders, A and B.[1] If these fragments do not originate from another independent composition,[2] they must be assumed to have come from an otherwise unknown portion of the Cylinder inscriptions.

But the most important evidence for the existence of an additional

1.   Baer (1971) published the fragments and attempted to place some into the lacunae at the end of Cylinder B. Van Dijk (1983: I, 11 n. 25) denies that any of the fragments belong to Cylinder B, stressing their stylistic difference.

2.   Falkenstein (1966: 187 n. 2) and Sauren (1975) hold that these fragments belong to a parallel inscription.

cylinder is found in the colophon. Colophons usually refer to the entire writing surface (tablet, cylinder, etc.) on which they are inscribed and not only to the precise locus in the text at which they stand. For this reason, the note *zà-mí mu-ru-bi-im* should not be seen as a marker identifying the middle point in the composition, but as an indication that the present first cylinder was actually the middle cylinder in the entire composition. It should not be translated as suggested above, but rather, 'the hymn, (this cylinder) is its middle (section/cylinder)'. Not only this, but the colophons to both cylinders contain the words *é-^{d}nin-gir-su-ka-dù-a*. W. Röllig has recently characterized these lines as 'doxologies'.[1] However, they may be (as suggested by A. Shaffer and accepted by T. Jacobsen)[2] the incipit of the entire text. Shaffer has further pointed out (oral communication) that on the cylinders themselves the lines are separated from the rest of the text by a blank space—something characteristic of colophons, but not to be expected of doxologies, which would be considered integral to the composition. Since Cylinder A opens with the words *u$_4$ an-ki-a nam-tar-re-da,* one may conclude that the real first cylinder, which began with the words preserved in the colophon as being the name of the text, has been lost.[3]

Even if this opinion is correct—and it is quite widely accepted—the content of the missing Cylinder X remains the subject of conjecture and speculation. Various suggestions have been made according to which the building story, which is the sole subject of Cylinders A and B, is extrapolated forward so as to place its beginning in Cylinder X. A. Leo Oppenheim proposed that the missing cylinder told about the time at the beginning of time when the building of the temple was decided upon.[4] T. Jacobsen suggested that it described the selection of Gudea and the events which preceded and led up to the building of Eninnu.[5] Shaffer believes that the *Himmelsszene* which opens Cylinder

1. Röllig 1987: 42.
2. Jacobsen 1987a: 386.
3. Despite the persuasiveness of this argument, it should be pointed out nonetheless that a nearly identical line appears at the end of the mythological temple-building text *Enki's Journey to Nippur* and the possibility must therefore be weighed that this is not an incipit but, rather, a stereotyped title which may be given to various compositions about temple building. See Falkenstein 1951.
4. Oppenheim 1956: 211 col. b.
5. Jacobsen 1987.

A is an abbreviated recapitulation of a more elaborate picture which occupied part of Cylinder X.[1] He also suggests that the missing cylinder may have contained a composition similar to the Lagash King List which surveys the history of the world from the time of the Flood until the time of Gudea.[2] In the course of a historical survey, the author of the King List records a number of building projects in the City of Lagash, and reports a command of Ningirsu to build his temple (ll. 107-71 according to the reconstruction proposed by Sollberger). Most recently, van Dijk[3] has expressed the view that the missing cylinder contained myths concerning Ningirsu.

All of these opinions are certainly reasonable and possible individually. Nonetheless, they have little positive evidence behind them. Only van Dijk identifies a line in the fragments of the missing cylinder (frg. 1. col. III) as parallel with a line in the Lagash King List (l. 22)—a fact which could perhaps be adduced in support of Shaffer's theory. Furthermore, the proposals are not necessarily mutually exclusive or contradictory, which leaves open the possibility that several of them, or some combination of them, might be accurate. In order to offer a somewhat more educated guess about the content of Cylinder X, and about its function in the structure of the entire composition, it is advisable to examine a few building stories, which are complete, but which do not start at the beginning of the compositions in which they are included. There is only a small number of such stories, but this is sufficient to cast some light on the problem.

(1) A prayer to Numušda for Sīn-iqīšam[4] describes the selection of Sīn-iqīšam for the task of digging canals. The account of the selection and the subsequent canal digging begins in the middle of the composition, and continues down to the end of the hymn. However, it is preceded by a general hymn to the god Numušda, which has nothing to do with the theme of digging canals.

(2) A Hymn to the city of Nippur,[5] which seems to have been preserved only partially, tells about the selection of Nippur by the gods and the conscription of a divine work force to build the city.

1. In conversation.
2. See Sollberger 1967a.
3. Van Dijk 1985: 11 n. 25.
4. Sjöberg 1973; Duppret 1974; cf. Falkenstein in *SAHG*, 112-114 no. 23.
5. Oberhuber 1967.

However, the story is preceded by a hymn to the city or to a temple which is written according to the standard structure of hymns in honor of temples.[1]

(3) 'Enmerkar and the Lord of Aratta'[2] relates Enmerkar's attempts to build a temple for the goddess Inanna, and tells of the 'anything you can do I can do better' contest which broke out between him and the anonymous Lord of Aratta in the wake of this project. The narrative itself opens in line 6 with words reminiscent of the opening lines of Gudea Cylinder A (u_4-*ri-a nam-ba*-[*tar-ra-ba*]), and immediately thereafter offers a description of the rise in the river and abundant precipitation—also resembling the opening section of Gudea Cylinder A. However, the five preceding verses contain a short hymn to Enmerkar's city, Uruk.

On the basis of these compositions,[3] all of which contain an 'introduction' preceding the building account, there is reason to conjecture that the lost Cylinder X of Gudea may also have included some sort of hymn praising Ningirsu or his city Lagash or his temple Eninnu. In such a hymn, references to Ningirsu myths would not have been out of place. Whatever the case may be, there is no compelling reason to assume that the cylinder contained some important, integral part of the main narrative. On the basis of the analogously structured texts

1. Sjöberg and Bergmann 1969: 5 and see below.
2. See S. Cohen 1973.
3. Prefacing a narrative with a hymn is not limited to accounts of building and similar activities, but seems to be a common feature in Sumerian literature dealing with topics of all sorts. The myth *Enki and Ninhursag* opens with a hymn to Dilmun (trans. S.N. Kramer, *ANET*, p. 37, ll. 1-30). *Enmerkar and Ensuḫkešdanna* (Berlin 1979) starts with a twenty-three-line hymn to Uruk, while the body of the story begins in l. 24 with the formula u_4 *-ba* ... u_4 *en-na-am*. *Enlil and Ninlil* (Behrens 1978) starts off with a hymn to Nippur, while the story itself begins in l. 13 with the formula u_4 *-ba*. *Šulgi O* (Klein 1976), the main part of which is a dialogue between Shulgi and Gilgamesh, opens with a hymn to the Ekishnugal temple in Ur (pp. 274-77, ll. 1-28). This hymn itself has a structure similar to that of the Temple Hymns composed by Enheduanna (Sjöberg and Bergmann 1969: 5): praise to the temple, followed by praise to the god, starting with the word *nun*, 'prince'. In l. 38 of *Šulgi O* we find the formula u_4 *(?)-bi (?) nam-kalam-ba-tar-ra-ta*. From a much later time, in the inscriptions of Sennacherib (Luckenbill 1924: 94 ll. 63-65; 103 ll. 23-33), the accounts of building the 'Palace Without a Rival' in Nineveh start off with poetic passages extolling the city, but this may be an independent development rather than a return to archaic literary conventions.

mentioned above, there is sufficient room to assume that the connection between Cylinder A and that which preceded was rather weak. There is, therefore, ample justification to ignore totally the missing cylinder in an analysis of the literary and thematic structure of the building narrative.

b. *The Content of Cylinders A and B*

Cylinder A tells at its outset about a day on which destinies were determined. This may have been at some time in the distant past, around the time of creation, or it may have been on some more recent occasion, such as at the New Year. On that particular day, Enlil, the chief god in the pantheon, looked at Ningirsu, the head deity of the city of Lagash. Enlil was pleased with the city (Cyl. A I 1-9).[1] In reaction, Ningirsu[2] announced that the anonymous governor (*ensi*) would build Eninnu and do in it great things (ll. 10-16). That night, Gudea beheld Ningirsu in a dream and the god commanded him to build his temple, Eninnu.[3]

Gudea did not understand his dream (I 32), and in order to have it interpreted, he travelled by boat to the goddess Nanshe, the dream interpretress (I 23–IV 4). On his way to the goddess, he visited the temples of Lugal-Bagara and Gatumdug in order to enlist their assis-

1. See Jacobsen's translation in Frankfort 1948: 240. For an up-to-date transliteration and notes see Sauren 1971–72. For cols. I–XIII, see Kramer 1969: 23-34.

2. So Kramer and Falkenstein. Lambert and Tournay, however, attribute these words to Enlil.

3. In ll. 20-21, we read *é-ninnu me-bi gal-gal-la-ám igi mu-ši-na-ni-gar*, which may be translated, 'He (Ningirsu) directed his (Gudea's) glance towards Eninnu whose *me-s* (attributes, ordinances) are very great'. If this interpretation is followed, it would appear as if Ningirsu showed to Gudea in a dream a heavenly temple or a heavenly plan for a temple which he was to build (but cf. the comment of M. Eliade cited by Alster [1976: 19 n. 28]). However, the detailed account of the dream which appears later on makes no reference to this. The dream, according to the description of it put into Gudea's own mouth, was a symbolic dream (on this phenomenon, see Oppenheim 1956: 206ff.). At most, Gudea saw in his first dream a plan for the temple drawn on a tablet held by the goddess Nisaba. Furthermore, Gudea must ask Ningirsu to reveal to him the plan of the temple. All this goes against the interpretation suggested, and leads us to seek a non-literal explanation of vv. 20-21, or to interpret them differently, as T. Jacobsen, who translates 'Ningirsu turned to him (Gudea) about Eninnu's offices which are all great'.

tance.[1] Upon reaching Nanshe, he told her his dream in all its details
(IV 5–V 10), and she interpreted it for him, point by point (V 11–VI
23).[2]

After interpreting the dream, Nanshe told Gudea what to do in
order to receive additional instructions and learn about the form and
nature of the temple he was to build.

Following the advice of the goddess, Gudea prepared a glorious war
chariot for Ningirsu (VII 9–VIII 3) and brought his gift before the
god.[3] Gudea then prayed to Ningirsu, after which the deity appeared
to him in a second dream (VIII 4–XII 11). This time, Ningirsu praised
his temple (IX 11-19; X 15-29), himself and all his deeds (IX 20–X
15),[4] even revealing to Gudea the blessings which would come upon
him and his city the moment the temple would be founded.[5] Gudea
woke from his sleep and sought confirmation for his dream through
the (already) standard divinatory practice of extispicy (XII 12-20).

Gudea immediately commenced preparations for the building
project. He imposed peace and tranquility in his city, introduced a bit
of social equality,[6] and purified the city (XIII 3–XIV 6). He even

1.   See van Buren 1952a for another interpretation of these visits. In her opinion,
Gudea did not approach these gods in order to clarify his dreams, but in order to
enlist their help in transferring certain gods from Eridu to Lagash. Against this
proposal, see Ellis 1968: 7-8.

2.   See Jacobsen's translations in Frankfort 1948: 255-88 and in Oppenheim
1956: 254, as well as the comments of Frankfort and Oppenheim.

3.   For divine chariots in Sumerian literature, see briefly Civil 1968. In the hymn
which he publishes here, it is said (among other things) that the chariot was made by
command of Enlil: 'O chariot! Enlil. . . in Ekur, his great temple, has spoken concerning your manufacture'. Although there is no hint of such in the Gudea Cylinders,
it is not impossible that a hymn such as this one would have been composed and
recited when Gudea presented the chariot to Ningirsu in his temple. The converse of
this possibility is that an event such as the one described in the Gudea cylinders
would suggest itself as a possible *Sitz im Leben* for a hymn like the one published by
Civil. The structure of this hymn should also be noted: ll. 1-2, the divine command
to make a chariot; ll. 3-90, a description and praise of the chariot; ll. 91-96, a prayer
on behalf of the king (see now Klein 1989 for new edition of the hymn).

4.   See Jacobsen 1970a: 12-13 and also 1970b: 328 n. 20 II A, and most
recently 1976: 80ff. Cf. also Kinnier-Wilson 1979: 26-27.

5.   See Appendix 1.

6.   For this passage and parallel passages in Cylinder B and Statue B see
the translation and comments of Kramer (1971). A similar incident from a much
later period is mentioned in the Weld–Blundell Cylinder of Nabonidus (Langdon

prepared a storeroom for the bricks which were to be molded, and ritually cleansed the building site. Afterwards he levied corvée labor *(zi-ga)* upon the inhabitants of the city (XIV 6-7),[1] and imported necessary building materials—wood and stone—from distant lands (XIV 27–XVI 25).[2] He brought the wood to his city as rafts, while the stones he transported aboard boats (XV 26-34).

Gudea is depicted as zealous and eager in all he does, and there are no preparatory activities in which he does not participate personally (XVI 25–XVII 9).[3] He measures the building site (XVII 10-28), molds the first brick amidst a glorious and festive ritual (XVII 29–XX 1),[4] and sets it in its place. At this point he lies down, and, as promised, is granted a third dream in which the Eninnu temple itself is revealed to him (XX 2-12). The remainder of the first cylinder details the building process and describes the edifice itself. First mentioned are measuring the area and laying the foundations (XX 13–XXI 12) with the participation of the gods Enki, Nanshe, Gatumdug, Bau, and all the Anunnaki gods. Afterwards there is an elaborate and highly poetic description of the temple under construction, and of all its sections and furnishings.[5] The description of the temple, and the cylinder itself, conclude with a hymn of praise to the temple (XXIX 14–XXX 13).

Cylinder B deals entirely with the dedication of the new temple. The cylinder is framed at its beginning and end by two short hymnic passages in praise of Eninnu. Despite a certain difference in the

1923: 36, ll. 21-31; see below for discussion of this text).

1.   See Poebel 1947: 64ff. and 77ff. For the term *zi-ga*, see Sjöberg 1967: 205 n. 7, and, more recently, Alster 1970. For the term *im-ru-a* and for Cylinder A XIV 14-27, see Sjöberg 1967.

2.   For a translation of this passage and parallel descriptions in Statue B and on a macehead, see A.L. Oppenheim in *ANET*, pp. 268-69 and cf. Sauren 1977. This passage will be examined in greater detail in Chapter 10, as part of the discussion of acquiring building materials.

3.   See Appendix 2.

4.   See Ellis 1968: 170 and Heimpel 1987: 205.

5.   These descriptions are not exact architectural accounts, and do not enable the reader to visualize the shape of the temple, even partially or schematically. They are somewhat reminiscent of the descriptions of temples found in the Temple Hymns (see Sjöberg and Bergmann 1969). Many parts of the temple are described in animal imagery. For these passages, see Heimpel 1968. For Ningirsu's trophies which adorned the temple (Cylinder A XXV 24ff.), see Cooper 1978: 145-46.

lengths of the two framing hymns, they are strikingly similar in
language (Cyl. B I 1-11, XXIV 9-15). The two passages serve as a
literary framework for the longer account of the dedication rites and
celebrations.[1] Compared with the first cylinder, the course of events
described in the second cylinder is not as clear. There seem to be
some gaps in the narrative which must be filled, and certain incon-
sistencies which call for explanation. When the action gets under way
following the introductory hymn, the governor[2] kisses the ground 'as
befits the divinity' (I 12-13).[3] Afterwards, Gudea offers sacrifices and
prays (ll. 14-21).[4] In this prayer, which is addressed to the Anunna
gods (I 21–II 6), Gudea requests the assistance of the gods in bringing
Ningirsu into his new house which has just been built for him.

The seven lines following (II 7-13) describe a procession. Gudea is
surrounded front and back by two gods (ll. 7-10; cf. the 'Gudea and
Ningishzidda stela', *ANEP*, no. 513), and afterwards it is said that he
brought gifts in exchange for the old temple (ll. 11-13). Line 14
reports that he went to his lord in the Eninnu. This passage must
describe certain activities done in the old Eninnu, for Gudea has yet to
invite Ningirsu and his spouse Bau to enter their new house, and such
an invitation, which comes later on, would make little sense if they are
already to be understood as dwelling in the new residence.

On the other hand, the activities and the prayers which were described previously in I 12–II 6 took place in the new Eninnu. If this is
the case, then v. 11, which was the last line of the introductory hymn,
can be understood as a description of the gathering of the gods in the
new Eninnu.[5] The line reads: ^{d}*a-nun-na ù-di-de im-ma-šu$_4$-šu$_4$-ge-éš*,

---

1.   For the chiastic relationship between these two hymns and several other
stylistic minutae, see the excursus at the end of this chapter.

2.   As in Cylinder A, here too Gudea is not mentioned by name, but only by his
title, *ensi*. The delay in mentioning the name of the main character creates a certain
amount of dramatic tension, which is relieved only after a few more lines. On this
literary device in Cylinder A, see Kramer 1969: 142 n. 10.

3.   For the expression *nam-dingir-e* in l. 13, see Rosengarten and Baer 1977: 8
n. 3, 204.

4.   It is not clear how many series of prayers and sacrifices are described in the
passage. Especially problematic are ll. 16-19.

5.   This sentence serves a double literary function. On the one hand it concludes
the introductory hymn, and as such, it describes the regular, permanent state of the
Eninnu temple—the Anunna gods are constantly to be found there. On the other
hand, it sets the stage for the cycle of cultic acts described in Cylinder B, and informs

'The Anunnaki gods made their way hither to admire'. This statement implies that all the Annunaki gods are present, already at the beginning of the cylinder, in the new temple (as guests for the impending celebrations), and Gudea approaches them to request their help. From the new temple, which is filled with divine guests, Gudea goes out in a procession to the old house in which the divine couple Ningirsu and Bau still reside. While standing in the old Eninnu, he turns to the divine couple and invites them to come and take up residence in their new domicile (II 14–III 1). His prayer is heard and his sacrifice is accepted (III 2-4).[1]

The 'invitation' passage is followed by another short passage, the meaning of which is also obscure (III 5-9). It is reported that on the third day of the new year, Ningirsu returned from Eridu.[2] Since there has been no indication in Cylinder B that Ningirsu left Lagash, it must be assumed that, following Gudea's invitation in the preceding passage, the god departed from his city and made a trip to Eridu, where he would have announced the building of a new temple and have been granted the blessings of Enki. The reason for the silence on the matter of Ningirsu's departure from the city is not entirely clear, and indeed nothing would be known about it, were it not for the reference to his return to Lagash. It is possible that the silence concerning Ningirsu's

the reader that, at the time of the dedication ceremonies, the Anunna gods were present in the temple so that Gudea was able to turn to them and request their assistance in bringing Ningirsu into the new temple. It is significant to point out that the Kesh temple hymn (Gragg 1969) states at the beginning of the description of the temple dedication rites (ll. 103-21, esp. 105) that the Anunna gods were lords of the temple. In other words, both in the Gudea Cylinder and in this temple hymn, the description of the dedication ceremonies commences with a statement about the presence and participation of these gods.

1. The account of this incident is similar in its structure to the descriptions of Gudea's trips and visits to the various temples found in the beginning of Cylinder A.

2. See Al-Fouadi 1969: 47-98 and Sjöberg 1973b: 428. Divine journeys between cities are well documented in Sumerian literature. For journeys mentioned in literature and in economic documents, see Sauren 1969. For a general discussion of the phenomenon, see in brief Ferrara 1973: 1-7, and in greater detail, Green 1975: 229-76. As Al-Fouadi pointed out, Ningirsu's journey to Eridu apparently resembles Enki's journey to Nippur, and its purpose was to report the building of the temple to the gods dwelling in the religious capital, and to secure their blessings. Hallo (1970: 134) suggests that the hymn *nin-mul-an-gim* may also be related to a journey of Nisaba from Lagash to Eridu to receive Enki's blessing.

departure has a purely literary reason, since the topic of the cylinder, and, indeed, the focus of the ceremonies described, is the god's entry into his new house. In this context, mention of his journey to Eridu, even though obligatory ritually, would go completely against the current, and for this reason the author may have seen fit to gloss over it.[1]

Ningirsu's return from Eridu and his immediate entry into the new temple should be the high point of all the activities described in Cylinder B. Nonetheless, we are not told at this juncture in the narrative about the arrival of Ningirsu and Bau, but rather about the completion of the building (III 13-15),[2] the removal of the builders from the building (III 16-17),[3] and other preparations made for the central event (offering III 17-18; purification of the temple by the gods, IV 1-14; and imposition of social equality and tranquility, IV 15-21). These passages, or parts of them, seem to constitute a sort of parenthetical statement reporting events which must have already occurred. The digression from the strict chronological order was intended, perhaps,

1.   In the opinion of van Buren (1952a: 296ff.), Ningirsu's departure from Lagash was mentioned already in Cylinder A II line 1. Mann (1977: 81-82) suggested a different solution to the problem, based on the assumption that Ningirsu's presence was 'fluid', and that the god could be found simultaneously in different forms in different places. 'For the author it surely would not have been at all paradoxical to suggest that the transcendent Ningirsu was present in the form of his emblem, yet came to the temple himself to take up his dwelling, an event that had eternal validity, yet was re-enacted regularly.'

2.   The ritual described here resembles, strangely, a 'foundation' ritual, and raises the question whether rituals involving depositing valuable materials in a structure were done only at the beginning of the construction process, or whether such rites may also have been performed at its completion, or perhaps both. But see below in our discussion of the Lugalannemundu pseudepigraphic inscription.

3.   The removal of the builder (*muš-dam*) may be compared, perhaps, to the removal of the brick god Kulla from a completed house. For this custom see Ellis 1968: 18 and the prayer cited on pp. 185-86. For Kulla and his relationship to another god named ᵈMušdam, see W.G. Lambert 1987. The removal of the architect and artisans may be comparable or somehow related, perhaps, to the practice of mutilating the hands of the artisans who have made a divine statue upon completion of the statue, a practice mentioned in the *mīs pî* ('mouth washing') ritual. Jacobsen (1987a) has explained the latter act as part of a ritualistic denial or abrogation of the human manufacture of idols. We would like to suggest that removing the builders from a temple may be taken as a ritualistic statement that the temple was not built by human hands, but that the gods, who are so frequently mentioned in the building process, are really the ones who built the temple.

to slow down the flow of the story and delay the climax, creating thereby some dramatic expectation.

At long last, the entry of the gods into their new temple is described (entry of Ningirsu IV 22–V 9; entry of Bau V 10-18), along with the appropriate sacrifices and purificatory rites which accompanied the crucial event (V 19–VI 10).

The next twelve columns tell about the appointment of the temple staff (VI 11–XII 25)[1] and about gifts which Gudea showered upon the temple and the divine couple (XIII 11–XVII 16). These two long passages are separated by a short account of certain things done for the temple by a group of seven different gods (XII 26–XIII 10). These passages are all constructed on the basis of the same repeating formula.[2]

After all this, the story returns to the celebration itself (XVII 18). Once again attention is called to the peace and social tranquility prevailing in Lagash throughout the festivities (XVII 18–XVIII 16). The celebration lasted seven days, all filled with eating, drinking and song. At the same time that the human citizens of Lagash were celebrating, divine festivities were also going on, participated in by Ningirsu, An, Enlil, and undoubtedly, other gods as well.[3] Most unfortunately, the text is broken at this highly significant point, more being missing than is preserved. We are thus deprived of an essential part in what is otherwise the longest description of a Sumerian or, for that matter, Mesopotamian temple dedication ceremony.[4] Nonetheless, enough of the text has survived to let us know that destinies were determined for

1. See Jacobsen 1976: 81-83 in his discussion entitled 'Divine Manors'. In the opinion of Cooper (1978: 159 n. 2), this long passage describes a procession of minor gods who pass in front of Ningirsu. Kramer (1963: 140) mentions the similarity between this passage and certain parts of the mythological composition *Enki and the World Order*. For more on this similarity, see Rosengarten and Baer 1977: 124-27. In their opinion the Gudea passage is a 'miniature ordering of the world'. This explanation accords well with the overall idea that on the day a temple is dedicated destinies are determined for the coming year.

2. See, perhaps, Num. 7.

3. For this ceremony and its parallels in *Enki's Journey to Nippur* and in Ugaritic literature, see Ferrara and Parker 1972.

4. Kingsbury (1963: 27) suggests that the seven-day ritual which he has published may have a parallel in Gudea's seven-day ritual, thus making that particular text the longest and most detailed document relating to a temple dedication ceremony. Nonetheless, as Kingsbury himself is quick to point out, there are other equally feasible candidates for the cultic setting of his text.

the temple and for Gudea. At the end, Ningirsu turns directly to Gudea and blesses him, and this is certainly a reference to another revelation to Gudea (XXII 1–XXIV 8).

The text concludes with a short hymn to the temple, as already mentioned.

The central event of all the activities described in Cylinder B is the gods' entry into the temple. The importance of this occurrence is expressed especially in XVII 18 where we read, 'on the day when his master entered his house' (*u₄ lugal-ni é-a tur-ra*). This line, which is in fact a temporal clause, expresses in only a few words and great conciseness the essence of the dedication ceremonies (and see perhaps Cyl. B III 25, 'the day of the coming of the good god' (*u₄ dingir zi-da DU-da*; following Falkenstein, *SAHG*, but cf. Jacobsen, 1987b [*Harps*], who translates 'With the sun stepping into the trusty sky...'). In Gudea's prayers to the Anunna gods, his words to Ningirsu and Bau and in other passages as well in Cylinder B, the god's entry into the temple is recalled repeatedly.

Despite the central role played by the god's entry into the temple, there is another event of great consequence, and even if it seems to be understated, it is alluded to now and then. This is the marriage of the two gods, Ningirsu and Bau. It is possible that Gudea played an active role in the consumation of this marriage, representing Ningirsu, although there is no unambiguous evidence for this.[1]

1. The importance of the sacred marriage—*hieros gamos*—in the Gudea Cylinders is emphasized by the French scholars Lambert and Tournay in their introduction to Cylinder B (1948: 520-25). In their opinion the dedication ceremonies focus on this act in particular. These two scholars speak of the governor mating with the goddess, but this is not certain and is not mentioned explicitly in the text (see also the Ur-Nammu hymn to be discussed below, ll. 35-55, and *Enuma Elish* Tablet I). The nuptials of the gods, or the preparations for them, are alluded to in Cylinder B XIV 21-23 and especially XVI 7–XVII 2. These passages stress the bed of the divine couple, Ningirsu's entry into the innermost part of the temple and his confinement with Bau. E. Douglas van Buren's suggestion (1944), that Gudea was received among the gods as befits the human participant in the sacred marriage rite, strengthens the possibility that he did in fact take an active role, representing Ningirsu. Frankfort's opinion (1948: 297, 330, 405 n. 7) on the question of Gudea's participation in the sacred marriage remains unclear. See also Pallis 1926: 199ff., 184-86. Most recently, J. Renger (1972–75: 251-59) supported Gudea's participation as follows: 'Die Hochzeit zwischen Ningirsu und Bau wird gewöhnlich als ritueller Nach vollzug eines "Fruchtbarkeitsmythos" verstanden'. Van Buren (1944: 46-48)

The union of the two gods, the aim of which is to guarantee a favorable destiny for the fertility of the land,[1] along with (a) the divine banquet, (b) the performance of the dedication rites in proximity with the New Year, and (c) Ningirsu's journey to Eridu to report and receive a divine blessing, all form a coordinated battery of activities, the combined purpose of which is to secure a good future for the city, the temple and the governor.

c. *The Literary Characteristics and Structures of the Cylinder Inscriptions*

Despite the great detail in which events are described, the Gudea Cylinders are not to be seen as a work having the sole purpose of recounting the events as they were witnessed by a detached bystander. Just the opposite! The story before us is a literary composition with well-planned style and structure, and with a clear message.

At the center of the work stand three 'characters'—the *ensi* Gudea, the god Ningirsu and the temple Eninnu—and the author spares no words wherever he has the opportunity to praise them. Furthermore, there is so much divine participation in the events that the story takes on nearly mythic character. The story opens and concludes in the divine circle, and although it tells of the terrestrial Eninnu temple, built and dedicated in the Girsu quarter of the earthly city Lagash, gods are ubiquitous, taking part in whatever is going on. To separate the divine sphere from the human would be totally artificial, something

finds allusions to the sacred marriage rite throughout both cylinders and in the statues: (1) Gudea's appointment as shepherd (A I 26; XIII 19; Statue A 6); (2) purification rites (Cyl. A XVIII 3); (3) presents and libations in the bedroom (A II 24-25; Statue E 1-3; B 1-7); (4) flute-playing for the enjoyment of the goddess (Cyl. B X 9; XV 20-22; XVIII 22–XIX 1); (5) deification of Gudea (B VI). To her textual considerations, van Buren adds a few iconographic factors. Nonetheless, there is a certain difficulty in her suggested reconstruction. Gudea celebrated the sacred marriage rite as an integral part of the dedication rites for the temple, but dedicatory rites are not mentioned and, indeed, have no place anywhere but in Cylinder B. In van Buren's reconstruction, certain phases of the sacred marriage celebrations are mentioned already in Cylinder A. If we accept her opinion, we have to assume that all the building process described in Cylinder A was fitted, somehow, around the ritual drama of the sacred marriage rite. If we do not accept this, then we must postulate that within the ritual drama it was not obligatory to observe the events in a fixed sequence. Neither of these suggestions is appealing.

1.   See van Buren 1944.

not intended by the author, and the figment of the modern reader's imagination and theological prejudices. Even if one is to admit that the gods mentioned in the work were embodied in their statues, emblems, priestly proxies, or activities associated with them, the story only occasionally takes this into account.

The Narrative 'Skeleton'

Despite the length of the work, the narrative skeleton, (or nucleus of the story) is a stereotyped story, the likes of which are well attested in Sumerian, Old Akkadian and Old Babylonian literature. The gods make a decision and select a human king to carry it out for them, and in return for his efforts and success in fulfilling the divine decision, he is rewarded with their blessings (or he requests their blessing).

This tripartite story (divine decision, implementation, blessing) is the basis of narratives told in numerous royal inscriptions and royal hymns. The task performed can be any one of the various deeds befitting a king. The pattern is found in relationship to temple building in inscriptions of Naram-Sin,[1] Ur-Nammu,[2] Ipiq-Ishtar[3] and Samsuiluna.[4] It is used in connection with building of cities and city walls in inscriptions of Warad-Sin,[5] Hammurabi,[6] and Samsuiluna.[7] Digging of canals is described in inscriptions of Ur-Nammu,[8] Sīn-iqī̌sam[9] and Rim-Sin.[10] The pattern even appears in the framework of the so-called 'law-codes' of Lipit-Ishtar[11] and Hammurabi,[12] and in a

1. See W.G. Lambert 1973. Naram-Sin of Agade (on the identity, see most recently W.G. Lambert 1986) builds a temple for Erra on divine command.
2. See Castellino 1959 and our discussion below. Ur-Nammu builds Ekur on command of Enlil.
3. See Schroeder 1917–18 and cf. *IRSA*, 255 (cf. Veenhof 1985b for some improved readings). Ipiq-Ishtar builds Emahtila on command of Ea.
4. Samsuiluna B—see Sollberger 1967. The king restores Ebabbar on command of Shamash.
5. See Falkenstein 1964. The text tells of building the walls of Ur.
6. Clay Nail Inscription—see Gelb 1948. The text tells of building the walls of Sippar.
7. Samsuiluna A (in Borger 1973c: 47) tells of the restoration of the walls of six different cities. Samsuiluna C (*ibid.*: 48) describes the restoration of the walls of Kish.
8. See Hallo 1966.
9. See Sjöberg 1973.
10. See *IRSA*, 205 IV B 14d.
11. See translation of Kramer in *ANET*, 159.

victory inscription of Lugalzagessi,[1] as well as in an inscription
describing the social reforms of Uru-KA-gina.[2]

However, these many inscriptions differ from each other not only
in their specific subjects, but also in the details of their structure. For
example, the process by which the gods select the king varies from
story to story. When the subject is the construction of a temple in a
certain city, or the building of a city and its walls, Enlil (or Anu and
Enlil) selects the patron god of the city and this god in turn selects the
king. This sequence of events occurs in Gudea Cylinder A. On the
other hand, when the story describes some other type of project, or
mission, such as digging canals, promulgating laws or vanquishing an
enemy, Enlil, after choosing the god, bypasses him and selects the
king directly. But despite the differences in main topic and certain of
the details, all these inscriptions are written according to the same
overall narrative structure described above. This distinction reflects
the belief that individual gods, given the proper authority, became
responsible for the cities under their tutelage, but when the welfare of
humanity in general was at stake, the head of the pantheon remained
responsible.

The Gudea cylinder inscriptions thus belong to the broad category
of narratives concerning kings who were selected for specific divine
missions, and more particularly to the group of stories about divinely
elected temple and city builders.

The Drama

Despite the routine nature of the story's broad outline, the account of
Gudea building Eninnu is by no means a rote playing out of a literary
formula. The story plot in Cylinder A is clear and simple. The gods
ordain the building a temple for Ningirsu, and the governor Gudea,
after making the appropriate clarifications, carries out the command
of the gods. But, notwithstanding the simplicity of the plot, it is
developed with considerable drama and noteworthy artistry. The story
concludes with the building of Eninnu. That this is the only possible
outcome of the story is obvious as early as the first few lines which

    12. See Borger 1973: 5ff. Cf. Paul (1970: 11-26), concerning the relationship
between the literary framework of the law codes and the royal inscriptions.
    1. See Kramer 1963: 323 no. 28.
    2. See Kramer 1963: 317 no. 24.

describe the divine conclave. Since the gods desire that a temple be built, there can be little doubt about the eventual result and the successful completion of the building. Furthermore, all the events described lead toward the accomplishment of the divine design. Nonetheless, the attempt to fulfill the gods' wishes meets with advances and setbacks. The factor which continuously hinders the immediate accomplishment of the plan is the uncertainty which incessantly plagues the leading human character in the story. Gudea acts with good will and decisiveness in performing his assignment, but, even so, the will of the gods is not always clear. Gudea must, therefore, not only carry out his mission, but must engage at every stage in clarifying precisely what that mission might be.[1]

When he experiences his first dream, Gudea does not understand its meaning and must seek out help. Nanshe, the dream interpretress, interprets his dreams, thereby relieving the first uncertainty. But, simultaneously, she introduces him to a new situation of doubt. Gudea now knows that he must build a temple, but before he can do so, he must ask Ningirsu himself what the form of the temple should be. However, when he experiences his second dream, the god tells him only about the 'spiritual' dimensions of the temple. The revelation of the architectural plan, without which no real work can be undertaken, is postponed to yet another occasion.[2] Only in a third dream, which is described with utmost brevity, is uncertainty totally eliminated and the long awaited confidence acquired.

This is not the end of matters. All these events of changing uncertainty are complicated by additional layers of questions. Gudea's initial dream is a spontaneous revelation for which he did not have to prepare himself at all. But such spontaneous dreams were considered unreliable, not to be believed without certification. Nanshe's interpretation of the dream, therefore, not only explains its content, but implicitly confirms its validity. The second dream, not spontaneous at all, was a revelation 'incubated' by staying overnight at a temple. Accordingly, when Gudea enters the temple and reposes (at the foot of the divine statue), he has no guarantee that he will in fact be graced

1. See Frankfort 1948: 267-74.
2. Gudea Statue B shows the *ensi* with an architectural plan spread across his lap (*ANEP*, 749). This statue has on occasion been associated with the revelation of the plan to Gudea by the gods, but there is no real support for such a suggestion.

with the desired revelation. Even if he has a dream, such revelations are not to be trusted hastily and outrightly, and it must be confirmed by other mantic means, in this case extispicy.

The interesting situation is created whereby actions which advance the plot—namely the dreams and the words of Nanshe—are the very same critical events which thwart and delay the successful achievement of the goal. The constant interplay between revelation and doubt certainly add dimensions of tension, anticipation and dramatic expectation to what might otherwise have been a rather dull composition.[1]

The Formal Structure of the Story

The narrative is divided into two large sections. The first cylinder describes the building of the temple, while the second cylinder tells of its dedication. Literary 'bracketing' is evidenced for the entire narrative as well as for each individual segment. Both cylinders are bracketed by hymnic passages. Cylinder A opens with Enlil's words of praise for Lagash and concludes by extolling Eninnu.[2] Cylinder B is bracketed by two hymnic passages praising Eninnu.[3] Cylinder A begins in the divine realm and ends in the earthly Eninnu, while Cylinder B inverts the order, starting in the earthly Eninnu, and concluding in the realm of the deities. Destinies are determined at the story's outset and at its conclusion, while Ningirsu addresses Gudea both at the beginning of the story and at its end.

---

1.   Kramer (1961: 254) writes: 'By and large the Sumerian writers show little feeling for closely knit plot structure; their narrations tend to ramble on rather disconnectedly and monotonously, with but little variation in emphasis and tone. Above all, the Sumerian poets seemed to lack a sense of climax; they did not appreciate the effectiveness of bringing their stories to a climactic head. The myths and epic tales show little intensification of emotion and suspense as the story progresses, and often the last episode is no more moving than the first.' It is hardly possible that Professor Kramer was thinking about Gudea when he penned these remarks. Despite the employment of a traditional literary pattern, and despite the use of many standard idioms which he learned in school, Gudea's writer managed to compose a wonderful piece of literature bearing all the traits (developed plot, sense of climax and so on), which Kramer would deny the average Sumerian inscription.

2.   For the structure of the hymns bracketing Cylinder B, see the excursus at the end of this chapter.

3.   See Excursus below.

The Formal Structure of Cylinder A

The account of building Eninnu, contained in the first cylinder, may be divided clearly into four parts. The division markers between each part are Gudea's three dreams. Each dream closes the series of activities which precede it, and introduces the series of activities following it, so dreams may be considered to be simultaneously both bridges and partitions.

The first dream, which is mentioned only briefly at first (I 17-21; a full account of the dream is found only later, when Gudea reports it to Nanshe), concludes the description of the divine conclave during which Enlil notified Ningirsu of his desire that Eninnu be built. The second dream, which is related at very great length (IX 7–XII 12), brings to an end the second phase of the story—the clarification of the will of the gods. The third dream, which is described with telegraphic conciseness (XX 8-12), concludes the phase of preparations for the building—purification and preparation of the site, enlisting workmen and importing various types of building paraphernalia (wood, precious stones and metals, and bricks). In the third dream the temple itself is revealed to Gudea. From this point onwards, the construction work is described, with emphasis being given to an exalted, poetic depiction of the temple being built.

The four sections, which are delineated and separated from each other by the three dreams, differ from each other not only in the activities described, but also in the participants involved and the location:

In the *first part*, which describes the divine decision, the players are Enlil, head of the pantheon, and Ningirsu, the patron god of Lagash. The scene of the action is the divine dwelling place, wherever that might be.

In the *second part*, which tells how Gudea clarified the divine will, the actors are Gudea and a number of personal, regional deities, who have technical functions. Only at the end of this section, in the dream which serves as a bridge leading into the following section, does Ningirsu himself appear. The locations of the events described in this section are the various temples in Greater Lagash.

In the *third part*, the participants are the citizens of Lagash, and for all intents and purposes, the people of the entire world. The arena is international, and the action is a stream of movement from the ends of the earth towards the city Lagash and the building site. The main topic is preparing for the building project.

In the *fourth part*, which describes the building work and the edifice itself, all the gods participate (XX 13-23). The stage is the temple itself.

Notice must also be taken of the internal structures of what have been designated the second and third parts. Both these parts conclude with descriptions of rituals. In the second part, the account of the dream is preceded by the festive presentation of a new war chariot to Ningirsu with the accompaniment of procession and song (VII 24ff.). Corresponding to this, the dream in the third part is preceded by the festive and somber molding of the first brick—which is also accompanied by a procession and song (XVIII 8–XX 6). These rituals both climax the activities which preceded them and enable Gudea to receive a dream revelation necessary for the next activity. Looking for a moment at the dreams which conclude the second and third parts, it is noticed that both are confirmed by routine oracular methods, namely, liver divination (XII 16-19; XX 5-6).

The second and third parts just discussed constitute independent literary units also from the standpoint of their respective internal substructures, which are indicated by the appearance of certain recurring formulae:

The second part is divided into two principal subdivisions. One tells of Gudea's visits to the various shrines in the quarters of Bagarra, Lagash and Nina. After Gudea visits the third of these places and receives Nanshe's interpretation of the dream, we read (VII 9-12):

	sipa-zi gù-dé-a	The able shepherd Gudea
A	*gal mu-zu gal i-ga-túm-mu*[1]	a. was greatly knowing and greatly too at the carrying out (so)—
Ba	*du₁₁ ᵈNanše-e mu-na-du₁₁-ga-aš*	b. to the words that Nanshe spoke to him
Bb	*sag-sig ba-ši-gar*	he bent his head.

The second subdivision tells of the presentation of the gift to Ningirsu according to Nanshe's command. After Ningursu has appeared to Gudea in a dream, we read (XII 14-15, 20):

---

1. The expression *gal mu-zu gal-ga-tum-mu* appears in Cylinder A VII 9-10, XII 20, XXV 22-23 and Cylinder B II 7-8, XIII 13. See Falkenstein 1941: 219 and most recently Alster 1970: 110 n. 5 for parallels from more ancient works.

Ba	*inim-du₄-ga ᵈNin-gir-su-ka-šè*	b. To Ningirsu's command
Bb	*sag-sig ba-ši-gar*	he bent his head

(a description of extispicy, ll. 16-19)[1]

A	*gal mu-zu*	a. Greatly knowing he
	gal ì-ga-túm-mu	was and great too at the carrying out.

This is to say that the two sub-divisions of the second part conclude with formulae different from each other only in the chiastic relationship of their respective components, and the switch in the name of the gods in accordance with the matter at hand. These formulae emphasize Gudea's submission to the will of the gods as well as his great wisdom which enables him to understand their (enigmatic) wishes and fulfill them appropriately.

The *third part* breaks down into four subdivisions, each of which tells about a different type of preparation for the building project. The first subdivision tells of the spiritual preparations of the city and of its cultic purification. The second subdivision depicts the work force, the importing of building materials, and the measuring of the building site. The third subdivision speaks of the molding of bricks, with emphasis placed on the festive manufacturing of the ceremonial first brick. The fourth subdivision reports the dream in which the temple appears before Gudea in its desired form.

The conclusion of each of these subdivisions is marked by the formula (XIV 5-6; XVII 28; XX 4, [7], 12):

(sipa-zi gù-dé-a)	(For the able shepherd Gudea)
ḫul-la-gim im-ma-ni-ib-gar	it was cause for rejoicing.

The *fourth* part of the cylinder, which describes the temple and its construction, may also be divided into two subdivisions, but by a division marker which also connects it with the first part of the Cylinder. In *part 1*, Enlil's thoughts concerning the temple and the city were described (I 5-7) thus:

šà gú-bé nam-gi₄	The heart was moved to overflow
šà ᵈEn-líl-la gú-bé nam-gi	Enlil's heart was moved to overflow
šà gú-bé nam-gi₄	The heart was moved to overflow.

1.   See Falkenstein 1965: 49.

In the middle of the *fourth part*, between the descriptions of the edifice and the description of some of the gifts which were granted to the building, a 'concluding' formula appears as follows (XXV 20-21):

mu-dù[1] *šu im-ta-gar-ra-ta*	He had built it! After he put hand off it (i.e. had completed it)
šà dingir-re-ne gú-bé gi₄-a-àm	the hearts of the gods were over-flowing.

The two lines which follow reinforce the recognition that we are dealing with a concluding refrain, for we read (XXV 22-23):

sipa-zi gù-dé-a	The able shepherd Gudea
gal-mu-zu	was very greatly knowing
gal ì-ga-túm-mu	and great too at the carrying out.

This is the same refrain which had structural significance in the second part of the cylinder. The recapitulation of the refrains from the first and second parts of the Cylinder gives the middle of the fourth part the character of a 'coda' to the composition thus far. It should be noticed that this time nothing is said of Gudea's submission to the divine will. Furthermore, the wisdom which is attributed to him this time is not the wisdom which enables him to understand the word of the god, but, rather, the wisdom which lets him do things for the gods of his own free will. The passage which follows immediately thereafter describes the presents which Gudea gave to his god, and these are most likely none other than the ornaments which decorated the new temple (XXV 24–XXVI 14).

The Formal Structure of Cylinder B

We have been unable to detect in the story in Cylinder B divisions and subdivisions with internal unity and outstanding formulaic markers of structure, such as those which were noticed in the first cylinder. Despite this apparent lack of explicit literary signposts, it seems that this part of the narrative too has a well-defined structure, and that it parallels to a certain extent that of the first cylinder.

Apart from the hymns which frame the narrative, the story itself divides into a short introduction and three additional parts, or three

1.   See the Keš Temple Hymn, Gragg 1969: ll. 118-19, *é al-dù giri_x -zal-bi al-du₁₀* ('the house is built, its abundance is good'), which appears between the description of the dedication rites and the announcement that the goddess has taken up her seat in the temple.

cycles of activity. In other words, the action takes place in this Cylinder, as in the first one, in four parts.

The *first part* (the introduction) is a continuation of the framework hymn. This introduction contains words of praise to the new temple, and these words constitute a background for the rest of the narrative.

The *second part* (the first cycle or round of activity) recounts how the gods entered their new temple. First described is Gudea's invitation to the gods, and this is followed by the actual entry.

The *third part* (the second cycle of activity) speaks of the 'gifts' which were dedicated to the temple. The enumeration begins with the personnel who were assigned to the temple staff, and this is followed by the other gifts.

The *fourth part* (the third cycle of activity) describes the festivities in the city and among the gods, and the fixing of destinies during the divine celebrations.

Parts 2, 3 and 4 of Cylinder B correspond to parts 2, 3 and 4 of Cylinder A. In part 2 of both cylinders, Gudea attempts to enlist the assistance of the other gods when he has to approach Ningirsu. Divine assistance is acquired by means of visits to the temples of the various gods, by trips from one temple to another, and by sacrifice and prayer. Ningirsu's appearance at the end of part 2 in Cylinder A is paralleled by his arrival at the new temple at the end of the second part of Cylinder B. The third part of both cylinders is marked by 'mass' movements of personages and property. Parallel to part 3 of Cylinder A, which speaks of drafting workmen and importing building materials, part 3 of Cylinder B describes a 'Pageant of gods',[1] and the presentation of sumptuous gifts. The final section of both cylinders concentrates on the Eninnu temple itself. Cylinder A describes how the temple was built and received its physical form, while Cylinder B relates how the temple's destiny was fixed.

Conclusions

The complete story, excluding the hymn which probably appeared in the missing first cylinder, consists of eight parts, as follows:

---

1.   Cooper 1978: 159 n. 2.

Cyl. A	(1)	The divine decision to build Eninnu, and notification of the decision to Gudea
	(2)	Clarification of the divine command by Gudea—revelation of the temple's spiritual dimensions
	(3)	The preparations for the building project—clarifications continued, the form revealed
	(4)	The construction process and description of the structure and its furnishings
Cyl. B	(5)	The gods assemble in the temple
	(6)	Ningirsu is brought to the new temple
	(7)	Presentation of gifts and appointment of temple personnel
	(8)	Determining destinies for the temple-seven day human and divine celebrations—revelation to Gudea

Anticipating the rest of our study, it is not difficult to see the great similarity between the structure of the Gudea cylinders and the structure of the story about building the Temple in Jerusalem by Solomon as found in 1 Kgs 5.15–9.25. The biblical Temple-building account opens with Solomon's notification to Hiram of his intention to build a temple. In his announcement, Solomon emphasizes the fact that he was chosen for the task by the Lord, this being an obvious allusion to Nathan's prophecy which appears in 2 Samuel 7. The divine selection of a temple builder and the revelation of the command to build the temple parallel parts 1 and 2 of the Gudea account. Solomon's announcement of his intention to fulfill his divine mission of building a temple is followed by a report about the preparations for the building projects. The king orders wood and drafts workers to transport the wood and to quarry stone. These matters parallel what is described in part 3 of the Gudea narrative. The detailed description of the temple and its furnishings found in 1 Kings 6–7 parallels part 4 of Gudea Cylinder A. The dedication ceremonies in 1 Kings 8 include transferring the Ark to the Temple, the entry of the Lord's *kābôd* into the temple, and a multi-day celebration which is participated in by the king and all the people, who together rejoice and offer countless sacrifices. This description parallels the events described in parts 5, 6 and 7 of the Gudea text. Finally, Solomon's prayer and the divine revelation to Solomon, described in 1 Kings 8 and 9, determine the function and fate of the Jerusalem Temple, this corresponding to part 8 of Gudea Cylinder B.

Along with these points of similarity, there are differences between the structures of the two accounts. So, for instance, Gudea is involved in clarifying the divine will all the way through the preparatory stages, and the revelation of the temple plan, which is part of this clarificatory stage, does not appear until the final moment of the preparations. Nonetheless, it is difficult to deny the overall similarity.

The story in the book of Kings will be discussed in greater detail later, showing that it and other Biblical building accounts follow the pattern seen here. But before doing so, several other extra-biblical building stories may be examined so as to demonstrate how well known, widespread and entrenched this pattern actually was.

2. A Hymn to Enlil with a Prayer for Ur-Nammu, the Builder of Ekur[1]

This hymn was written not long after the composition of the Gudea cylinders. It is considerably shorter than the Gudea cylinders, having only seventy-two lines. Furthermore, it is a *tigi* composition, whereas the Gudea cylinders were a *zà-mí* composition. Nonetheless, there is much similarity between the two works.

As for its external form, the hymn, like all *tigi* hymns is divided into two parts. The first part, which is called a *sa-gíd-da*, is a poetic account of building the Ekur, Enlil's temple in the holy city Nippur. The second section, which is designated *sa-gar-ra*, contains a blessing for Ur-Nammu for having built the Ekur, and words of praise for several of his other illustrious deeds. The second part differs stylistically from the first in that it makes use of the particularizing stanza, in which a word, an expression or whole sentence is repeated any number of times, adding a new compliment after each repetition. The first part is free of this style.

The hymn begins with a description of Ur-Nammu's selection by Enlil (ll. 1-6), and his commission to build the Ekur (ll. 7-12).[2]

---

1.   See Castellino 1959; Falkenstein in *SAHG*, 87-90, 376; Kramer in *ANET*, 583-84; cf. Sjöberg 1961. Komoroczy (1978: 44-45) suggests that this hymn was used on the occasion of (re)dedicating the restored Ekur and also pointed out influence of the Gudea cylinders on this composition. Castellino makes a similar suggestion about the cultic use of the hymn. (For the date of Gudea, see J. Klein 1989a: 289 n. 3.)

2.   To line 10, *á-bi mu-u$_8$-da-ág*, compare in Samsuiluna B (Sollberger 1967a, l. 32 [ll. 36-37 in the Akkadian version]): *tērtam šuāti uwa''eranni*. Also note in a newly published inscription concerning Hammurabi and the wall of a cloister (*gagû*)

Afterwards, the preparations for the building project are described (ll. 12-18). Ur-Nammu wisely prepared the brickmold,[1] Enlil suppressed the enemies of the king, the Sumerians joyfully laid the foundations of the temple, and the priests (or the gods responsible for the foundations) praised the foundations.[2] The following lines describe the temple in poetic language reminiscent of the language of the temple hymns (ll. 19-30).[3] The story concludes with a description of the dedication ceremonies (ll. 31-35) and the blessing of Ur-Nammu by the divine couple Enlil and Ninlil (ll. 36-38). The focus of the dedication ceremony is the sitting of the divine couple in their new temple.[4] A great celebration is prepared and the king presents sumptuous gifts. The whole temple is happy. It is possible that the mention of the divine couple is meant to be some sort of allusion to the marriage of the two deities. Enlil and Ninlil bless the king. The words of Enlil are cited in the first person (ll. 40-51) and this address may actually reflect a divine revelation to Ur-Nammu.[5]

This brief analysis[6] reveals that this hymn to Enlil contains a short

(Frayne and Donbaz 1984: 29 1. 12): *á-bi ḫu-ma-da-an-ág*.

1.   *sipa-zi. . . ˢⁱˢù-šub-ba si àm-mi-in-sá*; compare Gudea's dream (A V 6): *ˢⁱˢù-šub ku si-ib-sá*. Gudea was also praised for his wisdom in a recurring refrain in Cylinder A (see our discussion above).

2.   See Ezra 3.8-13. Opinions were divided about the meaning of *enkum* and *ninkum*, but it seems now that they are in fact priests and not gods. These priests function in similar circumstances in the Kesh Temple Hymn for which see Gragg 1969, and his comments to l. 112. The priests have recently been studied by C.B.F. Walker in his unpublished Oxford BPhil thesis on the *mīs pî* ritual (Walker 1966: 167-70); cf. *CAD s.v. enkummu* and *ninkummu*.

3.   It is particularly similar to the description of Enki's temple É-engurra found in *Enki's Journey to Nippur* (Al-Fouadi 1969).

4.   Compare Ningirsu's and Bau's sitting in their temple described in Cylinder B, and Ea and Damkina sitting in the newly built Apsu (temple) in *Enuma Elish* I 78, as well as W.G. Lambert 1973: 361 ll. 31-32, where Naram-Sin of Agade (or Eshnunna) has built a temple in which Erra and Laz reside.

5.   The overall structure of this hymn may be compared with that of Psalm 132, which praises David for his efforts to find a resting place for the Ark of the Lord. The first part (vv. 1-10) is phrased as a prayer in which the poet addresses God in the second person and asks 'O Lord, remember in David's favor his extreme self-denial, etc.' and goes on to relate David's deeds. The second half records the words of the Lord (vv. 11-18) which are phrased in the first person.

6.   Cf. also the analyses presented in the translations and articles mentioned above in the first note of the section.

narrative poem identical in its thematic structure and in several of its central ideas to the Gudea Cylinder inscriptions, and this is despite the great difference in the lengths of the two works.

Examination of this particular building story reveals that certain elements which some scholars have seen as essential to Mesopotamian stories about building temples are missing, and therefore not really that vital.[1] There is no hint that Enlil revealed the plan of the Ekur to Ur-Nammu, and even though it is stated that Enlil instructed Ur-Nammu to build his temple, the nature and content of the instruction are left unspecified. Furthermore, there is no trace of any uncertainty, concern or hesitation on the part of the king. It is also not stated that the king imported exotic building materials from distant lands.

The absence of these supposedly indispensable elements should indicate that, even within the Mesopotamian literary tradition, the building story was a somewhat flexible topos. Not every individual story need contain all the components and all the themes or ideas which seem to typify the pattern. The writer created according to an overall conception or according to a general literary pattern, but he permitted himself to mold the pattern and alter it according to his own views and needs, or in accordance with varying facts and changing realities.[2] What the Gudea Cylinders have in common with the Ur-Nammu hymn, then, is not only certain individual motifs but, more significantly, a shared outline or thematic structure.

It also appears that the topos may be employed for different purposes, as evidenced by the fact that it appears in one case in a *zà-mí* composition and in the other in a *tigi*. Indeed, it is employed in other types of writings as well, as will become clear below. The 'building account' thus displays characteristics of a distinct literary 'genre', such as fixed structure and recurring motives, but it may be used freely within the contexts of other 'genres'.[3]

---

1.   Cf. the studies of Weinfeld 1972 and Kapelrud 1963, as well as M. Lambert 1955.

2.   For a visual rendition of this building project, see the Ur-Nammu Stele from Ur discussed briefly in Appendix 3.

3.   Well after this book was completed and submitted for publication, a masterful new edition of the Ur-Nammu Hymn was published by my colleague J. Klein ('Building and Dedication Hymns in Sumerian Literature', *Acta Sumerologica* 11 [1989] 27-67). In his discussion, Professor Klein offers an independent analysis of this hymn's thematic structure utilizing the pattern for building narratives

3. Shulgi and Ninlil's Boat (Šulgi R)[1]

This text tells not of the building of a temple, but of the construction of a ritual boat for the goddess Ninlil by Shulgi, king of Ur. Despite its novel subject, it spins its narrative using the familiar literary form of a building story. In its thematic structure, language, and numerous individual motifs, it resembles both the Gudea cylinders and the above-mentioned hymn of Shulgi's father, Ur-Nammu.

Since the tablet ends with a catch line, it may not be a complete composition. Even so, the one tablet which has survived tells a complete story. Similarly to the Ur-Nammu hymn, this composition is divided into a *sagarra* and a *sagidda*, although the second part is not written in particularizing verse. Unlike the Ur-Nammu hymn, the second part continues and brings to an end the story started in the first section. As in Gudea Cylinder A, the first part of Šulgi R relates the construction of the boat, while, like Cylinder B, the *sagidda* speaks in its entirety of the dedication festivities for the boat and the divine blessings granted the king.

The first four verses recount the divine command to build the boat. Enki decrees a good destiny for the boat, Enlil looks upon it, and Ninlil, for whom it is to be made, orders Shulgi to construct it. Lines 5-8 tell of Shulgi's great intelligence and untiring efforts, and of the cedars which he felled to make the boat. The following section, lines 9-39, describes the boat in highly poetic language, using much imagery. Verses 41-82 portray the dedication festivities, which seem to focus on the bark's maiden voyage. Just as the temples built by Gudea and Ur-Nammu were dedicated by the act of the divine couples

discerned in the present study (see especially pp. 34-35).

1. This text was discussed by Professor J. Klein at the *Rencontre Assyriologique* in Istanbul, summer 1987, and he has now published it as 'Šulgi and Išmēdagan: Originality and Dependence in Sumerian Royal Hymnology', *Bar Ilan Studies in Assyriology* (Pinhas Artzi Jubilee Volume; ed. J. Klein and A. Skaist; Ramat Gan: Bar-Ilan University, 1990) 65-136. This article contains a detailed philological analysis, as well as extensive literary and form-critical remarks, including a comparison similar to the one offered here with the Gudea and Ur-Nammu hymns. In view of Klein's extensive treatment of this composition, my own comments have been kept to a minimum. I am exceedingly grateful to Professor Klein for showing me the manuscript of his article before its publication and for discussing with me this fascinating text.

sitting in them in marital bliss, here too the couple Enlil and Ninlil embrace and sit on their daises in the ship. The celebrations are marked by singing, offerings and general happiness. It is stated several times in this section that fates were determined for Shulgi (44, 65, 69-70). The last section of the hymn, lines 83-90, tells how Shulgi was blessed by Ninlil.

4. *The Pseudepigraphic Inscription of Lugalannemundu*[1]

This inscription, which has survived in two manuscripts from the seventeenth century BCE, reports the deeds of Lugalannemundu, king of Adab in the first half of the third millennium. The work is pseudepigraphic and reflects literary practices which were surely unknown during the so-called 'Heroic Age'. Its language is Sumerian (the tablets themselves contain some Akkadian glosses) although its literary style and structure are similar to those of later Akkadian royal inscriptions. The editor of the text, H. Güterbock, has pointed out that the text as a whole consists of all those components which typify royal dedicatory inscriptions,[2] namely: (a) the name and epithets of the goddess to whom the building is dedicated (I 1-3); (b) the name of the king and his titles (I 4-11); (c) an historical passage which tells of the background and circumstances of the building project (I 12–II 24); (d) the building account (II 24–IV); (e) a prayer (IV– end). It is easy to see that the building account, which occupies over half the inscription, is the major component, and it is this part which will be discussed now.

Although the building account makes up the major portion of the

1. See Güterbock 1934, esp. 40-47, and cf. Kramer 1963: 50-52. Concerning the historical worth of the text, Kramer writes optimistically: 'its contents are carefully, minutely and convincingly detailed, and ring quite genuine and trustworthy'. Nevertheless, it is difficult to assume that the scribe really had access to some ancient royal inscription which he only copied. This was already realized by Güterbock (1934: 14-15; 1938: 46-47). All the apparent details seem to be only stereotyped ideas. Even the lands mentioned in the inscription are 'legendary', and when taken all together they are to be understood as nothing more than symbols for all the ends of the earth. Finkelstein (1979: 76) classifies this text, along with the well-known 'Cruciform Monument of Manistushu' and the 'Agum-Kakrime' text, as a pious forgery recounting a revered, ancient king's devotion and generosity towards a particular temple, composed with the aim of influencing a subsequent king to support and generously endow the same temple. See now also Longman 1991: 92.

2. See Güterbock (1938: 46), for the structure of the inscription.

text, it has been very poorly preserved; for the most part, all that remain are the left ends of many of the lines. The building story begins by naming the temple to be constructed, Enamzu (II 25). We are told that the temple was old (II 26) and that the goddess Nintu commanded by her pure mouth to restore it (II 27).[1] The king measures the building site. It is possible that he laid out a building plan identical to the old layout, or it may be that he expanded the temple, but the text is broken at this point and we cannot know with certainty. Afterwards, the building itself is described, emphasis in the description being placed upon the temple's seven gates and their respective names (II 30–III 23). Following the description of the building is an account of the dedication festivities. The report begins with the words *é ù-til* (p. 42, A III l. 24), 'when the temple was completed'.[2] The dedication ceremony is called *u₄-sig₄-tab-ba-tu-ra*, i.e. 'the day of bringing in the double brick'.[3] It is likely that the entry of the goddess into the temple was mentioned in the broken line 26' which reads: *dingir-maḫ nin-mu šà-é(?)-x. . .*, 'The august goddess, my lady inside the temple. . .' At the dedication festivities, eight rulers sacrificed seven sacrifices each.

---

1. Compare Solomon's Temple dedication speech: 'Blessed is the Lord. . . who spoke with his own mouth to David my father' (1 Kgs 8.15). In the Sumerian inscription we read *dingir-maḫ ka-kù-ga-ni-ta*, 'the august goddess, cut of her pure mouth'. For a synonymous expression in an Akkadian building account of Takil-ilissu of Malgium, see Kutscher and Wilcke 1978, esp. 127 l. 9: *ᵈÉ-a-ma be-li i-na KA-šu el-li-im iq-bi-a-am-ma i-nu-mi-šu É-nam-ti-[l]a . . . [a]l-wi-šu-ma*, 'Ea my lord spoke to me by his pure mouth and at that time I surrounded Enamtila'; on this passage, see also Jacobsen 1937–39: 363-66 n. 10.

2. See also, for example, in the inscription of Warad-Sin, Falkenstein 1964: 25-40, l. 103. Sumerian *kin. . . til* is equivalent to Akkadian *šipram. . . gamārum*, and Hebrew *kalleh mĕlā'kāh*, 'to complete the work'. The synonymous Akkadian formula appears in various Assyrian building stories, as well as in the account of building Babylon found in the *Enuma Elish*. The Hebrew cognate expression is used as a structural marker in all the biblical building accounts. For a discussion of this and related expressions, see Chapter 10 section 3, below.

3. See the hemerology published by Labat 1939: 153, n. 21. In this context, bringing the brick is mentioned along with presenting gifts to the god and celebrating the *Akītu*. See *AHw, s.v. urubātu*. (Note also Charpin 1983: 58 l. 7. who makes reference to *inūma u-ru-ba-at É ᵈnin-a-ga-de* in unpublished TH 82.?.?(.). We should also perhaps compare Gudea Cyl B III 1.13-15, and the 'Kesh Temple Hymn', l. 107 (Gragg 1969; cf. the archaic version for Abu-Salabikh: Biggs 1971: 193-207, esp. 206).

People came from great distances (IV 8), and the king entertained them with song, sat them in honor on golden thrones, and placed golden vessels (?) in their hands.

The account (and the inscription itself) concludes with a prayer to the goddess, in which she is asked to bless the lands of these kings if they will offer continuous sacrifices in her temple (compare this with the end of *Enmerkar and the Lord of Aratta* as reconstructed by S. Cohen).

This building story shortens the description of the decision to build (the divine command) and expands proportionately the description of the edifice itself. The preparations for the building project are hardly mentioned at all, reference being made only to measuring the site. Yet, despite these deletions, there is no substantial distortion of the basic thematic structure, which remains identical to that of the Gudea Cylinders, the Ur-Nammu prayer and Šulgi R studied above.

This inscription is particularly significant for the present study in that it is a pseudepigraphic text, perhaps with a propagandistic purpose,[1] and not an eyewitness account of events seen by the narrator. It demonstrates that the building story functions at an early date as a literary topos which may be exploited by a writer to portray an idealized situation.

5. *Building Stories in Old Babylonian Royal Inscriptions:*[2] *Samsuiluna B*

Not many building stories have come down to us from the Old Babylonian period, but from among the extant material there is one text which is of interest, for its similarity both to the Solomonic building story and to the general pattern of ancient Near Eastern

1.   See Finkelstein 1979: 76.

2.   For the complete corpus of Old Babylonian Royal Inscriptions see Kärki 1983 and Frayne 1990. See also Sollberger and Kupper, *IRSA*. The corpus of Old Babylonian royal inscriptions written in Akkadian is relatively small, and the inscriptions are short, but there are several unique texts of high literary merit, each deserving individual attention. For literary analyses of several of these texts, see Hurowitz 1984a and the studies of A. Shaffer (*Ipiq-Ishtar*) and J. Sasson (Yahdun-Lim Disc Inscription) mentioned there (p. 200 n. 14). Note as well the hymnic text concerning Naram-Sin of Agade (or Eshnunna) published and discussed by W.G. Lambert 1973.

building stories, and also for its particular structural resemblance to the Priestly account of the building of the Tabernacle (Exod. 25–31; 35–40; Lev. 8–10; Num. 7).[1] This is the bilingual 'B' inscription of Samsuiluna, son of Hammurabi, king of Babylon.[2] The entire inscription deals with the building of Sippar and the Shamash temple Ebabbar.

In order to avoid repetition, and for the sake of clarity and efficiency, analyses of extra-biblical building accounts will hereafter be presented in annotated outline form, avoiding summaries and synopses. Comments on interesting passages or significant characteristics of the individual texts will be made either following the outline or in the notes to the outline. The following symbols will be used to designate the components of the stories:

(1)	the circumstances of the project and decision to build
(2)	preparations, such as drafting workmen, gathering materials
(3)	description of the building
(4)	the dedication rites and festivities
(5)	blessing and/or prayer of the king, etc.
(6)	blessing and curses of future generations
[+]	intrusive elements

An outline of the Akkadian version follows:

(1)	1.1-7	*inu-* Enlil looks at Shamash
	8.24	Enlil commands Shamash to build Sippar and the Ebabbar temple—the command includes a brief, poetic, description of the buildings
	25-32	*inūšu*—Shamash rejoices at command
	33-38	Shamash transmits command to Samsuiluna
[+]	[*39-54*]	[*inūšu*—Rebellion against the king, and suppression of the rebellion]
	55-71	Introduction to carrying out command
(2)	72-78	Drafting laborers and molding bricks
(3)	79-87	Building of city and temple—includes description which repeats chiastically language of command (8-24)
(4)	88-95	Joyous introduction of Shamash, Aya and Adad into new temple
	96-101	Summary statement—king did all he was commanded
	102-106	Naming the wall of the city
(5)	107-123	*ana šuāti*—Shamash blesses the king

The major innovations in these inscriptions are: (a) the repetition of the description of the buildings, first in the command section (1) and again in the implementation section (3); (b) the incorporation of a

1. See Hurowitz 1985 and 1983–84.
2. See Sollberger 1967b.

brief account of a rebellion [+] between the command section (1) and the preparations section (2);[1] (c) the summary statement and the naming of the wall between the dedication section (4) and blessing section (5). Yet, despite these innovations, which are nothing more than an expansion in one structural component and intrusions between several others, the basic structure of the building accounts remains the same as the one noticed in the Sumerian monolingual texts analyzed above.

EXCURSUS: CHIASMUS AND INCLUSIO

Part and parcel of the growing present-day interest in literary aspects of ancient texts is the awareness of the use of balanced structure, and especially chiasm in biblical and ancient Near Eastern literature. The phenomenon has been discussed very briefly in relation to Akkadian literature by Hecker (1974: 124, 144, 154) and in relation to Sumerian literature by Wilcke (1975: esp. 218ff.). These two studies mention only chiasm in adjoining verses, but they say nothing about long-distance chiasm and its structural use. In my own study of the literary structures of Samsuiluna A and the Hammurabi Clay Nail inscription (Hurowitz 1984), I pointed out the chiastic structure pervading the two texts. As another small contribution to what will undoubtedly become an unending scholarly enterprise, I offer the following observations about the phenomenon in the Gudea Cylinders and in the temple-building mythic poem *Enki's Journey to Nippur* (Al-Fouadi 1969).

Cylinder B is enveloped by a pair of hymns, as was pointed out in the discussion above. These two hymns contain nearly identical language, and close comparison of the two reveals that there is a chiastic relationship between them.

		I			XXIV
a	1	*é* dim-gal kalam-ma	d′	9	é **kur-gal**-gim an-ni-sa$_4$
	2	***an-ki-da mú-a***		10	ní-me-lam-bi-kalam-ma-ru-a
	3	é-ninnu sig$_4$-zi ^{d}en-líl-e		11	an-ni ^{d}en-líl-e
b		*nam* du$_{10}$-ga *tar-ra*	b′		*nam* Lagaš^{ki} *tar-ra*
				12	^{d}Nin-gir-su-ka nam-nir-gál-ni
	4	hur-sag še$_{15}$-ga u$_6$-e gub-ba			
c	5	*k̂ur-kur*-ta è-a	c′	13	*kur-kur*-re zu-a
d	6	é-**kur-gal**-àm an-ni im-uš	a′	14	***é-ninnu an-ki-da mú-a***
				15	^{d}Nin-gir-su zà-mí

1. For parallels to this intrusive element in some later inscriptions, see Hurowitz 1983–84. Note also, perhaps, Ur-nammu's reference to Enlil subduing his enemies. This reference also appears between the command section (1) and the preparations section (2).

The repeated elements stand in an a b c d //d′ b′ c′ a′ relationship.

	I		XXIV
1	The house, mooring stake of the country,	9	With the house like a *great mountain* abutting heaven
2	**grown up 'twixt heaven and earth,**	10	its awe and glory cast upon the country
3	Eninnu, right true brick structure *assigned good destiny* by Enlil,	11	Lagash's *fate determined* by An and Enlil
4	green foothill confronting the beholder	12-13	all *countries* taught Ningirsu's excellence
5	jutting out from the *highland*		
6	As the *great mountain* that it was, the house abutted heaven,	14	and Eninnu **grown up 'twixt heaven and earth**
		15	Praise be unto Ningirsu!

Cylinder A also ended with a hymn (A XXIX–XXX 13), and this hymn to Eninnu at the end of the cylinder counterbalances the words of Enlil in praise of the city Lagash at the beginning of the cylinder (A I 4-9). A near repetition of the description of Enlil in A I 6-7 appears in A XXV 21:

I 5	XXV 21
šà gú-bi nam-gi₄	*mu-dù*
šà ᵈEn-líl-la gú-bi nam-gi	*šu im-ta-gar-ra-ta*
šà gú-bi nam-gi₄	*šà dingir-ri-ne*
	gú-bi-gi₄ -a-àm
	He (Gudea) had built it!
	After he put hand off it,
The heart was moved to overflow	the hearts of the gods
Enlil's heart was moved to overflow	were overflowing.
the heart was moved to overflow	

There is, therefore, an 'envelope' structure to the two cylinders. Cylinder A is bounded by a very simple envelope consisting of the repetition, at the end of the text, of a key phrase which occurs three times at the beginning, while Cylinder B is bracketed by two hymns, the components of which are the same, but the order of which is inverted.

It should be pointed out here that the sentence *é . . . an-ki-da mú-a* is apparently a standard introductory sentence in temple hymns. The collection of so–called *zà-mí* hymns from Abu-Salabikh (Biggs 1974: 31-32, 46-56) begins with the sentence, *uru an-da-mú an-da gú-lá*, 'City which has grown together with the heavens, which embraces the heavens'. In the Kesh Temple Hymn (Gragg 1969), which begins with a description of the selection of the city by Enlil and the composition of the hymn by Nisaba, the actual praise of the city Kesh itself opens with the words:

é . . . é kes^{ki} ḫur-sag-da-mú-a an-da gú-lá-a
é-kur-da-mú-a kur-ra sag-íl-bi

Temple. . . Kesh Temple growing up like a mountain embracing the heaven
Growing up like Ekur when it lifts its head in the Land.

Finally, the opening section of *Enmerkar and Ensuhkesdanna*, which praises Uruk-Kuluba, starts off (Berlin 1979: 38, ll. 1-2):

sig$_4$ mùš-za-gìn-ta è-a	Brickwork rising out of the shining plain Kulaba,
kul-aba$_4$^{ki} uru^{ki} an-ki-da mú-a	city grown (high) between heaven
	and earth.

Another illuminating example of the use of chiasm in the parallel limbs of a literary envelope is found in the mythological composition, *Enki's Journey to Nippur*. Isimud's words extolling the newly built É-engurra temple, which are themselves structured like a standard temple hymn, are surrounded by an inclusio. This wrapper emphasizes perhaps the literary independence of the passage which it surrounds (for an inclusio in the Nungal Hymn, setting off a poetic description of the 'day of judgment', see Frymer-Kensky 1985):

18	lugal ^{d}en-ki-ra (I) *sukkal* ^{d}*isimu-dè*
	(a) mí-**du$_{10}$** -ge-eš im-me
19	(b) *é*-e im-ma-gub gù im-ma-dé-e
20	(c) *sig$_4$*-e im-ma-gub *gù* im-ma-**sum**-mu
	21-69 Temple Hymn
70	(I') [*sukkal*] ^{d}*isimu-dè* (C) *sig$_4$* -e *gù* ba-an-**sum**
71	(B) *é-engur-ra-ke* (A) šìr-**du$_{10}$** -ge-eš i**m-me**

The repeated elements stand in a I a b c // I' C B A relationship.

18	To the king Enki, the vizier Isimud speaks gently.
19	By the temple he stands and speaks to it.
20	By the brickwork he stands and speaks (about it).
	21-69 Temple Hymn
70	The vizier Isimud beside the brickwork speaks,
71	The E-Engurra he praises with sweet songs.

Chapter 2

BUILDING STORIES IN THE ASSYRIAN ROYAL INSCRIPTIONS

The Assyrian royal inscriptions, the earliest of which date back around the beginning of the second millennium BCE, provide the richest collection of building stories to have reached us from ancient Mesopotamia. This corpus is also potentially the most significant for the present study because the later and longer Assyrian texts represent a span of time overlapping the period of the First Temple in Israel, at which time the biblical traditions about the building of the Tabernacle and the Jerusalem Temple were either starting to crystallize, or perhaps even reaching their near-final form.

It would not be feasible in the present framework to deal separately with every single building account and all the variations in content and structure.[1] Discussion must be limited, therefore, to short investigations of only ten stories which display striking similarities to the Sumerian and Old Babylonian building accounts already studied. Several of the accounts to be discussed in this chapter are not concerned with temple building, but with the construction of certain types of secular edifices. However, it will become clear that even stories such as these had much the same content and structure, and for this reason it is appropriate to include them here.[2] I will of course point

1.   For an excellent and thorough discussion of Assyrian building accounts until the time of Tiglath-pileser I (1115–1077 BCE), see Lackenbacher 1982. For brief studies of the later material, until the time of Tiglath-pileser III (and, in particular, the stereotyped formulae employed), see Borger 1961 and Schramm 1973, *passim*. The extremely important material in the building accounts of the Sargonid kings, which constitute most of the texts to be discussed below, has not been systematically examined except in studies of building terminology or building rites such as Ellis 1968 and Baumgartner 1925. Grayson 1987 and 1991a were unavailable when this book was completed.

2.   Note *Shulgi R* (dealing with a boat) discussed above.

out where there are elements peculiar to the story of building a
secular building as opposed to a temple.

1. *The Annals of Tiglath-pileser I*[1]

This inscription, which was composed about a century and a half
before the building of the Jerusalem Temple by Solomon, describes in
its concluding section the restoration of the temples of Anu and Adad
in the city Ashur. Here is the content of the account in outline form
(King, *AKA*, 95-108; Grayson, *ARI*, II, 17-19 §§54-63):

(1)	VII	60-70	History of the temple from the time of Shamshi-Adad until demolition by Assur-Dan
		71-75a	Anu and Adad command to build the temple
(2)		75b	Molding of bricks
		76	Identifying[2] the building site
		77-84	Laying the foundations
(3)		85-108	Construction and description of the building
(4)		109-112	Bringing the gods and seating them in the temple
		113-114	The king makes the gods rejoice
(1a)	VIII	1-4	History of the *bīt ḫamri*
(3a)		5b-8	Description of the building
(4a)		9-10	Sacrifices
		11-16	Depositing precious stones in the building
(5)		17-38	Prayer on behalf of the king who built the temple
(6)		39-49	Erection of a memorial stele in the temple
		50-62	Request for future generations to restore the temple and honor inscriptions, request for blessing on those who do so
		63-88	Maledictions on those who efface the king's inscriptions

The story outline is identical to that found in the Sumerian and Old
Babylonian inscriptions. Note that a minor building account, relating

---

1.   For this inscription, see most recently Tadmor 1977. This document has a
special place in the history of Assyriology, because it served as a trial text for the
successful decipherment of cuneiform. It is surprising that in the nineteenth century,
when Assyriologists actively sought out Old Testament parallels, the resemblance of
this building account to the one in 1 Kings 5–9 was not pointed out. For the special
similarity between the concluding prayer in this text and Solomon's Temple
dedication prayer in 1 Kings 8, see below, Chapter 13.

2.   See Appendix 3.

to a *bīt ḫamri*, is inserted in the middle of the main description. This account, set off in the text above, itself follows the regular pattern. The major new component is part (6), blessings and curses to future generations who will respectively honor or disrespect the works and inscriptions of the present builder. This section, which becomes a standard part of Assyrian building inscriptions, has precedents in older inscriptions, but not in the ones discussed above.[1]

2. *The Inscriptions of Sargon II of Assyria*

Sargon spent more than half the years of his reign building a new capital city, Dūr-Šarrukēn (Fort Sargon). This grand project is described in most of the building inscriptions found at Khorsabad[2] as well as in a number of inscriptions discovered at Nimrud (Kalḫu).[3] The building of the city is mentioned as well in the contemporary *līmu* lists,[4] but additional data concerning the project come mainly from a number of administrative documents of grant associated with the purchase or requisition of real estate for the building site.[5] In addition, over one hundred letters relating to the project have survived.[6] In the temples within the city, several inscriptions containing prayers were found.[7] These prayers are not attached to any building story or inscription, but they are identical in character to the regular *Schlussgebete* which conclude such inscriptions.

For lack of a modern critical edition of Sargon's inscriptions, it is not possible at present to discuss all versions of the building account

1. For the special character of this section in the Assyrian inscriptions, see Chapter 14.
2. See Luckenbill, *ARAB*, II, pp. 1-68.
3. See Gadd 1954.
4. See Tadmor 1958: 85.
5. See Postgate 1969 no. 32 and appendix B, p. 117.
6. See Olmstead 1908: 190 n. 91; Unger, 'Dûr-Šarrukîn', *RLA*, II, 250; and, most recently, Parpola 1981: 132 and cf. the index to *CT* 53. Some of the letters have now been edited in Parpola 1987. These letters deal with several aspects of the building project and the buildings themselves, such as gathering straw and making bricks, quarrying and transporting bull colossi, cutting down and transporting wood, work assignments for skilled and non-skilled laborers, and even such administrative or financial aspects of the project as granting land for certain buildings, as well as repaying loans made by private individuals.
7. See von Soden's translations in *SAHG*, 279-82.

and their relationship one to another.[1] We will briefly discuss here three inscriptions which bear a marked similarity to those already seen.

a. *The Bull Inscription*[2]

This inscription may be divided into two parts: (1) a synopsis of all the king's works in the manner of the 'Display' or 'Summary' inscriptions (ll. 1-39); (2) the building story (ll. 31-106). The first section concludes (ll. 36-39) with the words:

šarru etpešu	The wise king
muštābil amat damiqti	who contemplates good things
ša ana šūšub namê nadûte	who, to settle abandoned wastes,
u pete kišubbê zaqāp sippate	to open fallow fields and plant orchards,
iškunu uzunšu	set his mind. . .

In these words the king presents himself as a wise king and his works as the fruits of his wisdom. These words are to be seen as an overture, leading directly into the building account (compare 1 Kgs 5.9-14!), which begins with the standard opening formula *inūmīšu* 'at that time'. Here is the content of the building account itself:

	39-42	Introduction
(1)	43-46	Site ignored by 350 previous kings
	46-49	The king (Sargon) plans and commands that the city be built
(2)	49-52	Molding bricks
	52-57	Founding the city
(3)	57-92	Description of the buildings
	57-60	Temples
	60-69	Palaces
	70-79	Statues and Decorations
	79-92	City Walls and Gates
(4)	92-97	Populating the city
	97-100	Dedication Festivities
(5)	101-102	Prayer
(6)	103-106	Curses for those who obliterate the king's works

---

1. My own preliminary investigation, which was based on the existing editions, revealed that Sargon's building accounts may be divided according to content and structure into three families: (1) 'hidden' inscriptions—on the cylinder, behind the walls and on the foundation deposits; (b) 'revealed' inscriptions—on paving slabs; (c) 'compound' inscriptions combining elements of the first two categories—in the annals, on the Bull and in Hall XIV. I hope that in the future I will have an opportunity to expand this enquiry.

2. Lyon 1883: 40-47 = Luckenbill, *ARAB*, II, pp. 91-94.

b. *The Display Inscription from Hall XIV*[1]
The building account in this inscription is nearly identical with the one contained in the Bull Inscription just examined. These are the differences:

1. In the Display Inscription from Hall XIV, the introductory lines have been expanded as follows (ll. 27-28):

ina tenēšēti nakirē	With (the help of) foreign peoples,
kišitti qātēja	the captives of my hands,
ina šēpē šad Muṣri	at the foot of Mt Muṣur
elēnu Ninâ	above Nineveh,
kī ṭēm ilīma	according to the command of the gods and
ina bibil libbīja	at the desire of my heart,
āla ēpušma	I built a city.

2. The king's prayer following the description of the dedication festivities (p. 184: ll. 69-82) is several times longer than it is in the Bull Inscription.

3. Before the curses promised to those who would obliterate the king's works, blessings are promised to all of those who will honor them (p. 184: ll. 82-85).

As a result of these additions, this display inscription contains a fuller building account than that found in the Bull Inscription, and is even closer in its content and structure to the other inscriptions. Note especially that the passage cited includes a reference to the divine command as well as to the work force. The differences between the two are not very great or all that significant, and they demonstrate once again that deletion of one element or the other does not really detract from the existence of the underlying literary pattern.

c. *The Cylinder Inscription*[2]
The cylinder inscription is marked by an especially high literary level and character, which set it apart from the other, somewhat more stereotyped, inscriptions. The scribe expands his discussion of several matters—the king's wisdom, the benefits which the building project offers the populace, the acquisition of property for the construction

1.   Weissbach 1918: 161-87 = Luckenbill, *ARAB*, II §§383-40.
2.   Lyon 1883: 30-39 no. 1 = *ARAB*, II, §§116-23.

site, the king's prayer to Shamash, Adad and Ishtar (who are referred to by rare, poetic names) and the brick-molding rites. The inscription may be divided into two parts: (a) a display inscription type of summary of the king's works; (b) the building account. Here is the building account in outline:

(1)	34-38	The king's wisdom in city planning and desert reclamation
	39-43	The benefits to mankind from building the city
	43	Planning day and night
		A command to build a temple to Shamash
	44-46	Site ignored by 350 previous kings
	47-49	The king, in his wisdom, commands to build the city
	50-52	Acquiring property[1]
	53-55	Permission requested of Shamash, Adad and Ishtar
		Permission granted[2]
(2)	56	Drafting the work force
	57-60	Molding bricks[3]
	61	Laying foundations
(3)	62-71	Description of the buildings
	62	Temples
	64	Palaces
	65-71	Wall and gates
(4)	72-74	Populating the city[4]
(5)	75	The gods accepted the king's prayer and blessed him
(6)	76-77	Curse for the obliterator of the king's works

This inscription makes no reference to dedication festivities *per se*, although populating the city is certainly related to this aspect of the building account (as it was in the Bull Inscription). There is also no reference to blessings for those who respect the works of the king. Furthermore, instead of a prayer for the king, there is simply a statement that the gods accepted his prayer and blessed him.

In addition to these 'omissions' and changes, there is one 'innova-

1.   See Postgate 1969: 117 and Parpola 1987, *passim*.

2.   For prayers requesting permission to build temples or cities, see Langdon 1912: 100, *Nebuchadnezzar* no. 12 col. II, ll. 9-27; p. 238, *Nabonidus* no. 3 col. II, ll. 34-40 and the inscription of Warad-Sin, Falkenstein 1964, ll. 65-66, as well as Nehemiah 1 and Daniel 9.

3.   See Ellis 1968: 175 n. 4.

4.   For the similarity between teaching the new population the ways of the land in Sargon's inscriptions and in 2 Kgs 17.24, see Tadmor 1967: 201, and after him in greater detail Paul 1969.

tion', namely the description of acquiring property. The action itself reminds the reader of King Ahab's suggestion to Naboth the Jezreelite—'Sell me your vineyard for silver, or if you prefer, I will give you another vineyard in exchange' (1 Kgs 21.6). Sargon offers to buy fields for silver and those who do not accept this offer are offered new fields in exchange for their old fields.[1] This incident may also be compared with David's purchase of Araunah's threshing floor for the purpose of building an altar (2 Sam. 24.24).

3. *The Inscriptions of Sennacherib*

The major building project of Sennacherib's reign was the rebuilding of Nineveh as his new capital. I will examine here three 'Bauberichte' which tell about the 'Palace Without a Rival'.[2]

a. *The Inscription Containing One Campaign*[3]

	63-65		A hymn in praise of Nineveh[4]
(1)	66-69		Previous kings ignored the city
	70		Sennacherib, according to his own will and the command of the gods decides to build the city
(2)	71a		Drafting work force (taking of captives)
	71b		Molding bricks
	72		Clearing reed marshes with help of captives
	73-75		Demolishing the old palace
(3)	76-90		Building the new palace, and its description
		76-82	Building—exterior and interior
		83-86	Statuary

1.   For expropriation of fields for building purposes, see perhaps the Irišum inscription, but cf. the comments of Landsberger and Balkan 1950: 235-37 and Grayson, *ARI*, I, 11 n. 37.

2.   For Sennacherib's inscriptions, see Reade 1975 and Levine 1983.

3.   Luckenbill 1924: 94-98.

4.   The introductory hymn emphasizes the heavenly plan of the city and its great antiquity, an obvious desideratum for a totally new capital! The plan is revealed in the stars, referred to as heavenly writing *(šiṭir burummê)*. The attempt to associate Nineveh with Apsu, referred to here as *lalgar* (see *CAD* L p. 47a) is perhaps connected with a rivalry with Babylon, which according to Babylonian tradition was built opposite Apsu, or in imitation of Apsu *(meḫret apsî)*, but cf. W.F. Lambert 1954–56: 319. For the cosmic relationship between Babylon and Apsu, see Moran 1959b.

	87-89	Landscaping and gardening
	89-90	Digging canals
(4)	91-92	Dedication festivities
(6)	93-94	Appeal to future generations and promise of blessing to those who restore the palace when it becomes dilapidated

The only elements of the pattern missing here are the prayer or blessing for the king (5) and the threat of curses in part (6).

b. *The Inscription Containing Five Campaigns*[1]

	V 23-33	Hymn of praise to Nineveh
(1)	34-42	Previous kings ignored the city
	43-47	Previous kings ignored the palace
	48-51	Sennacherib, by his own will and by the command of the gods decides to rebuild the city
(2)	52-55a	Drafting work force (taking of captives)
	55b-56a	Molding bricks
	56b-84	Demolishing the previous palace[2]
	85-90	Diverting the river
(3)	91–VIII 64	Description of the buildings
	V 91–VI 14a	Preparing the site—measurements
	VI 14b-44	The palace buildings
	VI 45–VII 52	The palace statuary
	53-57	Gardening around the palace
	58–VIII 5	The city, walls and gates
	6-12	Moat around the city
	13-15	Wall
	16-64	Gardening and forestation
(4)	VIII 65-76	Dedication festivities
	65-73	Divine festivities
	74-76	Human festivities
(6)	77-87	Appeal to future generations to restore ruins and promise of blessing to anyone who does so

Like the inscription containing one campaign, this makes no mention of a prayer or blessing for the king (5).

1. Luckenbill 1924: 103-106; and see also Heidel 1953: 117-88.
2. Lines 64-83 are a parenthetical statement here concerning the making of the statues for the old palace, and not for the new palace, as Luckenbill would have it (cf. Luckenbill 1924: 104, 105 n. 1). Line 84 *ekalla ṣeḫra šâtu*, that small palace, is a resumptive repetition (*Wiederaufnahme*) picking up in brief lines 56-60: *ekallu maḫrītu. . . ṣuḫḫurat šubassu*, the earlier palace. . . its area was too small. For transporting statues, see Laessøe 1953: 19ff.

c. *The Undated Bull Inscription*[1]

This is basically the same building account as the previous two, but with the following adaptations: a single inscription is written over two bulls rather than on one cylinder; there are no curses or blessings for a future king (6), but there is a prayer for the good of the palace (5); the selection of the king, which emphasizes his divinely granted wisdom, replaces the first part of the building account, which, in the other texts, told of the decision to build on divine command or with divine approval.

	Bull 1, 1-2	Introduction
(1)	3-6	Selection of the king (line 4, granting wisdom)
(2)	6-7	Drafting workmen, molding bricks
(3)	7-53	Description of buildings
	Bull 2, 1-48	Description continues
(4)	48-52	Dedication festivities[2]
(5)	52-53	Prayer

4. *The Inscriptions of Esarhaddon*[3]

M. Weinfeld has already pointed out certain similarities between the Solomonic Temple-building account and Esarhaddon's description of the restoration of Babylon which had been destroyed by Sennacherib[4] (Borger 1956: 10-29), and there is no need to repeat his most appropriate observations. However, it seems that two other building accounts of Esarhaddon are even closer to the standard literary pattern which we have noticed, and which we will find in 1 Kings as well, than are the Babylon building reports.

1. Luckenbill 1924: 117-25.

2. The account of the dedication ceremonies starts with the fomula *ultu šipir ekallīja uqattû* 'When I completed the work of my palace. . .' For similar formulae, see our discussion of the Lugalannemundu inscription above, and especially below, Part 2, Chapter 10 section 3.

3. See Borger 1956. For additional texts, see Borger 1957–58 and Cogan 1984.

4. See Weinfeld 1972: 249. For Esarhaddon's Babylonian inscriptions, see Cogan 1983.

a. *The Restoration of the Assur Temple, Ešarra*[1]

(1)	16-41	History of the Assur temple from the time of its founding by Ušpia until its most recent collapse
	III 42–IV 6	Acquiring divine consent to rebuild the temple (liver divination)
(2)	7-15	Enlisting the work force
	16-18	Demolition of the former structure
	19-22	Sprinkling oil on the building pit (*tarrahu*, or mixing mortar with oil)
	23-26	Molding bricks
	27-40	King ceremoniously molds brick
	41-V 2	The people mold bricks for one year
	V 3-12	Founding the temple
	13-16	Depositing foundation deposits
	17-26	Lifting up the *libittu maḫrītu* and placing it in the foundations
(3)	V 27–VI 27	Description of the construction process and poetic account of the building
	V 27–VI 23	The structure
	24-27	The furnishings
(4)	28–VII 27	Dedicating the temple (Part 1)
	28-36	Seating the gods in their places
	37–VII 8	Sacrifices
	8-12	Gifts to the gods
	13-16	'Foreign seed'[2] is removed from the temple and Assur calmed down

1.   Borger 1956: 3 para. 2 Assur A col. III 16ff. and see also Borger 1957–1958: 113 for a partly parallel and more poetic account.

2.   This note is enigmatic. For the expression *zêru aḫû*, see B. Landsberger's reading of lines I 12 (*[ša za-r]a a-ḫi-tim*) and II 10 (NUMUN *a-ḫi-tim*) in the Puzur-Sin inscription (Landsberger 1954: 32, and see Grayson, *ARI*, I, 30, §175). However, in the recent re-publication of the inscription (Grayson 1985) the expression is read in both places *ši-bi-iṭ a-ḫi-tim* and translated 'foreign plague' (?) on the basis of a phrase *šibṭi aḫi'ati* in an incantation published by C.B.F. Walker, *CT* 51 no. 142.7. Esarhaddon removes non-Assyrians from the temple. By so doing he acts vastly differently from the legendary Lugalannemundu, who takes pride in the many foreign kings who did homage to the newly built Enamzu Temple. Perhaps Esarhaddon's actions are to be explained in light of cultic prohibitions of entry such as those hinted at in the Bible (e.g. 2 Sam. 5.8; Num. 5.1-14; Isa. 52.1), as well as entry prohibitions for Gentiles known from the Second Temple Period. For entry restrictions in the ancient Near East, see Milgrom 1970; Weinfeld 1982, and most recently Weinfeld 1985: 57ff.

(5)	VII 17-25	Assur blesses the king
(4)	26-34	Dedicating the temple (Part 2)
		Popular festivities for three days and Assur calmed down
(6)	35–end	Address to future generations—promise of blessings and
		curses to preservers and effacers of inscriptions

This inscription contains the complete pattern. Interestingly, the blessing for the king does not stand at the end, but comes in the middle of the dedication ceremonies, between the celebrations aimed at the gods and the popular festivities. We will see an analogous situation in 1 Kings 8.

b. *Restoration of the ekal māšarti (Armory)*[1]

(1)	40-47	History of the armory and the reason for reconstructing it (old
		building too small)
(2)	47-48	Enlistment of work forces
	49	Molding bricks
	49-50	Demolishing the old armory
	50-53	Founding the new armory
	54-73	Enlisting 22 kings of western provinces
	74-76	Transporting wood
	77–VI 1	Transporting stones
(3)	VI 2	Description of construction and of building
	2-14	The edifice
	15-26	The statuary
	27-29	Decorating the walls
	30-31	Planting an orchard
	32-33	The courtyard
	33-34	Horse troughs
	35-43	Conclusion, naming of the building
(4)	44-53	Dedication festivals (Part 1)
	44-47	Festivals for the gods
(5)	47-48	The gods bless the king
(4)		Dedication festivals (Part 2)
	48-53	Popular festival
(5)	54-64	Prayer for the king
(6)	65-75	Appeal to future generations
		Promise of blessing for those who respect the king's inscriptions

---

1.   Borger 1956: 59, Nin. A-F Epis. 21. On this building and the inscriptions which tell of its construction, see Turner 1970. For an additional manuscript and an English translation, see Heidel 1956.

This inscription obviously follows the pattern completely even though there are no curses in part (6). Admittedly, part (1) contains no hint of divine sanction for the building project, but this may probably be attributed to the totally secular nature of the building. As in the previous inscription, a divine blessing (5) is mentioned within the context of the dedication festivities (4), between those of the gods and those of the populace. However, in this text, it does not come as a substitute for a prayer for the king, which, as expected, appears subsequently in its normal position.

5. *The Inscriptions of Assurbanipal*

The end of the Rassam Prism reports the building of the *bīt ridûti*, the residence of the crown prince.[1]

(1)	X 51-56	History of the *bīt ridûti*
	57-73	Reasons to build/determining the building's fate
(2)	74-75	Demolishing the former building
	76-80	The building platform (*tamlû*)
	81-84	Founding the building
	85-95	Drafting workmen and molding bricks
(3)	96-106	Description of the new building
(4)	106-108	Dedication of the building, entry of the king
(6)	108-115	Blessings to those who respect the building
	116-120	Curses to those who destroy the king's inscriptions

This inscription too contains no prayer or blessing for the king (5), but the remainder of the expected elements are present. It is not stated explicitly that the king undertook the building project on divine command or that he attained divine permission or consent for it, but, it is stated that the gods determined a good destiny for the building (l. 73), which reminds us of the heavenly scenes from the Sumerian and Old Babylonian building accounts. Furthermore, among the merits of the building recounted by Assurbanipal (ll. 59-72) he states that his dreams on his bed were good and that in the morning his *egirrû* were excellent. This word, as seen by A.L. Oppenheim, refers to favorable revelations from the divine sphere.[2] It may be conjectured that the

1.   Streck 1916: 84-90 = *ARAB*, II, §§835-40; a somewhat shorter version of the same building account is found in Aynard 1957: 60.
2.   See Oppenheim 1956: 229, and compare *CAD* E, *s.v. egirrû*, and the comments of Aynard, (1957: 61).

dreams and the *egirrû* revelations mentioned were associated somehow with the king's decision to build, and that they indicate that he was urged or encouraged to do so by the gods.

Chapter 3

BUILDING STORIES IN THE NEO-BABYLONIAN ROYAL INSCRIPTIONS[1]

The inscriptions of the Chaldaean kings of Babylon are substantially different from those of the kings of Assyria. They tell close to nothing about the kings' heroic acts, and have abandoned the annalistic format developed over the long course of Assyrian historiographic writing from the end of the second millennium until the time of Assurbanipal. The Babylonian monarchs boast in their royal inscriptions almost exclusively about their building projects and their support of the cult. The royal inscriptions in general, and the building inscriptions in particular, cease to be historical inscriptions of the type we have come to know from the Assyrian corpus.[2] Although disappointing to the political or military historian, these inscriptions are an extremely important source of knowledge concerning such matters as building rituals, descriptions and inventories of buildings and cultic objects, religious views concerning building, and various customs attached to building. To be sure, these inscriptions provide several examples of building stories which, in their narrative structure, resemble those

1. For the Neo-Babylonian building inscriptions, see Berger 1979. Berger presents a complete catalogue of all the texts, as well as literary analyses of the individual inscriptions. S. Langdon's study (1912: 1-58) is still very valuable. Building stories are almost totally absent from the Babylonian inscriptions of the Kassite and post-Kassite period before Nabopolassar (see a catalogue of inscriptions in Brinkman 1968: 4-6). Of interest regarding particular motifs, however, are the Simbar-šīḫu inscription (Goetze 1965), the Nabuaplaiddina grant document (King 1912: XXXVI), the Nabû-šum-imbi inscription (W.G. Lambert 1968), the Late Babylonian historiographic piece about Nabû-šuma-iškun recently published by von Weiher (1984), and the fragmentary Adad-šuma-uṣur epic, Grayson 1985: 56-77.

2. The substitution of building accounts for military records appears as early as the end of the Neo-Assyrian period in the Thompson Prism of Ashurbanipal (see Cogan and Tadmor 1981: 230 n. 5).

found in the Bible and the older Sumerian, Old Babylonian and Assyrian inscriptions. At the same time, however, the pattern seems to have undergone somewhat of a metamorphosis.

As in the treatment of the previous inscriptions, the discussion of the Neo-Babylonian texts will be confined to a small selection of building stories which most nearly resemble the accounts already analysed, so as to establish the continuation (and slight deterioration) in this corpus of what has already become recognizable as a 'traditional' or accepted story format.

1. *The Inscriptions of Nabopolassar*

a. *Nabopolassar's Account of Building Etemenanki*[1]

(1)	21-29	Introduction—Nabopolassar defeats the Assyrians
	30-33	Collapse of the Ziqqurat
	34-38	Marduk commands to rebuild the temple
(2)	39–II 11	Drafting workmen
		Molding bricks and floating them down the canal
	12-32	Experts and wise men survey the site
	33-41	The gods confirm the measurements
	42-46	Purifying the site
	47-61	Founding the temple and foundation deposits
	62–III 27	The king and his sons ceremoniously mold bricks
(3)	28-37	Description of the building
(5)	38-59	Prayer for the king

This text makes no reference to the dedication ceremonies (4) and contains no concluding section appealing to future generations to respect the king's works (6). In this inscription as well as the next one to be discussed, building the temple is organically linked to the defeat of the Assyrians. This is not merely a historical fact. The linking of the two events may be related to the pattern of the 'victorious temple builder' or the 'divine warrior' frequently mentioned in the writings of biblical scholars (Gaster, Kapelrud, Ulshoeffer, F.M. Cross and his disciples).[2] This pattern in fact exists in all the Assyrian royal inscriptions in which the king's military victories are placed before the building account concluding the inscription. In these two texts of

---

1.   Langdon 1912: 60ff. *Nabopolassar* no. 1 = Wetzel and Weissbach: 1938 42; line numbering follows Wetzel and Weissbach.

2.   For more details and bibliography, see below, Chapter 5 on *Enuma Elish*.

Nabopolassar, the two events are placed into the same clause, thus strengthening the link and making it more explicit.

b. *Nabopolassar's Account of Building Egidriduntilla, the Ninurta Temple in Babylon*[1]

	2-4	*inu*—Historical Introduction—Selection of the king, vanquishing enemies, Assyrians expelled from land of Akkad (Babylonia)
	22	*inūšu*
(1)	23-24	The temple is built by a previous king but is not completed
	24	The king sets his mind ('ear') to completing the temple
(2)	25-26	Drafting workmen, labor assigned
(3)	27-30	Description of the building
(6)	31-37	Blessing is promised to visitors of the temple andthe righteous king
	38-41	Request to honor the king's inscriptions

This inscription makes no reference to a divine command to build the temple, nor is any explicit connection made between the selection of the king and the building of the temple. There is also no dedication ceremony (4) or prayer for the king (5), but this last element may be replaced by the blessings promised for visitors in the temple. (Lines 31-37 are of a unique exhortative nature, and will be discussed in Chapter 13)

2. *The Inscriptions of Nebuchadnezzar II*

Nebuchadnezzar's Account of Rebuilding Etemenanki[2]
This inscription is partially broken, but enough has survived to permit us to discern its content and structure.[3]

(1)	part III	
	8-21	Nabopolassar founded the temple but did not raise its head above 30 cubits
	22-26	Nebuchadnezzar undertakes to raise the temple's head to heaven

1. Langdon 1912: 66ff. *Nabopolassar* no. 4. The *Bauberichte* in a recently published cylinder of Nabopolassar (Al-Rawi 1985) tells somewhat poetically of building Imgur-Enlil, the wall of Babylon, but the framework of this inscription is identical to Nabopolassar no. 1.

2. Langdon 1912: 144ff., *Nebuchadnezzar* no. 17 = Wetzel and Weissbach 1938: 44-47.

3. Line numbers according to Wetzel and Weissbach: 1938.

(2)	27-49	Men are drafted from all over the empire
	49-53	The corvée is imposed on the armies of Shamash and Marduk (citizens of Sippar and Babylon?)
	54-58	Continuation of the draft description (break)
	part IV	
	1-32	Wood is dragged from Lebanon by foreigners
	33-38	Drafting workers, imposition of the corvée
	39-40	Foundation
(3)	41–part V	Description of the building
(5)	7-30	Prayer

There is no explicit statement that the gods commanded or approved the building project. Nonetheless, the passage which preceded the building account claimed that the king had been selected by the gods and that he heeded them (part II l. 2–part III l. 7). This is an echo of the literary topos found in the Sumerian and Old Babylonian inscriptions, in which the actual selection of the king is integrally connected with his specific mission to build a temple or city, or to do some particular deed. This inscription also contains no dedication ceremony (4) or address to future generations (6).

3. *The Inscriptions of Nabonidus*

a. *Nabonidus's Account of Rebuilding Ebabbar, the Shamash Temple in Larsa*[1]

(1)	I 31–53	History of the temple—last restored by Nebuchadnezzar, but too small and not built according to the original layout
	54–II 5	Shamash remembered his temple and desired that it be exalted
	6-9	Shamash waited for Nabonidus to do work
	10-26	A wind from Marduk uncovered for Nabonidus the original form of the temple
	26-33	The king's fear and contemplation
	34-40	Prayer
	41-47	The plan for restoration is approved by extispicy
	48-51	The king rejoices
(2)	52–III 4	Drafting workmen and founding the temple
(3)	5-26	Description of the building
(6?)	27-31	Erection of monuments
(5)	32-54	Prayer for the king

---

1. Langdon 1912: 234-43 *Nabonidus* no. 3.

This inscription mentions the setting up of monuments, which in the Assyrian inscriptions was usually included in part (6). Here the erection of monuments appears before the prayer for the king (5) and seems to be incorporated into the description of the building (3). There are likewise no blessings or curses to protect the monuments. Especially interesting is the description of how the original layout of the temple was revealed.[1] The passage is parallel in its subject matter to the description of surveying the building site found in the Nabopolassar inscription mentioned above, but it appears here as part of the first section (1) of the inscription, and is connected not with the preparations for the project (2), but with the acquiring of divine approval for the building plan and decision to build (1). Divine revelation of the building plan does not appear in these inscriptions in a revelatory dream, but comes about by natural miracles and through activities connected with the necessities of building itself. This inscription too makes no mention of dedication ceremonies (4).

It may be noted here that the idea of a divinely revealed temple plan is totally missing in the Assyrian inscriptions (except, as stated above, perhaps in the hymnic introduction to the Sennacherib building stories about Nineveh). In addition, the idea of the king's fear and hesitation, which permeated Gudea Cylinder A, and which is found here and in other Babylonian building stories, is absent from the Assyrian building accounts before Esarhaddon.[2]

---

1.   The miraculous event itself seems to be 'lifted' from an inscription of Nebuchadnezzar (see Langdon 1912: 96, *Nebuchadnezzar* no. 10 I 11–II 1). Galling (1961) suggested that this incident was the origin of Zechariah's words 'Not by might, nor by power, but by my spirit (literally 'wind', *rûḥî*)' in Zech. 4.6.

2.   Not so in the Babylonian inscriptions. See for instance Goetze 1965: 122 l. 22 (Simbar-Šīhu); Walker and Kramer 1982: 72 l. 11ʹ (Bēl-ibni); and cf. *CAD* N, *s.v. nakādu* 2b. Note also, perhaps, Hag. 1.12, 'Zerubbabel son of Shealtiel and the high priest Joshua son of Jehozadak and all the rest of the people gave heed to the summons of the Lord their God and to the words of the prophet Haggai, when the Lord their God sent him; *the people feared the Lord*', cf. also 2.5.

b. *Nabonidus's Account of the Rebuilding of Ebabbar, the Shamash Temple in Sippar*[1]

(1)	History of the Temple	
	I 10-15	Introduction—The king takes notice of Shamash Temple
	16-18	The temple in Sippar has lain in ruins for a long time
	19-22	A previous king had restored the temple in an inappropriate manner and it collapsed
	Divine approval	
	23-29	Nabonidus saw the building in ruins, was afraid and inquired through extispicy what to do, and received divine instruction to restore the temple.
	Revelation of Plan	
	30-31	The king places Shamash in a temporary dwelling[2]
	31-39	The king sends experts to search for the original foundations of the temple, and they discover the foundations laid by Naram-Sin
(2)	40–II 1	The king rejoices and lays new foundations
(3)	2-12	Description of the new temple
(4)	13-15	Anointing the doors and locks in honor of the gods' entry into the temple[3]
(5)	15-51	Prayer for the king

This building story is written according to the complete traditional pattern with the exception of blessings and curses (6). As in the previous inscriptions, one matter—Nabonidus' success in building according to a plan which was unknown to a previous king—is emphasized and presented in great detail and at considerable length, this being duly compensated for by brevity in other sections of the account. Emphasizing one particular aspect or incident causes the first part (1) of the pattern to swell out of proportion while section (2)—the preparations—is reduced to merely a single short sentence.

---

1. Langdon 1912: 252ff., *Nabonidus* no. 6.
2. See Appendix 4 and Hurowitz forthcoming 4.
3. This passage alludes to the dedication ceremonies, but the description differs from other accounts of dedication rites in that the god's entry into the temple is mentioned as something which is yet to occur. For the use of oil and the importance of the doors in the ceremonies described, see below in the excursus to the chapter on dedication ceremonies (Chapter 11).

c. *An Account from Sippar about Rebuilding Eḫulḫul, the Sin Temple in Harran*[1]

This inscription contains three separate building stories—building Eḫulḫul, the Sin Temple in Harran; building Ebabbar, the Shamash Temple in Sippar; and building Eulmash, the Anunnitum Temple in Sippar. We are concerned here with the first account.

(1)	I 8-13		History of the temple—destruction by the Umman-manda
	13-15		Sin is reconciled with Ebabbar
	16-27		The king's dream
		16-22	Command to build the temple
		23-25	The king's reply to the gods
		26-27	Marduk promises that the enemies preventing the rebuilding of the temple will be vanquished
	28-33		The promise is fulfilled, the enemy vanquished by Cyrus (the dream is verified)
	34-38		The king is joyful and confident
(2)	38-49		Drafting the work force
	50–II 5		Founding the temple (the king's joy is connected perhaps to uncovering the foundations laid by Assurbanipal)
	5-6		Foundation rites
(3)	7-17		Description of the building
		7-13	Overlaying the walls and doors with gold
		14-17	Statuary
(4)	18-25		Dedication—God is seated in the temple
(5)	36-43		Prayer to Sin on behalf of the king
(6)?	43-46		Monuments are set up

This inscription too displays the complete traditional pattern. There are, admittedly, no blessings and curses (6), but the monuments, the preservation of which is usually the purpose of this section, are mentioned where expected.

d. *Harran Inscription of Nabonidus, Another Account of the Rebuilding of Eḫulḫul*[2]

This inscription as well tells of the restoration of Eḫulḫul, Sin's temple in Harran.[3] Most of the inscription describes Nabonidus's exile

---

1. Langdon 1912: 218ff., *Nabonidus* no. 1.
2. Gadd 1958 = Röllig 1964 = A. L. Oppenheim, *ANET*, 562.
3. On account of the dream report, this text has already been mentioned by Weinfeld (1972) as one of the Mesopotamian building accounts with biblical parallels.

in the Arabian desert and his return from exile,[1] but this story has
been incorporated into the framework of the building story.[2]

(1)	I 11-14	A dream in which Sin commands Nabonidus to rebuild Eḫulḫul
[+]	14–III 17	The king wanders ten years in the Arabian desert
	17-18	The king observes the command of the god
(2)	18-21	Drafting workmen
(3)	21-22	Building Eḫulḫul
(4)	22-28	Dedication—Sin is seated in the temple
		Popular festivities
	29-35	Conclusion—The king fulfilled the god's command
(6)	35–end	Address to future generations

The two parts of the building account, which are separated from one
another by the description of Nabonidus's desert sojourn, are connected by means of a *Wiederaufnahme*. In the description of the
dream we find (12-14):

> *Eḫulḫul bīt Sīn ša Ḫarrani ḫanṭiš epuš*
> *mātāti kalašina ana qātēka lumallâ*

> Ehulhul, Sin's temple in Harran, speedily build!
> *All the lands* I will *deliver into your hands*

In the description of drafting workmen, with which the building
account resumes, we find (III 18-21):

> *ušadkâmma nīšē māt Akkadî u Ḫatti*
> *ultu pāṭ miṣir tâmti elît adi tamti šaplit*
> *ša Sīn šar ilāni umallû qātu'a*

> *I* called up *the people of Akkad and Hatti*
> *from the shore of the upper sea to the lower sea*
> which Sin, king of the gods, had *delivered into my hands.*

---

1. For the history of this period, see Beaulieu 1985: 234-87. Nabonidus's exile
described in this text was apparently the basis for the biblical tradition about
Nebuchadnezzar found in Daniel 4. But, typologically, this story should be compared with the story of Idrimi, king of Alalakh, and with its various biblical parallels,
such as the story of Jacob in Harran, Moses in Midian, Jephtah in the Land of Tob,
David in the desert, and Jeroboam in Egypt. In all these stories, a man flees from his
rivals and lives in a foreign land under the protection of his god; then, after a divine
revelation, he returns to his land of origin and suppresses his opponents. This is,
apparently, a type of story characteristic of the Mediterranean area; cf. Greenstein and
Marcus 1965.

2. See Hurowitz 1983–84.

The building story which appears in this inscription is actually an abbreviated version of the one found in the Sippar cylinder, analyzed above. W. Moran suggested that the two stories are in fact based on a common source, which was none other than one of the building inscriptions emplanted in the Eḫulḫul temple itself at the time of its construction.[1]

Comparing all the above Neo-Babylonian building stories—those of Nabopolassar, Nebuchadnezzar and Nabonidus—reveals that each author took interest in a different stage of the building process. Nabopolassar goes to great lengths to describe how the building site was surveyed, while Nebuchadnezzar silently skips over this stage, preferring to emphasize the participation of hordes of people in the building project. Nabonidus, in contrast to the two others, tells in detail about his efforts to reveal the most ancient and original foundations and layouts of the temples which he rebuilds. This activity has won him, perhaps unjustifiably, the title 'archaeologist' (Goosens 1948). But the miraculous ways in which he sometimes discovers the sought-after earliest foundations indicate that it is not purely antiquarian interest that motivates him. He is, in fact, intent on demonstrating that the gods themselves had revealed the temple plans to him, and have, thereby, also expressed approval of his designs.

Similar 'literary license' was noticed in the Assyrian building stories. Esarhaddon tells how he rebuilt the Assur temple Ešarra, stressing the ceremonious molding of bricks—an activity in which he participated personally, together with all the inhabitants of his empire. This same king, when describing how he rebuilt his Armory (*ekal mašarti*), provides a complete roster of all the subject kings who provided him with wood and stone. Sennacherib, as we saw, was most elaborate in describing the buildings themselves, and also spared no pains praising his own personal skills as engineer, craftsman and artist. Sargon, in his cylinder inscription, lauded his own wisdom in planning the new city Dūr-Šarrukēn, as well as his honesty and righteousness in acquiring real estate for the project.

By choosing and expanding upon a specific topic or a small number of subjects which interested the author or his royal patron, the stories were personalized and 'de-stereotyped'. The 'price' paid was that the underlying traditional plan of the story became distorted, somewhat

1.   See Moran 1959.

skewed, lopsided and asymmetrical. The lack of proportion becomes even more exaggerated when, in order to compensate for the expansion of one element, certain other story components are reduced and nearly eliminated.

Yet, despite the difference brought about by shifting centers of gravity, and despite the relative proportions of the narrative components, the stories do not differ from one another in their overall form. All of the scribes, Assyrian and Babylonian alike, wrote their building accounts on the basis of the same fundamental literary pattern, although they tailored the pattern to fit the particular tastes, needs and circumstances of their royal patrons. By maintaining the basic underpinnings of the story, the scribes were naturally preserving and reaffirming the venerated message of the composition, namely that the king, by building a temple, had fulfilled in the time-honored manner the traditional role of temple builder and divine servant.

Chapter 4

DIFFERENCES BETWEEN THE BABYLONIAN AND ASSYRIAN BUILDING ACCOUNTS

At the beginning of Chapter 3, certain differences between the general character of the Neo-Babylonian and the Assyrian royal inscriptions were pointed out. In the subsequent survey of some Neo-Babylonian building accounts, attention was also called to various motifs found frequently in one corpus, but rare or absent in the other. In addition to these types of differences, two important incongruities in the structures of the building stories themselves are notable:

a. Blessings and curses for those who respect or disrespect the inscriptions and buildings (6), which were regular and nearly fixed features in the Assyrian building stories, are almost completely absent from the Neo-Babylonian building stories (this includes both the texts studied explicitly above as well as the remainder of the known material). At most, there is a shadow of this section in occasional references, sometimes out of place, to the erecting of monuments. Blessings and curses are found in two inscriptions of Nabonidus (the Sippar Cylinder, Langdon 1912: 228 *Nabonidus* no. 1 col. iii ll. 43-50, and the Harran Stele, Gadd 1958: 64 ll. 35ff.) and in one inscription of Nabopolassar (Langdon 1912: 68 *Nabopolassar* no. 4 ll. 31-40). However, the two Nabonidus inscriptions were composed under the influence of Assurbanipal's inscriptions and contain other Assyrianisms as well. It is possible that the Nabopolassar inscription also was composed under Assyrian influence (this inscription is also exceptional in that it does not end with a prayer for the king as is the usual custom of Neo-Babylonian inscriptions).

b. Descriptions of dedication ceremonies (5) are rare and very brief. Four inscriptions of Nebuchadnezzar narrate that the king seated the gods in the temples in happiness and joy,[1] but in all these examples the statement comes not in the 'main' building account at the end of the inscription, and for which the inscription was composed, but finds itself in the 'secondary' building accounts which make up the 'historical background' section of the texts. Dedication ceremonies are described in a 'main' building story (the story concluding the inscription) only in Nabonidus' inscriptions, and, apparently, only under special circumstances. Two inscriptions (Langdon 1912, *Nabonidus* nos. 1 and 6) come from the Shamash temple in Sippar. Suffice it to say that one inscription (no. 1, The Sippar Cylinder) is composed of three different inscriptions, and is not the original inscription composed for the building of Ebabbar. This inscription was written after Nabonidus's return from Teima,[2] and therefore resembles the 'secondary' building stories in that it relates the dedication rites in retrospect. The other inscription (no. 6) tells of the entry of the god as something that *has yet to happen.*[3]

1. Langdon 1912: 72 *Nebuchadnezzar* no. 1 II 23; 142 no. 16 I 31; 172 no. 19B VIII 20-23; Unger 1970: 282 no. 26 2-4.

2. See on this matter Tadmor 1965: 350, and Beaulieu 1985: 59-60.

3. On this inscription and its special peculiarities, see above, Chapter 3, section 1b. Several concluding prayers as well speak about the entry of the god as something which has yet to occur and contain the formula '*DN ana* TN *bītīka ḫadīš ina erēbīka*', 'O DN when you happily enter TN your temple!' (see Langdon 1912: 76 *Nebuchadnezzar* no. 1 III 38; 96 no. 10 II 12-15; 102 no. 12 II 41-43: 222 *Nabonidus* no. 1 II 28; 226 III 13-14, 39; 252 no. 5 II 7-8; 257 no. 6 II 15-16).

Chapter 5

BUILDING STORIES IN MESOPOTAMIAN MYTHOLOGY

Enuma Elish. This so-called 'Babylonian Creation Myth'—in fact a hymn of praise to Marduk—represents, perhaps, the example *par excellence* of what some scholars call the 'Divine Warrior' topos, in which a victorious god returns from battle to a newly built temple, constructed in honor of his victory.[1] This pattern is attested elsewhere in Mesopotamian mythology (Inanna and Ebih)[2] as well as in Canaanite myths (the Ugaritic Baal Epic) and may even appear in several biblical passages (such as Exod. 15, Ps. 29).[3] In *Enuma Elish* itself the pattern appears twice. The first tablet tells that Ea killed Apsu and imprisoned Mumu, after which he built his dwelling upon Apsu (I 71-78). According to the fourth tablet, Marduk, after slaying Tiamat, built Ešarra (IV 141-46), and in the wake of that glorious victory Esagila in Babylon was built (V 113-30, VI 45-81). This mythological pattern is in fact related to a historiographic topos according to which a human king who is victorious in battle builds a palace or a temple (for only a few examples out of many see the Idrimi statue, Samsuiluna C and *Nabopolassar* no. 1; cf. 2 Sam. 7 and 1 Kgs 5).[4]

1.   See Gaster 1946.
2.   See Limet 1971 for an edition of the end of the text. On p. 18 ll. 49-50, near the end of the text, we read *é-gal mu-dù nì-diri al-ak $^{gi\check{s}}$gu-za mi-ni-gub suhuš-bi mi-ni-ge-en*, 'I have built a palace, great things have I made. A throne I have set up, its foundation I have made firm.' Limet (1971: 27) has already equated this passage with Baal's palace building in the Ugaritic Baal epic.
3.   B. Halpern (1978) suggests that this topos underlies the prophecies in the first six chapters of the book of Zechariah. Other scholars have claimed to have sighted it in such places as Habakkuk 3 and even the 'Isaiah Apocalypse' (Isa. 24–27).
4.   For this topos, see Kapelrud 1963 and more recently Ulshoefer 1977. The latter study is the most detailed inquiry so far into this pattern and its implications,

In addition to this pattern, *Enuma Elish* represents an example of another pattern in which temple building is represented as the climax or purpose of a creation story, this being especially apparent in Tablet V in which the ordering of the universe precedes immediately the building of Babylon and Esagila. A connection between these two events is expressed in the Bible especially in the Priestly document, as was pointed out already by the Rabbis,[1] and is known from other Mesopotamian literature (in a temple building ritual the creation myth *inu Anu ibnû šamê*—'When Anu built the Heavens' is recited)[2] and even Egyptian sources.[3] This is not the place to discuss these well-known motifs. Instead, we will turn to the similarity between the part of the text about building Babylon[4] and the other building stories discussed above. The similarity has already been pointed out by Kapelrud, but our somewhat different definition of the building account topos invites a new analysis.

(1)	V 113-116	The gods promise to do whatever Marduk commands
	117-130	Marduk accounces his desire to build a house which will be a sign of his kingship and a resting place for gods ascending from the Apsu and descending from Heaven
		The place will be called Babylon
	131-142	The gods clarify with Marduk what their future status is to be
	143-148	Marduk replies (text damaged)
	149-156	The gods accept Marduk's supremacy and volunteer to do work (?)
	VI 1-44	Marduk fulfills his part of the bargain
		1-34 Creation of humanity to relieve the gods of work
		35-44 Division of labor among the gods
	45-54	The gods suggest building a temple for Marduk
	55-58	Marduk commands to build Babylon (approval of the gods' previous suggestion)
(2)	59-60	Molding bricks for one year (preparations)[5]

exploring biblical, Mesopotamian, Ugaritic and even Egyptian texts. Nonetheless, only part of the material has been exploited.

   1.   See Weinfeld 1981 and most recently Weimar 1988.

   2.   See Thureau-Dangin 1921: 46.23ff. (= Sachs in *ANET*, 341 Text C, Heidel 1951: 65-66 and cf. Mayer 1978: 438).

   3.   See Reymond 1969 as well as J.A. Wilson in *ANET*, 3.

   4.   On the building of Babylon at the time of creation, see the bilingual myth concerning the creation of the world by Marduk (trans. Heidel 1951: 62ff.), ll. 12-16, and ll. 36-40 concerning Marduk's building of other temples.

   5.   For gods carrying work equipment and molding bricks, see the beginning of

(3)	61-66	Description of the building and its construction
(4)	67-75	Dedication festivities
(5)	76–end	Determining destinies and assigning tasks

The party described for the dedication festivities (4) resembles the divine celebrations reported in Gudea Cylinder B, *Enki's Journey to Nippur* and the Ugaritic Baal epic, as well as those found in certain royal inscriptions. These are the elements which appear in each:

Enuma Elish	*Enki's Journey*	*Baal Epic*
71 the fathers of the gods is seated	93 slaughter	VI 35-38 proclamation
72 proclamation 'this is Babylon'	94-95 musical instruments	38-43 slaughter
73 music and joy	96-103 brewing drinks	44-46 invitation
74-75 drinking and sitting	104-108 seating the gods	47-59 drinking wine
	108-14 drinking	
	115- proclamation	

The motif of the gods resting in their temple, which appears in Marduk's words and in the words of the gods, is probably related to the motifs of (a) David's rest found in 2 Sam. 7.1, (b) Israel's rest found in the Solomonic temple-building story, and (c) perhaps even to the Sabbath command in the Tabernacle story (Exod. 31, 35) and (d) God's rest mentioned in Ps. 132.8 and Isa. 66.1.[1] See as well, in *Enuma Elish* itself, tablet I line 75, where Ea and Damkina rest in the newly built Apsu temple.

It seems that the building story in *Enuma Elish* is no more than an adaptation of a mundane literary topos for use in a divine hymn. Just as the extensive literary pattern of 'victory + temple or palace building' typifies both royal inscriptions and this hymn as well, so the building story found towards the conclusion of the hymn resembles in

---

Atrahasis as well as the Sumerian hymn to Nippur, UET VI 118 (cf. Oberhuber 1967), which begins with a story about building the city. See also the myth about creating the pickax (Kramer 1972: 51). This motif has an echo in the Ugaritic Baal epic, for which see the next chapter. It is expressed as well in Sumerian art (for which see Perkins 1957: 58-59). Specification of a period of brick molding is found in several royal inscriptions: Warad-Sin (Falkenstein 1964), ll. 80-81; Samsuiluna A, ll. 66-67; C l. 142; Esarhaddon (Borger 1956: 4 col. V 1-2, 27-18 (building Ešarra in Ashur), p. 20 Epis. 22 (building of Babylon), and see Speiser 1967b: 58.

1.   For temples and divine rest, see Appendix 5.

its structure the building stories which regularly appear in the royal inscriptions.

Just as the 'historical' temple building stories displayed a tendency to emphasize a certain motif or segment in the story at the price of brevity in describing other segments, so in the myth: one story element has been blown out of proportion in such a way that it occupies most of the story. *Enuma Elish* describes in great detail the agreement between Marduk and the other gods, and as a result the first component (1) has reached considerable length. Just as a human king will not build a palace or temple without divine permission, so the gods themselves will not construct a temple city without the permission of Marduk, the head god in the pantheon.

Chapter 6

Building Stories in Northwest Semitic Writings

1. *Building Inscriptions*

Numerous Northwest Semitic building inscriptions have survived, and some of them closely resemble the Akkadian royal inscriptions in language and style.[1] Nonetheless, these inscriptions do not contain examples of building stories approximating those which we found in the Mesopotamian inscriptions, and the likes of which we will encounter in the Bible.

The one possible exception to this rule is the inscription of Azittiwada, king of the Danunians (*KAI* 26).[2] In this composition, the style and language of which resemble the Old Babylonian royal inscriptions,[3] five components may be distinguished: (1) Royal epithets (1-2); (2) the king's deeds in his own land (3-9); (3) building the city and cultic innovations (II 9–III 2); (4) a prayer for the king (III 2-11); (5) curses for anyone who will destroy the inscription (III 12–IV 3). Part 3, which is a *Baubericht* relating the building of the city, includes a number of elements found in the other building stories. Baal and Reshep-ṢPRM sent Azittiwada to build the city (II 10-12). This statement contains an echo of the divine commands to build temples or perform other missions as found in the Mesopotamian inscriptions. Seating Baal-KRNTRYŠ in the city (II 18-19) is reminiscent of the dedication ceremonies in the Mesopotamian inscriptions, in

1. See Tawil 1972; Tawil 1973; Tawil 1974; Avishur 1979: *passim*. For some recent studies emphasizing structural aspects of Northwest Semitic inscriptions, see Younger 1986; Farber 1986.

2. See also Gibson, *SSI*, III, 41-64. For an English translation and discussion of the Hieroglyphic Luwian version of the Karatepe inscription, see Hawkins and Davis 1978.

3. See comments of Avishur (1979: II, 219-39).

which the gods were seated in their temples.[1] The Azittiwada inscription thus contains elements (1), (4), (5) and (6) and perhaps even (3) of the standard pattern, the only element entirely missing being the preparations for the project (2). Giving the name to a city (or to a building; II 10, 18) is a feature which has numerous parallels in many Mesopotamian building inscriptions (see also 2 Sam. 5.9; Num. 32.38-42).[2]

The other Northwest Semitic inscriptions contain only rarely isolated elements or individual ideas from the building story pattern. The most important component found in numerous inscriptions is the prayer on behalf of the writer of the inscription.[3] Some individual inscriptions may hint that the god commanded the construction of the building from which the inscription originates. So, for example, in the Amman Citadel inscription (Horn, 1969) we find in the first line:

xxm]lkm. bnh. lk.mb' t.sbbt[

According to Albright's suggestion, the line should be completed and translated:

wy'mr l m]lkm. bnh. lk. mb't. sbbt[
'And Milkom said to me build. . . entrances'

This restoration implies a divine command to build some part of a building.[4]

---

1. See in particular the city dedication ceremonies mentioned briefly in the 'provincial' inscriptions of Shamash-resh-uṣur and Bēl-ḫarran-bēl-uṣur. In the first we read (Weissbach 1903: 4 col. III 1-4; trans. Dalley 1984: 201-203 [ll. 1-4] *ālam abnīma Gabbara-KAK* (?) *šumšu azkur Adad Apla-adad Šala Madānu atruṣu ina qereb ālīja Gabbari-KAK šubtu ṭābtu ušarmīšunūti* 'I built a city and named it Gabbari-KAK. Adad, Apla-adad, Shala and Madānu I set up and seated them in the midst of my city Gabbari-KAK in a good dwelling'. In the other text we find (Unger 1917; Peiser, *KB*, IV, 102 = Luckenbill, *ARAB*, I, §§823-26, ll. 15-16): 'I inscribed a stela and made on (it) an image of the gods. In a divine dwelling I erected (it). Sacrifices, bread offerings and incense for those gods I established forever.'

2. See the two texts mentioned in the previous note, as well as *CAD* N, I, 33 *nabû* A 1a, 2'c'd', 3'4'; Z p. 20 *zakāru*.

3. See, for example *y'rk. . .ymt. . .w šntw. . . 'l* (*KAI* 4.3-7; 5.2; 6.2-3; 7.4-5). The Ammonite 'Amminadab Inscripition' contains a similar prayer.

4. See Ahituv 1977: 178-79 and bibliography in n. 12. On p. 180 Ahituv compares the action described in this inscription with the divine commands to build temples known from Mesopotamian and Egyptian inscriptions and from the Bible.

In a votive inscription to Ishtar found in Pyrgi (*KAI* 277), it is written:

wbn. tw. k'štrt'rš bdy

According to one suggestion,[1] this line is to be translated: 'and he built the chamber because Ashtoreth asked[2] (it) of him. . .' This would then be another example of building upon divine command.

In the Eshmunazar inscription (*KAI* 14 = Gibson, *SSI*, III, 105ff. no. 28), there seems to be reference to seating a god in a temple. We read:

15.   *'m bnn 'yt byt 'lnm*
        'yt [bt 'štr]t bṣdn 'rṣ ym
        wyšrn [read *wyšbn!* [3]]*'yt 'štrt šmm' drm*

According to another interpretation, the inscription speaks about the city actually being built by the god Milkom. This idea is also well attested in the Bible (Exod. 15.17; Ps 78.69; 147.1 etc.) and in extra-biblical sources (see Appendix 6).

    1.   See most recently E. Lipiński in Beyerlin 1978: 244 and Gibson, *SSI*, III, 57 l. 6.

    2.   This interpretation relates *'rš* to Akkadian *erēšu*. It so happens that there are quite a few Akkadian inscriptions in which a divine command to build a city or a temple is expressed with precisely this word (see Chapter 8).

    3.   Y. Avishur (1979: I, 30) claims incorrectly that the word pair *bnh//yšb* is found only in Hebrew and in Phoenician. As a matter of fact, the word pair *banû// šūšubu* appears in inclusio in the Sippar Cylinder of Nabonidus (Langdon 1912: 222 *Nabonidus* no. 1 col. ii 8 and 12). Furthermore, this word pair should not be divorced from the synonymous pairs *epēšu//šūšubu*, *šurmû* found in Akkadian as well. In the inscription of Shamash-resh-uṣur (see above) we read:

        ālī **a b n ī ma** *Gabbari-KAK šum īšu azkur*
        Adad Apla-Adad Šala ^d*Madāna atruṣa*
        ina qereb ālīja Gabbari-KAK
        šu bta *ṭābtu u* **š a r m ī šu n ū t i**

        I built my city and called it Gabbari-KAK
        Adad. . . I established
        Within my city Gabbari-KAK
        I had them take up good residence.

In this inscription, *banû* and *šubtam šurmû* appear in an inclusio. In an inscription of Tukulti-Ninurta I (Weidner 1959: 22) we find:

        bīta **ē p u š** *u šeklil parakka arme*
        Annunita bēltī ina ḫidâte u rīš āti
        ina parakkīša **u š ēš i b**

> *w' nḥn 'š bnn bt l' šmn [š] r/d qdš*
> *nydll bhr*
> *wyšbny šmm'drm*
> *w' nḥn 'š bnn btm l' ln ṣdnm bṣdnm bṣdn 'rṣ ym*
> *bt lb'l ṣdn wbt l'štrt šm b'l*

A very fragmentary, twelfth century BCE inscription from Lachish, published recently by F.M. Cross (1984: 71ff., esp. p. 75), contains the words:

>] *'l'b*
>]*byṣ' hwšb*

These may be related somehow to seating the god Ilab in a temple.

Mesha, king of Moab, lists in his famous stela all of his building projects (*KAI* 181 ll. 21-31), and at one point he remarks (l. 25):

> *w' nk. krty. hmkrtt. lqrḥh. b' sry. yśr'l*
> And I cut down the cuttings for the beams with Israelite captives.

This remark brings to mind, naturally, the statements of the kings of Babylon and Assyria that prisoners of war cut down for them trees which were used in royal building projects (see the discussion of this motif in Chapter 9).

The bits of information gleaned here may perhaps be the remnants of a rich literary tradition which also included complete building narratives resembling those in the Mesopotamian and biblical corpora.[1] With the eventual discovery of new literary works and additional building inscriptions, more complete building stories may well be found.

2. *The Baal Epic*

This myth recounts Baal's victory over his rival Mot. The epic contains two building accounts. One is a short episode concerning building a palace for Yam (*UT* 129 = *ANET*, 129). The other, which will concern us here, is the long story about how Baal had a palace

> I built a temple and completed it and set up a dais
> Annunita my Lady in joy and happiness
> I seated on her dais

1.   See below concerning the inscription of Barrakab son of Panammu king of Sam'al.

built for himself. The complicated problem of the place of this event within the Baal Cycle cannot be discussed here,[1] and the present study will be confined to the building account itself (*UT* 51 I–VI = *ANET*, 131 II AB I–VI):

(1)   I 1-18   Baal has no palace[2]
         19-44   Hayin the artisan makes furniture[3]
         II–III   Baal and Anat visit Athirat[4]

   1.   The structure of the Baal cycle has been discussed in the Yale dissertation of Mark Smith on Kothar waHasis (M.S. Smith, forthcoming; and 1987). See also Olmo Lete 1983; Clifford 1979.

   2.   The pericope has been discussed recently by Tsevat 1978. In his opinion the text does not deal with building a new palace for a hitherto homeless Baal, but rather with building him a different house which will better suit his position as a rising god. See as well Gaster 1946. About twenty lines are missing at the beginning of the tablet, and it is not clear who is speaking when the text begins. In the opinion of Cassuto 1975 these words are said by GPN waUGR, who is speaking to Hayin on behalf of Baal and Anat. For young gods living at home with their parents, see Jacobsen 1957: 103 n. 19.

   3.   On this passage, see Dietrich and Loretz 1978, with bibliography (n. 3). In the opinion of certain scholars (Cassuto, Gordon and Bernhardt in Beyerlin 1978), Hayin is doing his work and as the story begins he is already making furniture for the palace which is to be built. This interpretation was opposed by Gaster (1946: 21), who translated 'just consider them who ingratiate. . . Asherat . . . (for them) Sir Expert goes up to the forge. . .' According to this rendition, the text describes the possible rewards which await those who appeal to or do homage to Athirat. This understanding was accepted as well by H.L. Ginsberg, who translated 'Hayin would go up to the bellows'. According to C.H. Gordon (1977: 89), the text refers to *bakshish* which Baal will give to Athirat for her services as intermediary. The presents were given to Athirat when visiting her (see II 26-28). For a similar interpretation, see also Van Selms 1975. In his opinion, Baal and Anat give Athirat a tent and furniture, which she may use for hosting her spouse Il when he calls upon her.

   4.   Columns II and III are only partially preserved, making it difficult to know exactly what happened when Baal and Anat were received by Athirat. In Cassuto's opinion (1975), the arrival of Baal and Anat at Athirat's place was preceded by a stormy confrontation between Baal and the supporters of Mot, who tried to thwart Baal's attempts to build himself a palace. Another confrontation between Baal and Mot himself —this one verbal—occurred at a meeting called by Athirat. Because this explanation depends on the interpretation of the previous passage which was rejected above, it is difficult to accept in its present form Cassuto's suggestion of a confrontation pitting Baal, Anat and Kothar waHasis against the supporters of Mot. But Cassuto's remarks about the confrontation between Baal and Mot at the divine assembly are more reasonable. Even if we do not concede the actual presence of Mot

	IV 1-19	Athirat travels to Il (accompanied by Anat) and Baal returns to Mt Saphon
	20-57	Athirat visits Il and asks his permission for Baal to build a palace
	58–V 1	Il consents to Athirat's plea and orders that a palace be built for Baal
	2-11	Athirat thanks Il
	12-19	Athirat commands Anat to tell Baal that a palace will be built
	20-35	Anat relays to Baal (verbatim) Athirat's message
(2)	35-40	Baal prepares building materials (as Athirat had commanded)
	41–VI 14	Baal summons Kothar waHasis and they plan the building in detail
	16-21	Wood from Lebanon and Siryon
(3)	22-35	Building the palace, short description
(4)	38–end	Celebration

The end of the story is broken away, but it may probably be assumed that it related how, on the occasion of celebrating the palace's completion, when Baal hosted his guests, they blessed him (compare in particular *Enki's Journey to Nippur*). If so, the building account in the Baal epic represents the complete pattern as seen in the Mesopotamian stories, the only component missing being the blessings and curses (6), which, as has been pointed out, is found nearly exclusively in Assyrian building inscriptions.

Although identical in structure to the Mesopotamian building accounts, this text introduces numerous novel details. Among the unique ideas characterizing this story, we find the petition to the chief god by the agency of his spouse, an argument between the potential palace owner and his architect concerning the design, and building by miracle (the palace rises on its own from building materials which have been cast into a fire). The last incident may have a distant parallel in the biblical account of making the golden calf, and may even be echoed in certain rabbinic Midrashim about how the Tabernacle and Temple of Solomon rose on their own.[1] The hiring of

at this meeting, it is still possible to admit to the actual existence of a confrontation between Baal and his opponents at the divine meeting. Cassuto's suggestion was opposed by Gaster (1946: 23), who opines that the text does not describe a specific incident of confrontation between the two gods, but speaks about Baal's complaint before the assembly of the gods concerning the gods' constant disrespect towards him.

1.   See Cassuto 1975 nn. 23, 91.

an artisan who is mentioned specifically by name is found here and in the Bible (Bezalel and Oholiab in the Tabernacle story, Hiram in the Temple account), and has practically no parallels in Mesopotamian writings.

Of particular interest is the refrain 'Baal has no palace like the other gods...' Students of the myth seem not to have noticed that something similar to this opening is found in an alphabetic inscription from the Sam'al. In the Ugaritic text we read:[1]

> [wn. in. bt. lb'l. kmilm. whzr. kbn.] a[trt]
> mtb.il.mzll. bnh. mtb. rbt. atrt. ym.
> mtb. klt. knyt. mtb. pdry. b{t} ar
> mzll. tly. btrb. mtb. arsy. bt. y'bdr

And now, Baal has no house like the gods or courtyard like the children of Athirat.

The dwelling of Il is his son's shelter. The dwelling of Lady Athirat of the Sea is the dwelling of the perfect brides. It is the dwelling of Padriya daughter of Ar, it is the shelter of Taliya daughter of Rab and it is the dwelling of Arsiya daughter of Yabdar.[2]

The Aramaic inscription of Barrakab (*KAI* 216 = *SSI*, II n. 15 = *ANET*, 655) concludes with a short building account in which we find (15-20):

> wby. tb. lyšh. l'bhy. mlky. šm'l.
> h'. byt. klmw. lhm. ph'. byt. štw' .lhm
> wh'. byt, kys'. w'nh. bnyt. byt'. znh

And (behold) my fathers the kings of Sam'al had no good house. They had the house of Kilamuwa and it (was) for them a winter house, and it (was) for them a summer house, but I have built this house.

In both texts, it is first stated that someone had no house, and afterward the text goes on to state what substitutes there were for the missing house. Incidentally, this parallel may be used to strengthen M. Tsevat's claim (1978) that what Baal lacks is not just any house,

---

1. Reconstruction of text according to Ginsberg 1936: 18-19 ll. 10-19. The restoration is based on the repetition of the plea in col. iv ll. 50-57, and see Ginsberg's translation in *ANET*, 131.

2. But see *Enuma Elish* V 155-56 (Landsberger and Kinnier-Wilson 1961: 168), which specifically mentions Ea as the god who will build Esagila.

but a *proper* house, for in the Barrakab inscription, the word *bt* is qualified by the adjective *ṭb*.

All of these items are, perhaps, signs of an independent, peculiarly western tradition which differed in numerous details from the Mesopotamian tradition of building stories.

These peculiarities notwithstanding, the overall structure of the story does not differ, as we have seen, from the standard pattern of Mesopotamian building accounts. Furthermore, in certain details the Baal epic loudly echoes several characteristically Mesopotamian ideas. We have already mentioned how similar the dedication festivities described in the Baal epic are to those in Gudea Cylinder B, *Enki's Journey to Nippur* and *Enuma Elish*. In addition, as will be seen later on, the idea that the head god of the pantheon must approve the building of temples and cities for lower ranking gods is also well documented in Mesopotamian building accounts. The use of silver, gold and lapis lazuli in buildings is also a sign of the Mesopotamian tradition (see, for example, *Enki's Journey to Nippur* ll. 1-17 and *UT* 51 V 80-81). It goes without saying that the use of bricks in monumental building is so characteristic of Mesopotamian architecture and literature that mentioning it in a western myth practically compels us to seek a Mesopotamian background.[1] Most significantly, Mesopotamian mythology may provide the key to understanding an enigmatic incident in the Ugaritic myth. In his response to Athirat, Il says:

wy'n lṭpn il dpid	And good, very merciful Il answered,
p'bd an. 'nn aṯrt	'Am I a slave, a servant of Athirat?
p'bd ank aḫd ulṯ	Am I a slave who holds a. . .[2]
hm amt aṯrt tlbn lbnt	Is Athirat a maidservant that she should mold bricks?
ybn bt lb'l km ilm	Let a house be built for Ba'al like the other gods
w ḫẓr kbn aṯrt[3]	and a courtyard like that of Athirat's children!'

In these lines, Il announces his consent to the requested building project. But, as a condition for his total agreement, he insists that neither he nor Athirat will have to do any work.[4] Gibson comments

---

1. M. Dahood (*RSP*, I, 246), on the basis of the Ugaritic text, proposed a Canaanite background for certain motifs in the biblical Tower of Babel story. This suggestion is quite astonishing and should be rejected outright.

2. See Held 1969: 72 for the expression *aḫd ulṯ*, 'hold a basket/brick mold'.

3. See Held 1969: 72.

4. But see in contrast Albright 1968: 122 n. 30, who claims that Athirat is a

that Il's reply is sarcastic,[1] while Gordon explains that such labor is undignified and ill befits the head of the pantheon.[2] Whatever the case may be, the very objection is surprising because it has nowhere been stated that Il had been asked to do work, and there is certainly no reason why he should be apprehensive and proclaim his refusal to do any. If so, what is he protesting about? It seems to me that the solution to this riddle lies in the Mesopotamian tradition. In *Enuma Elish* VI 59-60, the gods themselves bore work equipment and molded bricks with which to build a temple for the new head of the pantheon. Perhaps Il suspects that Athirat and Anat have come to him not only to ask his permission to build a palace for Baal, but to enlist him for the work gang which will build the palace of the young god, who is now ascending the ranks to become head of the pantheon. There may even be here an echo of the tradition found in Atrahasis[3] and in the Sumerian myth *Enki and Ninmah*,[4] according to which the young gods working for Ilu/Enlil and for Enki rebelled against them in order to cast off their yoke. Perhaps Il, in the Ugaritic myth, fears that the young gods will want to impose work upon the older generation of gods. In order to prevent any such attempt, he gives his consent to the building plan in principle, but explains at the same time that he will have no part in the work itself.[5] It may be surmised that the Ugaritic text reflects a different, unknown form of the 'Divine Strike' motif in which the striking gods tried to impose their work on the older gods.

building goddess, even suggesting that she was to have done the work of building the palace. It seems that this explanation has not met with wide scholarly approval.

1. Gibson 1977: 11.
2. Gordon 1977: 95, and see Gaster's comment (1966: 185).
3. See Lambert and Millard 1969.
4. See Benito 1969.
5. In *Enki and Ninmah*, the complaint of the crying gods was brought to sleeping Enki's attention by his mother Nammu. Enki awoke from his sleep to reply to Nammu, and, upon hearing his answer, she praised him about his wisdom. This is precisely what Athirat does when she hears Il's reply to her plea (*UT* 51 V 64-65): *wtʿn. rbt. aṯrt. ym rbt. ilm. lḥkmt*, 'The great lady Athirat answered—You are great, O Il, in wisdom'.

Chapter 7

BUILDING STORIES IN THE BIBLE AND POST-BIBLICAL LITERATURE

1. *The Building of the First Temple*

The building of the Temple in Jerusalem stands at the center of the account of Solomon's reign in the book of Kings. The matter of building the temple is also the focal point of Nathan's prophecy in 2 Samuel 7.[1] The establishment of an altar to the Lord on Araunah's threshing floor reported in the appendices to the book of Samuel (2 Sam. 24) is perhaps a related incident.[2] The book of Chronicles

1. Many scholars have considered this story a *Königsnovelle* of the type known from Egyptian literature. This evaluation follows a suggestion of A. Hermann (1938), as developed and applied to the Bible by S. Hermann (1953–54; see also his most recent statement on the matter: S. Hermann 1985). So, for instance, Whybray (1968) writes without reservation, 'It has been clearly demonstrated by a number of scholars that there are a number of passages in the narrative books of the Old Testament which so closely resemble the Egyptian royal novel that their dependence on it is beyond doubt'. Nonetheless, this approach has recently been strongly challenged. Tomoo Ishida (1977: 83-84) has argued convincingly that the type of tension between the god and the king such as is found clearly in 2 Samuel 7 is unthinkable in the Egyptian *Königsnovelle*. His reservations concerning Hermann's suggestion were viewed favorably by, for example, Malamat 1980: 68-82. In the continuation of his argument, Ishida points out a whole range of structural, stylistic and ideological parallels between Nathan's prophecy and Neo-Babylonian royal building accounts (Ishida 1977: 85ff.). Nathan's prophecy will be examined at greater length in the course of our chapter on building temples upon divine command (Chapter 8).

2. The building of the temple is not mentioned explicitly in this story, and if it is indeed an aetiological tale connected with purchasing the building site for the temple, this is somewhat surprising. Nonetheless, placing the account of this incident at the very end of the book juxtaposes it as closely as possible to the temple-building story. Cf., for example, the words of M.Z. Segal in his commentary on the books of Samuel (1965, p. 395): 'It was located here at the end of the book "to suggest" the

contains a revision of the story which might be termed 'midrashic'. I will discuss here only the version in the book of Kings.[1]

The building story is composite in several respects. Classical literary criticism has revealed that the building account contains Deuteronomic elements (1 Kgs 5.17-19; *8.1-11, 14-61; 9.1-9),[2] several Priestly expansions (1 Kgs *8.1-11)[3] and other material.[4] Form criticism has suggested that the story is a patchwork of genres including contracts and treaties (5.15-23),[5] archival-administrative records (5.27-32; 6.1; 7.2-8),[6] architectural descriptions (6–7), speeches (8.15-21, 54-61) and prayers (8.22-53),[7] a poem (8.12-13),[8] descriptions of rituals (8.1-11, 62-66),[9] and divine oracles (6.11-13, 9.1-9). Chronologically, it has been proposed that some elements in the story are contemporaneous with or of nearly the same date as the events reported (such as the poetic

building of the temple by Solomon in the next book', and note similar statements by other commentators. The two events were, to be sure, specifically connected by the Chronicler in 1 Chron. 21.28–22.1. On the relationship between the Samuel chapter and its counterpart in Chronicles, see Rofé 1979: 184-203.

1. For discussions of the Chronicles account, see Introduction. Psalm 132 should also be added to the biblical material relevant to the building of the temple. This psalm will not come under discussion here, however. For the relationship between Psalm 132 and the Northwest Semitic royal inscriptions, see Hillers 1968, and for parallels to some Egyptian and Mesopotamian texts, see Kraus 1960. See also the discussion of the Ur-Nammu hymn above (Chapter 1).

2. See Jepsen 1956.

3. See the discussion of the extent and significance of the Priestly interpolations in Chapter 12.

4. For the attribution of the remaining material to the Pentateuchal sources J and E, see Hölscher 1923.

5. But see the discussion below (Chapter 10), for a re-evaluation of the literary types found here. For a recent form-critical survey of the temple building story, see Long 1984.

6. See in particular Montgomery 1934: 51, and Montgomery and Gehman 1951: 137, and note against him (concerning 5.27-32) Noth 1968: 93.

7. See Weinfeld 1972: 35-38.

8. Most scholars accept the Greek version of this verse and hold that this is a passage quoted from *sēper hayyāšār*. This opinion I find unacceptable, and will discuss it below in Chapter 13. Even so, the poetic character of the passage is undeniable.

9. The account of bringing the Ark to the Temple highly resembles the account in 2 Sam. 6 of the bringing of the Ark into Jerusalem. For details of the similarities, see below, Chapter 12.

lines in 8.12-13)[1] while others are from late in the biblical period, at which time Priestly and Deuteronomic clichés could intermingle indiscriminately, in the imitative style of a single author (6.11-13).[2]

Despite the heterogeneity and composite nature of the pericope, the canonical form of the temple-building story presents, on the whole, a well ordered, logical literary continuity. Its unified, continuous character becomes even more apparent in light of the extra-biblical material presented above.

The story (1 Kgs 5.15–9.25) begins with Solomon's message to Hiram. In the first part of his message he announces his intentions to build a house for the Lord's name. Referring to the events of 2 Samuel 7, Solomon explains that this was not done during the time of David because of warfare which occupied his father, and goes on to specify that his plan has already received divine approval in the form of YHWH's word to David. The second part of Solomon's message, together with Hiram's message in response and some comments by the narrator, has to do with the bargaining between Solomon and Hiram for the purpose of acquiring building materials, and with the implementation of the trade agreement thereby concluded. There follows an account of the corvée duty which Solomon levied upon Israel, and of how it was organized and carried out. The work force was responsible for cutting timber in the mountains, quarrying stone, and transporting the building materials. Within this description there is an allusion to founding the temple (v. 31). This passage concludes with the statement, 'they prepared the wood and the stone to build the temple' (5.32). The unit 5.15-32 tells therefore of two topics: (1) *the decision to build the temple and the divine approval of the plan*; (2) *preparations in manpower and materials for the building project (and foundation of the building)*.

The story continues with a description of the construction process

---

1.   J. Liver (1971a) contends that all the stories about Solomon were composed close to the time of Solomon's reign. If the descriptions of the building are in fact archival records, as Montgomery (1934: 52) suggests, then 1 Kgs 6.2-10 is also contemporary with the events described. I will discuss the nature of these passages in Chapter 11.

2.   We must reject the view of Burney (1903: *ad loc.*), who attributes this passage to two different scribes. Similarly, the promise 'I will dwell in the midst of the People of Israel' stands in blatant contradiction to the Deuteronomic conception of the temple, and it is inconceivable to ascribe this phrase to this school.

itself, but the bulk of what follows is in fact a detailed picture of the buildings and their furnishings (chs. 6–7). The temple is described from without (6.2-9) and from within (6.14-32) and the description of the building concludes with a description of the courtyard (6.36). The description of the temple is enveloped by opening and concluding chronological statements (6.1, 37). The description of the temple continues in 7.15, with a descriptive inventory of the bronze implements (7.15-47) manufactured by Hiram (7.13-14), and with a short non-descriptive inventory of the gold cultic vessels (7.48-50),[1] said to have been manufactured by Solomon himself (7.48). Sandwiched between the detailed account of the temple edifice and the detailed description of the bronze furnishings stands a brief summary account of the private and secular buildings which Solomon built (7.1-12). The description of the secular buildings resembles literarily (although in miniature) the description of the temple. The description of the temple concludes with a time statement, 'and he spent seven years building it' (6.38), while the description of the secular buildings begins with the sentence 'And Solomon was thirteen years building his house' (7.1). The description of the temple and the description of the other buildings both begin with the buildings' measurements (6.2-3; 7.2, 6). The descriptions of both the temple and the other buildings conclude with the courtyards (6.36; 7.12).

Following the description of the buildings and their construction comes an account of the dedication ceremonies (ch. 8), and in the middle of this account are the speeches and prayers uttered by Solomon in honor of dedicating the temple (8.12-61). Finally, we hear of a divine revelation to Solomon in which God, answering the king's prayer, sets down conditions according to which blessings or curses will befall the coming generations (9.1-9). In brief, this is the outline of the story:

(1)	5.17-19	Decision to build and divine approval
(2)	5.20-32	Preparations for the building (materials, drafting workmen, laying foundations)
(3)	6.1-7.51	Description of the construction process and the buildings and furnishings

---

1. I discussed this passage in a lecture delivered at the IOSOT conference in Jerusalem, 1986. See Hurowitz forthcoming 3.

(4)	8.1-11	Dedication festivities (The Ark and God's glory enter the Temple)
(5)	8.12-61	Dedication prayers
(4)	8.62-66	Dedication festivities (popular festivities)
(6)	9.1-9	Divine promises/revelation
		Blessings and curses for the future

The brief analysis presented here shows that, as far as its thematic structure is concerned, the story of the construction of the Jerusalem Temple found in 1 Kings is highly similar, practically identical, to a large number of extra-biblical building accounts. On the basis of the analysis and comparison it can be stated that *this biblical building story is a typical ancient Near Eastern building story.*

2. The Priestly Account of Building the Tabernacle

The building of the Tabernacle stands at the heart of the Pentateuchal Priestly Source (P). According to the Priestly school, it was the most important event of the stay at Mount Sinai, perhaps being considered the climax of Creation as well as the high point of Israelite and human history. The manufacture and setting up of the Tabernacle is described at length and in painstaking detail in Exod. 24.15–31.18 and 34.29–40.38. These chapters are augmented by the description of priestly initiation and sanctification of the Tabernacle in Leviticus 8–10, and by the record of dedicating the Tabernacle and altar in Numbers 7.

I have presented elsewhere a detailed analysis of the structure of this story and of its relationship to 1 Kings 5–9 as well as to several ancient Near Eastern building stories.[1] The Tabernacle story was shown to follow in general the pattern under discussion here, although it is particularly close in form to the structure of the Samsuiluna B inscription as analyzed above. One segment of the story (Exod. 25.2-9 + 35.4–36.8) was shown to bear great similarity to a sequence in the Ugaritic Baal epic (*UT* 51 V 74–VI 21). The complex problem of the literary development of the Tabernacle story was also touched upon, and I offered observations about the inadequacies of the major theory which had been proposed to explain the growth and present form of this story.

1. Hurowitz 1985.

In another study[1] I discussed the relationship between the Tabernacle story and the account of building the Golden Calf, which, in the canonical form of the Pentateuch, is incorporated within it. In that study, an attempt was made to demonstrate that the combination of the two stories follows a pattern known from a small number of Mesopotamian building stories according to which a building account is interrupted after the divine command by a rebellion against the assigned temple builder. I also pointed out certain structural, linguistic and stylistic influences of the Tabernacle building account on the Calf-making account.

The Tabernacle story in its present form also serves as a framework for cultic regulations and for the fixing of priestly income from sacrifices (Lev. 1–7). Such a juxtaposition of a temple-building account with cultic tariffs also may have parallels in the Mesopotamian sources such as the Cruciform Monument of Manistušu and the pseudepigraphic Agum-Kakrime inscription,[2] but of particular interest in this respect is the Nabû-apla-iddina grant document (King 1912: XXXVI). This text opens with a historical account of the disappearance of the statue of Shamash and the disruption of his cult in Sippar. After generations of conducting the cult around a substitute sun-disk, a model of the original statue is miraculously revealed and shown to the king by a priestly family. A new statue is then produced by skilled artisans, given life and divine status by the 'mouth-washing ritual', and brought to the Ebabbar Temple amid festivities. The ancient, venerated cult is then restored. This account resembles in style and structure the royal inscriptions and the building stories, although it is somewhat abbreviated. The second part of the text is a list of sacrificial dues alloted to the priestly family in gratitude for their aid in restoring the cult. This grant is made 'forever', just as the portions allotted to the Israelite priests are allotted 'for all time throughout the ages' (Lev. 7.36a).[3] This inscription, which some have considered a

1. Hurowitz 1983–84.
2. See Gelb 1948: 348 n. 12; Finkelstein 1979: 76; Longmann 1991: 79-88; Powell 1991. The institution of sumptuous daily (*sattukku, ginû*) and holiday (*isinnu, akîtu*) offerings is recorded in several royal inscriptions of Nebuchadnezzar II. See Langdon 1912: 90, ll. 13-28; p. 92, ll. 27-53; p. 94, ll. 7-17; pp. 154-56 col. IV 23–V18; pp. 158-60, ll.1-20; p. 164 B, ll. VI 16-19; p. 168 B, ll. VII 10-31. Note also 1 Kgs 9.25.
3. An interesting example of priestly income being granted 'forever' by gods

pious fraud,[1] may serve as an analogy to the Priestly code in which the sacrificial laws find their place within the framework of an account of establishing a cult and cultic installation.

It is unnecessary to repeat here our discussion of the Tabernacle story and its relation to the other stories, so I will limit myself to presenting an outline of the story.

(1)	Exod. 24.15–31.18	God commands Moses to build him a Sanctuary and reveals its plan verbally and visually
[+]	32.1–34.28	The golden calf incident (apostasy and rebellion causing delay in fulfilling the command to build the tabernacle—restoration of order)
	34.29–35.19	The command to build is conveyed
(2)	35.20–36.7	Building materials are gathered
		Artisans and workers are enlisted
(3)	36.8–39.32	Manufacture of the pieces of the Tabernacle (prefabrication)
	39.33–39.43	Inspection of the components
	40.1–40.33	Assembling the Tabernacle
(4)	40.1–40.33	Consecrating the Tabernacle
	40.34–40.38	God's *Kābôd* enters the Shrine
	Lev. 8	Installation of the Priests
	(8.12-13)	Consecration of the altar
	9.1–10.19	Dedication rites for the Tabernacle
(5)	Lev. 9.22-23	Blessing the people
(4)	Num. 7	Dedicating the altar
	7.89	Revelation to Moses

(and *not* by a king) occurs in the grant document of Nabû-mutakkil published by F. Thureau-Dangin (1919: 141-43). If all the apposite divine titles are deleted from the text, what remains is: '(The gods) Nanâ and Mār-bīti. . . looked at Nabû mutakkil with their radiant countenances, and at that time they brought him in (inducted him) into the cella of Nabû in Borsippa, and they granted him daily 1 seah of. . . and so that there be no counterclaim they sealed (this document) and gave it to him forever'. Compare Lev. 7.35: 'These are the measured out portion (*mišḥâ* is related to Akkadian *mašāḥu* B 'to measure' and is etymologically unrelated to *mšḥ* [= anoint], but is used here as a play on the homonym *mošḥô* in the same verse, *pace* NJPSV *ad loc.*) of Aaron and the measured out portion of his sons from the Lord's offerings by fire, once they have been inducted to serve the Lord as priests; these the Lord commanded to be given them, once they had been anointed, as a due from the Israelites for all time throughout the ages'. See also Walker and Kramer 1982: 72-73 ll. 14'-20' (Bēl-ibni).

1. See Gelb 1949; Jacobsen 1987a; Powell 1991.

Admittedly, there are no blessings or curses in this story (6), and certain parts seem to have merged slightly (3 and 4 in ch. 40; 4 and 5 in Lev. 9; note that in 1 Kgs 8, as well as in some of the Assyrian building accounts discussed previously, the blessing or prayer is integrated into the description of the dedication ceremonies). Nonetheless, it is difficult to deny that this story, in its canonical form, is a fully developed example of the traditional pattern.

3. *The Rebuilding of the Jerusalem Temple (Ezra 1–6)*[1]

The rebuilding of the Temple in Jerusalem at the time of the return from the Babylonian Exile is the main topic of the prophetic books Zechariah and Haggai, and is mentioned as well in the words of Deutero-Isaiah (Isa. 44.24-28; 60). A description of the events is found, however, in the first six chapters of Ezra (see also Ezra 9.9).

This material is not of one cloth. Half is Hebrew and half Aramaic. The material has been arranged by the compiler of the biblical book Ezra–Nehemiah (it is not important for the present purposes whether he was the 'Chronicler' or some other, contemporary writer),[2] who has added freely of his own to whatever documents he had before

---

1.   For a comparison between the building account in Ezra and other biblical building accounts, see e.g. Porten 1977 and Talmon 1977 (see now also Halpern 1990: 112-16). For the literary structure of Ezra 1–6, see Talmon 1976. On other literary aspects of Ezra 1–6, see most recently Polak 1985. For the 'unity' of Ezra–Nehemiah as expressed by the literary structure of the two books, see Eskenazi 1988. The problem of history versus historiography in Ezra, as well as the date of Ezra 1–6, has been discussed by Japhet (1982, 1983). The relationship between Ezra the OT book and the apochryphal books of Esdras and Josephus' version of the same events has been studied recently by Japhet (1982, 1983) and Z. Talshir (1983).

2.   The question of the common authorship of Chronicles and Ezra–Nehemiah has been reopened by current scholarship. Japhet (1968) attacked the longstanding standard view of common authorship on linguistic grounds, and this position seems to be winning the day (see, for instance, Williamson [1977 and 1982]; Eskanazi [1988], by emphasizing the literary unit of Ezra–Nehemiah, has simultaneously driven a wedge between them and Chronicles). Haran, however, would wish to defend the unity of the two books on 'codocological' grounds. He points to the practical necessity of splitting in two what would otherwise be an inordinately long book, and the use of a 'catch line' to join the two severed parts (Haran 1985). D. Talshir (1988) has recently attacked the linguistic underpinnings of Japhet's theory.

him. Numerous documents of various types and forms have been incorporated into the composition. These chapters cite letters, and within these letters other letters are encapsulated.[1] The story opens with royal proclamation made in Hebrew to the Jews throughout the Persian Empire, while another passage in this story records a royal memorandum (*dikrônâ*), written in Aramaic, which had been put away for safe keeping in the archives.[2] A royal edict, concluded with a series of maledictions for those who would transgress its provisions, refers to the resumption of work (Ezra 6.6-12). The temple vessels and the names of the returnees from Exile are found in administrative lists. In addition to all this, there are some narrative portions written in both Hebrew and Aramaic. Finally, the expression *bēh zimnā'*, 'at that time' (5.3), is taken from the characteristic terminology of royal inscriptions (cf. Akkadian *ina ūmīšu*). Within the story of the building of the temple is an extraneous and chronologically disruptive account about interference in the rebuilding of the walls of Jerusalem at the time of Ahasuerus and Artaxerxes (Ezra 4.6-23; 6.14). But even this intrusive passage is integrated by literary means into the narrative.

The basic narrative line is simple. With Cyrus's permission, Jews returned to Judaea to rebuild the Temple. They commenced building, but work was halted because of opposition from the local populace. The work was eventually resumed because of the encouragement of certain prophets, and the builders succeeded in overcoming the opposition and completed the work, several years after it had begun. Let us now examine the story in greater detail.

The story begins with the well-known Proclamation of Cyrus about restoring the temple of YHWH in Jerusalem. Although the declaration is that of Cyrus, it is clear that in the opinion of the narrator it is YHWH who is the true instigator. God has 'stirred up the spirit' of Cyrus (see also 1.5), the restoration is the fulfillment of a prophecy of Jeremiah, and Cyrus himself declares 'The Lord has ordered me to

---

1. For the language, style and structure of the Ezra letters in light of nearly contemporary letters from Elephantine, see the studies of Porten 1978–79 and especially 1978 with regard to the Elephantine documents relating to restoration of their temple.

2. See the studies of Bickerman (1946), Tadmor (1964) and de Vaux (1971) relating to the authenticity of the biblical Cyrus declarations, and to the distinction between royal proclamations in a vernacular language and archival memoranda written in Official Aramaic.

build Him a Temple'... (1.2).[1] The story thus begins with a *divine command to build a temple* (1).

The Declaration relates to two matters: the building itself (vv. 2-3), and the funding of the return to Judaea and building (v. 4). If so, the second part of the Declaration introduces the *preparations for the building project* (2). Verses 5-6 describe the immediate positive reaction to the Declaration. Verses 7-11 tell of Cyrus's personal contribution to the temple building fund. Chapter 2 contains a list of all the people who returned to Jerusalem to join the building project. The list, to be sure, is a record of those who went up to Jerusalem, but in its present context it has the additional task of telling who the temple builders were. The list ends with an account of the contributions made by these people to re-establish the Temple (vv. 68-69). The story goes on to describe the restoration of the altar and sacrificial worship in the seventh month. Afterwards, there is an account of purchasing cedars from the Lebanon to construct the Temple and shipping them by sea to Jaffa. This is followed by a description of founding the Temple in the second month of the second year (3.8-13). This completes the account of the preparations (2).

The cessation of work on the Temple is reported in 4.1-5. This is followed by 4.6-23, which tells of the interference in work on the walls of Jerusalem at a much later time—during the reigns of Ahasuerus and Artaxerxes—and this has absolutely nothing to do with the rebuilding of the Temple. The main story is resumed in 4.24, by means of a *Wiederaufnahme* linking this verse to 4.5:[2]

4.5   *wĕsōkĕrîm ʿălêhem yôʿăṣîm lĕhāpēr ʿăṣātām*
      kŏl yĕmê kôreš melek pāras
      wĕʿad malkût dārĕyāweš melek pāras

---

1.   Porten (1978: 129) suggested that the Cyrus declaration and the memorandum issued may have been in response to a Jewish petition which would have resembled the petition for restoring the Elephantine Temple (Cowley 30). Note Fales' (1987) interesting new rhetorical analysis of Cowley 30. He finds (p. 467) a 'double level of reality. . . the level of men and the level of God', for 'While the Jews are asking Bagohi to turn wrong to right again (by rebuilding the Temple), they intentionally let him know that a higher justice has already been appealed to. . . ' For the divine element in the story in Ezra 1–6, see Japhet 1982: 73.

2.   See Talmon 1976: 322.

116   *I Have Built You an Exalted House*

4.24   *bē'dayin bĕṭēlaṭ 'ăbîdaṭ bêt 'ĕlāhā' dî bîrûšĕlem*
          wahăwāṭ bāṭĕlā' 'aḏ šĕnaṭ tartên
          lĕmalkûṭ dārĕyāweš melek pārās

The story resumes in ch. 5.[1] First mentioned are the prophecies of
Haggai and Zechariah. This parallels the prophecy of Jeremiah and the
inspiration of Cyrus in ch. 1. Afterwards (5.2) we read, *bē'dayin
qāmû Zĕrubbābel bar šĕ'al tî'ēl*, 'Then rose up Zerubbabel the son of
Shealtiel...'), which is parallel to what was found in 1.5, *wayyāqûmû
rāšê hā'ăbôṭ lîhûḏâ* ('Then rose up the heads of fathers' houses of
Judah'). The words *wĕšārîw lĕmibnē' bêt 'ĕlāhā'* ('they began to build
the house of God') (5.2) echo in Aramaic what was said earlier in
Hebrew in 3.8, *hĕḥēllû Zĕrubbābel...wĕyēšûa'* ('Zerubbabel and
Joshua began...')

Just as adversaries had risen against the Jews the first time they
started building, once again opposition appears. The account of the
renewed disturbances starts with the words *bēh zimnā' 'ātâ 'ălêhôn
tattĕnâ...wĕkēn 'āmĕrîn lehōm*, 'At the same time came to them
Tattenai...and said thus to them' (5.3), which is parallel to what had
been said about the 'enemies of Judah and Jerusalem' in 4.2:
wayyiggĕšu 'el zĕrubbābel...wayyō'mĕrû lāhem. 'they drew near to
Zerubbabel...and said unto them'. But this time, the opposition is to
no avail, for we read, *wĕ'ên 'ĕlāhăhōm hăwaṭ 'al śābê yĕhûdāye wĕlā'
baṭṭilû himmô* ('But the eye of their God was upon the elders of the
Jews[2] and they did not make them cease') (5.5), contrasting to 4.24,
where we read, *bē'ḏayin beṭelaṭ 'ăbîdaṭ bêt 'ĕlāhā wahăwaṭ bāṭĕlā'*...
('Then ceased the work of the house of God...and it ceased...').

There follows Tattenai's letter to Darius inquiring about the work
permit, the discovery of the original Cyrus memorandum, and
Darius's order to resume construction. In the present form of the
story, these incidents parallel the account of the original opposition in
ch. 4. This time however, instead of interrupting the work of the
builders, Darius takes all possible measures to guarantee that the work

1.   For parallels between the Rehum–Shimshai incident and the Tattenai incident,
see Porten 1978–79.
2.   With God's (gracious) eye upon the elders of Judah (Ezra 5.5, 'But the eye
of their God was upon the elders of the Jews'), compare the gracious, steady or
happy look of various gods upon selected royal temple builders mentioned in
Mesopotamian royal inscriptions.

will be successfully completed. The two incidents are parallel. In both, the royal decision is based on clarification of past precedent. We read in 4.19, *uminnî śîm ṭěʿēm ûḇaqqarû wehaśkahû dî qiryětā' dāḵ*, 'And I decreed, and search hath been made, and it is found that this city...' In 6.1 we read, *bě'dayin dārěyāweś malkā' śām ṭěʿēm ûḇaqqarû běḇēṭ siprayyā'... wěhištěkaḥ běʾahmětā'...*, 'Then Darius the king made a decree, and search was made in the house of the archives... And there was found at Achmetha...' (see also 4.15, which parallels 5.17).

The building itself (3) is described briefly in 6.14-15. The description of the building is actually part of the memorandum cited in 6.3-5. The building process is summarized in the words *bēnô wěśaklilû* (6.14), 'they built and completed'. It is stated explicitly that the work was accomplished, 'urged on by the prophesying of Haggai the prophet and Zechariah son of Iddo... under the aegis of the God of Israel and by the order of Cyrus and Darius and king Artaxerxes of Persia'. The work was completed on the third of Adar, sixth year of Darius (6.15).

The dedication celebrations are described in 6.16-17. As at the dedication of the Tabernacle, here too Levites and Priests are appointed. The celebrations are carried out joyfully.

The story ends with an account of celebrating the Passover (6.19-22a). This parallels the celebration of Sukkoth in 1 Kgs 8.65. The joy of the Passover is juxtaposed to the joy of the dedication festivities. In 6.22b there is a concluding refrain for the entire story. The dedication celebrations parallel and contrast with the account of founding the temple described in 3.8-13. In both celebrations Levites and Priests participated. But whereas the dedication ceremonies were conducted joyously, the foundation rites had been saddened by the cry of the elders (3.12-13).[1]

The story is concluded with an account of celebrating the Passover and a closing refrain, 'for the Lord had given them cause for joy by inclining the heart of the Assyrian king toward them so as to give them support in the work of the House of God, the God of Israel'. This may be considered a blessing bestowed upon the people (5).

An analysis of the story follows in tabular form:

1.   For this contrast, see Assurbanipal's statement (Streck 1916: 248 ll. 8-9): 'In sadness and crying that the enemy had desecrated it (the temple) I set my hand (to start reconstructing). In joy I completed it.'

(1)	1.1-4	The command to build	5.1	Encouragement to resume building
(2)	1.5-2	Preparations (workers, materials)		Arousal of the workers
	3.1-6	Worship is restored		
	7	Preparations (materials)		
	8.13	Founding the temple (joy and tears)		
[+]	4.1-5	Enemies interfere	5.3	Attempt to interfere
	6-23	Opposition to the walls (letters)	6.13	Opposition is thwarted (letters)
	24	Resumption		
(3)			6.14-15	Building the temple *(bĕnâ//šaklēl)*
(4)			16-18	Dedication (joy)
			19-22a	The passover
(5)			22b	Conclusion God blesses the people

The remarks above and the table indicate that the story is constructed of two parallel sequences of events. In the first sequence, God commands the building of the temple, preparations are made, and work is started. But difficulties are encountered which lead to cessation and failure of the project. In the second sequence as well (which reflects the first in language, as seen above), God commands that the temple be built, preparations are made, and the same type of difficulties are encountered. But this time interference is overcome and the project succeeds. The first attempt ends in a mixture of joy and sadness, whereas the second attempt concludes in happiness, which for the sake of emphasis is mentioned three times (6.16, 22 [× 2]). If the story is examined somewhat differently, it is found to be composed of two stories—one of the foundation of the temple in the time of Cyrus, and one of the building of the temple under Darius. However we look at it, it is clearly an additional exemplification of the overall pattern typical of ancient Near Eastern building accounts.

4. *The Repairing of the Walls of Jerusalem (The Memoirs of Nehemiah)*

The central theme in the memoirs of Nehemiah is his great project of repairing the walls of Jerusalem. Just as certain Mesopotamian inscriptions described secular building projects in the same way temple building was described, so Nehemiah tells of his restoration of Jerusalem's walls in the way the building of a temple could be portrayed.[1]

In order to analyse the building account embedded in the book of Nehemiah, it must first be isolated from its present literary matrix. This may be done rather simply, without taking lightly the complex problems of the structure of the book as a whole and the process by which it came into existence. The book of Nehemiah contains two types of material: (1) Nehemiah's memoirs, written by him; (2) additions of the author of Ezra–Nehemiah, the so-called 'Chronicler'. These additions refer to Nehemiah in the third person and are found in 7.72b–10.40; 11.3-36; 12.1-26, 44-47; 13.1-3. Nehemiah's personal memoirs are, therefore, found written in the first person in 1.1–7.72a; 11.1-2; 12.27-43; 13.4-31.

The memoirs themselves may be separated into five divisions:

1. 13.4-31 contains three passages telling of Nehemiah's religious reforms: reforms in temple administration (13.4-14); prohibition of commerce on the Sabbath (vv. 15-22); expulsion of foreign wives (vv. 23-31). Each passage begins with a temporal clause ('before this', 'in those days', 'also in those days') and ends with a short prayer 'Remember me, O my God, concerning this', 'remember unto me, O my God, this also', 'remember me, O my God, for good').

2. In ch. 5 Nehemiah describes some of his social reforms (vv. 1-19) and his personal abstinence from his due as governor (vv. 14-18). This passage has no special introductory formula, but concludes with the prayer 'Remember me, O God, for good' (v. 19). The word *hā'ām* ('the people') in the concluding prayer may be an inclusio-type echo

---

1.   In his studies of royal inscriptions (1923) and of the books of Ezra and Nehemiah (1964), S. Mowinckel suggests a stylistic and thematic similarity and genetic relationship between Nehemiah's memoirs and the ancient Near Eastern royal inscriptions. Unfortunately, he never fully developed his theory. Subsequent scholars looked at other literary types to explain the background of Nehemiah's memoirs, comparing them, for instance, to Egyptian wills and funerary inscriptions, or to the book of Job and individual laments (see most recently Blenkinsopp 1987). These later explanations unfortunately have diverted attention from the full extent and nature of the relationship which Mowinckel rightly indicated between the Nehemiah memoirs and the royal inscriptions.

120 *I Have Built You an Exalted House*

of the same word which appeared in v. 1, indicating that the passage was indeed considered to begin with v. 1.

3. A group of seven passages interspersed through 2.10–6.14 describes the interference of Sanballat and other enemies of the Jews. Each individual event begins with a nearly identical formula:

1.	2.10	*wayyišma' sanballaṭ*
2.	2.19-20	*wayyišma' sanballaṭ*
3.	3.33-37	*wayhî ka'ăšer šāma' sanballaṭ*
4.	4.1-8	*wayhî ka'ăšer šāma' sanballaṭ*
5.	4.9–5.19	*wayhî ka'ăšer šāmĕ'û 'ôyĕbênû*
6.	6.1-14	*wayhî ka'ăšer nišma' lĕsanballaṭ*
7.	6.16	*wayhî ka'ăšer šāmĕ'û kol-'ôyĕbênû*

The sixth of these passages ends with the prayer formula, 'Remember, O my God, Tobiah and Sanballat according to these their works' (6.14). The third passage also ends with a prayer of malediction (3.36-37), 'Hear, our God, how we have become a mockery, and return their taunts upon their heads! Let them be taken as spoil to a land of captivity! Do not cover up their iniquity or let their sin be blotted out before you, for they hurled provocations at the builders.' Note that in the first three passages only verbal opposition is expressed to persuade the workers to stop, while in the fourth, fifth and sixth incidents the enemies have resorted to violence and stratagem to put an end to the work. The account of the disruptions thus divides into two parts both in content and form. The two groups of three passages each end with a prayer against the opponents. The seventh passage describes the final failure of the opposition and the downfall of all (*kol*) the opponents, and is actually a cry of victory. We will see further on how the structure of these seven passages corresponds to the structure of the building account.

4. Two more passages about the enemies of Nehemiah and the Jews are found in 4.16-17 and 6.17-19. They each begin in the same way, 'and from that time forth', 'and in those days', and are to be seen as supplements to the passages which precede them.

5. When all these passages are excised from the memoirs, what remains (1.1–2.9; 2.11-18; 3.1-32 (38);[1] 6.15 (16); 7.1-72a; 11.1-2;

---

1. This verse, which comes immediately after the first malediction, belongs apparently to the building account and not to the Sanballat incidents. It is thereby similar to 6.16 which also comes after a malediction and belongs equally to both stories.

12.27-43) is nothing more than a building account written according to the traditional format.

The building account begins with the news brought to Nehemiah by Hanani and some men of Judah, according to which 'The survivors who have survived the captivity there in the province are in dire trouble and disgrace; *Jerusalem's wall is full of breaches, and its gates have been destroyed by fire*' (1.3). This announcement may be compared with information relayed in many Mesopotamian building accounts to the effect that a certain building has been destroyed or become dilapidated and must be restored. On hearing this report, Nehemiah mourns and prays (1.4-11).[1] His prayer consists of a confession (vv. 6-7) and a plea for mercy (vv. 8-11), but the most important element in it is the request with which it concludes: 'Grant your servant success today, and dispose that man to be compassionate toward him!' (v. 11). This request reveals Nehemiah's true intention, which is to petition the king. Some scholars have suggested that this request actually should come after 2.4, but if this were the case, we would have to assume that an original request in the first prayer was deleted and lost, for, without the request, Nehemiah's eloquent prayer remains but an aimless introduction, leading up to nothing.

Four months later, in the month of Nisan, while serving Artaxerxes, Nehemiah finally has an opportunity to place his request before him. The king notices that Nehemiah is depressed and inquires as to the cause. Nehemiah fearfully[2] explains to the king, 'How should I not look ill when the city of the graveyard of my ancestors lies in ruins, and its gates have been consumed by fire?' (2.3). The king continues his questioning, inquiring as to what Nehemiah would request, to which Nehemiah remarks, 'With a prayer to the god of Heaven, I answered the king'. Some commentators (e.g. Ibn-Ezra) take this to refer to the prayer recorded in ch. 1, while others (e.g. Rashi) see this

---

1. Nehemiah's prayer and mourning practices may be compared with prayers and mourning practices concerning destroyed temples and the desire to see them rebuilt, as found in Dan. 9.4-20 as well as Cowley 30.15-19; Langdon 1912: 110 *Nebuchadnezzar* no. 13 col. iii 25-30; p. 142 no. 16 col. ii 2; Adad-Guppi's inscription, Gadd 1958: 46-57 (= A.L. Oppenheim, *ANET*, 560-62); and Assurbanipal, Streck 1916: 262 ll. 26-34; CT 13.48 (concerning Nebuchadnezzar I, cf. Miller and Roberts 1977: 77ff.).

2. Nehemiah's fear may be a development of the motif of fear of a god's command to build a temple, as found in many Babylonian building accounts.

as an allusion to a short prayer uttered on the spot, while standing before the king. Certain recent scholars have suggested that the last verse in the previous prayer (1.11) belongs here (1.11 begins 'O LORD, I beseech thee', just as the whole prayer had begun, and this is taken as a sign that the verse was originally an independent prayer). Whatever the case may be, the inclusion of a prayer effectively turns the permission granted by the king into an act determined by God in response to the prayer. God's participation in the decision process is alluded to twice more in the story that follows. In connection with the letters sent to Asaph the keeper of the King's Park, we read (2.8): 'The king gave me these, thanks to my God's benevolent care for me'. Referring to his nocturnal inspection tour of the walls, Nehemiah states (2.18), 'I told them of my God's benevolent care for me, also of the things that the king had said to me, and they said "Let us start building!" They were encouraged by [his] benevolence.' (See also Rashi's comments on both verses. Both passages imply that it was God who has helped Nehemiah succeed.)

All this echoes the theme, well attested in building accounts, that divine sanction must be given to a building project. Verses 1.1–2.8 describe, therefore, the *decision to build* (1). This description contains perhaps five elements characteristic of this phase in the other building accounts: (a) description of the situation demanding repair; (b) request for permission; (c) the granting of permission; (d) divine sanction; (e) fear. There is no specific reference to divine inspiration in the architectural planning, but two subsequent passages do refer to divine inspiration in regard to specific details. At the beginning of the description of the nocturnal tour Nehemiah says (2.12), 'telling no one what my God had put into my mind to do for Jerusalem...' At the end of the building account, when describing the populating of the city, he writes (7.5), 'My God put into my heart to assemble the nobles... in order to register them by families'.

At the end of his audience with the king, Nehemiah asks that he be provided with letters including one to Asaph the keeper of the King's Park, that he be given wood for the building project (2.7-9). Verses 11-18 describe Nehemiah's tour of the walls,[1] at the end of which he tells the people what he plans to do and arouses them to participate in

---

1.   For the archaeological aspects of the wall of Jerusalem described by Nehemiah, see Tsafrir 1977.

the undertaking (vv. 17-18). Nehemiah invites them, saying, 'Come, let us rebuild...', and they respond, 'Let us start building'. These two passages, which relate to the acquisition of building materials and enlisting the work force, form the second stage of the account: the *preparations* (2).

Chapter 3 depicts the work on the walls and describs the walls and gates themselves (3.1-32, 38), thus representing the third stage of the story (3). Completion of the work is mentioned in 6.15, 'The wall was finished on the twenty-fifth of Elul, after fifty-two days'. At this point, the building account is linked to the account of the disturbances which concludes with a prayer (for curses) in 6.14. The passage in which the two stories are joined together (vv. 15-16) is bracketed by the words:

> *wattišlam hahômâ*   The wall was complete...
> *ne'eštâ hammĕlā' kâ*   the work was done.

This line contains the expressions *šlm* and *'šh mĕlā' kâ* in a refrain typical of numerous building accounts, as we will see in Chapter 10.

Next, Nehemiah tells how he populated the city (7.1-5a [5-72b]; 11.1-2) and then how the city was dedicated (12.27-43*). The populating of Jerusalem may be compared with what was found in the cylinder inscription of Sargon about the populating of Dur-Sharruken.[1]

The building story does not end with a prayer or a reference to divine blessings for the builder. But the prayers concluding each of the three appendices in ch. 13 may fulfill this function.[2]

The building account and the account of the disturbances are joined by literary links at two points: 3.38 and 6.16. The account of the disturbances presupposes the building account, but the building account is not dependent to the same degree on the story of the disturbances. Removing the accounts of the disturbances as well as some additional secondary material not directly related to the building of the walls does not affect the continuity of the building story. In addition, all the 'extraneous' material is well defined literarily by the use of stereo-

---

1. See translation of Lückenbill, *ARAB*, II, §122. Note also the similar statements on the bronze plaque (§108), and on the back of a stone tablet (§105). The populating of a city is also described in Assurnasirpal II's accounts of building his new capital Kalḫu (Grayson, *ARI*, II 591, 671, 677).

2. Examples of prayers beginning with the word *zĕkôr* can be found in Psalm 132 as well as in several building and dedicatory inscriptions. The formula has been discussed by Schotroff (1967), following a discussion by Galling (1950: 134-42).

typed introductory and/or closing formulae. From all this, it becomes clear that the building story is the backbone and torso of Nehemiah's memoirs, to which everything else is secondarily attached. There is something of a parallel here to the Mesopotamian royal inscriptions. There too, the main part of the inscription, structurally speaking, is the building account, even though quantitatively and from the author's viewpoint predominance may be given to some other element such as military campaigns. The building accounts and the accounts of other achievements are somewhat loosely joined by use of the formulae 'when. . . at that time'. The main difference is that in the Mesopotamian texts, the other achievements are always described before and totally separately from the building account, while Nehemiah has integrated them into the building account itself.

The building account in Nehemiah's memoirs thus resembles in structure and several linguistic and thematic features the building accounts known from Mesopotamia and the Bible itself. To be sure, it has its own undeniable, unique character, but it represents the penultimate link in a literary tradition of building accounts which lasted close to 2000 years.

5. Herod's Rebuilding of the Temple in Jerusalem (Josephus)[1]

The building account, born and bred in Mesopotamia, and eventually adopted by the scribes of Ugarit and biblical Israel, seems to have outlasted these cultures and may have put in a final appearance in the writings of Josephus. Another, much later, temple-building account, that of the Herodian temple, is found in *Ant.* 15.11.1-7 (§§380-425). It is instructive to compare this account with the building stories discussed above. Josephus tells at the beginning of his account of Herod's decision to rebuild the Temple in Jerusalem and how he presented his plan to the people. Among other things, the king states that he rules by divine selection (§387). The people were apprehensive lest he should tear down the existing structure and not have sufficient means with which to rebuild it (§§380-87). This section parallels part (1) of the traditional pattern which tells of the decision to build, the 'consultations' required, and the acquisition of permission. The concern of the people may be compared with the apprehension often

---

1.   I am grateful to Dr Daniel Schwartz for discussing this passage with me.

expressed by the Mesopotamian kings when faced with a command to build a temple. Note also that Herod feels the need to rebuild the Temple because the one built during the Persian period was too small and was not according to the original plan (§386). These considerations resemble the reasons given by Nabonidus for rebuilding certain temples. Josephus goes on to relate how Herod, in order to assuage the people's fear, gathered up huge amounts of building materials and selected tens of thousands of the most skilled laborers to do the work (§§388-90). This corresponds with part (2) of the traditional pattern. Afterwards, Herod tears down the old Temple and builds the new one, which is described fully (§§391-420) as in part (3) of the other texts. The joyous dedication ceremonies (4) are then briefly described (§§421-23), during which time the people blessed God (5) and countless sacrifices were offered by the king and the people. Josephus concludes his account with a tale (reported identically in *b. Taan.* 23b) that when the Temple was being built, it rained only at nights so that the work was not interrupted. This is considered a divine miracle, perhaps parallel to the divine revelation which concludes certain building accounts.

It should be left to scholars specializing in Josephus to look for additional, more specific points of similarity between this late account and the vast amount of material which preceded him. It is also for them to determine whether this story is the independent creation of the historian or whether he is inspired by his ancient Near Eastern heritage which has reached him, either directly through his knowledge of ancient Near Eastern historians and historical writings, or indirectly through the biblical building stories investigated above.

Discussion has focused so far upon the thematic structure of ancient Near Eastern building stories. Comparison of the structures of more than twenty extra-biblical building accounts and four biblical building accounts has shown that there is practically no difference between the biblical accounts and the accounts which have reached us from different areas and different periods. The essential similarity exists despite the composite literary nature of the biblical accounts and despite certain differences existing within the corpus of extra-biblical accounts itself. As far as the thematic structure of the biblical building stories is concerned, it is possible to state that they are all typical, routine ancient Near Eastern building stories.

It should be emphasized at this point in the discussion that the five- or six-stage pattern noticed above is not a trivial one, reflecting simply the natural course of building, as if any building project anywhere and from any time would necessarily be described in this fashion. As a matter of fact, the human imagination could very conceivably come up with different ways of describing a building project. Building stories are not known from Hittite sources. Ancient Egypt provides numerous building inscriptions but only very few resemble those known from Mesopotamia and Israel. Building inscriptions found in ancient synagogues record the names and contributions of donors, but they can hardly be considered 'building stories', and are certainly totally dissimilar to the texts we have examined.

The five- or six-stage pattern employed by Mesopotamian and biblical authors is not one to be taken for granted and considered a product of necessity. One need only look at a full century of biblical scholars who accepted Wellhausen's view about the development of the Tabernacle-building account. In Wellhausen's opinion, the 'original' story consisted of a command to build the Tabernacle, in the course of which God described the structure to Moses, and this was followed by a simple statement that the Children of Israel did all that

God had commanded Moses. Such a story is not inconceivable but in fact no other such story is attested in all the writings of the ancient Near East! Illustrative of a variant way in which a building project could conceivably be described in a culture chronologically and geographically removed from the ancient Near East are the following excerpts from the *New York Times* of 3 September, 1979. They tell of a new Krishna palace built in Limestone, West Virginia. The numbers refer to the components of the traditional ancient Near Eastern building stories employed above.

> (2) The International Society for Krishna Consciousness. . . has taken many of the dimes and quarters from. . . sales and used them here, in the rural panhandle of West Virginia, to build an ornate Indian palace.
>
> (4) The structure is being dedicated this weekend with processions, dances and vegetarian feasts. Hundreds of visitors from the surrounding area. . . have been coming to eat and watch. More than the foreign customs, it is the palace itself that has left many of the visitors gawking.
>
> (3) It has Italian marble floors, walls inlaid with Iranian onyx, gold leafed column caps, stained glass windows in the shape of peacocks, numerous crystal chandeliers, and downspouts outside in the shape of elephant heads. . .
>
> (2) The palace cost $500,000 in materials and was built over the last six years by the 250 members of the community, (1) first as a house and then as a memorial to the religion's spiritual leader A.C. Bhaktivedanta Swami Prabhupada, who died two years ago. (3) The palace includes statues and pictures of the swami, as well as a bathroom for him that has carved teak shower doors and a marble toilet.

This twentieth-century journalistic *Baubericht*, to be sure, mentions four of the elements found in the ancient Near Eastern texts described above. However, the order is dictated by totally different criteria.

It seems that the pattern used in the building accounts discussed here is not even necessarily a reflection of reality. Many people who have tried to build houses know from their own bitter experience that building projects are often undertaken without all the material and personnel being prepared and available. Contractors often begin work only partially funded and purchase material and equipment and hire workers as the project progresses. The fact that the ancient stories consistently mention the preparations before the description of the actual building is therefore not only unnatural but even a bit idealistic—something to be expected in a story meant to show that a certain king did everything in the best way possible (note Josephus's account of Herod's preparations to rebuild the Jerusalem Temple in which Herod calms the people's apprehensions by making all the preparations before he starts). In addition, blessings for the builder could imaginably be pronounced before a building project is described, as an incentive or something which the king can expect upon completion of his task (note the very late insertion in 1 Kgs 6.11-13). The fact that ancient Near Eastern scribes preferred one fixed formula for writing building accounts, despite conceivable alterations and other possible, logical alternatives, indicates that the pattern uncovered above was indeed a scribal convention rehearsing a literary stereotype rather than a habitual adhering to the actual course of events.

PART II

THE ACCOUNT OF BUILDING THE TEMPLE IN JERUSALEM
(1 KINGS 5.15–9.25) IN LIGHT OF MESOPOTAMIAN AND NORTHWEST
SEMITIC WRITINGS

INTRODUCTION TO THE SECOND PART

The remainder of this book will be devoted to a detailed analysis of what might be called the major biblical building story, namely the account of the construction of the Jerusalem Temple by Solomon in 1 Kings. In the following chapters, the various individual stages in this account will be examined, and, with the help of comparison to and contrast with other building stories and related documents of all sorts, an attempt will be made to fix more precisely the place of the biblical building story within the literary tradition and within the beliefs and ideas of the ancient Near East. The comparison and contrast between the biblical pericope and the extra-biblical documents will enable us to discover what the biblical passage has in common with foreign writings as well as what distinguishes it from them. Furthermore, comparing the biblical story with extra-biblical documents of all types will make it possible to identify correctly the types of documents reflected in the various parts of the biblical account. Finally, comparison of the biblical and extra-biblical stories will be of use in tracing both the process by which the biblical story came into being and the historical background of its various stages and present form.

In this part of the study, comparison will not be confined to the stories adduced in the first part. The basis of comparison will encompass the entire corpus of Mesopotamian, Northwest Semitic and biblical building stories along with numerous documents and literary types.[1] The topics touched upon in this part of the work will be from the areas of language, literary style, ideology, religious beliefs and practices, and material culture.

---

1.   See the sources listed in the index and bibliography.

Chapter 8

THE DECISION TO BUILD (1 KINGS 5.15-19)

1. *The History of the Temple*

The temple-building account begins with Solomon's message to Hiram, king of Tyre (1 Kgs 5.17-19):

> You know that my father David could not build a house for the name of the Lord his God because of the war that encompassed him, until the Lord had placed them under the soles of my (*Kethiv* his) feet. But now the Lord my God has given me respite all around; there is no adversary and no mischance. And so I propose to build a house for the name of the Lord my God, as the Lord promised my father David, saying, 'Your son, whom I will set on your throne in your place, shall build the house for my name'.

These three verses exhibit certain obvious Deuteronomic features,[1] but they can be compared from the point of view of their content and function within the story to the standard openings of building stories which appear in a number of extra-biblical sources.

In the Assyrian inscriptions, the building account (*Bauberichte*) usually opens with a brief history of the edifice. If the inscription deals with an old building which has collapsed or become dilapidated from age, the king surveys the history of the building—when it fell into ruin and when and by whom it was renovated—all the way down to his own time, proclaiming afterwards his own decision to restore the building once again, and in numerous cases mentioning the divine

---

1. For the Deuteronomic contributions to this passage, see the commentaries, critical introductions to the Bible and the discussion in the next chapter. Extra-biblical parallels (from letters and royal inscriptions) to the expression 'until the Lord had placed them under the soles of my feet' (v. 17) are cited by Greenfield 1978: 74. For the important motif of rest or victory over enemies as a condition for building a temple or palace, see Kapelrud 1963 and in detail Ulshoeffer 1977.

approval given to his plan. For example, Esarhaddon tells of the restoration of the temple of Assur (Borger 1956: 3 iii 16–iv 6):

> The previous temple of Assur, which Ušpia, my forefather, priest of Assur, had built long ago, collapsed and Erišum, son of Šuma-ilu my forefather, priest of Assur (re)built it. 126 years passed and it fell into ruin again, and Šamši-Adad, son of Ilu-Kapkapi, my forefather, priest of Assur, (re)built it. 434 years passed and this temple was destroyed by fire. Shalmaneser son of Adad-nerari my forefather, priest of Assur (re)built it. 580 years passed and the cella (*bīt papāḫu bītānu*), the seat of Assur my lord, the *bīt šaḫūri*, Kabu's temple, the temple of Dibar and the temple of Ea became weak, old and ancient. I was afraid and worried to restore that temple so I was negligent, (but) by means of the bowl of the (liver) diviner Shamash and Adad answered me with a firm 'Yes' and caused to be written in the liver (an instruction) to build the house and restore the temple.[1]

Even when the text speaks of a new building intended to replace or improve an old structure which was unsuited to new circumstances and the desires of a new king, the building story will open with a survey of the past, emphasizing the attention or lack of attention given by previous kings to the state of the edifice. So, for example, Sennacherib's inscriptions about building his 'Palace without a Rival' tell how

---

1.   The passage cited here encapsulates the entire history of the temple from the time of its foundation until its restoration by the king writing the inscription. The chronological information given in these passages may be based on king-list entries (see Na'aman 1984). The historical information provided, i.e. the names of the kings who built and rebuilt the individual temples, is possibly derived from information given in previous building inscriptions implanted in the building and discovered and read by the new king. The practice of reading old inscriptions found while restoring buildings is reported, for example, by Nabonidus, who was fond of reviving Assyrian practices (see Goosens 1948). The assumption that old inscriptions will in fact be read at some future time underlies the requests and appeals to future generations which conclude most of the Assyrian building inscriptions. In these pleas, the present king asks his followers to honor his inscriptions, to replace them in the restored building, to anoint them, and even to offer sacrifices. He offers blessings to the king who accepts his plea and calls down vicious maledictions upon the king who ignores his request. As for the literary typology of the 'building histories', these passages somewhat resemble the Sumerian 'Tummal' inscription. Grayson (1980: 164 n. 116) says that copies of royal inscriptions were kept on file in special archives. Certainly such archival copies could also supply the information needed in the composition of new inscriptions, in the event that the older inscriptions could not be found.

building a palace in Nineveh had been neglected by his ancestors, and afterwards he says (Luckenbill 1924: 103-104, col. V 23-51):

> It came into my mind, and I directed my attention to doing that work according to the command of the gods.

Esarhaddon tells of rebuilding the Armory (*ekal māšarti*) in Kalḫu (Borger 1956: 34 ll. 40-47):

> At that time—with the people of all the lands which my hands had conquered by the encouragement of Assur my lord—the armory in Kalḫu which Shalmaneser, king of Assyria son of Assurnasirpal the previous prince had made, its building platform no longer existed and its space was too small, so I, Esarhaddon, King of Assyria, the righteous prince, equal of the sage Adapa, endowed (with wisdom) by the prince Niššiku, that building platform came to my mind and I gave my attention. . .

The Assyrian inscriptions provide only few details about totally new buildings. Tukulti-Ninurta I, who built himself a new capital (Kar-Tukulti-Ninurta) alongside the city Assur does not present in detail the history of the site. On the other hand, Sargon tells in the highly poetic Cylinder Inscription how the site for his new city had been ignored by all the previous kings (Lyon 1883 34 no. 1 ll. 44-46 = *ARAB*, II, §119). Afterwards he describes his own decision to build a new capital at the site, and goes on to tell of his prayers to the gods in order to acquire their consent to his plans.

Just as in the inscriptions mentioned here, so Solomon's words to Hiram in 1 Kgs 5.15-17 recall the background of the building project, emphasizing the reason why the previous king did not undertake it. We are also informed of the present king's own decision ('And so I propose. . .') to build a temple and of the divine approval granted for the undertaking ('as the Lord promised. . .').[1] If so, Solomon's message to Hiram may be considered a close parallel to the routine introductions to numerous Mesopotamian building stories, only a few of which have been cited above.

I readily admit that the passages referred to thus far say nothing about rest from enemies preceding the building project. However, this

---

1. Similar matters open Solomon's temple dedication address in 1 Kgs 8.16-20. Both passages are based ultimately on 2 Sam. 7.1-2 (see Kumaki 1981). For the similarity between these two verses and the opening section of the account of the building of Baal's palace in the Ugaritic Baal epic, see Gadd 1948: 6-7.

idea[1] appears explicitly in the inscription of Nabopolassar, king of Babylon, which relates the reconstruction of Etemenanki, the ziqqurat in Babylon (Langdon 1912: 60 *Nabopolassar* no. 1 ll. 23-41):

> When, according to the command of Nabu and Marduk who love my reign, and with the weapons, the strong reed of Erra who frightens and destroys my enemies, I killed the Subartu (Assyrians) and turned their land into rubble heaps—at that time, Etemenanki, the ziqqurat of Babylon, which for a long time had been in ruins—the lord Marduk commanded me to lay its foundations in the breast of the earth and make its top equal to the heavens.

This passage, which introduces the building story, contains reference to the defeat of the king's enemies with the help of the gods,[2] an allusion to the history of the temple and the situation which requires restoration, and a description of the divine command to rebuild the building. Of the elements mentioned in Solomon's message to Hiram, the Babylonian text lacks only an explicit reference to the previous kings.

In Chapter 9, below, it will be shown that Solomon's message to Hiram as well as Hiram's reply to Solomon are styled and phrased as letters, and that there is room to assume that they are actually based on authentic letters which were preserved in the royal archive and which somehow came into the hands of the biblical writer. Since the beginning of Solomon's message reflects in its content the introductions to building stories in the extra-biblical inscriptions, we must assume that the biblical author supplemented the content of the 'original' (?) letters, but phrased his additions in the epistolic style.

1.   See Ulshoeffer's detailed discussion in 1977. The pre-deuteronomic author is the one who mentioned the victory over the enemies, while the Deuteronomist added the idea of the rest which came with the victory. For the idea of rest in relationship to temple building, see Appendix 5.

2.   In the passage immediately preceding the description of building the Armory, Esarhaddon says (Borger 1956: 59 §20 ll. 33-39): 'After Assur. . .made me stand victoriously over my enemies, and I did everything my heart desired, with the widespread captives of the enemies which my hands had conquered, with the encouragement of the gods. . .I had them build the temples of the holy cities in the Land of Assyria and Akkad and I decorated them with silver and gold and made them shine like the day.'

2. *Building Temples upon Divine Command*

And I propose to build a house for the name of the Lord my God, as the
Lord promised my father David saying, 'Your son, whom I will set on
your throne in your place, shall build the house for my name' (1 Kgs
5.19).

With these words, Solomon informs Hiram, king of Tyre, that his
plan to build YHWH a temple is actually the fulfillment of God's own
word given to David. He refers here to the events described at length
in 2 Samuel 7. As the story now stands, David expressed to Nathan,
although not explicitly, his sorrow and wonder that there is no resting
place for the Ark of YHWH. YHWH understood from David's words
that the king actually desired to build a Temple. Nathan, who had at
first and of his own volition given David a 'go ahead' to do whatever
he had in mind, was then commanded in a nocturnal revelation to
inform David that God objected to this initiative. Instead of David
building a temple for God, David's son would do so after David's
death. David's desire to build a Temple and God's rejection of the
plan are mentioned again, in a somewhat different version, in Solomon's
blessing of the people at the dedication of the Temple (1 Kgs 8.15-19).

The reason for God's rejection of David's plan has always been somewhat of an enigma, and exegetes and scholars have struggled with the
question time and again.[1] As a matter of fact, this incident is already
the topic of inner-biblical exegesis, both on the part of the Deuteronomist himself and of the Chronicler (1 Chron. 17; 28-29; 2 Chron. 6.4-
10). Similarly, modern scholarship has raised the complex questions
of the unity, literary development and historical background of the
chapter. It is not clear whether 2 Samuel 7 faithfully reflects religious,
social and political situations of the time of David, or whether the
chapter is the product of speculation of later scribes who tried to
explain after the fact how it came to be that Solomon, rather than
David, was the one privileged to build a temple. Furthermore, while
there is no doubt that Nathan's words in their present form include
both ancient elements and Deuteronomic expansions, there are nonetheless differing and even contradictory opinions among scholars

---

1. See most recently Kumaki 1981, as well as Ishida 1977: 81-118 and Cross
1973: 241-65.

about the extent of the later additions and the literary development of the entire chapter.

Since the present study is mainly comparative and phenomenological, it is unable to advance, at least directly, the solution of all of these important questions, which are, by their very nature, connected with the internal problems of biblical literature and Israelite history and religion. Nonetheless, examination of extra-biblical sources may, at least, place in proper perspective and context the *religious phenomenon* expressed in this chapter, namely, the need to request and receive permission from a deity before building him a temple. Clarification of this phenomenon is important in its own right. It may also be of some consequence in evaluating certain theories suggested in current research concerning the literary and ideological background of the chapters under discussion.[1]

The decision to build the temple is mentioned, as stated above, in three different but interconnected passages: 2 Samuel 7, 1 Kgs 5.17-19 and 1 Kgs 8.14-19. In 2 Samuel 7 and 1 Kgs 8.14-19 it is clear that David is the one who first initiated the plan to build a temple. The king wanted to build a temple for (the name of) YHWH but it was YHWH himself who prevented the king from carrying out his desire. 1 Kgs 5.16-19 does not state explicitly that David wished to build a temple, but it is reasonable to assume that this is implied in the words of Solomon, *lō' yākōl libnôt bayit*. It was already suggested by Rashi (although for his own reasons) that *lō' yākōl* actually means 'was not permitted' rather than 'was not able', and this explanation has solid basis not only in Deuteronomic usage but in biblical Hebrew in general (see Deut. 12.17; 16.5; 17.5; 22.3; Gen. 43.32). The very fact of the prohibition implies the initial desire. If so, all the passages refer to the same event in a unified manner. The king wanted to build a temple,

---

1.   Numerous biblical scholars have recognized that building a temple on divine command is a phenomenon common to biblical and ancient Near Eastern literature. Even so, the phenomenon has not yet been systematically investigated, and what may appear (superficially) to be monolithic and homogeneous in nature is in fact complex and multi-faceted. Furthermore, the phenomenon seems to be known to biblical scholars through a random and not necessarily representative sample of extra-biblical texts, the best-known being Gudea Cylinder A. In this chapter I will present all the Mesopotamian sources I know of which attest the phenomenon, and where relevant examine its various manifestations.

but God rejected his plan and subsequently appointed an alternate builder.

This course of events is only one possible way of making a decision to build or not to build a temple, and several other methods theoretically exist:

1. A god may be the one to initiate a building project. In such a case, the god will have to make a decision that a temple should be built, select a potential builder, and inform the person of the plan. A king who is selected as a builder may want to ascertain whether he understands correctly what the god wants of him, and will have to take necessary measures for clarification;

2. A man (especially a king) will decide for some reason that he wants to construct or repair a building (a temple, palace or any other structure). He will want to see whether his plan meets with divine approval and will take the proper measures to find out, and the god wll give him a sign of consent;

3. A man will want to construct a building but the god will not agree. The god will inform the man of his disapproval either by an explicit negative answer, or by not responding to an inquiry (a 'pocket veto').

A man who starts building a temple without the express consent of the gods places himself in a dangerous situation. He might receive a signal of approval after the fact, but he is equally liable to receive a message of disapproval, and if this is the case he will have to abandon a project which he has already started. This is all the more serious if building a new temple entails first demolishing an old temple, for the god will be left homeless. The king who builds a temple without permission is courting disaster—either he will not complete the project successfully, or the completed building will not stand, and may collapse after completion.

The possibilities outlined above exist not only in theory, but (as will be seen) in actual texts as well, as is evidenced both in the Bible and in numerous extra-biblical documents.

The Bible itself provides several examples of building a temple on divine initiative. According to the account of building the Tabernacle, God, through the offices of Moses, commanded the Israelites to build a Tabernacle and even showed Moses a scale model while he explained to him verbally and in great detail the form (and function) of the Tabernacle and its furnishings. The account of the Tabernacle construction (Exod. 35–40) emphasizes time after time that the Israelites or Moses did what God had commanded. There is no need to confirm God's command, and God does not repeat his command, reflecting the belief that God spoke directly and unambiguously to Moses (cf. Num. 12.6-8).

The traditions concerning the rebuilding of the temple at the time of the return from Exile strongly attest the belief that the project was divinely initiated and sanctioned. The account of rebuilding the temple found in Ezra 1–6 as well as the prophecies of Haggai and Zechariah tell of God's commands to Cyrus, Zerubbabel son of Shealtiel, Joshua son of Jehozadak, the prophets Haggai and Zechariah themselves, and to the entire people. These sources even report that God 'stirred up the spirit' (*hē'îr rûaḥ*) of Cyrus, Zerubbabel, Joshua and the entire people. There seems to be no need to confirm the Divine command, although, in saying that God both stirred up the spirits of the people and also sent prophets, the author may be stressing that the stirring up of the spirit was insufficient. Also, the employment of two prophets may be tantamount to sending two messages, one confirming the validity of the other. (The duplication of divine messages as a sign of their validity is commonplace, as we will see below.)

An explicit and detailed command to build a temple at some unspecified date in the future concludes the book of Ezekiel (chs. 40–48).[1]

An example of the second way of initiating a building project, namely a human decision and divine approval, is found in the story of Nehemiah in the court of Artaxerxes. Nehemiah relates that, having heard of Jerusalem's continued state of destruction, he prayed to God

1.   Weinfeld (1972: 247) suggests including within the category of building by divine command the stories in the Pentateuch and Former Prophets about building altars in places where God has revealed himself to a person. It seems to me, however, that apart from the stories about David's altar at Araunah's threshing floor (2 Sam. 24.18-25) and about Jacob's altar in Bethel (Gen. 35.1-7), in which there are actually commands given to erect an altar, the stories all reflect a basically different (even if related) phenomenon. A theophany at a particular location marks that place itself as a place which God frequents, or the place where he resides and may therefore be found. Building an altar at such a site is not to be perceived as the fulfilling of a divine command, but as a spontaneous human reaction to the knowledge that God is present. On this phenomenon, see Lindblom 1961.

and asked that God would grant him a successful mission and make the king be merciful towards him (Neh. 1.11). By merit of his prayer (Neh. 1.4), Artaxerxes permits Nehemiah to travel to Jerusalem to restore it. It is clear that Nehemiah is the initiator of the building project, but his success in obtaining permission from the king is interpreted as God favorably answering his prayers. By force of circumstance, the course of 'initiative–request for approval–consent' is played out on both the human and the divine level.

Remarks about divine participation in decisions to build temples and other types of buildings appear in dozens of Mesopotamian texts and even in a few Northwest Semitic inscriptions. It will now be appropriate to review these sources, categorizing them according to the possible courses of decision-making outlined above:

The Gods Initiate the Building Project
a. Divine Conferences

In numerous Sumerian and Old Babylonian inscriptions, there are introductory sections which describe or allude to divine 'conferences' at which a certain project is decided upon and for which a king is chosen and commissioned to undertake. Gudea Cylinder A, Samsuiluna C and the inscription of Ipiq-Ishtar of Malgium report short conversations between the gods which preceded sending an order to the king. Participating in these consultations are the chief deity of the pantheon and the god for whom the project is being carried out.

Although opening sections such as these are most typical of the older Sumerian and Old Babylonian texts,[1] they are not unheard of in the Assyrian inscriptions. Even the later Neo-Babylonian inscriptions contain indirect references to decisions being made within the divine circle. Inscriptions of Merodachbaladan,[2] Nebuchadnezzar II[3] and Nabonidus[4] attribute the initiative to build (in such cases this involves reconciliation of the god with a destroyed city or temple) to the chief god in the pantheon (Marduk, Anu and Enlil, or Sin depending on the

---

1. See the inscriptions listed in the discussion of Gudea, Cylinder A, in Chapter 1, p. 47 above.
2. Gadd 1953: 123.
3. Langdon 1912: 142 *Nebuchadnezzar* no. 16 col. ii ll. 11-14.
4. Nabonidus, Weld–Blundell Cylinder Langdon 1923: 32 ll. 1-8; Langdon 1915–16: 108 l. 33.

prevailing theological preference), but the actual command to the king to carry out the divine decision is communicated by the god whom the project is to benefit. It seems, therefore, that, according to the assumptions of the narrator, a divine conference has taken place in which the main god has announced his decision to the lower ranking god who, in turn, gives a building order to his selected king.

An echo of this process is heard in the Azitiwadda inscription. The king states that he built a city and seated in it Baal-KRNTRYŠ because he had been sent by Baal and Reshep-ṢPRM (*KAI*, no. 26 II 10-11). It may be assumed that Baal and Reshep-ṢPRM were part of the decision-making body, Baal being the higher ranking member.

The Ugaritic Baal Epic and *Enuma Elish* speak explicitly of divine assemblies at which the gods made decisions to build temples. It is possible, however, that these myths in fact reflect a projection into the divine realm of another phenomenon, namely, that of asking permission to build a temple (see below for this phenomenon), for in both texts the original initiative to build a house for the god comes not from the head of the pantheon but from a god who has not yet made it to the top.

Monotheistic religion, obviously, has no room for divine conferences and conclaves in which several gods meet and decide among themselves that a temple should be built for one of them. Nonetheless, a metamorphosis of this topos may possibly be found in Zech. 1.12-17. In this passage, an angel asks YHWH, 'O Lord of Hosts! How long will you withhold pardon from Jerusalem and the towns of Judah, which You placed under a curse seventy years ago?' This may be a monotheized variation of the *Himmelsszene* known from the Mesopotamian sources, with all secondary gods being replaced by angels. On the other hand, there may be a situation analogous to that in the Baal Epic, whereby the process of a king asking permission from a god to build a temple has been elevated to the divine sphere, and a member of the divine court asks the head god permission to build a temple.

b. *Reconciliation of a God with his Temple or City which Has Been Destroyed for a Predetermined Period of Time*
The destruction of a temple or a city was, in the ancient Near East, attributed to a god's anger with his or her city, while restoration of a destroyed building required a special divine decision and the assuaging

of the god's wrath against the city or temple. Reconciliation of a god with a city or temple is therefore a widespread theme in Assyrian and Babylonian texts, including some of those already mentioned in the previous paragraphs. It should be pointed out, however, that, although the Assyrian inscriptions do contain this motif, it is confined to compositions from the time of Esarhaddon and Assurbanipal which are connected specifically with Babylon and Babylonian temples. It would be hasty to say, therefore, that this is a universal motif, or even a pan-Mesopotamian theme.

Reconciliation of a god with a temple or city is often connected with the conclusion of a predetermined span of time. The best-known example of this topos is found in Esarhaddon's inscriptions relating to the restoration of Babylon. They tell how Marduk decreed that Babylon was to be destroyed and lie in ruins for seventy years, but before this time elapsed he had mercy on his city and by a trick rotating the tablets of destiny and reversing the numerical signs, he was able to lighten the sentence, thereby reducing the seventy years of destruction to a mere eleven (Borger 1956: 15 Episode 10).[1] The similarity of the seventy years decreed for Babylon's destruction and the seventy years of destruction decreed for Jersusalem (Jer. 25.11, 12; 29.10; Ezra 1.1) was noticed long ago by scholars. However, it is also possible that lessening the punishment by a numerical trick is somehow a precedent for Daniel 9, where a new interpretation is given to the seventy years decreed for Jerusalem.

Assurbanipal tells that Nana sat in exile in Elam for 1635 years before calling him to return her to the Eanna temple in Uruk. In this inscription too, the selection of Assurbanipal had been decreed some time in advance (Streck 1916: 58 ll. 116-18):

amat qibīt ilūtīšun	The word of their divine command
ša ultu ūmē rūqūte iqbû	which they had spoken in days of yore
eninna ukallimū nišē arkûti	they revealed now to latter-day people.

There is a similar statement about the restoration of Eḫulḫul, Sin's temple in Harran.[2] These texts are, of course, *vaticinia ex eventu*, but just as in Esarhaddon's inscriptions, so in those of Assurbanipal, the period for a temple's destruction has been predetermined, as has been

---

1. See most recently Shaffer 1981.
2. Streck 1916: 216 no. 13; Thompson 1931: 17 l. 26; Cogan 1978 (Assurbanipal Prism T).

the time for the god's self-imposed exile, and only at the termination of the period is the king called.

In the Cylinder inscription of Merodachbaladan mentioned previously it is written (Gadd 1953: 123 ll. 10-11):

> When the days were full and the predetermined time arrived, the great
> Lord Marduk became reconciled to Akkad which he had scorned.

The expression *ikšuda adannu* (the time arrived) refers to a time set in advance—an appointed, predetermined time, implying that, as in the other texts, so here a period of destruction and a date for restoration had already been set at the time of destruction.

These two ideas—reconciliation or pacification of the god and the predetermination of a period for destruction and a date of restoration—are found individually or together in additional inscriptions of Nebuchadnezzar[1] and Nabonidus.[2] All these sources report that the time arrived, and that, after the god was pacified, some sort of sign was revealed to the selected king, on the basis of which he knew that he had been appointed to restore the destroyed building (see below for the signs).

The idea of reconciliation of a god with his temple after a predetermined period of destruction is found in the Bible in the prophecies of the Restoration Period. The expression '*ēt bō*', which is the exact Hebrew equivalent of *adannu kašādu*, is found in Hag. 1.2 (see also Jer. 27.7, cf. Ps. 102.14. 'Thou shalt arise, and have mercy on Zion: For *it is time* (*kî 'ēt*) to have pity on her, yea, *the set time is come*'

---

1. Langdon 1912: 96 *Nebuchadnezzar* no. 10 i 17-19; p. 142 no. 16 col. II 11-13.

2. Langdon 1912: 270 *Nabonidus* no. 8 col. i ll. 34-36; 284 col. x 8-10; Gadd 1958: 46 ll. 35-39 (Adad-guppi inscription); Langdon 1912: 218 *Nabonidus* no. 1 col. i 13-15. cf. also Nabû-apla-iddina's grant document (King 1912: XXXVI iii 13). A divine decision concerning the building of a temple in the future is mentioned in a text which is, apparently, a collection of *ex eventu* prophecies (Borger 1971: 8 ll. 12-27). In this text Marduk speaks in the first person, predicting that a king will arise and restore the temple Ekursagil, change its form, and bring the god into it in a procession. See also Hunger and Kaufmann 1975: 372 ll. 12-15 as well as Weinfeld 1979: 267, 271-74. In addition to these texts, the Papulegarra Hymn (Pinches 1924 = Seux 1976 p. 46 and cf. von Soden 1982: 195-97) mentions the building of a temple in an announcement (precative used). The Akkadian expression *adannam šakānum* has a parallel in the Hebrew *śām mōʿēd* (Exod. 9.5; cf. Eccl. 3.17b emended '*ēt . . . śām*).

(*bā' mô'ēd*).[1] Zech. 1.2-3 mentions the idea of YHWH becoming reconciled with his temple which he had cursed. An allusion to a fixed time may be heard in the angel's question (v. 12), '*How long* ('*ad mātê*) wilt thou not have mercy on Jerusalem... against which thou hast had indignation these seventy years', as well as in the opening of the book of Ezra (1.1) and in Daniel 9.

c. *Communicating the Divine Will to the Selected King*
When the building or restoration of a temple was initiated by a divine decision, the god had to reveal his wish to the chosen builder. Such revelations are not portrayed as sought by the king, but come to him unawares, taking him by surprise. The gods had several ways of informing the kings of their desire:

Dreams. The best-known (to us) way for the god to deliver a message to the king was by means of a dream. In a dream the god would reveal to the king, either explicitly through words or symbolically through visual means, what was demanded.

We have already made several references to Gudea's dreams. The first of his dreams was a symbolic one. He saw a huge man wearing a divine crown, winged like a lion-headed bird whose lower body was a flood wave flanked by two lions. This figure was the god Ningirsu who commanded him to build the Eninnu temple. Gudea's personal god Nigishzidda appeared in the dream as the breaking day, while a woman and a hero holding styluses and writing on tablets of gold and lapis lazuli represented the goddess Nisaba and the god Nindub. Gudea appeared in his own dream as a donkey impatiently pawing the ground. We must emphasize once again that this dream was a spontaneous vision, initiated by the god himself. It was unexpected and was not solicited or induced through incubation or by praying to and petitioning the deity. Furthermore, two of the other three dreams, in which Ningirsu revealed to Gudea the attributes and form of the temple, were dreams procured through incubation—once in the temple and once on a brick pile. But even in these cases, the incubation procedure was ordered by the gods. Only the dream in the Nanshe temple was totally the doing of Gudea, and the purpose of this induced dream was to clarify the previous, uninduced revelation. Most important, in none

1. See, in brief, Tadmor 1984: 262.

of the dreams is there any hint that the initiative for building the temple was that of Gudea. Just the opposite, Gudea is pictured as a ruler who tries with all his might to perform the will of his god, and there is no sign of any personal initiative or independence.[1]

Dreams are mentioned in the building accounts of the Assyrian kings Assurbanipal and (perhaps) Esarhaddon.[2] Assurbanipal tells in one place that Ishtar abandoned her temple Emashmash in Nineveh, and after becoming reconciled to it she sent the king constantly recurring dreams (Thompson 1931: 31 ii l. 14; cf. Streck 1916: 59 n. 5):

> In order to complete her august divinity
> and glorify her most precious rites
> through dreams, the business of ecstatics
> she kept on sending to me constantly (*ištanappara kajāna*).

Although there is no explicit reference to a dream, it is possible that there is at least a hint of one in Assurbanipal's inscription describing the restoration of Eanna and Eḫulḫul. In connection with Eanna he says (Streck 1916: 58 ll. 111-17 and see also Bauer 1933: 34 K 2664 III 18-29, 43 K 2628 vv. 1-8):

> For mastery of the lands and returning her divinity
> she entrusted me saying: 'Assurbanipal
> from wicked Elam will take me out
> and will bring me into the midst of Eanna.
> The word of their great divinity which they said in days of yore
> they now revealed to the latter-day people.

1.   Jacobsen 1987 interprets this passage differently. In his opinion, the dream is indeed invited and incubated. Nonetheless, he adds that Gudea had been given previous indications that the gods wanted something of him, namely the rising in the river mentioned in the opening lines of Cylinder A. If so, the building of Eninnu remains divinely initiated.

2.   Oppenheim (1956: 354 [additions to p. 193]) claims most surprisingly that a text concerning the fashioning of statues of Zababa and Ishtar by Sennacherib (Ebeling 1954) mentions a dream of Sennacherib (Postgate 1969: 73, referring to *bīru* in no. 36: 6' 8', similarly takes the word to refer to some sort of revelation or vision). However, the word *bīru* which Oppenheim interprets here as a dream, is the regular term for extispicy. Furthermore, the gods responsible for showing the king a *bīru* are Shamash and Adad, the well-known patrons of extispicy. We must therefore reject Oppenheim's contention and regard this text as referring to extispicy (see W.G. Lambert 1983: 82-86). I will further discuss this text below.

In connection with Eḫulḫul he relates (Thompson 1931: 31 II 31-51):

> To rebuild Eḫulḫul
> Sin, who created me for kingship, called me by name
> saying: 'Assurbanipal will build that sanctuary.
> He will set up for me in its midst
> an everlasting dais.
> Sin's word which he said
> in days of yore,
> now he revealed to the latter-day people.

Streck, following a suggestion of Jastrow, suggests that the words of Nana and Sin came to the king in a dream. This is not impossible, but the possibility is not to be excluded that the text actually refers to a question posed to a diviner but rephrased as a direct divine utterance to the king (see below for another possible case of such a conversion in an Esarhaddon text).

Assurbanipal mentions good dreams in connection with his building the palace for the crown prince (The Rassam Prism and the Louvre Prism AO 19.939 [Aynard 1957]). However, as mentioned above when analyzing the text, the circumstances of these dreams are not entirely clear. Whatever the case may be, it seems that the dreams mentioned in this text inspired the king to build the *bīt ridûti*.

It is possible that a dream is referred to in a poetic inscription of Esarhaddon telling about the restoration of Ešarra, Assur's temple in the city Assur (Borger 1957–58: 113 ll. 4-8):

> He gives him an instruction, and sends him a command
> to the restorer of Ešarra, the perfecter of the rites
> he called him by name for kingship (saying):
> 'Build August Ešarra, dais of my delight!
> Like the writing of Heaven make its forms artistic'.

In this text, the god (probably Assur) is speaking to Esarhaddon. It is difficult to imagine that a divine revelation involving direct speech to the recipient of the revelation could be anything but a dream. Even so, it is to be noted that the building inscription itself (see analysis in Chapter 2, 4a) makes no reference to a dream. Just the opposite! The building inscription says explicitly that the king received permission to build a temple by means of liver divination. If the author of the building inscription had knowledge of a dream, why would he not mention it? We may conjecture that the author of the poetic text converted the answer of the *bārû* (the extispicer) into a direct divine command to the king in which he refers to the king in the second person and to himself (speaking for the god) in the first person. It is not impossible that the author of the poetic account really wanted to ascribe a dream revelation to the king—perhaps considering this more prestigious—but if he did, he invented the dream.

Dreams concerning temple building are found as well in Nabonidus's inscriptions. The Sippar Cylinder tells how Marduk and Sin appeared to the king in a dream and commanded him to build Eḫulḫul.[1] In this

---

1.   Langdon 1912: 218 *Nabonidus* no. 1 col. i 20-23. The words of Marduk and Sin to Nabonidus may be compared to two biblical passages. According to Nabonidus, the gods commanded him to build the Eḫulḫul temple as follows:

> Nabonidus King of Babylon!
> With the horses which you ride
> carry bricks! (*iš ši libnāte*).
> Build Eḫulḫul and (*Eḫulḫul epušma*).
> Sin the great lord
> cause to take up residence
> within its midst! (*ina qerbīšu šurmâ šubassu*).

A command of similar content and structure is found in the Priestly account of the building of the Tabernacle. YHWH commands Moses (Exod. 25.2-8):

dabbēr 'el bĕnê yiśrā'ēl	Speak unto the Israelites
wĕyiqḥû lî terumâ	and they will take for me a contribution. . .
wĕ'āśû lî miqdāš	and they will build me a sanctuary
wĕšākantî bĕtôkām	and I will dwell in their midst

Another similar divine command is found in the prophecies of Haggai (Hag. 1.8):

> Go up to the mountain and bring wood
> and build the temple
> and I will desire it
> and will be glorified by it
> says YHWH.

The first two passages contain commands in synonymous language (1) to gather building materials; (2) to build a temple; (3) to bring the deity into it. The passage from Haggai contains the first two elements explicitly, and the third element in an altered form, for the word *wĕ'ekkābĕda(h)*, which means 'I will be glorified by it' (cf. Hag. 2.7-8) alludes to the word *kābôd* which means divine presence, and the *nip'al* form may actually mean 'I will be present in it in my *kābôd*'. The Rabbis have already explained the deficient spelling of the word as hinting at the five things present in the First Temple which will be absent in the Second Temple, their list including the Ark, its covering and the Cherubs, the miraculous fire on the altar (cf.

dream, in contrast to those mentioned so far, the dreaming king actually participates. Nabonidus speaks with Sin and with Marduk. The same dream is referred to in the Harran inscription (Gadd 1958: 56 ll. 11-14) but this time there is no reference to Nabonidus speaking. In addition, only Sin is mentioned and there is no hint of Marduk. These differences stem either from the fact that the Harran inscription summarizes the building account, or from the fact that it shows a later stage of Nabonidus's religious development and the tendency to worship Sin as the major god in the pantheon. Another inscription reports that Shamash commanded Nabonidus to build Ebabbar in Sippar.[1] This dream was experienced not only by the king, but by many other people. This is a rather rare example of the revelation of a divine command to the entire people and not only the king.[2] In the same inscription (which contains four tendentious reworkings of four separate building accounts), there is reference to yet another dream in which Anunitu of Sippar commands the building of her temple Eulmash.[3] Lastly, Nabonidus's aged mother Adad-guppi mentions a dream in which the gods inform her that her son Nabonidus will build Eḫulḫul (Harran Stele A).[4]

Attention should be given to the fact that a large number of the dreams mentioned in building accounts are centered around two personalities: Assurbanipal, king of Assyria and Nabonidus, king of

Lev. 9.24; 2 Chron. 7.1), the Shekinah (divine presence), the Holy Spirit of Prophecy, and the Urim and Thumim. The first items are symbols of God's tangible presence (*b. Yom.* 21b), and their absence indicates that the Temple has undergone a fundamental transformation in its meaning.

1.   Langdon 1915–16: 105 l. 63, and cf. Oppenheim 1956: 209 col. a.

2.   See below in connection with the letter from Dilmun. Recently published is a text from the reign of Bēl-ibni king of Babylon (Binning no. 1: See Walker and Kramer 1982), which tells of the return of the plundered image of ᵈba-KUR, to the temple Etenten, where we read (ll. 8-11):

> Ninurta showed him a sign
> concerning Ba-KUR, the mistress
> of oracles and
> made him understand in his heart.
> The whole city of Sapija
> saw Ba-KUR and
> (the king?) was fearful and trembled.

3.   Langdon 1915–16: 108 l. 36.

4.   Gadd 1958: 48 ll. 5-11.

Babylon. It is possible that this is no coincidence but yet more evidence of the conscious imitation of Assurbanipal by Nabonidus.[1]

As in the cases of Assurbanipal and Nabonidus, it is not unlikely that some other kings allude in their inscriptions to dream revelations even though they do not say so explicitly. So, for instance, in Samsuiluna C we find (Borger 1973c: 48 ll. 53-69):

> Zababa and Ishtar. . .
> to Samsuiluna. . .
> . . . lifted. . . their countenances
> and spoke happily with him.

There follows a nineteen-line address to the king ending with a command to build the walls of Kish.

Takil-ilissu, king of Malgium, says about building Enamtila (Kutscher and Wilcke 1978: 127):

> Ea, my lord,
> spoke to me with his pure mouth,[2] and
> at that time, Enamtila
> in its entirety
> I surrounded with a great wall.

In these two inscriptions it is difficult to imagine what divine word to the king can be referred to if not a dream.

In addition to the dreams mentioned in the building stories in royal inscriptions, dreams concerning temple building (and other sorts of building projects) are reported in various letters sent to the kings:

A letter sent by Ili-ipšara to Iliya of Dilmun[3] mentions ominous and threatening dreams which occur time and time again, demanding that the king restore a certain temple which has grown old. These dreams seem to have been seen by the people of the city and not by the king himself. The repetition of the dream is to be taken as a sign that the dreams are reliable.[4] Even though this looks like a clear case of divine

---

1. See Oppenheim 1956: 186; and Tadmor 1965: 353 n. 16.
2. See also my comment on the Ur-Nammu Hymn, and also Jacobsen, 1937–39. Cf also Langdon 1912: 284 *Nabonidus* no. 8 col. X 10 (= Oppenheim, *ANET*, 311), but this text probably refers to Marduk's command uttered within the divine assembly.
3. Goetze 1952.
4. This principle of dream interpretation is articulated explicitly by Joseph, the 'master of dreams', in Gen. 41.32: 'As for Pharaoh having had the same dream

initiative and the gods making their wishes known to the king without his asking, the content of the letter makes it clear that the gods were in fact waiting for the king to take the initiative and repair the temple (this is, after all, one of the major tasks of a king), and since he did not do so the god's anger was provoked. We may cautiously compare this with Haggai's complaint that the people are facing drought and agricultural failure because they are running to their own homes while letting God's temple lie in ruins (Hag. 1.3-10).

A letter from Kibri-Dagan to Zimri-Lim, king of Mari, mentions yet another dream. In this dream, which was experienced several times by a *muḫḫu*, the god expressed his objection to building a certain 'house'. We will return to this text below.

Omens. In certain cases, the gods expressed their desires to the king not through a dream, but through some sort of sign, or omen. It is probable that astral omens are referred to in an inscription of Warad-Sin, although this is not completely certain.[1] He relates (Kärki 1968: 47, Warad-Sin no. 10 ll. 25-33):

> when Ašimbabar showed me his good signs
> and cast a glance of life at me
> and commanded me to build and restore his temple. . .

It may perhaps be assumed that the moon god's good signs are in fact astral omens connected with the phases of the moon or its position in the heavens. That this is the case is indicated, for instance, by the much later inscription of Nabonidus (Böhl 1939: 162 ll. 9-10), in which the setting of the moon on the thirteenth of Ululu while eclipsed is taken as a sign that Sin requests a high-priestess, who is the king's daughter.[2]

A detailed report of astral omens can be found in Esarhaddon's inscription concerning the restoration of Babylon.[3] He tells that in his

---

twice, it means that the matter has been determined by God, and that God will soon carry it out'. See also the inscriptions of Assurbanipal and Nabonidus where they report that their dreams recur constantly by employing verbs in the *-tn* forms.

1. For astral portents in the Gudea cylinders, see Falkenstein 1965: 65 and Alster 1976.

2. See Böhl 1939: 162 ll. 9-10 and for discussion identifying the omen, see Reiner 1985: 7ff., 15 nn. 8-9 and see *CAD* A I *s.v. adāru* A 8 (iv).

3. The scarcity of astral portents in Assyrian royal inscriptions has been pointed out by Oppenheim 1960: 137.

first year he witnessed signs indicating the gods' command to rebuild Babylon (Borger 1956: 16-18 Episodes 12–14). The stars had gone in incorrect paths and afterwards they returned to their correct courses. The stellar movements symbolized the return of the gods to their proper places, which they had abandoned in their wrath. These signs recurred again and again, and just like constantly recurring dreams, this is a sign of reliability.

Another type of omen—this one partially meteorological—is mentioned in Nebuchadnezzar's account of restoring Ebabbar in Sippar (Langdon 1912: 96 *Nebuchadnezzar* no. 10 cols. i 17–ii 1). This inscription relates that after Marduk was reconciled with his temple, the god stirred up some strong winds which blew away the sand covering the original outline of the ruined temple, and by so doing he signaled his selection of Nebuchadnezzar to restore the temple.

A grant inscription from the time of Nabû-apla-iddina, king of Babylon, (King 1912: XXXVI cols. iii l. 15–col. iv l. 13)[1] informs the reader that Shamash, who had been wrathful with Akkad, became reconciled to it and turned to it once again. On the other side of the Euphrates a symbol of the Sun god was found which the priest revealed (*ukallim*) to the king, who in turn rejoiced, and made a new symbol just like the old one.

In these two cases, the gods reveal the form of an old building or cult object to the king. By doing so, they inform him of their desire to restore the building or cult object, and also reveal to him the plan (see below for more on this idea).

It is quite possible that, in an Old-Akkadian inscription of Šar-kali-šarrī (Thureau-Dangin 1907: 162 no. 1c), the words *dEn-líl u-gal-lim* refer to some sort of omen which encouraged the king to restore Enlil's temple (cf. the use of the verb *kullumu* 'to reveal', in several of the texts cited above).

In Samsuiluna C, the king's victory over his enemies, in the wake of which he rebuilds Kish, is described as the good sign (*ittakunu damiqtum*) of the gods Zababa and Ishtar (Borger 1973c 48 ll. 40-41). But in this case the victory serves to confirm the word of the gods which, as suggested before, may have come to him in a dream. A similar combination of events is found much later in Nabonidus's Sippar Cylinder (Langdon 1912: 218 *Nabonidus* no.1, col. i 24-36). Sin and

1. See Frankfort 1948: 270.

Marduk command Nabonidus in a dream to build Eḫulḫul, and, in reaction to the king's apprehension, they promise him that the Umman-manda, who have been preventing him from building the temple, will be vanquished. After their rout by Cyrus king of Anshan, we hear that Nabonidus feared the word of the gods and untiringly built the temple. If so, then in this text as well a victory in war (albeit of another king) served as a sign confirming a dream. In the Deuteronomic ideology, too, rest from the enemies is taken as a sign that the time has come to build a temple (Deut. 12.10; 2 Sam. 7.1; 1 Kgs 5.17-18).

The gods' command communicated to the king by a third party. It is well known that apostolic prophecy was not one of the regular phenomena of the main stream of Mesopotamian religion. The desires and plans of the gods usually became known to the king through divination or through decipherment of all sorts of occurrences considered ominous. If the gods wished to communicate directly with the king, they could do so through dreams, or through numerous signs which would be recognized by the appropriate experts, as we saw previously. Nonetheless, there are cases in which the gods would communicate with the king not directly, and not even through the offices of the *bārû*, but through some other individual. It is not impossible that the divine utterances interpreted above as possible dreams were in fact prophecies delivered to the king by some third party, but there is no evidence for this, nor would it be in keeping with what is known otherwise about divine–human communication in Mesopotamia. Examples of dreams experienced by all the people of the land or by the mother of the king have already been mentioned. Nabonidus claims that Sin's request for an *entu* priestess was revealed to the inhabited world.[1] He refers to an astronomical omen which, obviously, can be observed (even if not understood!) by anyone who bothers to look up and see it, but the king's emphasis of the fact shows that he is interested in the 'public' nature of the revelation (a 'media event'!). In the grant inscription of Nabû-apla-iddina it was noted that the emblem of Shamash was revealed to one of the priests—a *bārû* to be sure, but not in the course of his performing divination of any sort.[2] According to the Weld–Blundell cylinder of Nabonidus, experts informed the king

1. See Böhl 1939: 162 col. i 1 and Reiner 1985: 2. CAD A I *s.v. adnātu.*
2. King 1912: XXXVI 123 iii 19–iv 10.

that Shamash was waiting for him to rebuild Ebabbar, the ruins of which he beheld.[1] The Mari correspondence, which offers much information about practices not typical of Mesopotamia proper but more symptomatic of the West Semitic world, provides two additional examples of this phenomenon. One letter (*ARM* 3 78) says that time after time the restoration of a city gate was demanded by an ecstatic (*muḫḫû*). Another letter states that a youth informed the king (through the agency of Kibri-Dagan) of the gods' opposition to completing a building (perhaps a temple) presently under construction.[2]

To be sure, this method is the one most prevalent in the Bible. Divine commands to build (or not to build) temples are expressed to kings and the people through the agencies of Moses, Nathan, Ezekiel, Zechariah and Haggai. We can also include, perhaps, Gad who commands David to build God an altar (2 Sam. 24.18). This is in keeping with Israelite views that YHWH communicates with his people and their leaders through prophets. Only if one were to accept the proposal of A. Kapelrud and M. Weinfeld that Solomon's dream at Gibeon originally concerned building the Temple would there be a case of God communicating directly with the selected temple builder, but this proposal is otherwise problematic, as will be seen below.

Divine inspiration. There are instances in which the divine command to build a temple has no external, discernible expression, but even so the king attributes his plan to build a temple to the intervention of the gods. Nebuchadnezzar, for example, credits all his construction undertakings to divine inspiration (Langdon 1912: 76, *Nebuchadnezzar* no. 1, col. ii 55–iii 4):[3]

> To build the holy cities of the gods and goddesses
> which the great lord, Marduk
> commanded me (*iāti umarrannimma*) and
> inspired my heart (*ušadkânni libbam*)
> fearfully I did not desist from it,
> I completed its work.

These passages may be compared to various biblical statements that YHWH stirred up the spirit (*hē'îr rûaḥ*) of Cyrus, of Zerubbabel son

---

1.   Weld–Blundell Cylinder of Nabonidus (Langdon 1923: 33).
2.   Cf. *ARM* 13.112 and Malamat 1967: 238 and Oppenheim 1967 no. 57.
3.   See as well p. 111 no. 13 col. iii 7; p. 98 no. 11 col. ii 5-6.

of Shealtiel, and of the entire people to rebuild the temple in Jerusalem (Ezra 1.1, 5; Hag. 1.14).[1]

Non-explicit ways of relaying the divine command. In addition to the texts cited above which describe or allude to the way in which the gods made their desire to build a temple known to the king, there are additional passages which say only that the building project was commanded by the gods, that it was done at their request, according to their will, and the like. I will cite just a few examples: Tukulti-Ninurta I claims to have built Kar-Tukulti-Ninurta because Assur 'asked it of him' (Weidner 1959: 28 l. 88; p. 31 l. 44):

> Assur my lord asked of me (*ēriš animma*) [2] a holy city and
> commanded me (*iqbâ*) to build his temple.

Tiglath-pilesar I tells concerning the Anu-Adad temple (King, *AKA*, 96 ll. 71-75):

---

1. Cf. Weinfeld 1979: 266 and Tadmor's comments cited by Weinfeld in note 14.

2. For the use of the word *'rš* in an inscription from Pyrgi, see above, Chapter 6, section 1. The term *erēšu* is used in several Akkadian building reports: inscription of Ad-da-hu-šu from Susa (Scheil 1939: no. 5 l. 7): *É.KI.A[GA.NI] ša i-ri-šu*, 'his beloved temple which he requested'; inscription of Salim-ahum, king of Assyria (Ebeling 1926, 4.8; *Aššur bītam īrussumma*, 'Assur asked from him a temple'; Tukulti-Ninurta I (Weidner 1959: 17): *Ištar bēltī bīta šanâ ša el maḫrî ajakkīša quššudu īrišannimma*, 'Ishtar my Lady requested of me another temple which was holier than her previous sanctuary'; Weidner 1959: 24 l. 40; p. 28 l. 88; p. 31 l. 41: *Enlil bēlī māḫāza ēriš annimma epēš atmanīšu iqbâ*, 'Enlil my Lord requested of me a holy city and commanded to build his temple'; and cf. the Ipiq-Ishtar inscription (Shroeder 1917–18: 92) *ina šurri Ea Damkina ana wardūtīšunu ēršūninni ēpušma abni bītam*, 'as soon as Ea and Damkina requested me for their servitude, I made and built a temple'.

The word *erēšu* appears as well in the Neo-Babylonian period to express divine wishes for other types of cultic implements. So the inscription of Nabonidus in which he tells how he consecrated his daughter to be priestess of the moon god Sin begins (Böhl 1939: 162 i 1; p. 170; for recent discussion of the inscription, see Rainer 1985: 1-16): *inu Nannari īrišu enta*, 'when Nannar requested an *entu* priestess'. Note also *Enuma elish* IV 11 *zanānūtum eršat parak ilānīma*, 'when maintenance is requested in the temple of the gods', and see on this passage Oppenheim 1943: 224 n. 2. The term also appears in some omen apodoses to signify that the gods request sacrifices.

> At the beginning of my reign
> Anu and Adad, the great gods, my lords
> commanded me (*iqbûni*) to build their temple.

In these inscriptions it is possible that the gods expressed their wishes to the king in one of the ways mentioned above, and that the building project was divinely initiated. On the other hand, it is not impossible that the texts actually refer to divine approval granted a project initiated by the king. These texts may refer to a positive answer given to a request made by the king, since an answer to a query may also be considered a divine command (see especially the inscriptions of Sargon and Sennacherib, in which it is clear that the divine command did not precede but only succeeded a royal initiative).

The King Clarifies the Divine Will

Dreams, natural portents, the words of wise men, priests or divine messengers, and even *vox populi* were not considered reliable expressions of divine desires and demands. Furthermore, when a king himself was the initiator of a building project, even if his decision was made wholeheartedly, and with the best of intentions, and even if it was a product of profound, even divinely granted wisdom,[1] it was not always certain what the gods themselves wanted. For these reasons, it was always necessary to certify by tested and recognized means that the project under consideration by the king met with the approval of the gods and would merit their blessing.

In the first Cylinder of Gudea, the reader has no doubt that the rebuilding of Eninnu is what the gods desire—one is told so by the author in the very first scene. Even so, Gudea does not know what the audience has been told and the author goes to the trouble of mentioning no fewer than six different ways in which Gudea clarified and

---

1. The wisdom of the king, granted by Ea and sometimes compared to that of the primordial *apkallu* ('sage') Adapa, is frequently mentioned at the beginning of a building story, leading us to believe that the actual decision to build, as well as the architectural planning, is depicted as a product of the king's wisdom. This motif is especially prominent in Neo-Assyrian royal inscriptions, and found only rarely elsewhere (for a partial listing of sources, see the recent study of Kalugila 1980). It is possible, although by no means certain, that this is somehow related to the juxtaposition of the Temple-building story and the description of Solomon's divinely granted wisdom in 1 Kgs 5.9-14 (he is also compared with several well-known sages) and the reference to Solomon's wisdom again in v. 26.

verified Ningirsu's command: (1) Ningirsu himself appears to Gudea three times before the building project gets underway; (2) Gudea's dreams are interpreted by a dream interpretress who is herself a goddess; (3) Gudea witnesses certain natural phenomena; (4) Gudea has a sign performed in his own body;[1] (5) the molding of the first brick is successful; (6) following every dream, and after the molding of the first brick, Gudea slaughters a lamb and performs extispicy.

If Gudea, who was commanded by the gods to build a temple, needs so many means of verification of the gods' wishes, how much more so would a king who took building a temple upon himself of his own initiative. I will cite here several additional examples in which the king verifies the divine will, some where the initiative was originally of the gods themselves, and others in which the suggestion was that of the king. The examples cited will also illustrate certain aspects of the clarification process.[2]

Sumerian and Old Babylonian building accounts provide no indication that permission to build a temple was requested of a god by means of liver divination, and only the Gudea cylinders mention that dreams were certified by extispicy. However, a somewhat different picture is seen outside the narrow confines of building stories *per se*. In a letter from Kibri-Dagan, governor of Terqa, sent to Zimri-Lim, king of Mari, the writer informs his master that he has started to repair the dwelling of an *ugbabtum*-priestess, and this is after he, in accordance with the king's order, performed extispicy and received from the gods a reliable 'Yes!' (Kibri-Dagan, *ARM*, 3 no. 42. trans. A.L. Oppenheim 1967 no. 56):

> Now to the matter at hand: as I recently wrote to my lord, I had extispicies made concerning the house in which the *ugbabtum*-priestess of the god Dagan should live, and my extispices were propitious with regard to the house of the former *ugbabtum*-priestess. And since the god has thus given me a positive answer (*ilum annam īpulannimma*), I have started to bring that house into good repair and to. . . its enclosed part. The *ugbabtum*-priestess whom my lord will bring to Dagan can now live in this house.

Extispicy and divination are mentioned frequently in Assyrian

---

1. See Falkenstein 1965.
2. T. Ishida (1977: 85 n. 27) follows Ellis (1968: 6) in claiming that asking divine permission for a building project is a practice limited to southern Mesopotamia, with the exception of Esarhaddon. This claim is refuted by the evidence adduced here.

building accounts in the inscriptions of Tukulti-Ninurta I, Bel-harran-beli-usur,[1] Sargon, Sennacherib, Esarhaddon and Ashurbanipal.[2] They are also referred to in building accounts of the Chaldaean kings of Babylon—Nabopolassar, Nebuchadnezzar and Nabonidus.

The actual questions posed to the gods or diviners are found in the inscriptions of Tukulti-Ninurta I and Sennacherib. The king would ask a question demanding a positive or negative response, and according to the answer delivered he would know whether or not to carry out his plan. Tukulti-Ninurta I (Weidner 1959 36 §25) asks:

> Whether Assur my lord loves his mountain,[3] Ebiḫ
> (and whether) he commanded me
> to build the exalted dwelling
> which is within it—
> I asked his reliable 'Yes!'

Sennacherib (Ebeling 1954: 10) reports:

> I performed extispicy[4]
> and I asked Shamash and Adad
> saying: 'Is Zababa the son of Anšar?'
> Shamash and Adad informed me through extispicy.

Prayers which preceded the performance of extispicy are reported by the Assyrian kings Sargon and Esarhaddon[5] and the Babylonian monarchs Nebuchadnezzar[6] and Nabonidus.[7] The latter records his prayer

1.   Unger 1917 l. 10 (*ina qibītīšunu ṣīrti u annīšunu kīni*, 'through their exalted command and their reliable "Yes!"').

2.   Thompson 1931: 31 ll. 18-19; see as well Schramm 1975–76: 44 col. ii 5. For the rest of the kings mentioned here, see below.

3.   *kīma Aššur bēlī Abeh šadâšu irammu*. See Ps. 78.68, 'He did choose the tribe of Judah, Mount Zion, which he loved (*'āḥēb*); 132.13-14, 'For the Lord has chosen Zion; he has desired it (*'iwwâh*) for his seat. 'This is my resting-place for all time; here I dwell, for I desire it' (*'iwwîṯîhah*). For a god loving a city, see the Harab Myth, recently re-edited by Jacobsen (1984: 11 l. 12), where we read *ina ᵘʳᵘDunnu ša irammu ušnīlšu*, 'He laid him down in the city of Dunnu which he loved' (see also Miller 1985: 239).

4.   Deller 1987; Galter 1984.

5.   Sargon's Cylinder Inscription, Lyon 1883: 36 ll. 53-55; Borger 1956: 82 ll. 11-20; and see below.

6.   Langdon 1912: 100 *Nebuchadnezzar* no. 12 col. ii 12-27.

7.   Langdon 1912: 238 *Nabonidus* no. 3 col. ii 34-49; p. 254 no. 6 ll. 26-29, and cf. Nabonidus, Weld–Blundell Cylinder (Langdon 1923: 34).

to Marduk which he recited prior to visiting the temples of Shamash, Adad and Nergal in order to obtain permission to restore Ebabbar (Langdon 1912: 238 *Nabonidus* no. 3 ll. 35-40):

> O lord, first among the gods,
> Prince Marduk!
> Without you a dwelling is not founded,
> its outline does not come into existence.
> Something not from you, who will do it?[1]
> O lord, by your exalted command,
> what is good before you,
> may I cause to have done!

The technical details of extispicy are mentioned in several building accounts. The king would pray in the temples of Shamash and Adad and would offer a sacrifice[2] and the entrails of the victim would be put in a bowl called a *mākalti bārûti*, a diviner's bowl.[3] The gods would 'cause (a sign) to be written' on the liver *(ušaštiru amūtam)*[4] or 'cause a sign to be placed' in the liver *ušaškinū tērtam*.[5] The king, when seeing the signs, or having them deciphered for him, would 'take confidence' (*takālu*) in the divine command.[6]

Extispicy was performed not only for the purpose of confirming the actual decision to carry out a building project, but also for approving several of the activities which this project would entail. Sennacherib used extispicy to receive approval of his artistic and architectural innovations.[7] Nabopolassar informs us that through liver divination Shamash, Adad and Marduk approved the measurements which the king had designed for the walls of the Ninkarak temple Ehursagsikilla.[8] Nebuchadnezzar, after having the site for Etemenanki surveyed by expert surveyors, reports that Shamash, Adad and Marduk approved

1. See Ps. 127.1, '. . .Unless the Lord builds the house, its builders labor in vain on it'.
2. Langdon 1912: 254 *Nabonidus* no. 6 l. 26.
3. Winckler 1889: II, pl. 49 no. 17 (Sargon); Thompson and Hamilton 1932: 103 l. 7; Borger 1956: 3 l. 45; p. 19 episode 17 and see p. 81 l. 52.
4. Borger 1956: 81 l. 52.
5. Langdon 1912: 102 *Nebuchadnezzar* no. 12 col. ii 24-27.
6. Langdon 1912: 254 *Nabonidus* no. 6 col. i l. 30.
7. Luckenbill 1924: 137 ll. 29-30; p. 140 l. 3; p. 140 ll. 8-9, 12, 13, 16; p. 144 ll. 8-15.
8. Langdon 1912: 76 *Nebuchadnezzar* no. 1 ll. 18-30.

the measurements he had planned.[1] Nabonidus boasts that his success in uncovering the ancient, original foundations of Eulmash was promised ahead of time by extispicy.[2] In another place he states that the appropriate day for founding Ehulhul was selected by divination.[3] Esarhaddon, who fashioned some new divine statues as well as a new crown for the image of Assur, prayed to the gods and requested that skilled craftsmen be selected for him by the gods (Borger 1956: 82 epis. 53 ll. 11-20):

> O great gods! With whom will you send me to make the (images of the) gods and goddesses, to a place to which there is no approaching, to a difficult task, to the task of restoration? Will it be with human beings who do not hear and do not see, who do not know themselves and whose lives are unknown? Making the (images of) gods and goddesses is in your hands! Build by yourselves the temple of your exalted divinities![4] (Then) everything which you desire will be done without deviating from your command. The wise craftsmen whom you have said, give them a high ear (great wisdom) so that they may perform this work like Ea their creator. Teach skill to their heart. By your exalted command, may everything their hands touch succeed.

Following this prayer, Esarhaddon tells how he selected the artisans through extispicy:

> In order (to learn) the decision of Shamash and Adad, I prostrated myself fearfully. In order (to learn) the certain decision, I arranged the extispicers. I performed extispicy (concerning) whether to enter the workroom of Baltil (Assur) or Babylon or Nineveh. About the matter of the craftsmen who would do the work and be introduced to secrets, I set up group opposite group. The signs (in the livers) were identical and thus they (the gods Shamash and Adad) answered me with a reliable 'Yes!' They

1. Wetzel and Weissbach 1938: 42 col. ii ll. 33-41 (cf. *CAD* K 314, *s.v.* *keṣēpu* 2).

2. Langdon 1915–16: 106 l. 53.

3. Langdon 1912: 226 *Nabonidus* no. 1 col. II l. 60. Another, much earlier case may be a text of Ur-Nanše, king of Lagash, where we read (Jacobsen 1985: 70 col. iii 1-3): 'May Enki perform the seeking of prognostics'. Jacobsen compares this passage with Gudea Cylinder A xx 16 and explains, 'omens were taken after invocation of the deity in question to determine a suitable time for beginning work'.

4. On the idea that it is not a man who builds the temple but God himself, and especially in connection with this passage, see Weinfeld 1970: 286. And compare Ps. 127.1.

commanded me to enter the workshop in Baltil, the city of rule, the dwelling place of the father of the gods Assur, and they made known to me the names of the artisans who would do the work.

Extispicy may have been known and practiced in ancient Israel, but it was rejected by 'biblical' religion, and there is no hint of it in the various building accounts recorded in the Bible. Nevertheless, the activities which according to the Mesopotamian inscriptions required special confirmation through divination—these were done in the biblical texts according to explicit divine commands.[1] So we find that God showed Moses the plan of the Tabernacle and its vessels (Exod. 25.9, 40; 26.30; 27.8; Num. 8.4) and explained to him the details of its form. Similarly, Ezekiel is shown and told the form of the Temple to be built in the future (Ezek. 40–48 and see also Zech. 2.5-9). According to the Chronicler's account of the building of the first temple, the plan for the temple to be built by Solomon was given to David in writing (1 Chron. 28.11-19, and see Ezek. 43.11). Nabonidus's statement that the date of founding Ehulhul was fixed by extispicy may be compared to God's command to Moses that the Tabernacle be erected on the first day of the first month (Exod. 40.1, 17). Esarhaddon's use of extispicy for selecting skilled artisans to restore the images of the gods is comparable to God's selection of Bezalel and Ohaliab to manufacture the Tabernacle and its vessels (Exod. 31.1-11; 35.30–36.1). Finally, we find that in Mesopotamia divination was used to promise the king that the building project would reach a successful conclusion. So Nabonidus states (Langdon 1912: 254 *Nabonidus* no. 6 ll. 28-29):

> A 'Yes' of wellbeing and a firm decision
> about completing my work
> and establishing the temples
> Shamash and Adad
> placed in my (divinatory) entrail.

This divine promise of success is perhaps comparable to an explicit revelation to Solomon mentioned in 1 Kgs 6.11-13:

> Then the word of the Lord came to Solomon, 'With regard to this House you are building—if you follow my laws and observe my rules and faithfully keep my commandments, I will fulfill for you the promise that I gave to your father David: I will abide among the children of Israel, and I will never forsake my people Israel'.

1. See Excursus, this chapter.

Although the technical methods of expressing divine approval or revealing the divine will differ, it is clear that in the Bible as well as in ancient Mesopotamia divine guidance was desired and considered crucial throughout all stages of the building project and regarding any aspect where human judgment could lead the builder astray.

Witholding Permission to Build a Temple
The very necessity and custom of requesting divine permission to engage in a building project imply that the gods reserved for themselves the option to reject or ignore a request. Now a king who had not received a divine building permit would certainly hesitate to build, and it is obvious that inscriptions would not be written to commemorate buildings which were never constructed. In addition, divine rejection of a building request might have been considered a sign of disfavor, and it was hardly a matter to be boasted about by a king in a royal inscription memorializing his great acts. For these reasons, it is obvious that one should not expect to find many references to building requests which were turned down. Nevertheless, the historical surveys of building histories which introduce building accounts do, on occasion, contain information about previous kings who desired to restore the building but were unsuccessful. Furthermore, writings of types other than royal inscriptions also on occasion provide information about events which would not be recorded in the standard royal building accounts.

Warad-Sin,[1] Samsu-iluna,[2] Nebuchadnezzar[3] and Nabonidus[4] claimed in their inscriptions that the buildings they constructed had not been built previously because the gods had not made it possible. Samsuiluna writes:

> Since. . . among the previous kings
> Šamaš did not agree to any king,
> so he did not build for him the wall of Sippar.

An inscription of Enlil-bani tells that two bronze statues manufactured by Iddin-Dagan for Ninlil had not been brought to Nippur before

1.   Kärki 1968: Warad-Sin no. 6 ll. 13-15, and see Falkenstein 1965b: 92 l. 97 for interpretation of the inscriptions under discussion.
2.   Inscription B—Sollberger 1967b: 41 ll. 58-62.
3.   Langdon 1912: 100 *Nebuchadnezzar* no. 12 col. ii 4.
4.   Langdon 1912: 240 *Nabonidus* no. 3 col. iii ll. 20-22.

Enlil-bani's reign, and it has been suggested that the delay in dedicating the statues was caused by the gods' disagreement with the deed.[1]

The Sumerian tale *Enmerkar and the Lord of Aratta* relates that the Lord of Aratta was not favored by the goddess Inanna as was Enmerkar, lord of Uruk-Kulaba, and as a result he built no temple for her. The narrator seems to assume that he wanted to build her a temple, but that she would not allow it.[2]

Two literary texts about Amar-Suen, a so-called *Unheilsherrscher* of Ur, tell of the king's repeated attempts to restore Enki's temple.[3] One tablet says that for seven years the king wore mourning garments and tried in vain to uncover the outline of the temple.[4] His failure to uncover the temple's original outline prevented him from proceeding with the building project. Only after seven years did Enki finally speak to him, enabling him to build the temple. The second tablet reports that the king was unable to receive a divine answer to his query through extispicy.

These stories are reminiscent of the incident told in *The Curse of Agade*, in which Naram-Sin mourned for seven years and tried relentlessly to acquire Enlil's permission to build a certain temple.[5] The god did not answer, so the king went ahead and tore down Ekur, perhaps in order to be able to rebuild it—without the express consent of Enlil.[6] Thus Naram-Sin, as a result of his impetuous behavior,

1.   Shaffer 1974: 252 l. 7.

2.   S. Cohen 1973: ll. 30-32.

3.   See Michalowski 1977.

4.   This incident has much later counterparts in Nabonidus's frequent claims that the kings who preceded him were unable to uncover the outlines or original forms of the temples which they wished to rebuild.

5.   See Kramer's translation in *ANET*, 646, Falkenstein 1965; Cooper 1983 and Attinger 1984. Kramer and others assumed that the temple which was not allowed to be built was Ekur itself, but Cooper suggests that it was in fact a yet unbuilt temple for Inanna in Agade.

6.   See Jacobsen 1978–79: 7 n. 14 and Westenholz 1979: 122 n. 32 for the historical background. According to Jacobsen, Naram-Sin tore down the temple in order to rebuild it, but didn't complete the work. Note also *Erra* I 149-62 in which Marduk objects to having his divine regalia laundered lest the materials for refurbishing the statue should not be available, and the cosmos be thrown into chaos for lack of divine rule. An interesting, considerably later parallel to the scenario proposed by Jacobsen is found in Josephus, *Ant.* 15.11, describing the rebuilding of the Jerusalem Temple by Herod. According to Josephus, the people were afraid that

brought calamity upon himself and his kingdom.

In a letter, Kibri-Dagan, governor of Terqa, informs his king Zimri-Lim of Mari that it has been revealed to him in a dream that it is forbidden to restore a certain house—probably a temple—and that if the king should persist in restoring it, it will collapse and fall into the river.[1] The dream is said to have recurred, and this is to be taken as an indication of its reliability.

Nabonidus (Langdon 1912: 262 *Nabonidus* no. 7 l. 28; Dhorme 1914: 111 col. I 35) says that the god (Marduk in one version, Shamash in another) waited for him (*uqa''ânni*) to build Ebabbar, the Shamash temple in Sippar.[2] In another account of the same project (Langdon 1912: 254, *Nabonidus* no. 6 ll. 16-30), he reports that a previous king had searched for the earlier foundations of the temple but with no success. That king then went and built the temple 'of his own accord' (*ina ramānīšu*) and as a result it collapsed before its time (*ina lā adannīšu*). Interestingly, Nabonidus himself is accused by his rivals, the authors of the so-called *Verse Account*, of building temples and designing cultic objects which were not commanded by the gods (see S. Smith 1924 = A.L. Oppenheim, *ANET*, 312-15).

The *Verse Account* is not the only polemical text which accuses a king of unwarranted cultic innovations. In a recently published Late Babylonian text from Uruk concerning Nabû-šum-iškun (Weiher 1984) we read (p. 204 rev. III 34-35):

> In the sixth year, he set his face/mind to restoration of Esagila, the palace of the Ellil of the gods (Marduk).

Herod would pull down the whole edifice and not be able to rebuild it as he had promised. For this reason, Herod went to the trouble of preparing all the building materials before demolishing the temple.

1. ARM 13.112.

2. It may be of some significance that the previously mentioned inscriptions of Samsuiluna and of Nebuchadnezzar are also connected with building in Sippar. Similarly, a grant inscription from the time of Nabû-apla-iddinna (King 1912: 120-29), which reviews the history of Ebabbar in Sippar tells that Simbar-Šīḫu, king of Babylon, searched for the missing statue of Shamash, but because the god was not favorable, the king was unable to find the statue and the divine regalia and symbols. Whereas the connection between Nabonidus's inscription and that of Nebuchadnezzar is clear and obviously genetic, the parallels with similar incidents indicate that the Nebuchadnezzar inscription itself may be firmly rooted in a local literary or religious tradition native to the city of Sippar.

This is a report of a royal decision to restore a temple, with no indication that divine sanction was sought for the undertaking. The text goes on to say that the king appropriated to himself treasures contributed to Esagila by previous kings, and that he misused them (ll. 36-45), even shipping them off as far as Hatti and Elam—i.e. the ends of the earth (cf. the *Curse of Agade*, which accuses Naram-Sin of shipping off the precious materials of Ekur). The silence concerning divine approval of the building project is in itself to be taken as a negative sign, given the polemical nature of the text which tells abundantly of the king's cultic offenses.

These sources[1] demonstrate not only that it was not customary to build a temple without express divine consent, but that such an action was frowned upon, and that the builder as well as the building could expect dire consequences as a result.

3. *Conclusions and Implications for the Biblical Building Accounts*

a. The preceding survey demonstrates that in Mesopotamia (as among biblical authors) it was considered important and even essential that a temple should be built only with explicit divine consent. The acquisition of the needed license was a complex process which could take two basic courses:

1. *Divine Initiative.* When the gods desired that a new temple be built or that an old one be restored, they would reach a decision among themselves, select a king to implement their plan, and notify him of their wishes, either through a dream revelation, or by some sign, or by inspiring him to their desires. A king who received one of these indications would validate and clarify them by one of the usual mantic devices available to him. If the sign were confirmed, the king would fervently accept his assignment, carry it out, and successfully complete it.

2. *Human Initiative.* When the king himself desired to build or restore a temple (or any other building), he would decide

---

1.   A late example of divine rejection of a plan to build a temple is found in Jub. 32.15-22, where we read that Jacob wanted to build a temple in Bethel, but he was dissuaded by God who appeared to him in a dream and expressly prohibited it. On this passage, see Schwartz 1985.

upon it personally, and afterwards he would seek divine approval.[1] If the gods agreed to the king's plan, they would inform him through the accepted mantic devices. If they did not consent, they would either send negative messages, or not answer him at all. A king who built a temple without divine permission could expect to see his project fail.

b. The stories in 2 Samuel 7 and 1 Kings 5 and 8 assume that the king of Israel also needed divine permission to build a Temple. As far as this is concerned, there is total agreement between the biblical attitude and that of the numerous extra-biblical texts cited above. As for God's refusal to agree to David's plan, this too was found to be in keeping with Mesopotamian outlooks, both in theory and in practice. David asked permission to build God a temple, and by so doing he is no different than any of the Mesopotamian monarchs whose inscriptions were cited above. But even in receiving a negative response, David is not alone. In being denied permission to build a temple, David has equals in Mesopotamia from the days of the Dynasties of Akkade and Ur III until the Neo-Babylonian period. In one place, at least— Sippar—there are even indications that a tradition of divine refusal developed.

Does the story of God's refusal to allow David to build a temple have any basis in reality? This is obviously a question for the historian, and not for the literary critic. Even so, the texts presented above permit us to determine whether such a refusal would be considered possible. The letter from Kibri-Dagan to Zimri-Lim, which is not a polemical document or in any way tendentious, shows that divine refusal to approve a building project was not limited to the realm of literature and royal image-building, but was regarded as a normal occurrence in reality. But, it seems that most of the information provided in the 'historical-historiographic writings' is retrospective information, based on hindsight, and not necessarily the historical truth. In the royal inscriptions, for example, a king might well claim that one of his predecessors was denied a building license, but this information

1.   Unlike the Egyptian *Königsnovelle*, in which Pharaoh would announce his plans to his privy council, there is little indication that the Mesopotamian king took counsel with his advisors, but this is probably a reflection of the royal inscriptions' concentration on the character of the king, and not a reflection of what really happened.

is intended more to glorify himself, and his own accomplishments and closeness to the gods, than to pass on the truth about previous kings. Similarly, the literary texts about Amar-Suen and Naram-Sin are retrospective, and their purpose seems to be that of explaining certain tragedies which befell these kings, or which were attributed to them. If so, the report of divine rejection of a building plan may be told *ex post facto*, in a reflective manner, and in order to account for some surprising, incomprehensible situation confronting the author.

The implication of this survey is that anyone who desires to view the Nathan–David story as realistic may do so, because such events actually did occur. Nonetheless, anyone wishing to attribute the story to later thinkers and ideologues who tried to explain, after the fact, how it was that Solomon rather than David was granted the great privilege to build God a new Temple, can also bolster his or her position with sufficient extra-biblical analogies. The biblical accounts are unique, however, in being the only ones which venture to explain why the deity responded negatively to the request of a king who is otherwise viewed in a positive light.

c. I turn now to comment on the suggestion of A.S. Kapelrud and M. Weinfeld about Solomon's dream at Gibeon as reported in 1 Kings 3. These scholars made the interesting proposal that the dream in which Solomon was promised wisdom (with which to rule his people) actually has replaced an original dream account in which God either commanded Solomon to build a temple, or expressed his consent to Solomon's request to build a temple.

Their proposal is based mainly upon the overall structural parallel between the biblical temple-building account and the extra-biblical accounts. As discovered in the first part of this study, some of these stories begin with a dream revelation in which the king is commanded to build a temple. The Kapelrud–Weinfeld suggestion assumes that such a dream was an essential, integral and *indispensable* part of the building story pattern, such that without a dream, or an explicit divine command of some other sort, the story would be incomplete.

This survey has shown that such dreams are, indeed, not considered uncommon, and as far as this is concerned, it would not be surprising to find a dream at the beginning of the biblical account. Even so, we encountered a large number of extra-biblical building accounts which contain no dream, and which do not assume that the building project was undertaken on divine initiative. To the contrary, quite a few stories, especially Assyrian and Neo-Babylonian building accounts, explicitly state that it was the king who initiated the building project and requested divine permission to build. In such cases, divine approval was expressed through ordinary, accepted divinatory means. This being so, for the literary pattern to be complete, it is enough that divine consent to a royal plan should be expressed. Such an expression of divine agreement is found, as we saw, in a pre-deuteronomic passage telling of Solomon's correspondence with Hiram.

It turns out, then, that the evidence upon which the Kapelrud–Weinfeld suggestion is based is only partial, not fully representative. For this reason, the hypothesis cannot be proven and must remain just a conjecture. Certainly it is possible, but this is mainly because it is difficult to disprove it. Nonetheless, the suggestion is neither proven nor a necessary conclusion from the overall structural similarity between the biblical and extra-biblical building accounts.

d. Finally, several observations are in order concerning a theory advanced and recently restated by S. Hermann. Hermann contends that 2 Samuel 7 reflects an Egyptian *Königsnovelle*,[1] an example of which is the Inscription of Sesostris I (Lichtheim 1973: 115-18). In this text, the king decides to build a temple for Atum and announces his plan to his advisors. They all agree with him and tell him to proceed with the work. Hermann compared this with David's announcement of his desire to build a temple to Nathan, who immediately told him to do as he pleased. Hermann explained the subsequent rejection of the plan by God as a revolutionary Israelite modification of the traditional Egyptian literary pattern. This theory can, in our opinion, be safely rejected. The Egyptians believed Pharoah to be a god, and as such, he had no need to consult with the gods about his plans. Pharoah's consultations with his advisors were meant for his own self-aggrandizement, demonstrating his wisdom to his courtiers. It would be unthinkable that a

---

1.   See Hermann 1953–54, 1985. Ishida (1977: 92-94) has already pointed out that divine rejection of a royal plan is improbable in the Egyptian view of the world. Hermann's restatement of his view came in response to Malamat 1985, who presented a letter from Mari as a parallel to Nathan's prophecy. This letter, however, has nothing to do with the central issue of whether a royal building plan can be rejected by a deity, so Hermann's objection to its admissibility as evidence is irrelevant.

plan to build a temple would be rejected. All this is missing in 2 Samuel 7. David takes counsel with Nathan, who is a prophet and not merely a wise man. David's plan, although considered meritorious by later scribes, is not meant to aggrandize him, but is a sign of his piety and concern for the unsuitable accommodations enjoyed by the Ark. Most importantly, however, David's initiative to build a temple is ultimately rejected. All this is quite at home in the world view of the Mesopotamian king and quite foreign to Egypt, so if parallels are to be sought, the place to look is not Egypt but Mesopotamia.[1]

1. For the similarity between the biblical story and the Mesopotamian tradition, see Ota 1974.

EXCURSUS: *tabnît*

Revelation of temples and cultic objects in dreams or visions is a well-known phenomenon. For biblical and extra-biblical sources, see Oppenheim 1956: 193. Another way of revealing a plan of a cult object to its potential fashioner is by revealing a prototype. This is the manner in which Moses is instructed how to build the Tabernacle (Exod. 25.9, 40; 26.30; 27.8; Num. 8.4), and how, according to 1 Chron. 28.11-19, David is shown how Solomon is to build the Temple.

What Moses and David are shown is designated *tabnît*. Two views have been expressed as to the nature of the object so designated. According to one view (see e.g. *b. Men.* 29a, Rashi and Ramban to Exod. 25.9, 40), Moses was shown a model of the Tabernacle and its furnishings. Traditional exegetes ascribed a didactic function to the *tabnît*, holding that it was necessary to help Moses understand the complex instructions. To be sure, the model conceived of by these commentators was one of all sorts of fire, yet despite its miraculous substance, it was envisaged as a teaching model. S.E. Loewenstamm (*Miškān, Encyclopaedia Miqra'it*, V, col. 534) cites an incident from the Atrahasis myth in which Ea draws a boat for Atrahasis (who claims to have had no experience in boat making) as a parallel to the didactic function of the *tabnît* (see Lambert and Millard 1969: 128 DT 42 (W) 14-15: [*ina qaq*]*qari eṣir u*[*ṣurtu*] [*uṣur*]*tu lūmurma* ᵍⁱˢ*eleppa* [*lūpuš*], 'Draw the design on the ground that I may see [the design] and [build] the boat').

An alternative view, found in Jewish and Christian sources from the Hellenistic period onwards, contends that Moses was shown God's heavenly dwelling, and that the Tabernacle was to be an earthly replica and counterpart thereof (for traditional sources, see Aptowitzer 1931; Kasher 1961: 22; Goppelt 1972: 256-57). This view has become popular today, especially among scholars with a comparative approach and a tradition-history inclination (see for instance the more recent articles of Cross 1947; Levine 1965: 308a n. 4; Freedman 1981; Weinfeld 1980). To the texts adduced by these scholars we should add the Hittite texts in which a dreamer sees a god in a dream and is commanded to make a statue exactly according to what he has seen and dedicate it to the deity (see Oppenheim 1956: 193). U. Cassuto, in his commentary on Exodus, suggests joining the two views and explains that Moses was shown a model of the heavenly temple.

In my opinion, the plain meaning of the verses referring to Moses' revelation is that he was shown an exact model of the Tabernacle which he was to make. If so, he was *not* shown the divine heavenly dwelling. This evaluation is based on an analysis of the use of the words *tabnît* and *mar'eh* in several biblical passages (some of which

are from cultic contexts and even originate in priestly circles) and on my understanding of Exod. 25.40 and Num. 8.4, which are the most unambiguous of the
relevant verses. The word *taḇnît*, which has the basic meaning of 'form', 'structure'
or 'shape', is employed to indicate a 'replica' (Josh. 12.28; 1 Chron. 28.18; cf.
Ezek. 8.3, 10; 10.10; Deut. 4.16, 17, 18; Ps. 106.20 [this last verse may reflect the
meaning of *taḇnît* in the Tabernacle story as understood by an early Midrashist]; Ps.
144.12; Isa. 44.13). In 1 Chronicles, in a passage which probably expresses the
same idea as found in the Tabernacle story, the word *taḇnît* means '(written) model-
blueprint' (1 Chron. 28.11, 12, 19). This is in addition to the meaning of 'replica'
found later in the same chapter (1 Chron. 18.28). In the Chronicles passage, therefore, the word has two meanings according to the context of its appearance. In
vv. 11, 12 and 19 it is the 'blueprint' for what Solomon is to build. In v. 18 it is the
(earthly, yet to be constructed) replica of the heavenly *mērkāḇâ*. In 2 Kgs 16.10 the
word bears the same two meanings, only this time simultaneously. In this passage
the *taḇnît* sent by King Ahaz to Uriah the Priest is a depiction of the 'original' altar
seen by the King in Damascus, and is at the same time a 'model' for the duplicate
altar to be built and installed in the Jerusalem Temple. In neither case is it the original
object that is to be imitated. The usage of *taḇnît* in Exod. 25.40, however, is not
'double-duty', and is closest to the usage in 1 Chron. 28.11, 12, 19. This becomes
clear from the passage itself: 'and look and make according to their *taḇnît* which is
shown to you on the Mountain (*bĕṭaḇnîṭām 'ăšer 'attâ mor'eh bāhār)'*. The *mem*
suffix in *bĕṭaḇnîṭām* is anteceded by 'all these implements', mentioned at the beginning of the previous verse. In other words, Moses is shown the *taḇnît* of what he
himself is called upon to manufacture. What he is to produce is not referred to as the
taḇnît of what he is shown. The *taḇnît* is therefore a 'replica' of the earthly, as yet
unconstructed, Tabernacle. Since the word (even where it is 'double duty') never
designates the 'real thing', but only a representation of it, it cannot be taken to refer
to the heavenly abode of God.

Just as *taḇnît* does not indicate the object itself, so *mar'eh* does not. According to
Num. 8.4, Moses was shown a *mar'eh* of the lampstand which he is commanded to
duplicate. Moshe Greenberg has kindly informed me that *mar'eh* is frequently used
as a 'buffer' between an object and a viewer, when it is desired to indicate that the
viewer is hesitant about identifying that which has been seen as a real object, despite
the exact visual identity between the two (see Judg. 14.6 and Ezek. 1 *seriatim* and
Greenberg 1983: 52-53). It is not unlikely that the earthly Tabernacle was considered
to be a replica of a Heavenly Divine Abode, but this cannot be derived unequivocally
from the description of Moses' visual experience on Mount Sinai, and can only be
inferred from comparative material.

There are several less known examples of revelations of models involving cult
objects in certain Babylonian inscriptions.

1. In the Nabû-apla-iddina grant document (King 1912: XXXVI) we read that
Shamash's divine regalia had disappeared and had been sought after by Simbar-
Šhipak, but had not been found for lack of divine cooperation. Many years later,
during the reign of Nabû-apla-iddina (p. 123 col. III 11–IV 11) 'Shamash. . .

relented (and) a model of his statue made of kiln-fired clay and showing his appearance and regalia (*uṣurti ṣalmīšu ṣirpu ša haṣbi šikinsu u simātīšu*) was found/seen (*innamir*) on the west bank of the Euphrates'. The high priest and diviner of Sippar showed (*ukallim*) it to the king. The king 'who had been commanded and entrusted to make the statue' saw the model, rejoiced, and set about making a new statue. From the details about Simbar-Shipak's inability to find the statue and the remark the Nabû-apla-iddina had been commanded and entrusted with (re-)fashioning it, it is clear that the revelation of the clay model was regarded as an act of divine intervention and no freak discovery. The model, referred to as an *uṣurtu*, which is semantically identical with *tabnît*, serves as a link between the lost original statue and the new one to be manufactured.

2. In a text about the selection and commissioning of Nabonidus's daughter as a priestess (Böhl 1939; Reiner 1985), we read:

> Because for a very long time the office of high priestess had been forgotten and her characteristic features were nowhere indicated, I bethought myself day after day. The appointed time arrived, the doors were open for me (*uptattani bābāni*); indeed I set my eyes on an ancient stele of Nebuchadnezzar. . . on which was depicted the image of the high priestess. Morever, they had listed and deposited in the Egipar her appurtenances, her clothing, and her jewelry. I carefully looked into the old clay and wooden tablets and did exactly as in the olden days.

The expression 'the appointed time arrived' indicates that the discovery of Nebuchadnezzar's stela was no accident, but an act of divine providence. The statement 'the doors were open for me' is enigmatic, but it clearly is meant to be a miraculous event. This granted, Nabonidus is stating not only that he made the priestess's regalia according to an old plan, but that the old plan was made known to him through divine revelation. Here too, he does not see the original objects themselves, but depictions of them.

3. A final example, probably of the same phenomenon, is found in another inscription, related as well to the consecration of Nabonidus's daughter (Dhorme 1914: 113). In this text the king states that he made a chariot for Sin:

> His divine riding chariot. . . which no previous king had made for a very long time—
> in the foundation (document?) of the Eigikalama temple its fittings and furnishings was
> seen on stones (?), and I made that chariot anew.[1]

The phenomenon of revealing a model or replica of a cult object to a king charged with fashioning such an object lends comparative support to the understanding of Moses' visual experience set forth above. Even when the object to be manufactured is to be a copy of a previously existing object, it is not the preexisting object itself which is revealed to the builder, but a model.

---

1.   *narkabtu rukūbu ilūtīšu . . . ša ištu ūmē rūqūtu šarri mahrî lā īpušu ina temen Eigikalama NA$_4$ .MEŠ tiqnīšu u unūssu innamirma narkabti šuāti eššiš abnīma.*

Chapter 9

THE ACQUISITION OF BUILDING MATERIALS: THE LITERARY AND MATERIAL CULTURE BACKGROUND OF 1 KINGS 5.15-26

The description of the negotiations and conclusion of a commercial agreement which opens the temple-building account contains elements of diverse literary backgrounds. In order to appreciate better its composite nature and the literary forms which it contains, this pericope must be examined in light of various types of writings known to us from outside the Bible, such as royal inscriptions, domestic and international contracts and treaties, and—above all—letters from Israel and the surrounding peoples. In this chapter, I will attempt to place this passage in its proper context literarily and form-critically. Afterwards, I will investigate the practical background of the actions described. Finally, there will be an opportunity to make a contribution to the question of the story's origin and its historicity.

1. A Literary and Form-Critical Analysis

1. The Extent of the Deuteronomic Reworking

From the very beginning, higher (literary-historical) criticism of the book of Kings has recognized that this pericope contains several blatant Deuteronomic expansions: '(A House for the) name of YHWH God' (vv. 17, 19 [2×]); 'YHWH my God gave me rest all round' (v. 18).

Despite the general agreement about the Deuteronomic nature of these expressions in particular, there are two fundamentally different approaches concerning the *extent* of the Deuteronomist's contribution to the pericope as it now stands. According to one opinion, the Deuteronomic hand contributed only these expressions, or, at most, the verses in which these expressions appear (and some would include v. 21 as well). According to this approach, which may be termed 'minimalist', these expressions were added by an editor or redactor before whom lay a pre-deuteronomic form of the narrative. Burney, for instance, writes: 'The verses have, in their present form, been amplified by R upon the lines of 2 Sam. 7'.[1]

Suggested candidates for the pre-deuteronomic substratum are J (Hölscher)[2] and 'The Book of the Annals of Solomon' referred to in 1 Kgs 11.41 (Skinner, Liver, Kittel and Snaith).[3] But, according to another opinion put forth recently in detail by Martin Noth, in his unfinished commentary on the book of Kings, the *entire* pericope is a Deuteronomic production.[4] Attribution of the complete unit to the Deuteronomist is based on: (1) the smooth, uninterrupted flow of the narrative; (2) the theoretical possibility that the Deuteronomist himself drew all the factual material given, as well as the technical language (such as the word *ḥēpeṣ*), either from other biblical passages which were at his disposal, or from his own conjectures, or from his own common sense, or from common knowledge.

The correct view may be the one which attributes to the Deuteronomic redactor more than just the peculiarly Deuteronomic expression, but we doubt whether it is possible to find his traces much beyond vv. 17-19 in which these expressions are actually imbedded. Perhaps his voice is heard in the words *kol hayyāmîm* (v. 15), but this term, even if it is favored by the Deuteronomist, is not his exclusively.[5] Hiram's statement in v. 21 *bārûk YHWH hayyom* are akin, admittedly, to the view expressed by the Deuteronomist concerning the recognition of the great name of YHWH God of Israel even among foreign nations (see Josh. 2.9-11; 1 Kgs 8.41-43). Furthermore, the

1.   Burney 1903: 53. The 'minimalist' view is held by Stade 1883: 131-32; Burney, Skinner, Eissfeldt, Snaith, Montgomery and Gehman and Gray in their commentaries to the book of Kings; Liver 1971a; Weinfeld 1972: 250.

2.   Hölscher 1923.

3.   In their commentaries and articles listed above in note 1.

4.   Noth 1963: 88. This evaluation is found as early as Šanda, in his commentary to Kings (1911: 116), and Jepsen (1956: 21), and was accepted most recently by Würthwein (1977) and B. Peckham (1965). Gray, who wrote a revised second edition of his commentary to Kings, and was aware of Noth's commentary, continues to hold the minimalist approach.

5.   See Weinfeld 1972: 358 §16, on the basis of Driver 1895: lxxxi n. 41. Note, however, that the expression in 1 Kgs 5.15 means 'from days gone by', while in Deuteronomy it means 'continuously' or 'forever more', and in any case in Deuteronomy the expression always refers to the future and never to the past. I will discuss this expression further below.

continuation of the verse connects well with the story of Solomon's dream at Gibeon, which has been worked over by the Deuteronomist. Nonetheless, these considerations do not prove conclusively that the passage is of Deuteronomic origin. The Deuteronomist did not invent the idea or belief that foreigners can recognize the greatness of YHWH (see, for instance the story of the Aramaean army commander Naaman in 2 Kings 5, and the sacrifices brought by Gentiles mentioned in the Holiness Code, Lev. 22.25 and elsewhere). Similarly, since the extent of Deuteronomic reworking in 1 Kings 3 is itself the subject of much controversy, and since it is likely that 1 Kgs 3.8 and 9 are in fact pre-deuteronomic, they may not be used as evidence for the deuteronomic origin of Hiram's similarly phrased statement, 'Blessed be YHWH this day, who gave David a wise son (to rule) over this vast people'.

As for Noth's claims, it must be remembered that smooth narrative cannot serve as a proof of unity of authorship—why should one assume that every instance of combination, expansion, addition or interpolation will be done in such a haphazard manner as to show give-away scars and stitches? The fact that in one verse there is a concentration of obvious Deuteronomic touches, while in the next there is not a single clear sign, should be enough warrant to conclude that the hand of the redactor is no longer at work. Noth's claim that the author could have known all the facts from other sources is inconsequential. That the author could have known something is no proof that he actually did know it. In addition, it must borne in mind that 2 Sam. 5.11, from which, according to Noth, the redactor supposedly drew his information about Israel's prior connections with Hiram, king of Tyre, is not without its own problems and might even be dependent on 1 Kings 5ff.!

The debate about the extent of the Deuteronomist's contribution to this particular story will continue for as long as there is no solution to the rest of the problems involved in the process of the composition of the book of Kings in particular, and the Deuteronomic History in general. Even so, the considerations presented above lead towards the 'minimalist' camp as regards the account of Solomon's dealing with Hiram.

2. *The Literary Forms in the Pericope*[1]

An attempt will be made now to clarify and identify the various literary forms found in the chapter. This will be done primarily through detailed comparison of the content, the structure and (especially) the language of the biblical passage with various types of extra-biblical writings. The passage is written, to be sure, in a free-flowing narrative style, and is not simply a patchwork of independent, definable documents of different types. However, a penetrating, precise investigation of numerous expressions in the narrative will reveal signs characteristic of various different and distinct literary types which have influenced the narrator in varying degrees.

We already saw above that vv. 17-19, which were expanded upon by the Deuteronomist, reflect in their content the regular introductory sections of building accounts found in royal inscriptions. In addition, acquiring trees from the Lebanon mountains, the employment of cedars and cypress in building projects, and even the transporting of logs or beams by water—these are all motifs found in abundance in the royal inscriptions of the ancient Near East. Nonetheless, more numerous and decisive are the factual and stylistic elements drawn from other literary genres, and these elements will be examined now. Attention will first be directed to the frame (vv. 15 and 26), and then to the body of the passage (vv. 16-25).

The Frame (vv. 15, 26)

Diplomatic customs. Scholars commenting on the book of Kings[2] have already indicated that v. 15 reflects a well known custom by which a reigning monarch would send emissaries to a new king upon the latter's accession to the throne. The purpose of this custom was, naturally, to preserve friendly relations between the two states, and to assure their continuation in the future. This particular practice, as well as the general tendency to maintain amicable ties between states, is alluded to several times in the Bible as well as in ancient letters.[3]

---

1. Cf. Long 1984.
2. See Noth 1968: 89 and Würthwein 1977: 53.
3. This custom is best documented in the international correspondence from the El Amarna archive, for which see the commentaries on Kings as well as Moran 1963a: 80-81. In *EA* 33, the king of Alashiya writes to the king of Egypt saying, 'I heard that you have sat on the throne of your father's dynasty. . .' (ll. 9-11), to which we may compare 1 Kgs 5.15, 'King Hiram of Tyre sent his officials to

The custom was observed when David sent messengers to Nahash, king of Ammon, to comfort him after the death of his father, and perhaps to bless him on his succession to the throne (2 Sam. 10). It is likely that the same custom underlies the description of Hiram's mission to David as found in 2 Sam. 5.11.[1]

Diplomatic and Legal Terminology
'ohēb and *šālôm*. In addition to the similarity in the diplomatic *practice* reflected in these biblical passages and inscriptions, the frame of the unit describing the trade negotiations also contains echoes of the *terminology* of international diplomacy. The best known example of this terminology is the word *'ōhēb*. In the opinion of W. Moran, this term indicates that the friendly relationships between the two lands

---

Solomon when he heard that he had been anointed king in place of his father'. In *EA* 6, Burnaburiash king of Babylon writes to Pharaoh Amenophis III, saying, 'Formerly, you and my father did well (*ṭābatunu*) with one another, and now, you and I, let us not let other things come' (ll. 8-12). In the continuation of this letter (ll. 13-16), the king of Babylon offers his Egyptian peer a trade agreement identical in language to that in the Kings passage under study (see below).

1.   According to the present arrangement of events in 2 Sam. 5, Hiram's envoys to David arrived at the time David started to rule in Jerusalem, and it is likely that the *redactor* desired to make events accord with this diplomatic custom. Verse 12, 'Thus David knew that the Lord had established him as king over Israel and had exalted his kingship for the sake of his people Israel', may indicate (a) that there is more intended by the 'new' order than merely juxtaposing the building of a house for David to the description of David's other building works (v. 9) and (b) that the important aspect of Hiram's mission which is emphasized here is the recognition the foreign monarch has given to the new king of Israel. Similarly, building a palace in itself is a sign of monarchic stability. So, for example, the statue of Idrimi, king of Alalakh, states that the king built himself a palace at the time he seized the crown from his rivals. (On the Idrimi Inscription, see Greenstein and Marcus 1976. An account of building the palace is found in ll. 77-80.) Similarly, in the Baal epic, recognition of Baal's sovereignty is contingent on his having his own palace. In *Enuma Elish* as well, the gods build Marduk a temple as a sign that they recognize him as their king. In any case, placing Hiram's mission to David at the beginning of David's reign in Jerusalem is impossible historically, because of internal biblical chronological difficulties (as well as contradictions between the biblical tradition in its present form and the account of Josephus). For these problems, see the commentaries on 2 Samuel and the history books, as well as Liver 1971b and A.R. Green 1983.

were rooted in a treaty between David and Hiram.[1]

Similarly, the word *šālôm* appearing in v. 26 has also been noted by scholars. This word, which has been related in its technical use to Akkadian *salīmu*, also designates friendly relationships and the existence of a treaty between two states.[2] M. Noth related the formula '*šālôm bên* X *ubên* Y' with the formula *salīmum birit* X *u birit* Y in a letter from Mari (*ARM* 2 37.13-14) which reports the conclusion of a treaty.[3]

This explanation is quite reasonable. Nonetheless, it seems that another explanation of the expression *wayhî šālôm bên Hîrām ubên Šělōmōh* is equally possible and should be explored. Middle Assyrian and neo-Assyrian legal documents as well as their Aramaic counterparts employ the expressions *šulmu ina birtīšunu* (lit. 'well being between them') or *wśmw šlm bynyhm* (lit. 'they placed well being between them'), which S. Kaufmann translates figuratively as 'they made a settlement'. This expression refers to the settlement of accounts and claims between two parties involved in litigation, and follows statements concerning the payment of debts or the settling of claims. Since *wayhî šālôm bên Hîrām ubên Šělōmōh* appears immediately after a statement that the conditions of the trade agreement had been fulfilled (vv. 24-25), it is not impossible that the verse reflects this somewhat later expression, rather than the treaty-making formula known from the earlier Mari documents. In this case, the following formula *wayyikrětû běrît šěnêhem* is not a synonymous formula or one telling us that after they were at peace they made a treaty (treaties usually precede states of peace), but is a supplementary statement.[4]

kol hayyāmîm. The expression *kol hayyāmîm*, 'all the days', well known from the Bible, may reflect in the present context a certain

1. Moran 1963a; cf. Weinfeld 1973, and 1972; Moran 1963b.

2. Munn-Rankin 1956: 85, and see the bibliography in Fensham 1969: 77 n. 4. See most recently Wiseman 1982.

3. Noth 1966a: 113. Note as well the documents from Ugarit cited below which contain the formulae *kitta ina berīšunu* and *rikiltu ina beri* X *u beri* Y. On the history of the treaty between Tyre and Israel, see Fensham 1969, and most recently Peckham 1976: 231-32.

4. See Kaufmann 1977 for a detailed discussion of the term and previous literature, and note most recently Lackenbacher 1983: 49 l. 10: *šul-mu ina bir-ti-šu-nu* in a seventh-century document concerning the payment of a debt.

diplomatic parlance or diplomatic custom, but if it does, the similarity is not etymological or lexical but only semantic and conceptual. The expression *kol hayyāmîm* expresses in the present context the view conveyed in Akkadian idioms such as *ultu dārīti* and the like, expressions which appear in international letters and treaties discussing the existence of contractual relationships between two states.[1] In an Amarna letter (*EA* 74) Rib-Addi writes:[2]

> May the king, the lord know
> that it is well with Byblos,
> the loyal maidservant of the king
> since the time of his fathers

In *EA* 19.11-16, Tushratta suggests to Amenophis III that they should 'love' each other forever, and he begins his letter by describing the good relationships which their fathers maintained.

The letters, which spell out the periods of faithfulness between the two sides, and which view them as rooted in the period of the fathers, reflect the language and spirit of the treaties themselves. Such treaties are enacted 'forever', and they assume that the state of relationships which they determine have actually existed 'from eternity'. So we find, for instance, in the treaty between Ramesses II of Egypt and Hattusilis III of Hatti (Weidner 1923: II, 112 l. 9, Akkadian version):[3]

> See! The way of the great king
> the king of Egypt
> and of the great king
> the king of the Land of Hatti
> *From all time (ultu dārīti)*
> the god does not permit
> making hostility
> between them
> because of the treaty
> (which is valid) *forever (adi dārīti).*
> (ll. 9-11 and see also ll. 11-18).

We can also mention in this connection a decision in a territorial

1. Concerning the validity of a treaty in the future, see Weinfeld 1976: 65, and 1973: 199.
2. See also *EA* 75.7-9.
3. See *ANET*, 199-203 for a translation of the Egyptian and Hittite versions of this treaty.

dispute between the king of Ugarit and the king of Siyannu, found in the archives of Ugarit (*MRS*, IX, 230, no. 17.123 ll. 5-6):

> and now
> they have established
> justice between them
> as had been *from all time* (*kima dārīti*).

Verse 26

Obviously, the words *wayyik̲rĕtû bĕrît̲ šĕnêhem*, which conclude the description of the negotiations, are from the language of treaties. In their function as a concluding refrain they have parallels in the inter-national treaties known from the archives at Ugarit. So, for example, the commercial agreement between Hattusilis of Hatti and Niqmepa, king of Ugarit concludes with the sentence (*MRS*, IX, 103-105, 17.30 ll. 34-37):[1]

anumma	And so
Š amšu sarru rabû	the Sun, the great king
rikilta	a treaty
ina beri mārī Ú-ra tamkārī	between the some of U-ra, the merchants,
u ina beri mārī Ugarit	and the sons of Ugarit
akanna irkussunītī	herewith concluded for them.[2]

If the phrase *wayyik̲rĕtu bĕrît̲ šĕnêhem* does indeed function in the same way as the parallel Akkadian formulae mentioned here, the result is that the entire pericope (1 Kgs 5.15-26) is presented as a treaty document between Solomon and Hiram, and the words of the two kings take on the character of the terms of the treaty.[3] If the expres-sion *wayhî šālôm bên Ḥîrām ubên Šĕlōmōh* is related to the *šulmu ina*

1.   Note Loewenstamm's Hebrew translation of this document in Malamat 1977: 179.

2.   See as well *MRS*, IX, pp. 154-57 (17.46) l. 4-5, 45-47; pp. 40-44 (17.227) ll. 16-19, 46-48; p. 52 (17.369A) ll. 6, 19'-20'; pp. 80-83 (17.382+380) ll. 60-63; pp. 152-54 (17.230) ll. 1-3; p. 158-60 (18.115) ll. 1-3 (in the last two documents, such a sentence appears in the introductory section, while in the rest of the documents it appears in both the introductory and concluding sections). See also the introduction to the treaty between Ramesses II and Hattusilis (Weidner 1923: 112 ll. 1-3 and Deut. 28.69).

3.   Noth (1968: 92) remarks that these words are clumsy, but this irregularity may be explained on the basis of the assumption that the verse is a concluding for-mula like the ones mentioned here.

birtīšunu formula, as suggested above, then the whole preceding unit takes on the additional character of the terms of an *egirtu ša šulmu* document proclaiming the final settlement of some sort of agreement. Nevertheless, we will see immediately that the 'body' of the document, whichever type it may be, is neither a treaty document nor an *egirtu ša šulmu* type document, but is in fact a pair of letters exchanged between the two parties to the agreement. It should be emphasized at this point that the elements in the story which derive from the realm of treaties are confined to the frame of the pericope—that is, the introductory and the concluding sentences. All these considerations indicate that the passage is form-critically eclectic and that the narrator has combined or seeks to reflect a mixture of literary types.

The Letters (vv. 16-23)

As stated above, the body of the pericope is the exchange of messages between Solomon and Hiram. Already the Chronicler was of the opinion that the negotiations were conducted by way of letters between the two sides, and he states explicitly: 'Huram, king of Tyre, sent Solomon this *written message (biktāb)* in reply...' (2 Chron. 2.10). Josephus goes so far as to claim that the letters exchanged between the two kings were still preserved in the royal archives in Tyre.[1] Yet despite this ancient 'testimony', modern scholars have reservations about this way of viewing the events. So, for example, Montgomery and Gehman speak about 'the initial "conversation"' (their quotation marks),[2] and only in connection with the Chronistic report do they refer to 'the diplomatic correspondence'. M. Noth as well speaks of 'Botschaften', messages, and not about actual letters.[3] S.E. Loewenstamm, and most recently D. Pardee,[4] in long, detailed

---

1. See Katzenstein 1973: 77ff. for sources and discussion.
2. Montgomery–Gehman 1951: 132.
3. Noth 1968: 87.
4. Loewenstamm 1962 (*s.v. miktab̲, EM* 4) mentions neither this passage nor the parallel in Chronicles. Even in his discussion of passages referring to the dispatching of messengers with the intention being that letters (*sĕpārîm*) are being sent he disregards the Solomon–Hiram correspondence. Pardee (1978) mentions the Chronicles account and points out in note 53 that in Kings the word *sēper*—'letter'— does not occur, and suggests translating 'Hiram sent Solomon the following (message)'. In his list of biblical letters on pp. 330-31, he includes 2 Chron. 2.11-15

articles about letters in the Bible, do not include the passages from
1 Kings 5 in their lists of biblical letters. Among the standard Bible
introductions and handbooks with a form-critical bent, we find
O. Eissfeldt listing our unit with the contracts,[1] G. Fohrer including
them among the treaties and covenants,[2] and A. Bentzen placing them
with 'documents'.[3] Among the scholars who recognize the messages of
the kings as letters we may mention Gray and Würthwein in their
commentaries to the book of Kings, as well as Knutsen,[4] Aharoni and
Rainey[5] in various studies. The most balanced and explicit statement
on the matter is that of B. Long,[6] who writes:

> Possibly the form of a letter is in the background. . . In this text, however,
> we have no way of distinguishing between a letter and a message spoken
> by a diplomatic messenger (cf. Isa. 36.13-20), and since there are abun-
> dant parallels to the style of Solomon's petition, we may safely conclude
> that the text was shaped primarily by OT literary styles without denying the
> substantive and stylistic connections with letters in the ancient Near East.

(Hiram's letter) but makes no reference to the parallel text in Kings. See also his
recent book (1982: 179-80).
1. Eissfeldt 1966: 20.
2. Fohrer 1970: 72 and cf. Avishur 1988.
3. Bentzen 1961: 209.
4. Knutsen, *RSP*, II, p. 214 VI 14. Even if these scholars recognized the fact
that the pericope is phrased in epistolary style, they did not indicate which literary
considerations led them to this evaluation. For that matter, most of the scholars who
classified the pericope as a treaty, agreement, contract or the like offer no substantia-
tion for their judgment apart from pointing to the rather innocuous word *wĕ'attāh*.
Only Avishur (1988) suggested that the sequence *šm'-ḥdy-'mr* is characteristic of
treaty terminology. However, he supported his suggestion by referring to Adler 1976
for citations, but most of the passages listed come from letters, just reinforcing the
epistolary provenance of the formula. It seems to me that scholarly judgment on this
matter has been somewhat arbitrary and lacks foundation (apart from the scholarly
fashion to look for treaties or covenants everywhere). Even if we are to agree that the
letters are cited within the *framework* of a treaty (see above), this use is secondary,
and a precise examination shows that the basic, principal formulation is that of
letters. Cf. now Weinfeld 1988.
5. Rainey (1967: 35) and Aharoni (1962: 122 n. 38) took note of the connection between the word *'el* which starts off the Lachish letters (and the Arad letters)
and the expression *wayyišlaḥ 'el* in the Hiram–Solomon correspondence (1 Kgs
5.16, 22). They interpreted the expression 'to send notice to'.
6. See Long 1984: 79 on vv. 15-26, which he classifies form-critically as a
'Report'.

It goes without saying that excessive credence should not be afforded the form-critical opinion of the Chronicler, and even less authority should be granted Josephus's testimony about the actual existence of letters. The Chronicler's reference to a written exchange may be little more than an instance of his known tendency to claim written evidence for his own assertions, even if he has to 'write' them himself. Josephus may have done the same thing independently, or he may have already taken cognizance of the Chronicler's claim in writing his own account. All this notwithstanding, even if these ancient authorities have no reliable tradition upon which to rely, it seems that their description of the way in which Solomon and Hiram communicated may be essentially accurate. A comparative analysis of this unit will reveal very strong similarities in both language and content between the words of these two kings and a number of authentic ancient letters.

The epistolary language in the Solomon–Hiram communication. The language of our unit resembles that of ancient letters. In contrast to all the letters known to us from the ancient Near East, as well as from the Aramaic portions of the book of Ezra, the Solomon–Hiram letters preserve no 'Introductory' section. It is likely that the absence of this important component is what has led scholars of epistolography (who have given much attention in particular to this section) to ignore the epistolary character of this pericope. But the absence of this element should not be sufficient to eliminate the pericope from the category of letter literature, and, to be sure, we find that even those biblical narratives which explicitly use the term *sēper* ('letter') invariably mention only the body of the letter, while deleting or forgoing the preamble. Only the author of the book of Ezra went to the trouble of reproducing letters in their entirety. Moreover, the expressions typical of ancient letters are not restricted to the introductory sections of the letters, and even within the bodies of letters one may encounter idioms, expressions and stylistic features not less characteristic of epistolary diction than the introductory formulae themselves. It is precisely these formulae that bind the messages of Solomon and Hiram and the narrative connections between them (v. 21a) closely to the language of various ancient letters—more closely than any of the letters recorded in the Hebrew sections of the Bible. These are the signs:

A. *Direct speech.* The words of the two kings are phrased in the first and second persons, as in direct speech and conversation. This is characteristic of letters, and of legal and administrative documents. Admittedly, international treaties as well are phrased as direct conversations between the parties, but this in itself does not make the messages of Solomon and Hiram more like the treaties than the letters. B. *wĕ'attâ.* Solomon's message to Hiram (vv. 16-19) may be divided into two parts—an introduction in which Solomon notifies Hiram of his intention to build a House to the Name of the Lord, and a second part in which Solomon asks Hiram to send him wood (v. 20). Since all the explicit Deuteronomic language is concentrated in the first part of this message (as stated above), there is, perhaps, room to assume that the word *wĕ'attâ,* 'and now', in v. 18 reflects the well-known rhetorical diction of the Deuteronomic school (even if this word is quite common and not all that prevalent in Deuteronomic literature). Be this as it may, the second appearance of the word in v. 20—this time in a context devoid of obvious deuteronomisms—seems to belong to the stereotyped language of the ancient letters. This has already been pointed out by Gray and Würthwein[1] in their commentaries on the book of Kings, and, because the matter is so well known, it need not be elaborated upon here.[2]

---

1.   Würthwein (1977: 54 n. 9) holds that *we'attâ* is parallel to Akkadian *umma,* and this is on the basis of Brongers 1965: 296. It seems to me, however, that *wĕ'attâ* should be associated rather with Akkadian *enna,* for *umma* (derived etymologically from *enma*) means 'behold' while *enna* means 'now' See for *(u) enna* in letters Ebeling 1930–34 (*NBU*) I 30.5; 56.8; 65.7; 108.5; 139.4; 270.20; 296.9; 331.9 and *CAD* E *s.v. enna* (a). As for the structural function and the semantic meaning *wĕ'attâ* is also comparable with Akkadian *anumma,* for which see *CAD.*

2.   Here are only a few examples:

(a) In letters mentioned in the Hebrew portions of the Bible, *wĕ'attâ* appears as an opening word in the body of the letter in: 2 Kgs 5.6, *wayyābō' hassēper 'el hammelek lē'mōr we'attâ kēbō' hassēper hazzeh 'elâw.* . .; 2 Kgs 2.1-7 *wayyiktōb Jēhû sĕpārîm wayyišlaḥ šōmĕr'ōn.* . . *lē'mōr wĕ'attâ kēbō' hassēper hāzzeh 'ălêkem.* . . (and see the parallel to our passage in 2 Chron. 2.6, 12, 14).

(b) In the Aramaic letters cited in the book of Ezra, the words *ûk'enet* or *ûk'an* appear in the same function (*ûk'enet,* Ezra 4.10, 11, 17; 7.12; *ke'an* Ezra 4.13, 14, 21; 5.17; 6.6).

(c) In the Hebrew letters from Arad and Lachish *w't* appears (Aharoni, 1975): 1.1-2, *'el 'elyāšib wĕ'attā nātōn lakKTYM yayin* . . . ; 5.1-2, *'el 'elyāšib šălōaḥ mē'tĕkā.* . . (and see letters 1, 2, 3, 5, 6, 7, 8, 10, 11, 16, 17, 18, 21, 40). From Lachish, *KAI* I, 194, *yšm' yhwh['t 'dny] 't kym šm't ṭb w'th kkl 'šr šlḥ 'dny.* . . The transfer of the word *wĕ'attâ* from the head of the message section of the

C. *ṣawwēh*. Following the transitional word *wĕ'attâ* comes the word *ṣawwēh*. This word is an imperative expressed in the infinitive absolute. In ancient Hebrew letters as well, the word immediately following the transitional term *wĕ'attâ* is frequently an imperative, and this imperative is sometimes expressed in the infinitive absolute. So we find in Arad letters 1, 2, 7, 8 and 11 *wĕ'attâ nātōn* in infinitive absolute (this along with the short, imperative form such as *wĕ'attâ tēn* in nos. 3 and 18) and perhaps *wĕ'attâ šālōaḥ* (but possibly *šĕlaḥ*) in nos. 5 and 6.[1] In Ezra 4.21 we find *kĕ'an ŝîmû tĕ'ēm* with a simple imperative following the transitional word. In Ezra 5.17 (*ûk'an hēn 'al malkā' ṭāb yitbaqqar bĕḇêt ginzayyā'...*) the imperative is replaced by a jussive and distanced somewhat from the transitional word, but this deviation from the pattern is to be attributed to court or diplomatic etiquette.

D. *Hiram's reaction*. Hiram's reaction to Solomon's message as well as his reply are described in vv. 21-23, starting with an introduction by the narrator:

wayhî kišmōa' ḥîrām 'et dibrê šĕlōmōh wayyiŝmaḥ mĕ'ōd.
When Hiram heard Solomon's message, he was overjoyed.

Joy at hearing the words of a messenger or hearing a letter read is described frequently in literary contexts.[2] When Baal hears from Anat's messenger that Il has agreed to his request to build a palace, we read *šmḫ aliyn b'l* (*UT* 51 V 97-98). Mot, upon hearing the messengers' report of Baal's surrender, rejoices: *šmḫ bn ilm mt* (*UT* 67 ii 20). According to Isa. 39.1-2: 'At that time Merodach-baladan sent...letters and tribute to Hezekiah...and Hezekiah rejoiced over them'. It is obviously possible to compare the description of Hiram's joy with the passages just cited and go no further,[3] but the description

letter to a transitory position within the message section itself has been described by Levine (1978–79: 291) as a regular feature of the letters which are cited in the Bible, and he explained this dislocation as the result of literary adaptation. This may be relevant to the present discussion as well, and as we will yet see, this is not the only case of the reworking of the letter form for the purposes of narrative.

1. See Pardee 1978: 293 as well as Levine, 1978–79: 287, 291, 292.
2. On the genetic relationship between the style of the letters and the accepted speech patterns of messengers, see Loewenstamm 1962 (*s.v. miktāḇ* in *Encyclopaedia Miqra'it*).
3. Those who wish to categorize the present passage as a treaty may adduce as

is even more similar to certain formulae which appear in a number of extra-biblical letters. Rib-Addi, king of Byblos writes (Rainey, *EA* 362 ll. 5-7):

> (And) now, I have heard
> the words of the king, my lord
> and my heart rejoiced greatly.

Ammunira, King of Beirut writes (*EA* 142 ll. 6-10):

> When I heard
> the words of the tablet of the king my lord
> then my heart rejoiced
> and my two eyes shone greatly.[1]

Similar formulae are found in other letters from El-Amarna,[2] Ugarit,[3] Mari[4] and certain other Old-Babylonian archives.[5]

E. *The reply.* Hiram's reply, as presented in the story before us, opens with the declaration: 'I have heard what you sent to me... ' This sentence is nearly identical with a common formula which appears dozens of times in letters from El-Amarna and Mari. Here are several examples:

1.   In *EA* 1, Amenophis III writes to Kadashman Harbi (l. 10):

> (And) now, I have heard the words
> which you sent concerning her
> to me saying...

2.   In *EA* 254 Labaya writes (ll. 6-7):

> I heard the words
> which the king sent me.

3.   In *EA* 364 Ayyāb of Ashtartu says:

> I heard the message of the king my lord
> to me (sent) by Atahmaja.

---

evidence for their opinion the words of Matiwaza in his treaty with Shupiluliuma (Weidner 1923: 42 ll. 2-7): *amāti ša šarri bēlīja altemīma aḫtadu*, 'The words of the king, my lord, I heard and I rejoiced'.

1.   For the glow of the eyes as a sign of happiness see most recently Gruber 1980: 383-598.

2.   See *EA* no. 17 ll. 49-50; no. 27 ll. 7-8; no. 171 ll. 8-11; no. 154 ll. 5-6.

3.   *MRS*, IX, 132 l. 5'-7'.

4.   *ARM*, V, 21 ll. 4-5.

5.   F.R. Kraus 1932: 41 no. 5 l. 5.

4. All the previous formulae seem to be only abbreviated or alternate forms of what we find in a letter from Labaya (*EA* 253 ll. 7-10; and see as well *EA* 304 ll. 15-17):

> I heard the words
> which the king, my lord,
> sent me on a tablet.

5. In the Mari letters a synonymous formula occurs as, for example in *ARM*, II, 6.14:

> I heard your tablet which you sent me.

(See as well *ARM*, I, 9.5; 10.4; 20.5; 22.4; 37.5; *ARM*, II, 17.5; 60.5; 62.3; 63.4; 94.4; *ARM*, V, 43.5; 62.4 and dozens more letters).

6. Closer to home, we find in a Lachish letter (*KAI* 194.2):

> And now, according to all that my lord sent
> so has your servant done
> I wrote on the (writing) board
> as all that. . . sent to me
> and that my lord sent about the matter of. . .

F. At times, the two formulae appear together in the very same letter.

1. In *EA* 142, mentioned above, we read (ll. 6-10):

> I heard the words of the tablet which the merciful (?) king my lord sent
> and when I heard the words of the king, my lord my heart rejoiced and
> my two eyes shone strongly.

2. In *EA* 144[1] Zimriddi mayor of Sidon writes (ll. 13-18):

> And when I heard the word of the king my lord
> which he sent to his servant.
> then my heart rejoiced
> and my head was uplifted[2]
> and my two eyes shone
> upon hearing the words of the king my lord.

1. For a new translation see Oppenheim 1967 no. 70.
2. For *rēšu šaqû* ('lifted up head') as an expression in Akkadian for happiness see Gruber 1980: 609 and note also Samsuiluna A ll. 103-108 (Borger 1973: 48): *in rēšīn eliātim in rīšātim u hud libbim attallukam*, 'to walk constantly with uplifted head(s) in joy and happiness of the heart'.

G. *Commercial language*. In his message to Solomon, Hiram suggests a 'commercial' agreement for exchange of goods and he says (vv. 22-23):

> I will do all your desire (*ḥepsĕkā*)
> and you will do my desire (*ḥepṣî*)

The Hebrew word *ḥēpeṣ* (see also 1 Kgs 5.24 relating the fulfillment of the agreement achieved), which is rendered by the Aramaic Targumim with *ṣby* and *ṣrk* (see, for instance, Onqelos on Deut. 25.7, Jonathan on 1 Kgs 5.22-23 and note 2 Chron. 2.15), parallels the Akkadian words *ḥašḥu*, *ḥišḥtu*, as well as *ṣebû*, *ṣibûtu* and *erēšu* and *mērēštu*, all having connotations of desire or need. The verses in 1 Kings are comparable to sentences found in letters of trade from El-Amarna and Ugarit.[1] So, for example, in *EA* 6 Burnaburiash writes to Amenemophis (ll. 13-16):

> What you need/want from (*ša ḥašḥata*) my land
> send me (notice) so they may take it for you (*liqûnikku*)
> and what I need/want (*ša anāku ḥašḥāku*) from your land
> I will send (notice) so they may take it for me (*lilqûninni*).

Suggestions in nearly identical formulations[2] are found in *EA* 7.33-36, 61-65; 16.32-34; 19.66-69; 37.8-18; 41.36-42; 43.29; 44.25-29.[3] An example of the same formula in the Ugaritic language occurs in *MRS*, XI, p. 93 no. 65.15-20:

> Whatever is your wish (*irštk*)
> which you lack, (*dḥsrt*) behold, I
> will place (at the disposal) of my brother
> And I too, whatever
> I lack, behold my brother
> will carry it there ([y]*'msn. šmn*).

Perhaps we may also compare the last three words cited from this

---

1.   The similarity between these verses and the Akkadian letters of trade mentioned here was already pointed out by Elat 1977: 191. For similar formulae, see *CAD* M II *s.v. mērēštu* A II; S II, p. 170 *s.v. ṣibûtu* A 3a2' p. 168 1a2'3'. To the passages listed we should add now the Akkadian letter from Ugarit found at Tel Aphek, for which see Owen 1981. See also Weinfeld 1982: 44-45 and 1982: 278-79 n. 18 for the relationship between the Hebrew, Aramaic and Akkadian terms.
2.   See *CAD* under the words derived from *ḥašāḥu*.
3.   See also *ARM*, V, 5.18-19, Ebeling 1942: 39 no. 53.22-23.

letter with Hiram's words to Solomon about transporting the wood which he is to be sold (1 Kgs 5.23[1]). Note that the Ugaritic letter uses the word *irštk*, just as the Akkadian letter from Ugarit uses *mēreštu*.

In addition to the above-mentioned expressions, where there can be little doubt that the Hebrew is an exact equivalent of the Akkadian, Ugaritic or Aramaic cognates, there are two additional expressions which *closely resemble* common epistolary phrases even though they are not completely synonymous with them. Since strong testimony as to one aspect may enhance the weaker evidence of other aspects, these following expressions may be included as possible signs of the pericope's epistolary character.

H. *Statement of cognizance.* Solomon starts his message with the words (v. 17):

'attâ yāda'tā 'et dāwid 'ābî	You knew David my father
kî lō' yākōl...	that he was not allowed...

Fensham,[2] on the basis of a study by H.B. Huffmon,[3] proposed that this is a case of treaty language, but his suggestion is unacceptable. The text has nothing to do with the 'treaty knowledge' of David, and the verse must be taken to mean 'You know that David my father was not allowed/unable...' This, in fact, was how all the mediaeval exegetes understood the passage.[4] In its immediate literary context, this expression, along with *kî 'attâ yāda'tā kî* in v. 20 are to be taken together and seen as an inclusio bracketing Solomon's words. However, in the wider context of epistolary style, these expressions are to be seen as related to extremely common expressions such as the Aramaic *yĕdia' lehĕwē' lĕ...*[5] and the Akkadian expressions *lu tīdi, lu īdi, lu īdi kî, tīdi inūma, īdi kî, ata tīdi, kīma iddu, kīma iddu, kīma tīdû, lu tīdi, lu tīdi inūma, lu tīdi kî* found in numerous letters.[6] All

---

1. The words *we'attāh tiśśā'* in 1 Kgs 5.23 correspond not only to this phrase in the Ugaritic letter, but also to the expressions *lilqûnikku* and *lilqûninni* in *EA* 6 ll. 13-16 mentioned above. This correspondence is based on the well-known equivalence between the Hebrew words *lqh* and *nś'* and the Akkadian terms *leqû* and *naśû*.
2. Fensham 1969: 75-76.
3. Huffmon 1966.
4. See also GKC 106g, 117h; NAB, NEB, NJPS.
5. Ezra 4.12, 13; 5.8.
6. *lu-ú ti-i-du* (*NBU*, I, 33.4; II, 115.6) (this formula appears in Old Babylonian letters as a concluding formula); *at-tu (-nu) ti-da-am ša...* (*BB* 149.14;

these expressions serve as phrases introducing the writer's message or as transitional phrases within the body of the letter. Some of them indicate the transmission of new information to the addressee (*yĕdia' lehĕwē'*, *lu tīdi*), while others draw the person's attention to something he or she is already assumed to know (*kīma tīdû*, *atta tīdi*, *lu īdi*, *īdi PN inūma kî*. Categorization of these expressions is obviously beyond the scope of the present study. The expanded expression *kî 'attâ yāḏa'ta kî* found in v. 20 has an exact equivalent in the Aramaic letter of Adon king of Ekron (?) to Pharaoh (l. 6) where we read:[1]

> *ky mr' mlkn pr'h ydy' ky*
> For the lord our king Pharaoh knows that. . .

I. *Blessing*. The narrator states that when Hiram heard Solomon's words he was very happy and exclaimed (v. 21):

> Blessed be the Lord this day
> for granting David a wise son.

These words may contain an echo of one of the important and prominent components found in countless ancient letters—the blessing formula. These formulae, in which the writer blesses the addressee, are well known from Hebrew,[2] Aramaic,[3] Ugaritic[4] and Akkadian[5] letters. Montgomery and Gehman[6] pointed out the similarity between Hiram's benediction and a letter sent by Tushrata king of Mittani to Amenophis III of Egypt (*EA* 21 ll. 18-23):[7]

221.18, 19; 186.12; 158.10-22; *ARM*, II, 65.8; *NBU*, I, 81.6; 155.6 (rvs); *at-ta ti-i-di ki-i* (*NBU*, II, 198.6; III, 222.5); *ki-ma ti-de-e/ ti-du-ú* (*AbB* I 39.4; 77.5; 106.4; 108.3; *ti-di i-nu-ma* (*EA* 102.3, 7, 12, 25, 31); *lu-ú i-di. . .i-nu-ma* (*EA* 68.9; 74.5; 76.7; 78.7; 81.6; 114.6; 116.6); *PN i-di. . .i-nu-ma šum-ma* (*EA* 92.51; 110.8-9; 106.47; 114.18-22); *at-ta ti-di* (*EA* 69.15); *LUGAL be-li u-da ki-i* (Parpola 1970: 114 = *ABL* 421 ll. 17-18). For additional references, see the indexes of these collections of letters *s.v. idû*

1. For the letter of Adon, see Porten 1981 as well as Porten 1986: 6. Note also Gibson, *SSI*, II, 115, who remarks that *kî* with the meaning 'that' is not found in Aramaic.
2. See Loewenstamm 1962 (*s.v. miktāḇ*, *EM* 4) and Pardee 1978.
3. See Fitzmeyer 1974: 214-17.
4. See Ahl 1973.
5. See E. Salonen 1967.
6. Montgomery and Gehman 1951: 134.
7. See the edition of Adler 1976.

May Shamash and Shaushga
give my brother great blessing
and beautiful joy
may they bless him
and my brother, may you live
forever.

The Arad letters contain blessing formulae such as (Aharoni 1975: 15.1-3):[1]

Your brother Hannanyahu has sent (regarding) the wellbeing of Elyashab
and the wellbeing of your house
I have blessed you to YHWH (*bēraktîkā laYHWH*)

The formula in the Arad ostracon may be compared to similar blessing formulae in neo-Assyrian and neo-Babylonian correspondence such as:[2] 'May DN bless my brother', or 'Before DN. . . I have blessed my brother'.

Hiram's blessing parallels the blessings from the ancient extra-biblical letters in a general manner although the similarity is admittedly rather small. Hiram, by saying *bārûk YHWH 'ăšer* . . . is thanking the God of Israel for something and praising him, and this would not seem to be a blessing of Solomon. In contrast, the writers of the extra-biblical letters ask and pray that the gods bless the addressee, or announce that they have blessed the addressee[3] (*bēraktîkā laYHWH*). It would seem at first glance that there is no relationship between the two. Even so, there may be some way to relate them a bit more closely. Several biblical passages mention that one person blesses another using a formula with the simple meaning 'Praise YHWH or be blessed!' For instance, 1 Kgs 8.14 states 'Then. . . the king faced about and blessed the whole congregation of Israel', but when the 'blessing' itself is cited, we do not find the expected *bārûk yiśrā'ēl laYHWH*—Blessed be Israel of the Lord—but, rather, 'Praised be the Lord, the God of Israel, who has. . . ' (1 Kgs 8.15 and see also v. 55). Likewise, when Malkizedeq blesses Abram (Gen. 14.19-20), he says first *bārûk 'abrām lě'ēl 'elyôn*, and adds immediately, *ûbārûk 'ēl*

---

1.   Aharoni 1975. See also 21.1-3; 40.1-4 and Aharoni's bibliography (1975: 32); Pardee 1976: 221-23 and 1978: 311. Note as well the Aramaic letters from Hermopolis in Gibson, *SSI*, II, 129 l. 2, p. 132 l. 2 *brktky lpth*.
2.   See *CAD* K, p. 194 *s.v. karābu* 1b and E. Salonen 1967: 50, 70, 96ff.
3.   See Pardee 1976, 1978.

'elyôn 'ăšer . . . '—first announcing that Abram is blessed, and then actually praising God. Finally, Noah's blessing of his son Shem (Gen. 8.26) is expressed *bārûḵ YHWH 'ĕlōhê šēm*. . . These verses show that it is possible to invoke a blessing upon a person by praising God, and that it is not necessary to say explicitly that the person is blessed. In view of this, we may conjecture that Hiram's 'original' blessing may have been something like *bēraḵtîḵā laYHWH,* or *yĕbārekēkā YHWH*, by which he announced that he indeed wished for God to bless Solomon, but the biblical author who recorded the benediction reformulated it and 'translated' it to make it more suitable for his narrative. In other words, Hiram's blessing underwent a literary 'adaptation', transforming it from epistolary to narrative language.

A literary 'adaptation' similar to this one is found in the beginning of the description of Hiram's reaction, where we read *wayhî kišmōaʿ ḥîrām 'et diḇrê šĕlōmōh wayyišmaḥ mĕʾōd*. In actual letters, such statements would be made by the sender/writer, and would be expressed in the first person, but in the given narrative they are placed in the voice of the narrator.[1]

There is an interesting corollary to the identification of Hiram's blessing as some sort of offshoot of the standard greeting formulae of the extra-biblical letters. It is well known that in ancient correspondence blessings were found in letters addressed either to an equal or to a superior, while a letter from a superior to an inferior would not contain a blessing formula.[2] Since only the message of Hiram contains a reflex of the blessing formula, we are to assume that the author is portraying him as inferior to Solomon.

3. *The Content of the Letters*

The epistolary nature of the account of Solomon's dealings with Hiram is reflected not only in language and style, but in content as well. Trade agreements such as the one negotiated and concluded by Solomon and Hiram were made in the ancient Near East not through treaties (to the extent that the documents correctly identifiable as 'treaties' permit us to assume), but through exchange of letters

---

1. For literary adaptation of administrative and cultic documents for the purposes of narrative use, see Levine 1965, and 1978–79: 291.

2. See Loewenstamm 1962: 970 and Levine 1978–79: 285.

between the parties.[1] To be sure, several examples of letters dealing with the purchase or acquisition of building materials have survived.[2] It should be emphasized at this point that trade agreements are not mentioned anywhere in Mesopotamian building accounts.

Requests for Building Material

a. In a letter from Assur-uballit, king of Assyria, to Amenemophis III of Egypt (*EA* 16 = Grayson, *ARI*, I, 311-18) the king of Assyria informs Pharaoh that he is building a new palace and asks that he be sent gold (ll. 14-16):

> I am building a new palace. Whatever gold is needed for its decorations and appointments send me!

He prefaces this request with an announcement that he has sent Pharaoh horses, and after making his request he writes (ll. 32-34):

> If you are well disposed towards friendly relations, send me much gold. This is your family. Send me and what you need/wish (*ḫašḫata*) they (the messengers) will take.

b. In a letter from Burnaburiash to Amenemophis IV (*EA* 9 = Oppenheim 1967: no. 59), the king of Babylon tells old Pharaoh that he is building a temple and asks gold to be sent (ll. 15-18):

> Now my work in the temple is great[3]
> and I am very anxious to do it.
> So send me much gold,
> and you, whatever you desire (*ḫašḫāta*)
> from my land, write me
> so that (the messengers) can take it to you.

At the end of this letter, following a blank space of about five lines,

1. For royal purchasing agents, see *Enmerkar and the Lord of Aratta* and the *Journey of Wenamun*, both of which will be discussed in detail below.
2. For a 'literary' letter of trade, see 'The Letter from Gilgamesh' published first by Gurney 1957, and recently re-edited and translated by F.R. Kraus 1980. In this letter, Gilgamesh asks the addressee for numerous sorts of merchandise in immense quantities. Among other things he orders 120,000 talents of some type of metal (the text is broken) in order that a smith can do work on a temple (l. 27).
3. To Burnaburiash's words in this letter, compare Solomon's message to Huram in 2 Chron. 2.4: 'The House that I intend to build will be great, inasmuch as our God is greater than all gods. Who indeed is capable of building a House for him?'

Burnaburiash states that he has sent Pharaoh lapis-lazuli and horses. Another letter between these same two kings alludes apparently to the same building project (*EA* 7 = Oppenheim 1967: 58) and says:

> I am busy with work so
> I have sent to my brother.
> May my brother send me
> much good gold so
> I may put it towards my work. . . [1]

c. The king of Carchemish sends a letter to Ibirani, king of Ugarit (*MRS*, IX, 194 B17.385) in which he asks that he be sent beams of *dupranu* (juniper)-wood of certain dimensions. Unfortunately, the reverse of the tablet is broken so the circumstances of this request remain unknown, but it is phrased (ll. 6-14):

> Now I am sending you the
> dimensions, length and width.
> According to those dimensions
> send me 2 beams of *dupranu*!

The order for only two trees or only two pieces of wood with given dimensions seems to indicate that the king of Ugarit is not involved in an extensive building project but only in light restorations or redecoration—perhaps he is repaneling some walls or making new doors.[2]

Shipping Arrangements

Hiram, when writing to Solomon about his willingness to sell him wood, also makes some proposals about transporting the goods. In 1 Kgs 5.23 we read:

> My servants will bring them down to the sea from the Lebanon; and at the sea I will make them into floats and [deliver them] to any place that you designate to me. There I shall break them up for you to carry away.

Arrangements for shipping building materials in general, and for transportation of wood in particular from the place of origin to the building site, constitute a well-known literary/artistic topos in royal inscriptions and palace reliefs. Some of the sources have already been

---

1.   See also Kadashman-Harbi's letter to Amenemophis III in *EA* 4 ll. 36-50.
2.   See *CAD* D, p. 289 *dupranu* b. This wood served at times for building palaces.

referred to in the modern commentaries.[1] The relevant royal inscriptions will be discussed below, but first I will mention several letters in which the matter appears.[2] Most of the letters dealing with transporting building supplies are domestic, administrative letters, but there is no reason that such shipping arrangements would not have been the topic for international trade letters as well. As a matter of fact, in *EA* 7, mentioned above, Burnaburiash adds to his request for gold the following stipulation regarding the manner in which it is to be handled (reverse 66-68):

> (But) the gold which my brother sends (me), let him not give it over to the hands of any reliable (official). (Only) [the eyes] of my brother should keep watch over it, and my brother (personally) should seal it and send it. . .

a. In the literary text known as a 'Letter from Gilgamesh' (because it is written according to letter format [F.R. Kraus 1980 = Gurney 1957]), Gilgamesh orders precious metals to make a pectoral ornament for his friend Enkidu. There we read:

> New [boat]s
> fill with silver and gold,
> and with silver and gold
> let them float down to Sippar.
> Send to the quay of Babylon
> and may my eyes see and my heart be confident.

b. A letter from the time of Sargon II, king of Assyria (attributed by Waterman to Ṭab-šār-Aššur) relates (*RCAE* 490):

> 470 beams, for 3 days (already)
> are found on the river. . .
> Altogether 100 men
> along with Assur-riṣua
> within Ura
> are transporting beams.

c. A letter to Sargon from Ša-Aššur-dubbu reports that timber was

---

1.   See especially Montgomery and Gehman 1951.
2.   For the corpus of letters and administrative documents concerned with shipping wood see Elat 1977: 64-65. For additional letters from the time of Sargon II concerning the transportation of raw and finished building materials see Parpola 1987, *passim*.

cut in the mountains of Ararat, and in order to transport them the writer says (*RCAE* 705 rev. 9-10):

> I will free 100 workers
> and they will place the beams
> in the river (in order to float them).

d. A letter from Nimrud (Kalḫu) which was sent to the king of Assyria by Qurdi-Aššur-lāmur does not actually deal with providing timber for building projects, but it is nonetheless important to our study for its description of the logging industry in the Lebanon during the Assyrian period. The author of the letter is the royally appointed customs official in Tyre, and he is making a report to the king about his activities (Saggs 1955: 127 no. 12 ll. 6-11):

> His servants among them (the Tyrians)
> come and go at the customs house.
> They sell and buy and
> the Lebanon is theirs.
> As they like they go up and come down.
> They bring down logs (?).[1]
> Whoever brings down logs,
> I collect his customs.

At the end of his letter, following a description of some recent local disturbances, the official describes some new regulations which he has instituted (ll. 23-27):

> I ordered them as follows:
> from now on bring down the logs (?) hither.
> Do your work in it.
> To the Egyptians and the Philistines
> you may not sell.
> If not, I will not free you,
> and to the mountain you will not ascend.

These passages demonstrate that the matters discussed by Solomon and Hiram were topics regularly dealt with through letters in the ancient Near East. Once again it should be emphasized that trade agreements are not discussed in royal building accounts found in the royal inscriptions, nor are they the subject of the international treaties which have reached us.

1. Postgate 1974: 131 reads *GIŠ.MEŠ*.

4. *Summary of the Literary and Form-Critical Analysis*

Summing up the literary and form-critical analysis of 1 Kgs 5.15-26, it may be said that comparison of the language and content of the body of this unit (vv. 16-25) has shown striking resemblance to epistolary writings from ancient Israel and the neighboring peoples. The verses framing the correspondence (vv. 15, 26) reveal signs of ideas and language characteristic of treaties and, perhaps, certain types of legal documents. These elements are missing, however, from the body of the correspondence. Furthermore, the narrator seems not to have cited his letters in their original form. Deuteronomic elements have infiltrated the beginning of Solomon's letter. In addition, epistolary language has been incorporated into the narrative matrix (vv. 21, 24-25) by making small stylistic changes. More specifically, those parts of Hiram's letter in which he reports his reactions to receiving a letter from Solomon have been excerpted from the letter and placed in the mouth of the narrator. Nonetheless, the epistolary character of the pericope remains prominent. Even if the letters have been utilized in a broader context of describing treaty stipulations or contract terms, this use is at most secondary and does not diminish from the primary epistolary nature of the messages. It would be a mistake to go astray after the secondary use of the letters in a treaty or a contract context and categorize the words of the two kings exclusively or even primarily as treaty or legal language, and one who wishes to do so must shoulder the burden of proof.

2. *Analysis of the Content*

The literary nature of the description of Solomon's trading with Hiram having been determined, attention must now be turned to placing the content of this description in its proper place among descriptions of similar events. So far I have dealt mainly with 'comparison'; from now on the element of 'contrast' will enter the discussion.[1] I will now analyze the content of the Solomon–Hiram correspondence. Afterwards, I will compare and contrast it first with two extra-biblical accounts of negotiations for the purchase of building materials, and then with those passages in extra-biblical building accounts concerning the acquisition of building materials and their transportation to the building site.

1. See Hallo 1977.

1. *The Solomon–Hiram Incident as a Story about Trading*

Bible commentaries seem to have frequently ignored the obvious (but fundamental) fact that Solomon and Hiram did not simply exchange letters of friendship and mutual admiration, but actually engaged in commercial negotiations leading to a trade agreement. As in all cases of bargaining, this story too knows of an initial price offer by the buyer and a counter-offer made by the seller, and at the end a compromise is reached. Solomon, who wishes to acquire wood, suggests to Hiram that his own workers will work together with those of Hiram, and offers to pay as much wages to Hiram's men, as Hiram will demand. It seems, therefore, that the price Solomon proposes to pay for the wood is quite small. In fact, Solomon has offered to pay only the cost of labor, and even this stands to be minimal since Solomon's workers will be doing most of the work. Hiram, so Solomon would have it seem, is asked to do nothing more than give the order that trees be felled and supply some technical expertise to Solomon's workers. The wood itself is to be provided to Solomon free of charge! This may sound somewhat astonishing, but in the two extra-biblical texts to be examined next, this is precisely what happens. There may even be a political claim implicit in Solomon's offer, namely, that the forests do not belong to Hiram, whose sovereignty extends only to the city of Tyre, and he cannot expect therefore to profit from them as if they were his property.

Hiram, for his part, does not consent to this offer and demands quite a high price. He makes it clear to Solomon that it is wood he will supply, and not expertise alone. Similarly, whereas Solomon ordered only cedars, Hiram offers to throw in cypresses as well. Moreover, Hiram rejects Solomon's proposal that Israelites do the work. He suggests instead that his own men will be the ones to cut down the trees and tend to their transportation, while Solomon's men[1] need only pick up the wood after it has been delivered to wherever he wishes—presumably far away from Tyre! In exchange for the wood and the labor, he requests *makkōlet̲ bêt̲î* 'my household provisions', and it

---

1.   R. de Vaux (1945: 48 n. 4) suggests reading *'ăb̲ād̲êk̲ā*, 'your servants', rather than *'ăb̲ād̲ay*, 'my servants', in v. 23, and in his opinion Solomon's servants are to work as porters in the Lebanon while Hiram's men and the Tyrians will cut the trees. *BHK* also suggests this emendation, but with a question mark. Nonetheless, the emendation is unnecessary and has no basis in the ancient versions.

may be assumed that this is more than or in addition to the wages of his workers.[1]

Comparison of these two proposals makes it clear that the price demanded by Hiram is considerably higher than the one Solomon has offered to pay. Not only this, but Hiram's proposal promises extensive employment for his own workers and very little for Solomon's, leading one to assume that he was not thrilled by the prospect that myriads of Solomon's men would enter the Lebanon to work.

There is no way of knowing just how many letters were exchanged before concluding the agreement—the Bible cites only the initial pair of letters—but the final agreement shows signs of compromise. According to v. 25, Solomon agreed to Hiram's price demand and gave him his 'household provisions'[2] However, v. 28, which in the present form of the account lies outside the formal limits defined by the opening and closing sentences (vv. 15 and 26—see the discussion above),[3] indicates that Hiram accepted Solomon's terms concerning the labor force.[4]

There is obviously nothing special or unique about commercial bargaining and trading. It went on in the ancient Near East just as it does in the modern world. Even so, a brief look at two extra-biblical stories—the Sumerian tale of *Enmerkar and the Lord of Aratta*, and the Egyptian *Journey of Wenamun*—which tell of trading and the bargaining involved, will help emphasize by comparison and contrast certain noteworthy features of the biblical account. The stories are of particular interest because they tell, respectively, of acquiring building materials for a temple and for a divine boat.

---

1.   See Montgomery and Gehman 1951: 136 and against this view see Gray 1970: 153.

2.   Additional details of the trade agreement and its implementation are to be found in 1 Kgs 9.10-14. See also 10.22.

3.   Verse 28 is not to be seen as contradicting v. 23, as Noth and Gray propose. Hiram's refusal to receive Solomon's workers in his land was apparently his initial position in the negotiations, but he compromised on it.

4.   The Chronicler introduced numerous changes into the details of the negotiations, and according to his version Huram accepted Solomon's conditions. As a result, the Israelite king comes out in a much more positive light, as seen by the commentaries to Chronicles.

'*Enmerkar and the Lord of Aratta*'.[1] This lengthy text, containing more than 630 lines, is one of four literary compositions telling about the rivalry between the cities Uruk-Kullaba and Aratta. The contest described in this particular text arose as a result of Enmerkar's plan to decorate the temple of the goddess Inanna in his city Uruk-Kullaba. The king needed building materials—in particular lapis lazuli and other precious stones—as well as skilled craftsmen, and he intended to acquire them by subjugating the city of Aratta which was well endowed with all that Enmerkar needed. As it happened, Aratta was suffering at that very time from a drought, a heavy famine and a grain shortage.

Enmerkar, commanded and encouraged by Inanna, sent the Lord of Aratta a messenger bearing demands and threats. The Lord of Aratta refused to submit to Enmerkar's demands and was able to initiate a 'war of nerves' in which the two kings, rather than engaging in physical combat, exchanged challenges of skill through the agency of the messenger. The account of the exchanges—a sort of 'anything you can do, I can do better' science and technology competition[2]—which is reminiscent of the well-known Sumerian debate genre (*a-da-man du$_{11}$-ga*), makes up most of the poem, and it may be assumed that it was composed for the purpose of court entertainment. In any case, the people of Aratta did not submit to Enmerkar's threats, and their ruler's cunning kept them safe until the rain started again. In the end, the two cities reached a peaceful agreement. Unfortunately, the end of the text is lost, but we may assume that Aratta agreed to supply Enmerkar with the required building materials and artisans, while Uruk-Kulaba agreed to pray for the land of Aratta and its continued fertility, and to furnish grain.

---

1. The text was published along with a commentary by S. Cohen 1973. See more recently the comments of Kramer 1977: 61 and the new translation of Jacobsen 1987b: 175-319.

2. It seems to me that hiding behind this war of wits and challenges is an actual exchange of gifts or merchandise which preceded full commercial relations. That is to say, that by the one party sending wet grain, then a sophisticated type of scepter, and then undyed cloth, he is actually making the down payments on the merchandise he requires from the other. Recently Berlin (1979: 3-34), pointing out the similarity between *Enmerkar and Ensuhkeshdanna* and the well-known Sumerian debate or contest literature, also mentioned that it most closely resembles *Enmerkar and the Lord of Aratta*.

As mentioned above, this story was probably meant as court entertainment, but it has been suggested that it also was intended to explain aetiologically the restoration of trade in lapis lazuli—a trade which stopped at the end of the Early Dynastic I period and was restored during ED II.[1] Jacobsen has pointed out other aetiological elements as well—namely, attributing to the genius of Enmerkar such important cultural inventions as transporting grain as malt, cultivation of the 'resplendent reed', and even the use of letters.[2]

This amazing story is generally reminiscent of the biblical account of Solomon's dealings with Hiram. Both of them tell about the exchange of essential building materials as well as expert craftsmen (see 1 Kgs 7.13 and 2 Chron. 2.6, 12-13) for agricultural produce.[3] In addition, both stories describe negotiations which start off with minimal offers and maximal demands of the two sides and which conclude with compromises acceptable to both partners. Furthermore, the two stories have what may be called a 'wisdom' background. At the heart of the Enmerkar tale stands the war of wits between two wise kings. In this connection we may recall the Queen of Sheba's visit to Solomon. She came to hear Solomon's wisdom and test him with riddles, but the ultimate outcome is a commercial agreement (1 Kgs 10.10, 13). Similarly, Hiram's initial emissary to Solomon comes to hear his wisdom (1 Kgs 5.14-15) and the conclusion of the negotiations is portrayed by a biblical narrator as a sign of Solomon's wisdom (5.26). Interestingly, rabbinic literature and the writings of Josephus refer to riddle contests between Hiram and Solomon which paralleled the trade negotiations.[4]

Nonetheless, the stories differ considerably in length and in form. These significant differences will be discussed below.

1. See G. Hermann 1968: 38-39.
2. Jacobsen 1987b: 277; Vanstiphout 1989.
3. See ll. 347-62. It is likely that at the end of the story the people of Uruk undertook not only to pray for the land of Aratta and its fertility, but to supply her with fruit as well.
4. Josephus attributes the stories about the riddle contests to his sources Deus and Menander. It is not impossible that the later reports preserve memory of an ancient custom. See Katzenstein 1973: 98-99. Katzenstein mentions in this connection Ezek. 28.3: 'Yes, you are wiser than Daniel; in no hidden matter can anyone compare to you'.

'*The Journey of Wenamun*'. Because of the practical, chronological and geographical similarities between this story and the Solomon–Hiram negotiations, I will deal with the Egyptian text at some length. This composition[1] is in fact an official report, perhaps in the form of a letter, written by Wenamun, a purchasing agent of the temple of Amun in Karnak under Ramesses II (1050 BCE).[2] The writer relates that he was sent to Phoenicia in order to purchase cedar wood for the holy boat of his god, Amen-Re. After trouble-laden stops in Tanis, Dor and Tyre, Wenamun reached Byblos where he was delayed for more than a year. During the fifth month of his voyage, after a wait of over a month in the port of Byblos, Wenamun was reluctantly invited to the upper-storey room[3] of Zakar-baal, Prince of Byblos, who finally agreed to receive him (l. 49) and to enter into negotiations for the acquisition and transportation to Egypt of the needed lumber.

The Egyptian agent is asked to present the books and letters provided him by the priest of Amun. The required documents are apparently to have been letters of recommendation, identifying Wenamun as an authorized purchasing agent.[4] The governor also demands to know in which vessel Wenamun plans to ship the wood which he seeks to buy. The Egyptian has no documents and no ships, but despite his inability to defend his lack of credentials, he seems to succeed in convincing the governor that he is not an impostor, and the negotiations continue.

After having investigated the man's identity, the governor goes on to inquire as to the purpose of the visit. To his inquiry 'Why have you

---

1.   This document has been frequently translated. The passages cited here are from Wilson's translation in *ANET*, 25-29. My discussion is not based on use of the text in the original language, but, rather, on the translations and accompanying notes found in *ANET*, 25-29; Lichtheim 1976: 223-30; Erman 1966: 142-45; Simpson 1973: 174-85; Gardiner 1961: 306-13 and Grintz 1975: 23-33. The most extensive study of this work is Goedicke 1975. I am grateful to Miss Deborah Sweeney of the Hebrew University Department of Egyptology for discussing this text with me.

2.   See Breasted 1906: 319-24, for a report of an agent for purchasing stones.

3.   See Judg. 3.20, but cf. now Ward 1985, who dissociates Egyptian *ar.yt:* from Hebrew '*ăliyyôt*.

4.   See Neh. 2.7-9: 'Then I said to the king, "If it please the king, let me have letters to the governors of the province of Beyond the River, directing them to grant me passage until I reach Judah; likewise, a letter to Asaph, the keeper of the King's Park, directing him to give me timber for roofing the gatehouse of the temple fortress etc. . . ." '

come here?', Wenamun replies, 'I have come after the woodwork for the august barque of Amen-Re King of the Gods; that which your father and your father's father have done, you too shall do'. Zakar-Baal's response to these somewhat enigmatic words shows that Wenamun has in fact suggested that the Prince of Byblos give him wood as has been done in previous generations. (Wenamun's words remind us, interestingly, of Solomon's message to Hiram as recorded in 2 Chron. 2.2: 'Solomon sent this message to King Huram of Tyre, "In view of what you did for my father David in sending him cedars to build a palace for his residence... "'). The governor admits that his ancestors have indeed provided wood to Egypt, but he adds that a fair price has always been paid, and even sets before Wenamun his account books.[1] In other words, he agrees in principle to provide wood to Wenamun, but only for a price, and a high one at that. It is perhaps fitting to compare Solomon's request, 'Please, then, give orders for cedars to be cut for me in the Lebanon' (1 Kgs 5.20), with Zakar-Baal's boast, 'If I cry out to the Lebanon, the heavens open up and the logs are here lying on the sea-shore'. Zakar-Baal acknowledges the greatness of Amun and the antiquity of Egypt and her culture, but he characterizes Wenamun's voyage as silly and expresses his surprise at the humble conditions in which the Egyptian agent is forced to travel (so Goedicke explains), and he seems to have pity on the Egyptian. Wenamun tries in any case to convince Zakar-Baal to give him wood free of charge, claiming that the entire world belongs to Amun, including the Lebanon, which, according to the governor, is his own personal property. Wenamun also explains to the governor that previous, illegitimate, Egyptian kings paid for timber they received only because they did not possess any 'more spiritual' rewards to offer, and suggests that instead of payment, he, as messenger of Amun, has the power to offer divinely granted life and health in exchange.

Putting aside his attempts to persuade with these rather strained theological arguments, Wenamun suddenly becomes quite pragmatic and suggests an interim agreement. He will send a message to Smendes and Tentamun requesting that they forward some sort of payment. In response to this suggestion, the governor has an advance of seven beams loaded upon the vessel carrying the letter of request. Several

---

1. Demsky 1976: 85 mentions this passage in reference to 2 Chron. 2.10-15, and especially the word *biktāb*—'in writing'.

months later, the messenger who carried the letter returns, bringing with him fine Egyptian merchandise. Upon seeing this merchandise, Zakar-Baal rejoices and sends 300 men and supervisors to cut down some trees. But even though the trees are felled and brought down from the forest, they are left on the sea-shore, and the Prince demands payment for any additional handling of them. He informs Wenamun that he has not received the customary payment, and suggests that the Egyptian load the wood on his boats by himself. He also makes a rather transparent threat that he has the power to kill Wenamun if the work is not done with the utmost dispatch. Wenamun, however, does not succumb to the threats, and even answers that the workers of Khaemwese (whose death had been recalled by Zakar-Baal) were mere mortals, while he, Wenamun, is protected by the god, and threats against him are therefore meaningless. As compensation to Zakar-Baal, he suggests that the governor make himself a monument upon which he will write 'Amen-Re, King of the gods, sent to me his messenger. . . and Wenamun his human messenger after the wood-work for the great and august bargue of Amen-Re, King of the gods. I cut it down, I loaded it in and I provided it with my ships and with my crews. I caused them to reach Egypt, in order to ask fifty years of life from Amun for myself over and above my fate'. This monument and the inscription which it was to bear may be compared with the monuments set up by Mesopotamian kings who reached the Lebanon and the coast of the Mediterranean.[1]

The conversation ends in a stalemate, leaving the Prince unconvinced and still not agreeing to help Wenamun. Wenamun, for his part, does not do the work alone, and he stays where he is for a considerable amount of time. But, when the men of Tjeker arrive, who are pursuing Wenamun for a supposed robbery he has committed in Dor, and they demand his extradition, Zakar-Baal loads the ship and expels Wenamun from his land so that his pursuers might apprehend him on the high seas.

The Wenamun story provides an additional case of negotiations leading to the purchase of building materials, this time for making a ritual boat. As in the account of Solomon and Hiram, here too the

---

1. See below for the ascent of Mesopotamian kings to the mountains of the Lebanon. For requests for long life in the royal inscriptions and the Bible, see recently Malamat 1982, 1982b and the bibliography listed there.

opening positions and proposals are diametrically opposed. Wenamun wishes his wood for nothing, while Zakar-Baal demands its full price, just as Solomon wanted cedars *gratis* and offered to pay only the wages of Hiram's workers. Enmerkar, as well, wanted lapis-lazuli free of charge. Afterwards, a round of bargaining ensues—something described in the Enmerkar story but not mentioned in the Bible—and in the end the two sides reach an agreement whereby goods will be traded. It may be that all three stories refer to payments being made in stages. The Wenamun story specifies seven beams sent in advance of full payment, while in the Enmerkar tale, the king of Uruk sent his rival bags of grain, an unusual scepter and undyed cloth. According to the Bible, Solomon paid Hiram year after year for the wood (1 Kgs 5.25). He eventually ceded to Hiram twenty cities in the Galilee, apparently in return for gold which Hiram provided but which was not mentioned in the initial agreement (1 Kgs 9.11-13). In the Egyptian text as well as the Sumerian story, the atmosphere is charged with tension. Such tension is apparent in several letters from the El-Amarna archive as well. In these letters, the king demands with unabashed arrogance that the addressee send him what he requires.[1] Comparable animosity is not apparent in 1 Kgs 5.16-26, but may be hinted at in the appendix (9.11-13) where Solomon's payment of twenty cities in exchange for gold is not to Hiram's satisfaction. The three stories thus convey similar pictures of the methods and ambiance of trade negotiations in the ancient Near East.

But in contrast to the Egyptian and Sumerian texts, the biblical account of the negotiations is incomplete. The biblical text lays out in detail the opening demands of the two sides. The results of the negotiations are also incorporated and alluded to in the narrative, but readers must fill in for themselves the intermediate steps in the bargaining and the drawing together of the initially opposing positions. Not only is the story not entirely complete, but, as we saw above, the description of the negotiating is not completely unconstrained, the narrative having been subordinated to the style of international correspondence.

---

1.   See, for instance, *EA* 16 from Assur-uballit to Amenophis IV, and *EA* 35, where the king of Alashiya (Cyprus) complains to the king of Egypt that he has taken wood from his land without paying for it (ll. 27-29); and cf. *MRS*, IX, 221 no. 17.383, where the messenger of the King of Ugarit in the Hattian court expresses the complaint of the king of Hatti that the lapis-lazuli sent him is of inferior quality.

Since the reality described in the three stories is for all intents and purposes equivalent, there is reason to suggest that the peculiar literary character of the biblical account stems from the fact that the author may not have composed the story out of whole cloth. It seems, rather, that existing letters available to the author may have been tailored to the purposes of the narrative, for if the writer had been free of pre-existing strictures, a fuller and more spontaneous story might have been expected.[1]

3. *The Acquisition of Building Materials according to Extra-Biblical Building Accounts*

The main building material used in Mesopotamia was the brick.[2] Large, important buildings such as royal palaces and temples were decorated with wood, stone and precious metals, which were imported, luxury commodities. Biblical authors were familiar with Mesopotamian building practices,[3] and in particular the use of brick and wood. According to the story of the Tower of Babel (Gen. 11.3), the planners said to one another, 'Come, let us make bricks and burn them hard'. Thus 'brick served them as stone, and bitumen served them as mortar'. The prophet Nahum chides the people of Nineveh, saying (Nah. 3.14): 'Draw water for siege, strengthen your forts;

---

1.   A complete biblical account of a commercial negotiation is to be found in the story of Genesis 23 about the purchase of the Cave of Machpelah. This story uses precise legal terminology, but the dependence on language taken from non-literary genres (such as contracts) does not remove the story from the category of a description of a commercial negotiation (cf. Melamed 1984). Note that whereas Abraham starts his negotiations by offering any price and Ephron starts off by asking for nothing, Solomon, Enmerkar and Wenamun start off by demanding everything and offering next to nothing.

2.   See *CAD* and *AHw, s.v. libittu* (brick) and *agurru* (baked/burnt brick); also cf. A. Salonen 1972 and Dunham 1982.

3.   See Speiser 1967a: 58-59, who is of the opinion that the relation between the biblical Tower of Babel story and the Mesopotamian ziqqurat is a literary one, one not based on the biblical author's personal knowledge of this peculiar feature of Mesopotamian architecture. According to M. Dahood (*RSP*, I, 246; II, 325-26), the appearance of the pair *lāḇan lěḇēnîm // bānâ* in the Tower of Babel story and in the Baal epic (*UT* 51 V 61-62) indicates a Canaanite background for the biblical story. This suggestion is surprising. On the expression *lāḇan lěḇēnîm*, see Held 1965: 277 n. 25.

tread the clay, trample the mud, grasp the brick mold!' Isaiah recalls
the cutting down of trees in the Lebanon by the kings of Mesopotamia.
In one place he mocks the king of 'Babylon' with this taunt (Isa. 14.8):
'Even pines rejoice at your fate, and cedars of Lebanon: "Now that
you have lain down, none shall come up to fell us"'. In a message to
Hezekiah, he complains about the king of Assyria (2 Kgs 19.23; Isa.
37.24): 'Through your envoys you have blasphemed my Lord.
Because you thought, "Thanks to my vast chariotry, it is I who have
claimed the highest mountains, to the remotest parts of the Lebanon,
and have cut down its loftiest cedars, its choicest cypresses, and have
reached its remotest lodge/highest peak, its densest forest"'. (Also cf.
Hab. 2.17, where the prophet both threatens the king of the
Chaldaeans and recalls one of his iniquities, saying: 'for the lawless-
ness against Lebanon shall cover you'.) These verses reflect
Mesopotamian reality and ideology as expressed in the royal inscriptions in general[1] and several building accounts in particular.

We will now analyze the passages from these inscriptions which
describe how wood was cut in the mountains of the west, and how
building materials—wood, stone and even bricks—were transported
to building sites. This survey will include only the texts which mention the *manner* in which the wood and stone were acquired, and will
not list the dozens of texts which mention the fact that wood and stone
were used, or even that the wood and stone originated in foreign
lands. Nothing at all will be said about the molding of bricks.[2]

Mesopotamian Sources
The most ancient and detailed descriptions of transporting wood and
stone for building projects are found in the inscriptions of Gudea of
Lagash.[3] According to Cylinder A col. XV, the people of Magan and

1. See Machinist 1983a.
2. The Mesopotamian, Egyptian and post-biblical Hebrew sources are mentioned in part by Montgomery and Gehman 1951: 134-36, 151-52). Other lists or
collections of sources are found in various places such as Aharoni 1962 (*s.v.
Lebanon, EM*); Elat 1977: 58-68; Brown 1969: 175ff. The most detailed and
penetrating survey is that of Elat, and I can add little to the sources he already cites.
Even so, the discussion presented here is of a somewhat different nature than Elat's,
and my conclusions about the meaning of the royal pilgrimage to the mountains are
not entirely identical with his.
3. Sauren (1977) doubts the historical reliability of these descriptions. His

Meluhha (Elam and Susa) brought him, on their shoulders[1] wood
from the mountains (ll. 6-10). Copper and wood were brought from
Tilmun (ll. 11-18). Concerning Gudea himself, the text states:[2]

> To the cedar mountain, which a man does not enter,[3] Gudea, for the lord
> Ningirsu, directed his step. Its cedars he cut with great axes. . . like giant
> snakes which float upon the water, from the cedar mountain, rafts of
> cedars, from the cypress mountain rafts of cypress, from the juniper
> mountain rafts of juniper, great pines, *tu-lu-bu-um* wood, *e-ra-lum* wood
> float in great rafts, [Gudea, for the lord Ningirsu directed to the exalted
> quay of Ka-sur-ra.]

Following immediately afterwards is a similar description of quarrying stone and shipping it to Lagash. Obviously, stone cannot be made
into rafts to be floated on the water, so the text speaks instead of
shipping by boat (col. xvi 3-12):

> To the stone mountain which a man does not enter, Gudea, for the lord
> Ningirsu set his foot. Its great stones he made into blocks. In *ḫa-sig-na*
> boats and *na-lu-a* boats, bitumen and pitch and gypsum from the moun-
> tains of Madga like grain boats coming from the fields, Gudea, for the
> lord Ningirsu, directed.

The text then reports the mining of copper, gold and silver. Statue B[4]
presents an even more detailed description of the building materials
and their places of origin. It specifies the lengths of the logs which
were floated to Lagash, and even records the function of each type of

suggestion is possible, but not for the reasons he gives, for he is of the opinion that
the Gudea Cylinders were actually the libretto of an annually performed cultic drama
(see our remarks in Chapter 1). For an older text, see the inscription of En-anna-tum
I (Steibel 1982: 183 En I = Sollberger, Kupper, *IRSA*, p. 62 IC6a 2.2): 'White
cedar he brought out for him (Ningirsu) from the mountain (or: from the enemy
land). His house he made luxurious, and placed white cedar in its walls.' See also
Steibel 1982: 228 Entemena 27 = *IRSA* I C7f and Leemans 1960: 10-12.

 1.   The passage probably refers to shipboard transportation. See Falkenstein
1966: 47 n. 3.
 2.   Cylinder A col. XV l. 19–col. XVI l. 2 = A.L. Oppenheim, *ANET*, 268 =
Jacobsen 1987: 407.
 3.   Compare the description of Solomon's and Hiram's fleet which brought trees
and stones from distant lands, where we read: 'Such a quantity of almug wood has
never arrived or been seen to this day' (1 Kgs 10.11-13). See also Luckenbill 1924:
107 ll. 49-53, 54-64 (Sennacherib).
 4.   See Lambert and Tourney 1951.

wood and stone in the building. But this time it is not said that Gudea 'directed his step' (*gir mu-na-ni-gar*) to the mountains, but, rather, that Ningirsu 'opened the way for him' (*gir-bi gál-mu-na-kid*, Statue B col. V 27), which Oppenheim interpreted 'opened up for him (all) the (trade) routes'.[1] Nor does the statue mention that Gudea went to a place to which no one had gone before.

A similar account of bringing stones from the quarry is found in an Old Babylonian copy of an inscription of Manistushu, King of Akkad (Hirsch 1963: 70 l. 58]):[2]

> From the mountains across the Lower Sea
> he brought their black stones
> and loaded them on ships
> and at the quay of Agade he tied them (the ships) up.

Anam tells that he built a *gipar* (a high priestess's residence or a place for performing the sacred marriage rite) for Ishtar, and claims to have made immense doors of cedar and *elammaku* wood 'brought from the mountains' (Kärki 1983: Anam 4 ll. 22-24).

Looking once again at the passages cited from the Gudea cylinders (note also all of Cyl. A xv–xvi), we find that they contain three ideas (1) building materials flow into Lagash from the ends of the earth; (2) Gudea goes ('directs his step') to the sources of the wood and stone; (3) building materials are brought to Lagash by water transportation. These three ideas recur time and again in the later royal inscriptions, sometimes individually, and sometimes in combination with each other.

Foreign peoples bring building materials from the ends of the earth. The clearest expression of this idea is found in a text dating from the twilight of Mesopotamian civilization. Darius, king of Persia, built a new palace in Susa, and in honor of this great undertaking, he composed a trilingual (Persian, Elamite and Akkadian) inscription[3] which describes several aspects of the building project. Following the custom

1.   *ANET*, 269. See Falkenstein 1966: 46 n. 2.

2.   See also concerning Naram-Sin (Thureau-Dangin 1907: 166b = Hirsch 1963: 17.

3.   See Koenig 1930. A translation of the Persian version may be found in Kent 1950: 143. This translation is also cited by Girshman 1961: 165-66. I have based my discussion on the Akkadian version and on Kent's translation of the Persian.

of Mesopotamian royal inscriptions, this text contains a historical preamble followed by a building account. The building account proper starts with the declaration, 'This is the palace which I built in Susa' (l. 16). Immediately thereafter, the king proclaims, 'from far away the decorations (for the palace) were brought', and in so doing he presents one of the main ideas of the standard building stories. In a manner similar to the custom of the Assyrian building accounts, Darius describes the laying of the palace's foundations on bedrock and specifies the dimensions of the building's area (ll. 17-20). But the main part of Darius' building story is a detailed enumeration of all the building materials and the way they were brought to Susa, as well as a list of the many foreigners who performed the various types of work. Heading the list is the molding of bricks by the 'Akkadians'. Despite the rather mundane nature of this work, it is mentioned first because it is, nonetheless, the most important. Second in the list are the cedars from the Lebanon. Darius says: 'The cedars of which this (building) is made are brought from a mountain whose name is Lebanon. Hordes from across the river carried them to Babylon, and from Babylon the Karshu and the Ionians/Greeks brought them to Susa' (ll. 21-24). The text goes on to mention other varieties of wood. Next after the wood come gold and precious stones, and each time these are mentioned Darius states that they were brought from their place of origin prepared for use at the building site (*ša aganna ipšu*). The text then enumerates silver, ebony wood, ivory and wooden pillars. Following this catalogue of materials, he mentions the workmen and their lands of origin. The inscription concludes with a short prayer on behalf of the king.

Darius's inscription is reminiscent of the passage from Gudea mentioned above, and the two of them together bring to mind various biblical passages which describe the flow of building materials and gifts from the ends of the earth into Jerusalem. Especially prominent are Isaiah 60, 1 Kgs 10.24-25 and Hag. 2.7. I may also mention the passage in the Baal Epic .[1] On the literary level, it is worth noting that

---

1.   *UT* 51 VI 18-21. For the flow into the center, see also the Lugalannemundu pseudepigraph in which the kings of the four corners of the earth celebrate the dedication of Enamzu. This idea finds expression in several accounts of palace and temple dedication festivities (see Liverani 1973). The passage from the Baal epic will be discussed in greater detail at the end of this chapter.

the repetition of the words 'they brought/were brought' (*ittašû/našû* in every sentence achieves the same effect as the repetition of the word *hēbî'û*, 'they brought', in the account of collecting materials for building the Tabernacle (Exod. 35.21-29). Both texts lead readers to feel as if an unending caravan of contributors and tribute bearers is passing before them.

The similarity between the Gudea passage and the Darius passage masks the fact that they actually represent quite divergent literary, historical and political realities. Gudea, to be sure, ruled more than his own city. As a matter of fact, he built temples in Ur, Nippur, Adab, Uruk and Badtibira, and was in a sense the heir of the great Akkadian empire. In addition, he undertook campaigns against Anshan and Elam. Nonetheless, he does not seem to have been much of a conqueror or warrior.[1] In contrast, Darius ruled the entire Persian empire, which embraced much of the world. It is generally assumed that the merchandise which streamed into Gudea's Lagash was purchased, whereas the building materials brought to Darius were the proceeds of tax, tribute or booty. Neither passage mentions or alludes to actual conquest or subjugation, but neither do they mention trade and commerce. Both texts conceal the 'facts' and by so doing they have drawn identical pictures of a world which universally recognizes the centrality of the king and the centrality of the building which he is constructing; accordingly, the building materials are portrayed as presents sent by free will.[2]

Quite a different picture is painted by the Assyrian and neo-Babylonian building accounts. These texts frequently relate that the kings of foreign lands (especially to the west of Mesopotamia) brought wood to the kings of Mesopotamia, but they also state explicitly that these kings were subjects, conquered by the king of Assyria (or Babylon). Such statements are found in the inscriptions of Tiglath-pileser III, Sennacherib, Esarhaddon, Assurbanipal and Nebuchadnezzar.[3]

---

1. Gudea's campaigns may have been the events inspiring the composition of *Lugal-e* and *An-gim dim-ma*. See Hallo 1974: 184; 1981: 255. For Gudea's military and trade activities and the extent of his domination see Falkenstein 1971 and Bottero 1965: 120-25.

2. For the roots of this custom, see Edzard 1960 and Liverani 1973.

3.   Tiglath-pileser III   II R 67 1. 73 = *ARAB*, I §804
        Sennacherib   Luckenbill 1924: 95 ll. 71-72; p. 132 ll. 68-71.
        Esarhaddon   Borger 1956: 60 epis. 27.54

For example, Sennacherib reports in connection with building the back wing of his palace at Nineveh, the *bīt kutalli* (Luckenbill 1924: 132, ll. 68-71):

> By the mighty strength
> of the gods, my lords,
> all the kings of the Amorites
> whom I subdued at my feet
> I commanded,
> and great beams of cedar
> they cut down in the Amanus,
> they brought them to Nineveh
> and I stretched them over the them (the palaces).

The inscriptions of Tiglath-pileser III, Sennacherib and Darius all deal with the building of various palaces, while the inscriptions of Gudea, Assurbanipal and Nebuchadnezzar describe the building of temples: Eninnu in Lagash, Eḫulḫul in Harran and Etemenanki in Babylon. From this it may be learned that wood from the forests of the west was considered suitable for both sacred and secular buildings. We will return to this matter later.

The king goes to the forests to cut down trees. This motif is known from the Bible (2 Kgs 19.23 = Isa. 37.24; 14.8) as well as from the Gilgamesh epic (Tablet III, see *ANET*, 79ff.). These sources, however, make no explicit connection between the king's journey to the Lebanon to fell trees and any particular building activity. Although it is hard to assume that the kings would have cut down trees and then just left them there in the forest, the ultimate disposal of the timber is irrelevant to the literary context. As for the royal inscriptions, the felling of trees is on occasion mentioned in connection with their use in building projects, i.e. within the building accounts themselves. But in most instances this motif appears within the context of the kings' military campaigns. As a result, it appears in royal inscriptions which are not building inscriptions, but rather memorial inscriptions inscribed and erected within the forests themselves. Nonetheless, even

Assurbanipal   Streck 1916: 170 l. 45.48
Nebuchadnezzar   Langdon 1912: 146 *Nebuchadnezzar* no. 17 III 2-18.
Note also the Agum-kakrime inscription (Unger 1970: 279 col. IV).

in such contexts there are frequent indications that the trees cut down have been utilized in fact for building projects.

One of the oldest and fullest descriptions of a royal journey to the mountains appears in the great foundation inscription of Yahdun-lim, king of Mari. The inscription was written in honor of building the Shamash temple Egirzalanki, and this project is described briefly in the building account concluding the text. However, in the long historical introduction making up most of the text, we read (Dossin 1955: 13 ll. 38ff.):[1]

> And whereas since days of old (since) the god built the city of Mari,[2] a king who sat (enthroned) at Mari had not reached the (Mediterranean) Sea, and had not reached the cedar forests and the boxwood forests, the great mountains, and had not cut down their trees, (now) Yahdun-lim, son of Yagid-lim, the mighty king, the wild ox among the kings, with power and strength marched to the shore of the sea, and sacrificed sacrifices to the sea (as befits) his royal splendour, and his army washed in the water of the Sea. To the mountains of cedar and the mountain of boxwood, the great mountains, he entered, and boxwood, cedar, *taskarinnum*, juniper, and *elamakku* wood—these woods, he cut down. He prepared a commemorative monument, established his name and proclaimed his might.

This inscription does not mention how Yahdun-lim disposed of the many trees he cut down, but since it was composed in celebration of building the Shamash temple, it would certainly not be out of place to conjecture that the wood was shipped off or carried away to Mari where it was incorporated into the new temple. By emphasizing that no former king of Mari had reached the west and cut down trees, the author is using precise language by which he on the one hand preserves historical accuracy, and on the other hand follows the demands of a literary topos. Yahdun-lim is the first king of Mari who has performed such a notable deed, but he knows full well that he has been preceded by other kings from other cities.

The account includes several components: (1) a journey to the

---

1.   Translation in *ANET*, 556-57 and *IRSA*, 245-49 IV F6b. For the journey to the Mediterranean, see Malamat 1965; 1987: 186 and 1992: 214. For individual passages, note Machinist 1988, *passim*. Note also a new inscription of Šar-kali-šarri (Frayne 1982), which tells how a king reached the source of the Tigris and Euphrates and they (?) cut down (*ib-tu-qu*) cedars in the Amanus for some part (*ba-qí -iš*) of the temple of Inanna.

2.   See Appendix 6.

Mediterranean; (2) sacrifices to the sea; (3) purification of the army in the sea; (4) ascent to the mountains; (5) the felling of trees; (6) the setting up of monuments. These elements appear sometimes all together, and sometimes individually in similar descriptions contained in inscriptions of Tukulti-Ninurta I, Tiglath-pileser I, Assurnasirpal II, Shalmanesar III, Adad-nerari III and Nebuchadnezzar. Brief allusions to royal ascents to the mountains to cut down trees are found in inscriptions of Esarhaddon and Nabonidus,[1] but these inscriptions do not contain detailed reports as found here.

Utilization of the wood. Since several forests provided wood for Mesopotamian building projects, and since wood could be acquired in various ways, the question arises whether there is any correlation between any specific source of wood or means of acquiring wood and any specific type of building. We have already seen above that wood brought from the west by foreign subject kings was used at times for temples and at other times for secular buildings. Examination of the sources reveals, so it seems, that wood cut down by the kings themselves was also seen as fit to be used in both sacred and profane buildings.

1.   See also Malamat 1965. The sources are as follows:
Tukulti Ninurta, Weidner 1959: 3 ll. 12-20.
Tiglath-pileser I, Weidner 1957–58: 343 ll. 24-30: p. 352 ll. 59-76; Millard 1970, pl. xxxiv no. 122630 ll. 9'-10'; *KAH*, II, 67 = Grayson, *ARI*, II, 110.
Assurnasirpal II, King, *AKA*, 372 III 84-92; p. 170.2-9; Thompson and Hamilton 1932: 109 ll. 28-30. E. Ebeling, *LKA* 64, an unedited prayer on behalf of Assurnasirpal associated with dedicating booty from his western campaign, mentions ascents to the Hamanu mountains (obv. 19) and sacrifices, perhaps to the Sea (ll. 21-22 broken). The inscription concludes with broken references to the king carrying beams from the Hamanu mountains (rev. 7) and perhaps dedicating them to the temples of Assur (rev. 8), Sin (?) and Shamash (rev. 8-10).
Shalmaneser III, Michel 1947–52: 12 ll. 1-7 (1st campaign): p. 15 l. 3 (1st year); p. 458 ll. 42-45 (1st year); 1954–59a, p. 28 ll. 23-30 (1st year); p. 144 ll. 26-31 (1st year): p. 38 ll. 37-41 (17th year); p. 152 ll. 96-97 (17th year) and see Michel 1954–59b to the 1st and 17th years. See now also Grayson 1991b.
Adad-nerari III, Page 1968: 141 (= Tadmor 1973: 142-43).
Esarhaddon, Borger 1956: 87 epis. 57 ll. 21-23.
Nebuchadnezzar, Langdon 1912: p. 94 *Nebuchadnezzar* no. 9 III 36-37; p. 126 no. 15 III 21-32; p. 152 no. 19. A iv 4-9; p. 158 A vi 16-23; p. 174 IX 13; p. 194 no. 27A II 4-8; p. 174 no. 19 IX 13; Zablocka and Berger 1969: 123 ll. 10-13.
Nabonidus, Weld–Blundell Cylinder (Langdon 1923: I, 35 II 59–III 15).

There are kings—Yahdun-lim and Shalmanesar III in particular—who do not specify how they utilized the trees which they personally cut down. But most of the kings state explicitly that they used wood which they cut personally for building temples— thus in the texts of Tiglath-pileser I, Assurnasirpal II, Adadnerari III, Esarhaddon, Nebuchadnezzar and Nabonidus. However, even among these kings, there are those who used such wood not only for temples, but in other projects as well. Tukulti-Ninurta I even says that the wood which he brought from the mountains of Mehru was incorporated in his palace, making no reference to any use in temples.

Even so, despite an appearance of arbitrariness, there seems to be a discernible pattern in the exploitation of wood of varying origins. As already noted, even though it is not stated in so many words, it is reasonable to suggest that Yahdun-lim utilized the wood he cut in the Shamash temple mentioned in his inscription. Shalmanesar III also does not claim to have built temples with the trees he cut down, but he does mention in the account of his seventeenth year that he sent the trees to Assur. Since his political capital was Kalhu, it may be plausibly surmised that the trees were shipped to Assur to be used in temples in the old capital, still venerated as the religious center of Assyria. As for Tukulti-Ninurta I, the information provided by the text must be carefully examined. According to this text, the king made a trip to the mountains but the trees were felled not by him but by the troops of the land of Quti which he had conquered. For this reason, the description should be placed in the first group and not in the second. Finally, we find that Tiglath-pileser I and Nebuchadnezzar, who used trees from the west which they cut down personally in both palaces and temples, hint at a certain difference between the holy building and the secular building. Tiglath-pileser, in describing the *bīt šaḫūri*, says (Weidner 1957–58: 352 l. 59 = Grayson, *ARI*, II, §102):

> With cedars and beams which at the command of Assur and Anu, the great gods, my lords, I had gone to the mountains of the Lebanon, cut down and carried off beautiful beams—the temple of Anu and Adad, the great gods, my lords, I established. With the remaining cedar (*ina šītet erēni*), that *bīt šaḫūri*, from foundation to parapet I built. . .that palace, with cedar wood and oak wood I built, I completed, I made magnificent, I made appropriate.

In describing the construction of a boxwood leisure palace (*ekal* GIŠ. TÚG *ana multa'it bēlūtīja*),[1] he says (Weidner 1957–58: 352 l. 72 = Grayson, *ARI*, II, §104):

> and with *taskarinnu* wood which together with beams of cedar (*ša ištu gušūrē ša erēni*) I had cut down and carried off, alongside that cedar palace, I built a boxwood palace for my lordly leisure...from its foundations to its parapets I built, I completed (it).

These two passages mention the use of wood imported from the west. We should note the fact that the campaign to the west is portrayed by the scribe as one carried out on divine command (*ina siqir Aššur u Anim ilāni rabûti*—Assur is the god of the empire and chief god, and Anu is the god of the temple involved) with the purpose of cutting down cedars to be used in the Anu-Adad temple. The other fruits of this campaign are to be seen as secondary by-products of this primary goal. The first passage cited stresses that the cedars used in the *bīt šahūri* were 'the remaining cedars' (*šītet erēni*). The second paragraph emphasizes that the *taskarinnu* wood was imported from the mountains 'along with' the cedars, and is thereby somewhat of an afterthought, the importing of cedars (for the temple) being the true purpose of the mission. Nebuchadnezzar emphasizes that he cut down trees with his very own pure hands, and proclaims in a number of his inscriptions that he utilized the wood in the temples Esagila and Ezida as well as in his palace. This would make it seem that the wood cut by the king was used equally in all sorts of building. However, one inscription contains a slightly different version of the events (Langdon 1912: 126 *Nebuchadnezzar* no. 15 col. II ll. 21-26):

> The first/best of my cedars (*rēšāti erēnīja*)
> which I brought from the Lebanon,
> the holy forest,
> for roofing Ekua
> the temple of the god of his lord-ship
> I sought out (*ašte'ma* selected).

'The first fruits of the cedars' (*rēšāti erēnīja*) is a cultic term, *rēšāti* being cognate and semantically equivalent to Hebrew *rē'šît*.[2]

---

1. For the reading *ekal taskarinni*, see Lackenbacher 1982: 44 and *CAD* M II 192. Weidner and Grayson read *ekal kakkē*, 'weapons palace'.

2. See Postgate 1983: 155-59 for *rēšēti*, as a term for a temple loan, and for comparison with Hebrew *rē'šît*. Also see Fales 1984: 66-71 for *rēšēti* as first fruits.

Nebuchadnezzar is saying that a 'first fruit offering' from the cedars was dedicated to a certain temple. The verb *še'û,* 'select, chose, pick out' indicates that the wood used was not necessarily the first to arrive, but was the best.

From this survey we can surmise that the kings of Assyria and Babylon distinguished between wood which their own woodcutters had felled and wood which was cut for them by other, subject kings. Both types of wood were deemed appropriate for use in both palaces and temples, that is, in building of any sort. But wood which the king cut himself was to be used first in temples, and only after its 'desacralization' by means of such sacred use was it permitted to be put to other purposes. This is in keeping with the religious and ritual nature of the royal pilgrimage-campaigns to the west, as indicated also by the sacrifices and ablutions performed in the course of these campaigns.

Transportation of building materials. The transporting of building material by floating it on water was a regular practice, mentioned not only in royal inscriptions, but in letters and administrative documents as well.[1] Even so, the court scribes and artists considered it a great feat, worthy of mention when glorifying their patron sovereigns.

Sargon, king of Assyria, does not mention water transportation of wood for the building of Dur-Sharrukin in his inscriptions, but it is described in his palace reliefs. These pictures show boats pulling beams of wood which are tied together.[2]

Sennacherib, in the account of building his new palace, reports what previous kings have done.[3] They have quarried out great statues in the

1.   See above and also Elat 1977: 58-68.
2.   See Olmstead 1923: illus. 108; *ANEP*, illus. 107; Orthmann 1975: 223; Parpola 1987: 53-59 fig. 17a-20d and the discussion of the Sargonide reliefs in Linder 1986.
3.   According to Luckenbill (1924: 104 n. 1), the incident described here was from the time of Sennacherib himself, when building the palace at Nineveh. From his comment and translation, it seems as if the men who built the ships were the ones who constructed the palace. However, the entire incident is to be related to the time of the previous kings. The pronominal suffix *-šun,* 'their' in the word *mātīšun* ('their land') in l. 69, is anteceded by *šarrāni ālikūt mahrî abēja,* 'the previous kings, my ancestors', in l. 61. Similarly, the entire passage from ll. 34 to 47 describes the dilapidated condition of the previous palace (Nineveh had a long history and Sennacherib

quarries of Tastiate[1] and transported them to Nineveh in ships made of wood from the forests (Luckenbill 1924: 104-105 col. V 61-78).

Nabopolassar, king of Babylon, in his description of restoring Etemenanki, makes no reference to the felling of trees, but in his account of molding bricks describes how he shipped them by water (Wetzel and Weissbach 1938: 42 = Langdon 1912: 60 *Nabopolassar* no. 1 col. II 2-17):

> Upon numerous troops
> I imposed my land's corvée,
> I had them mold bricks without number,
> I had them strike baked brick.
> Like countless raindrops
> like a mighty river-tide
> bitumen and pitch
> I made the Arahtu canal carry.

Nebuchadnezzar, in his Wadi-Brissa inscription, reports that he floated cedars of Lebanon down the Arahtu canal as if they were reeds carried by the river (Langdon 1912: 174 *Nebuchadnezzar* no. 19 col. IX 13ff. = *ANET*, 307).

Finally we should mention the remarks in the inscriptions of Sennacherib and Esarhaddon about dragging colossal statues from the quarries to the building sites. Sennacherib (Luckenbill 1924: 107 ll. 45-75) reports that the gods Assur and Ishtar (the god of the empire and the goddess of the city Nineveh) revealed to him how to exploit the ancient forests growing in the mountains of Sirara (ll. 45-53) and also showed him the marble quarries around Nineveh, from which he brought the statues to his new capital (ll. 54-75). According to the description, it seems that the statues were actually sculpted in the quarries and brought to Nineveh in their completed state. This is borne out by the palace reliefs which clearly show the workmen dragging not a block of stone but a statue.[2] This event is reported as well in the short epitaphs inscribed on the statues themselves

was not the first to build a palace there), and only in ll. 48-51 does the king tell of his own decision to build the palace anew.

1. Note Parpola 1987: 96 no. 120 for reference to Tastiate in a highly broken letter to Sargon. Parpola entitles this fragment 'On Bull Colossi in Tastiate'.

2. See Orthmann 1975 n. 234a, b.

(Luckenbill 1924: 126-27).[1] Esarhaddon too, in describing the preparations for building his armory in Nineveh, relates that the kings of the lands of the west who cut down and dragged trees from the mountains of Sirara and Lebanon also hauled to him various types of statues of all sorts of stone (Borger 1956: 61 epis. 21 col. V 77–VI 1):

> Giant bull statues of red stone,
> protective genies, bull statues,
> stone slabs, flagstones
> of red. . . stone [further types of stone]
> from the depths of the mountains
> where they are created
> for the requirement of my palace
> with great difficulty and trouble
> to Nineveh, my lordly city,
> I caused (them) to drag.

The pictures and these inscriptions may, perhaps, provide a key to a better understanding of 1 Kgs 6.7: 'When the House was built, only finished stones, cut at the quarry were used, so that no hammer or ax or any iron tool was heard in the House while it was being built'. Just as the Assyrian reliefs and texts depict complete statues being brought from the quarries, and not simply raw, undressed stone, it is possible that the biblical verse means to state nothing more than the fact that the building stone was dressed in the quarry, and there was no need to do anything more to it at the building site (also 1 Kgs 7.46, which informs us that the bronze vessels were cast 'in earthen molds, in the plain of the Jordan between Succoth and Zarethan').

Sennacherib's inscription boasts about new natural resources which were either unknown or unexploited previously. He claims to be the first to have discovered and utilized them. By so claiming he is developing in his own way the motif of the king being the first to do something, as noticed in the inscriptions of Gudea, Yahdun-Lim and Nebuchadnezzar (Wadi-Brissa inscription, Langdon 1912: 174 *Nebuchadnezzar* no. 19 col. IX 33). It is possible that this idea is

---

1.   See the reliefs of Sargon which show men dragging a colossal statue (Olmstead 1923: illus. 129; *ANEP*, illus. 107; Reich 1979: 11). See also Alkim 1968: 219-20 pl. 154 for a picture of a quarry and 'workroom' for making statues at Yesmak from the late 2nd millennium or early 1st millennium BCE. At this site were found partially completed statues which were destined to be marketed in various cities (I am grateful to Dr A. Kempinski for calling this find to my attention).

expressed in the biblical account of Solomon's reign in 1 Kgs 10.11-12, where we read: 'Moreover, Hiram's fleet, which carried gold from Ophir, brought in from Ophir a huge quantity of *'almûg* wood...Such a quantity of *'almûg* wood had never arrived or been seen to this day' (and see 2 Chron. 9.10-11).

Ugaritic Literature
The Baal Epic. Acquisition of building materials for constructing Baal's palace is mentioned in two places. One passage relates that Athirat (accompanied by Anat) visited Ilu in order to attain his consent that Baal should build himself a palace. After some encouragement from his spouse Athirat, Ilu agrees to the request, and Athirat informs Anat of his agreement as follows (*UT* 51 V 74-81, 91-102):

> Let it be said to Mighty Baal
> Call *ḥrn* into your house
> *'dbt* into your palace!
> May the mountains bring you much silver,
> the hills, precious gold.
> May they bring you the costliest of stones (?).
> And build a house of silver and gold
> a house of pure lapis-lazuli.

This passage is not free of linguistic difficulties, the words *ḥrn* // *'dbt* proving especially enigmatic. H.L. Ginsberg translated them as 'weeds and herbs', leaving the passage to mean that Il has given a command to demolish and abandon an older house in order to rebuild a new one.[1] M. Pope accepted this translation but explained that the weeds and herbs are to be tinder for the fire which will burn and out of which the new palace will spring.[2] Ginsberg and Pope notwithstanding, this translation has not been widely accepted and alternate renditions have been suggested such as 'caravans and companies of traders' (and workers),[3] 'caravans and building materials',[4] 'caravans and furnishings',[5] 'workers and builders',[6] or 'building materials'.[7] I am inclined

1. H.L. Ginsberg in *ANET*, 133 and see also Ginsberg 1936: 31.
2. Pope 1955: 100-101.
3. Albright 1934: 124 nn. 119, 120; Driver 1956: 97; Gaster 1966: 118, 185, 186; Cassuto 1975: 147.
4. Gibson 1977: 61.
5. Gordon 1977: 95.
6. Bernhardt in Beyerlin 1978: 209.

to think that this passage speaks about caravans bringing building materials from the mountains, in which case it resembles the passages cited above from inscriptions of Gudea, Darius and Isaiah 60.[1] The text may refer to building materials which could be acquired through commercial means and we should translate 'caravans and merchandise'. The term *ḥrn* is to be associated with Akkadian *ḫarānu*, while *'ḏbt* is related to Hebrew *'izzābôn* found numerous times in Ezekiel 28, and perhaps Akkadian *ezēbu*, both terms from the field of trade and commerce. The word *'ḏbt* probably means 'merchandise delivered', namely, that which is left by the merchant or caravan (cf. Koehler and Baumgartner 1983 *s.v. 'izzābôn*).

The importing of wood from the Lebanon is mentioned in *UT* 51 VI 18-21, where we read:

> y[tl]k(?). llbnn. w'sh
> l[š]ryn. mḥmd. arzh
> h[l]bnn. w'sh
> šryn. mḥmd. arzh

This passage (in which all the verbs are unfortunately broken off)[2] is difficult to interpret, but it is clear that it speaks of bringing cedars from the Lebanon and Sirion mountains, and the passage appears right before the description of the building of the palace by burning the silver and gold. The use of cedars in the construction of the palace is mentioned also by Athirat, who says (*UT* 51 V 72-73):

> A house of cedars he will complete
> Lo, a house of bricks he will erect.

Egyptian Literature

A survey of several collections of translated Egyptian texts yields a number of passages mentioning wood brought from the Lebanon in order to make ritual boats for the gods (compare Shulgi R which tells of a divine boat made out of cedars cut by the king in Lebanon). The

---

7. Tsevat 1978: 153.
1. See Waldman 1981 and Paul 1968; Lipiński 1973.
2. All scholars restore l. 18 as we have done here. However, opinions are divided about v. 20. G.R. Driver restored *h[lk]*, but this suggestion was opposed by Cassuto who proposes *h[pl]*. Collation (see *KTU*) shows that the line is to be read *hn*[.l]*, and Gordon translated accordingly 'Behold. . . ' However, the context demands some verb which will describe either bringing trees or cutting them down.

Wenamun journey, to which much attention was given above, was for just such a purpose. This account may be compared with a fragmentary papyrus of an official of Thutmosis III (15th c.) in which he states (*ANET*, 243) that he entered the forest, paid for the wood,[1] took beams sixty cubits in length, brought them down from Lebanon and returned to Egypt by sea.[2] An inscription of Amenhotep III reports (Lichtheim 1980: 451; *ANET*, 375):

> I made another monument to my father Amon-re. . . by making for him the great boat of the Nile (named) 'Amon-Re of the strong forehead' out of new pine wood which my royal majesty cut down in the countries of the land of the god and dragged from the mountains of Retinu by the great ones of all the foreign lands.

This passage is reminiscent of the Mesopotamian texts which describe how the king personally cut down trees in the Lebanon and then had them shipped home by foreign kings. Thutankhamen reports that he built boats for the gods out of new cedar from the land of Nagu (*ANET*, 252). From the time of Merineri, a Pharaoh of the sixth dynasty, comes an inscription of Oni, the governor of Upper Egypt, which describes the governor's journey to Elephantine and Hat-neb to bring back stones with which to make furnishings and decorations for the pyramid of the queen (?) (Breasted 1906: 319-24). The text not only specifies the types of stone and furnishings, but also the dimensions of the cargo ships which were prepared for the voyage.

4. *Conclusions*

The above survey demonstrates the important function which trees, especially from the Lebanon and the mountains of the west, played in both secular and religious building throughout the ancient Near East.[3] Certain kings boast of their personal role in acquiring such trees, and

---

1. See *ANET*, 243 n. 1. The payment is described in the text as presents to the goddess, lady of the mountain.

2. See Ahituv 1970: 319.

3. See Elat 1977, concerning the sanctity of the Lebanon as a factor in their importance as a source of wood for building materials. Note that in evaluating the Mesopotamian material, we should be aware of the probability that the location of the holy cedar forests has changed and is not the same in later texts as it is in earlier ones. On this aspect, see for instance Tigay 1982: 78ff., and most recently Hansman 1986.

in particular trees used in temples. They also boast about wood for their own building projects being provided by foreign kings. Nautical transportation of building materials, whether aboard boats or made into rafts, in spite of being a mundane, day-to-day activity, was deemed impressive enough to mention in texts meant to praise noteworthy activities of the monarchs, and it is mentioned in not a few royal inscriptions.

Solomon too was personally involved in acquiring wood from the forests of the Lebanon and having it provided by a foreign king, although he makes no claim to have gone to the forest and chopped the trees down with his own hatchet. In addition, the story in 1 Kings (and the parallel version in 2 Chronicles) refers to the maritime transportation of the wood. The element of domination over the forests of the Lebanon, so typical of much of the extra-biblical evidence, seems to be absent from the biblical account. But even this element may be implicit if credence is given to juxtaposition of events as found in the present form of the biblical narrative. Hiram is one of the kings who sends messengers and presents to Solomon upon hearing of his wisdom (1 Kgs 5.14-15, and see the Greek version of v. 14). Furthermore, comparison of the letters of the two kings revealed that Hiram, who blessed Solomon, may have been regarded as the inferior of the two kings. Not only this, but Solomon's initial demand that trees be sent him without charge may imply a Solomonic claim for sovereignty over the Lebanon.

It seems therefore that the the biblical passage and the extra-biblical royal inscriptions have much in common. Even so, there are several significant differences in substance and ideas as well as in literary formulation. The biblical account contains not the slightest hint of the military dimension characteristic of the extra-biblical sources. Solomon may wield influence over the Lebanon, as indicated by Hiram's gifts and blessing, but there is no indication of any conquest or subjugation of the Lebanon and its inhabitants. Furthermore, the presents sent by the 'kings of the nations' (following the Greek of 1 Kgs 5.14) do not include the wood, which Hiram sends Solomon at a price. Solomon is personally involved in acquiring the wood, but only as a trader, and not as a conquering king plundering at will or demanding tribute. Above all, there are no religious or ritual overtones to the acquisition of wood from the Lebanon, and Solomon does not go there on 'pilgrimage'. Nowhere is there the slightest hint of the sanctity of the forests. The Lebanon, for the biblical writer, is not a divine dwelling, as it is in Gilgamesh, nor a 'holy forest' as it is, for example, in Nebuchadnezzar's inscription. It may indeed have been so considered by the average ancient Israelite, but so far as the present account is concerned, it is little more than the local lumber yard.

On the literary plane, we have seen that the biblical author is influenced in most of what he writes by epistolary style. This style is totally absent from the extra-biblical building accounts including the Gudea cylinders, the Baal epic and the report of Thutmosis III's purchasing agent—i.e. texts describing building materials evidently acquired through trade. Admittedly, the two texts describing trade negotiations (*Enmerkar and the Lord of Aratta* and the *Journey of Wenamun*) mention letters—the Enmerkar tale even relates how letters were invented by the messenger in order to assist his overtaxed memory! But even in these compositions, the letter is not used as a literary vehicle for relating the events. 1 Kgs 5.15-26, which describes routine activity, has employed irregular literary means, and this is innovative and quite exceptional.

The exceptional characteristics of our story make it somewhat difficult to accept M. Noth's contention that the Deuteronomist invented his story *ex nihilo*, having nothing available but other passages preserved in the Bible, general contemporary experience, and common sense. All of these factors would not have brought him to formulate a passage such as the one before us in 1 Kgs 5. Quite to the contrary! Had the biblical author followed current literary practice, the results would have been quite different (see 2 Sam. 5.11-12).[1] One factor which could have influenced the author to compose such an

---

1.   All the previously mentioned Mesopotamian accounts of royal journeys to the mountains for cutting down trees are found in historical inscriptions, and they are to be taken, apparently, as simple historical facts. However, the incident related in tablets III to V of Gilgamesh is obviously a legend. From the use of this type of deed in a composition describing a hero's attempt to find immortality through all types of conventional and unconventional means, we may learn that the act of going into the cedar forest to fell trees was considered a heroic deed suitable to be performed by any king who wished to make a name for himself (note as well Wenamun's advice to Zakarbaal, mentioned above). Even an Israelite scribe who would want to compose a story with which to glorify Solomon could have depicted him as a king who went up to the mountains of Lebanon to cut down trees. The possibility that several of the Mesopotamian accounts are in fact fictitious has been suggested by Malamat (1965).

account may have been the utilization of already existing, authentic source material. If the author did not have access to the actual letters of Hiram and Solomon, he may at least have had reliable knowledge that such letters still existed or had existed. But I tend toward the view that he actually had access to the letters. My view is based on the unfavorable outcome of the negotiations, as explained above, as well as on the tension between the letters and the passages preceding (5.15) and following (5.24-32) them.

In summary, comparative analysis has revealed that Solomon's and Hiram's exchanges reflect the genre of letters in content, language, style and form. Contrastive analysis shows that this passage is highly divergent literarily both from other building accounts and from other accounts of commercial negotiations, despite the similarity in the actual activities described. From this there is room to conclude that the author of the building account, whether he was the Deuteronomist or some previous author, neither composed this passage out of thin air, nor did he work totally independently, in a literary vacuum. It is more likely that he incorporated into his composition at the appropriate place ready-made, existing texts relevant to the matter about which he was writing. Instead of composing a totally original account of how wood was acquired for building the temple, the author worked into his account the original commercial letters, making the adaptations needed for use in a narrative context.

Chapter 10

THE DESCRIPTIONS OF THE TEMPLE
AND ITS FURNISHINGS (1 KINGS 6–7)

The heart of the Temple building account is the long, detailed description of the temple itself (1 Kgs 6), the secular buildings (The Royal Palace, a house for Pharaoh's daughter, the courtyard, 1 Kgs 7.1-12) and the bronze (1 Kgs 7.13-47) and gold (1 Kgs 7.48-50) furnishings and cultic vessels which stood in the Temple. The 'appendices' to the building account found in 1 Kgs 9.15-19 include an additional list of buildings which Solomon built 'in Jerusalem and in Lebanon, and throughout the territory that he ruled'.

The details of these descriptions and the physical aspects of the buildings and implements described will not be discussed here. These important matters have been studied often and reconstruction of the shapes, sizes, materials and weights of the objects pictured is something which should be dealt with jointly by philologists, archaeologists and art historians. In this chapter I will accordingly limit my remarks to certain literary aspects of the descriptions, attempting to elucidate their literary form and origin with the help of comparison and contrast with several extra-biblical documents of various backgrounds.

1. *The Date Formulae*

At five different places in the building story there are verses which convey chronological information: at the beginning of the description of the temple (1 Kgs 6.1); at the end of the temple description and beginning of the description of the secular buildings (6.37, 38; 7.1); at the beginning (8.2) and at the end (8.65-66) of the record of the dedication ceremonies; and at the beginning of the 'appendix' to the story (9.10). All the problems which these verses arouse cannot be studied here, but it seems that a comparative and contrastive treatment of these verses may illuminate at least two issues: (a) the chronology of the building project; and (b) the situation and literary formulation of the verses.

It should be pointed out immediately that, by providing exact chronological information, the biblical story is at variance with most of the Mesopotamian building accounts. Of all the Mesopotamian building stories available, such information appears in only a very few, and for clearly definable purposes. Gudea states that Eninnu was dedicated during the first month, and that Ningirsu returned from Eridu on the third of the month (Cylinder B III 5-12). In the Sargon Cylinder inscription, we are told that the king molded bricks during the month of Simanu and founded his palace in the month of Abu.[1] Nabonidus states that he founded Ebabbar in Sippar 'in the month of Tashritu on a good day and a propitious month which the gods Shamash and Adad had revealed to him through extispicy' (Langdon 1912: 226 *Nabonidus* no. 1 II 60-61). But the vast majority of Mesopotamian building stories state at most that the kings founded (or dedicated) their buildings 'in a propitious month on a favorable day', or something similar. In light of this, we should understand as well the information given exceptionally by Gudea, Sargon and Nabonidus. By specifying the months in which they performed specific acts, these kings are only informing the reader that they did them at the appropriate time.[2] Admittedly, non-tendentious chronological information

---

1.　See the passage and translation in Ellis 1968: 175 no. 14.

2.　Propitious months suitable for building activities such as restoring palaces, making platforms for building houses, tearing down houses, replacing old houses with new ones, returning to a house, entering a house, entering a temple, restoring a temple, or restoring various types of cultic installations are prescribed by the menology *KAR* 177 edited by Labat 1939: 146-53 (and cf. also Langdon 1935: 49 and *iqqur-īpuš*, Labat 1965). The propitious days within these months are listed further on in the text (Labat 1939b: 163-67). See also the composition *iqqur-īpuš* §§1-53, for the expected consequences of undertaking these activities in the various months of the year. Cultic texts also indicate that building activities were undertaken on such months and days. See, for instance, Thureau-Dangin 1921: 34 ll. 1-2 (trans. A. Sachs in *ANET*, 339ff.): 'When the wall of the temple of Anu will collapse [for the purpose of tearing up the foundations of that temple], in a good month and on a propitious day, in the night. . . ' (and see also Thureau-Dangin 1921: 40 ll. 1-2, and other texts). The royal inscriptions themselves indicate that these instructions were actually carried out, the result being that the three types of texts—the menologies, the ritual texts and the royal inscriptions—are supplementary, describing the

appears only rarely. In an inscription of Arik-din-ili we find (Ebeling 1926: 50 ll. 42-47):[1] 'I laid its foundations in the eponymy of Berutu [. . .], son of Eriba-Ada, king of Assyria'.

An inscription of Antiochus Soter (*ANET*, 317) tells that he founded Ezida on the 20th of Addaru in the 43rd year of Seleucus. Another text (Clay 1915: 82-83 no. 52.16), dated to the 58th year of Seleucus, reports that a certain Anu-uballit rebuilt the Resh temple in Uruk and introduced Anu and Antu into it on the 8th of Nisannu.

a. *The chronology of the building project.* It was a custom in Mesopotamia to ascribe an important act to a king in his first year. This act was often the building of a temple—or, at least, the decision to found and build a temple.[2] This custom is attested in the inscriptions of Tukulti-Ninurta (Weidner 1959: 16 l.34; p. 17 l. 82; p. 20 l. 17); Tiglath-Pileser I (*AKA*, 96 l. 71); Esarhaddon (Borger 1956: 16 epis. 12 l.9); Assurbanipal (Streck 1916: 172 l. 51); Sîn-šar-iškun (Böhl 1936: 98 l. 16); and Nabonidus (Langdon 1912: 218 *Nabonidus* no. 1 I 16).[3]

Echoes of this tradition are heard in the Bible as well. Cyrus's declaration permitting the rebuilding of the Temple in Jerusalem is dated to his first year (Ezra 1.1; 5.13; 2 Chron. 36.22). Even building the Tabernacle was commanded and carried out in the first year following the Exodus (see Exod. 40.1, 17). The Chronicler ascribes the cultic reforms of both Hezekiah and Josiah to their respective first years (2 Chron. 29.3; cf. 34.3).[4] Solomon, to be sure, is reported to have built the temple in his fourth year, and not his first, which would lead one to assume that he did not act according to this custom.

same phenomenon from three different points of view (see now W. Horowitz 1991). To these three types of evidence we may add as well the official correspondence which tells about inquiries made in order to determine what days were suitable for building activities. See on this matter Parpola 1970: I, 7 no. 8 (= Waterman, *RCAE*, 673).

  1.   Chronological information of another sort is found in the surveys of buildings' histories found in the beginning of numerous Assyrian building stories. For the so-called 'Time Spans', see above Chapter 8 as well as Tadmor 1961: 69-71. An annalistic text of Nabonidus (W.G. Lambert 1968–69) relates that he built the Shamash temple, Ebabbar, in the month of Elul.

  2.   For this custom in Israel and Mesopotamia, see Cogan 1980; Tadmor 1981: 21-25; and Cogan 1985.

  3.   See Tadmor 1965.

  4.   See Cogan 1985.

Nonetheless, it is clear even from the Deuteronomic historiography that Solomon was co-regent with David (see 1 Kgs 2), and it is possible that the author assumes the period of co-regency to have lasted precisely (or typologically?) three years, and that Solomon started to build the temple during his first year as king in his own right.[1]

Solomon spent seven years building the Temple (6.38). This number should be compared with an event related in the Ugaritic Baal epic according to which Baal's palace rose by itself out of a fire which burned for seven days. The Tabernacle too was regarded as having been built over a period of seven months.[2] It seems that this information may therefore be somewhat stereotyped and typological rather than historically accurate. To the best of my knowledge, there are no attempts in Mesopotamian building stories to cast an entire building project into a seven-year, seven-month or seven-day mold, although certain individual events, such as the dedication of Eninnu by Gudea, lasted seven days. If so, the similarity between the Israelite stories and the Canannite account may indicate a West-Semitic 'iso-motif'.

Construction of the palace and other governmental, private and secular buildings lasted for thirteen years (1 Kgs 7.1). This information as well is probably artificial, most likely calculated by subtracting seven from twenty (cf. 9.10), with the result being that building occupied Solomon for half of his forty-year reign.

b. *The situation and formulation of the date sentences.* It is not impossible that 1 Kgs 6.1 is in fact a biblical substitute for the standard Mesopotamian formula 'in a propitious month on a suitable day'. In the Mesopotamian building accounts this formula often appears in close proximity to the beginning of the description of the building (component 3 in the traditional building account pattern),[3] and this is precisely where the first date sentence appears in the biblical story. Furthermore, the descriptions of the buildings sometimes start by stipulating the measurements of the building. It turns out that building descriptions in Mesopotamian accounts start with a combination of two elements—the first is the stylized date formula, and the second is

---

1. See, for instance, Yeivin 1965 (*s.v.* David, *EM*), col. 687.
2. See Josephus, *Ant.* 3.3.201 and cf. Shalit 1967: lxxxix n. 147b for Midrashim. See also Fisher 1963: 41 and cf. MacNeile's Exodus Commentary (1931: 155-57).
3. Cf. Chapter 1, section 5, above.

the statement of dimensions. So we find, for example, in Esarhaddon's inscription reporting the restoration of the *ekal māšarti* (Borger 1956: 51 VI 2):

> In a propitious month on a favorable day
> great palaces
> for my lordly residence
> I built upon it.
> A royal house, 125 great cubits long
> 31 great cubits wide
> I constructed.[1]

Despite this interesting correspondence, the similarity remains only partial. It is clear that the actual language of the biblical date sentences, and the fact that precise dates are given, have no significant parallels in the Mesopotamian building stories, and related material is to be sought elsewhere. Let us now examine the first date sentence and see if we can uncover the source of its content and phraseology (1 Kgs 6.1):

> *wayhî bišmônîm šānâ wĕ'arba' mē'ôt šānâ*
> *lĕṣē't bĕnê yiśrā'ēl mē'ereṣ miṣrayim*
> *baššānâ hārĕbî'ît behōdeš ziw hû' hahōdeš haššēnî*
> *limlōk šĕlōmōh 'al yiśrā'ēl*
> *wayyiben habbayit laYHWH.*

The words *hû' hahōdeš haššēnî* are certainly an explanatory gloss aimed at an audience who did not know the month name *ziw*, and they may be ignored in looking for the original form of this date sentence. But even after they are deleted, the verse remains difficult and confused. It is clear, however, that the confusing factor is the phrase *bĕhōdeš ziw*. We expect the year stipulation *baššānâ hārĕbî'ît* to be followed immediately by *limlōk šĕlōmōh*, and we must, for sake of clarity, reverse the order of these two elements and read *wayhî*. . . *bĕhōdeš ziw baššānâ hārĕbî'ît limlōk šĕlōmō 'al yiśrā'ēl wayyiben habbayit laYHWH.* The reversal of the sentence components may perhaps be explained as the result of imitating v. 37. There is certainly not a copying out of 6.37, as has been suggested, and the reconstructed verse stands on its own merit.

The phraseology itself is comparable with date sentences found in

---

1. See similar passages in Luckenbill 1924: 96 l. 76 (Sennacherib); Borger 1956: 3 V 27 (Esarhaddon).

several Phoenician votive and building inscriptions. It is well known that the month names *ziw*, *bul* and *hā'ēṭanîm*, which appear uniquely in the building story, are of Phoenician origin, and the use of the word *yeraḥ* for month may also be a Phoenicianism.[1] But it seems to me that the Phoenician influence is not limited to the realm of vocabulary, and these particular lexemes, but permeates the content and structure of the entire sentence, perhaps even extending into the following sentence.

This can be demonstrated by comparing 1 Kgs 6.1 in its reconstructed, syntactically unencumbered form with date sentences found in several Phoenician inscriptions:[2]

> *wayhî*
> *bišmônîm šānâ wĕ'arba' mĕ'ôt šānâ*
> *lĕṣē't bĕnê yiśrā'ēl mē'ereṣ miṣrayim*
> 1. *bĕhōdeš ziw*
> 2.. *baššānâ hārĕbî'ît*
> 3., 4.   *limlōk šĕlōmōh*
> 5. *'al yisrā'ēl*
> *wayyiben habbayit laYHWH.*

KAI 38:

> *mrq'. ḥrṣ 'z 'š ytn mlk mlkytn mlk kty w'dyl bn b'lrm l'ly*
> *lršp mkl b'dyl*
> 1. *byrḥ bl*
> 2. *b šnt 2*
> 3., 4. *lmlky*
> 5. *'l kty w'dyl.*

Both passages contain a date formula which includes in fixed order five components: (1) a month; (2) a year; (3) the verb *mlk* in the infinitive construct form; (4) the name of a king (or a possessive pronominal suffix with the king as antecedent); (5) the king's realm. The prepositions before elements 1, 2, 3, and 5 are identical: *b-, b, l-, 'l*. Nearly identical formulae are found in several additional inscriptions. In *KAI* 32, 33 and 41, all the components are present but instead of the preposition *'l* before the last element, the word *mlk*, king, appears in construct state. In *KAI* 40 the last element is missing. In *KAI* 43 the

1. See Avishur 1979: 142.
2. Jirku (1923: 153) compared this verse to the Eshmanazur inscription and the Babylonian Chronicle II 46 (Grayson 1975b).

last element is absent and the prepositions vary. In *KAI* 18 and 19 the first and last elements are lacking.

I will discuss below the possibility that the biblical statement dating the building of the Temple 480 years after the Exodus has its parallel in the Phoenician dating of events to the foundation of the city (*KAI* 18, 19, 40 and 43). The similarity between the biblical formula and the Phoenician inscriptions is not limited to the date sentence, but it extends over into the following verse, 1 Kgs 6.2 where we read: *wĕhabbayit 'ăšer bānâ hammelek šĕlōmōh laYHWH...* Similar words appear in the inscriptions mentioned above:

KAI 38 *mrq' ḥrṣ*	*'z*	*'š*	*ytn*	*mlk mlkytn...*	*l'ly lršp mkl...*
KAI 19 *'rpt kbrt*	...	*'š*	*bn*	*h' lm ... mlk' št...*	*l'štrt...*
KAI 41 *sml*	*'z*	*'š*	*ytn wytn'*	*mnḥm ...*	*l' dny lršp 'lyyt...*

Each of these sentences contains (1) the name of an object or building; (2) a relative pronoun; (3) a verb of construction or dedication; (4) the name of a person who built or dedicated the object; (5) the preposition *l-* followed by the name of the deity to whom the object or building is built or dedicated. In all these instances, to be sure, the dedicatory formula precedes the date formula, that is, each has the reverse order of what is in 1 Kgs 6.1-2. But in other inscriptions, the same order appears as the one found in the Bible:

> *KAI* 33   *bymym 24 lyrḥ mrp'*
> *bšnt 37*
> *lmlk pmyytn mlk kty w'dyl...*
> *[s]mlt '[z] 'š ytn wytn' mhḥš y'š 'št [b'lt]ytn*
> *lrbty l'štrt...*

> *KAI* 32   *bymm 6 lyrḥ bl*
> *bšnt 21*
> *lm[l]k pmy[y]tn m[lk kty w]'dyl*
> *mzbḥ '[z] w'rwm 'šnm 2 'š ytn bd' khn ršp ḥṣ*
> *l'dny lršp ḥṣ ...*[1]

It must be admitted that the Phoenician inscriptions cited here are all very late, dating from the Hellenistic period, and the significance of the similarity between the date formulae in them and the date sentence in the Bible can well be called into question. Even so, earlier inscriptions may be cited which contain at least parts of the formulae, and stand even closer in some aspects to the date sentence in the Bible. The

---

1.   See also Amadasi and Karagheorghis 1977 nos. A27, A29 and A30.

date sentence very closely resembles the beginning of the Eshmanazour sarcophagus inscription,[1] where we read (*KAI* 14):

> *byrḥ bl*
> *bšnt ʿšr wʾrbʿ 14*
> *lmlky mlk ʾšmnʿzr mlk ṣdnm . . .*

Parallels to the votive formulae are found in votive and building inscriptions from Byblos, and their form is extremely close to that of the biblical passage:

> *KAI* 6   *mš. z pʿl. ʾlbʿl. mlk gbl. . . [lb]ʿlt gbl ʾdtw*
> *KAI* 7   *qr. zbny šptbʿl mlk gbl. . . lbʿlt gbl ʾdtw*
> *KAI* 5   *[mš (?) zy]bʾ. ʾbʿl mlk gbl. . . lbʿl[t. gbl ʾdtw. . .]*

Note also the sarcophagus inscription:

> *KAI* 1   *ʾrn zpʿl. [ʾ]tbʿl. . . lʾḥrm. ʾbh. . .*

It would be difficult to imagine that the similarity between the biblical verses and these Phoenician formulae is merely coincidental. There is certainly room to assume that the biblical writer intentionally begins the building descriptions with words sounding like those of authentic lapidary building or dedicatory inscriptions. It is not impossible that he even had before him some sort of building inscription or a votive inscription from the temple itself, written by one of the Tyrian or Byblian workmen involved in the project, and that he has integrated its language into his own narrative, making whatever literary adjustments he found necessary.

Even if it can be demonstrated that 1 Kgs 6.1 and the Phoenician date formulae are somehow related, a question remains whether the statement about the time elapsed since the Exodus is to be associated with the statements in some Phoenician inscriptions dating an event to the founding of the people (or colony—*KAI* 18, 19, 40, 43).[2] Even if

---

1. See Jirku 1923.
2. For the phenomenological similarity between the Exodus as the time of establishing the people of Israel and the foundation of cities as a date of founding for other peoples see Licht 1980. The number 480 in the biblical passage has been the subject of much scholarly conjecture and many studies. It is generally agreed upon today that this number is not to be taken as an exact and reliable historical datum (cf. however the neo-fundamentalist view of Bimson and Livingston 1987), but there is still much discussion concerning its meaning. It has been suggested that it reflects the time period of twelve Judges, or twelve priests, or twelve generations, all of forty-year duration. For the various opinions, see the lengthy discourse of Rowley 1951,

the biblical statement is considered part of the original date formula, the fact remains that in the rest of the world chronology was not reckoned from specific events in the past before the Seleucid period[1] (even though the recognition of the founding of a people as a crucial event is much more ancient).[2] An item such as this one must therefore be missing from building or votive inscriptions predating the fourth century BCE. Alternatively, the reconstructed Phoenician prototype demanded by the biblical verse can be adduced as evidence that reckoning by era in fact had more ancient roots than modern historians generally assume. If dating by era cannot be considered for the pre-Seleucid period, then the similarity between the two formulae in this particular detail may be considered a coincidence. However, the fact that there is no 'parallel' in this detail does not detract from the similarity between the biblical and Phoenician formulae in the other respects. (If we insist on the complete parallel and also on the impossibility of pre-Seleucid era dating we will be forced to the extreme, but not impossible conclusion that the date formula is a very late addition to the text. This would demand, of course, an explanation of the use of the Phoenician month names in such a late text.)

Attention must be directed finally to vv. 37-38. They differ in their formulation from v. 1, and, as stated above, there is no apparent reason to consider them the source for v. 1. It seems that these two verses are formulated in the style of royal chronicles. Montgomery and Gehman already compared these sentences to the Assyrian eponym list for the years 788–787, where we find:[3]

ina līme Adad-muṣammer ša Kakzi uššū ša bīt Nabû ša Ninua karrū
ina līme Ṣīl-Ištar ša Arba-ilu. . .Nabû ana bīti ešši ētarab

In the eponymy of Adad-muṣammer of Kakzi, the foundations of the Nabu temple in Nineveh were laid.
In the eponymy of Ṣil-Ishtar of Arba-ilu, Nabu entered the new temple.

and in a briefer form Loewenstamm 1962 (*s.v.* Exodus from Egypt, *EM* IV), col. 245.
    1.   For reckoning by era, see Samuel 1972: 245-48.
    2.   See Licht 1980.
    3.   See Hallo 1987, who investigates the possibility that the concept of era can be pushed forward to the time of Nabonassar. A much earlier predecessor of 'era' reckoning may be the 'Akkadê era' or *šu-lum Akkadê* (read, perhaps, *šullum Akkadê*, 'the completion of [the building of] Akkadê'), mentioned in an inscription of Shamshi-Adad I (see Grayson 1987: 53 n. i 15-18 for discussion and bibliography).

On the basis of these formulations, we may conjecture that the original chronicle formulation of 1 Kgs 6.37 was:

baššānâ hārĕbʿît bĕyeraḥ ziw yussad bêt YHWH. . .
bišnat 'aḥat 'eśrēh bĕyeraḥ bul killâ habbayit. . .

In the fourth year, in the month of Ziw the temple of YHWH was founded. . .
In the eleventh year, in the month of Bul, he completed the temple. . .

Even the concluding remark *wayyibnēhû šeba' šānîm* is reminiscent of some summary statements appearing in the Mesopotamian chronicles at the ends of the reigns of certain kings.[1] Since this statement relates to years in the history of the temple and not years in the history of the king, we may perhaps learn that the chronicle being cited is that of the temple, and that this is a passage from the first entry in the chronicle.[2]

In summary, vv. 1-2 and 37-38 are not duplicate sentences which are literarily dependent on each other, but are to be regarded as slightly revised citations from distinct sources. Verses 1-2 reflect a votive or a building inscription, while vv. 37-38 echo the royal or temple chronicle. Each source had its own way of expression. It is possible, nonetheless, that certain changes were made in v. 1 under the influence or in imitation of vv. 37-38. Similarly, the order of phrases in v. 38 has been altered for poetic considerations.[3]

1. See Ungnad, *s.v.* 'Eponymen', in *RLA*. The building of temples is mentioned in the years 720, 719, 713 and 707. The building and dedication of temples are mentioned in date lists as well, for which see Ungnad, 'Datenlisten', *RLA*.
2. See the religious and eclectic chronicles published by Grayson 1975b: 195. It is illuminating to compare the biblical passage with the Nabonidus inscription (W.G. Lambert 1968–69), which surveys the events of his reign 'annalistically'. In this composition, an account of the building of Ebabbar (an account known as well from other Nabonidus texts) is incorporated into an annalistic or chronicle-like framework—not as an independent building inscription, but as an individual episode in a longer text. In this framework, the building story starts off with the words 'In the month of Elul. . . ' This information is not found in the building inscriptions themselves, and we must conclude that the author knew it from some other source—perhaps a religious or temple chronicle. In this Nabonidus text there is a building story (and other stories as well) incorporated into a chronistic-annalistic framework, while in 1 Kings 6 there is a citation from a chronicle incorporated into a building story. In v. 37, the action *yussad bêt YHWH* is mentioned before the month, and this is done so as to form a chiasm with v. 38: *yussad bêt YHWH bĕyeraḥ ziw // bĕyeraḥ bul kālâ habbayit.*
3. In v. 37, the action *yussad bêt YHWH* is mentioned before the month, and

2. *Statement that the Temple was Built in an Appropriate Manner*

In the date formula concluding the description of the Temple, we read (1 Kgs 6.38):

> . . . *kālâ habbayit lĕkol dĕbārâw ûlkol mišpāṭô* (Qere' *mišpāṭâw*)

NJPSV translates this verse:

> The House was completed according to all its details and specifications.

NEB renders it slightly differently:

> The House was finished in all its details according to the specification.

NAB gives us:

> and it was completed in all particulars, exactly according to plan.

M. Noth comments on the verse (1968: 125):

> By the *dĕbārîm* of the Temple building are meant in general all of its special peculiarities, while by the *mišpāṭîm* are meant probably the instructions which form the foundation of the 'description' in vss. 2-36..

The assumption of all these translations and Noth's explanatory remark is that there was a pre-existing plan which was carried out. The Aramaic Targum Jonathan however, renders:

> *ištaklāl bêtā' lĕkol gĕzērātêh ûlkol dahazê lêh,*

> The house was completed according to all its ordinances and according to everything befitting it.

This translation also may assume a pre-existing plan (*gezērtah*) but it renders *mišpāṭîm* to mean something more general. The mediaeval commentary Metsudoth David, perhaps inspired by the Targum, interprets *lekol dĕbārâw* as 'all the things which are needed in it', and adds that *ûlkol mišpāṭâw* means exactly the same thing but in different words. In other words, the two expressions are understood as a hendiadys and should be translated 'in all its appropriate details'.

This statement seems comparable to pronouncements in numerous Akkadian texts to the effect that the temple was built in an appropriate manner, the Hebrew expression *lĕkol dĕbārâw ûlkol mišpāṭâw* being

---

this is done so as to form a chiasm with v. 38: *yussad bêt YHWH bĕyerah ziw // bĕyerah bul kālâ habbayit.*

equivalent to Akkadian *kīma simātīšu* (note also *kīma simātīšu labīrāti, simātīšu rēštātu, simat dāriātim*). So, for instance, Sennacherib is commanded (Ebeling 1954: 10):

[*bīt*] *Zababa u Bau kīma simātīšu epuš*

Build the temple of Zababa and Bau in a fashion appropriate to it.

Esarhaddon claims (Borger 1956: 74 l. 32):

kīma simātīšu labīrāti ina šipir Kulla arṣip ušaklil

According to its old manner I built it and completed it with brickwork.[1]

The idea of building according to plan is found of course in the Tabernacle account which repeats seven times that the priestly garments were made 'as The LORD commanded Moses' (Exod. 39.1, 5, 7, 21, 26, 29, 31), and which uses the formula 'the children of Israel did as all which the LORD had commanded Moses, so they did' (39.32, 43) to create an inclusio enveloping the 'inspection' of the finished Tabernacle components.

3. *The Use of Sentences Containing the Words bānâ, 'āśâ (mĕlā' ḵâ) + klh, ślm, tmm (mĕlā' ḵâ)*

The heart of the building account is a long, very detailed description of the buildings and cultic appurtenances built and manufactured by Solomon and Hiram. This description will be studied more closely further on, but attention is to be given now to its general structure, and in particular to the formulae serving as its internal structural markers.

The description is composed of several parts. In 1 Kgs 6.1-10, the temple is described from without. Verses 14-38 describe it from within. The secular buildings constructed by Solomon are listed in 7.1-12. Verses 7.13-47 describe the bronze vessels of the Temple, and 7.48-51 the gold ones.

The division by content is marked externally by the occurrence at critical places of what appears to be formulaic language or stereotyped refrains. The description of the Temple begins with the sentence:

wayhî bišmônîm šānâ wĕ'arba' mē'ôt šānâ wayyiḇen habbayit laYHWH
In the four-hundred-and-eightieth year. . . he built the Temple for YHWH.

---

1. For additional references see *CAD* S: 282 *s.v. simtu* 3c as well as A II, pp. 328ff. *s.v. asāmu* 2; p. 337 *s.v. asmiš*.

In the middle of the description (close to the transition from the account of the Temple from the outside to the account of the inside of the Temple) there is a reference to a divine revelation to Solomon (vv. 11-13). This revelation disrupts the description of the temple, is extraneous to the traditional pattern of building accounts, and contains very late stylistic and linguistic elements. It is highly probable that it is a very late interpolation. In the verse immediately following the revelation we find:

> *wayyiben šĕlōmōh 'et habbayit waykallēhû*
> and Solomon built the Temple and completed it,

and only two verses before the interpolation we read:

> *wayyiben habbayit waykallēhû*
> and he built the Temple and completed it.

It may be conjectured, in my opinion, that at an earlier stage of the development of the text there was no revelation, and that a later scribe added it at a transition from one matter to another, after the words *wayyiben 'et habbayit waykallēhû*. The same scribe returned to the main subject—the description of the Temple—by repeating after the interpolation the words which immediately preceded it. This is a simple employment of resumptive repetition or *Wiederaufnahme*. At a later stage in the transmission of the text, a copyist's error dislodged the words *wayyiben 'et habayit waykallēhû* from their place and mistakenly relocated them in their present position in v. 9. Whatever the exact mechanism by which these words were relocated, they form a refrain.

The description concludes with the sentence (6.38):

> *ûbaššānâ hā'ahat 'eśrēh . . . killâ habbayit . . . wayyibnēhû šeba' šānîm*

The description of the building thus starts with a statement about its being built (*bnh*) and ends with a statement that it was built (*bnh*) and completed (*klh*), while in the middle, at a place of transition from one matter to the next, there are two statements about building and completing the work.

Something similar is found in the description of the vessels. The account of the vessels begins a note describing Hiram, the Tyrian artisan. This note, which introduces the account of the bronze vessels which he produced, concludes with the words:

wayyāḇō' 'el hammeleḵ šĕlōmōh wayya'aś 'eṯ kol melā' ḵtô (7.14)

He came to King Solomon and did all his work.

The description of Hiram's works in copper concludes with a summary statement (7.40-47) providing the number of implements manufactured and the amount of material which went into the work. This summary begins with the sentence:

wayya'aś ḥîrôm 'eṯ hakkiyyōrôṯ wĕ'eṯ hayyā'îm wĕ'eṯ hammizrāqōṯ waykal ḥîrām la'aśôṯ 'et kol hammĕlā' ḵâ 'ăšer 'āśâ lammeleḵ šĕlōmōh bêt YHWH

After the description of the copper works is a brief inventory of the gold furnishings and implements said to be manufactured by the king himself (vv. 48-51). This passage opens:

wayya'aś šĕlōmōh 'et kol hakkēlîm 'ăšer bêt YHWH . . . (7.48).

It concludes:

wattišlam kol hammĕlā' ḵâ 'ăšer 'āśâ hammeleḵ šĕlōmōh bêt YHWH (7.51).

Within the description of the vessels, every individual item is described with a passage starting with the word *wayya'aś* (7.18, 23, 27, 38, 40). For the most part these passages do not have concluding formulae, but the description of the pillars, Yakhin and Boaz, concludes with the words:

wattittōm mĕle'ḵeṯ hā'ammûdîm (7.22).

Thus, just as each passage in the description of the Temple opened with a statement that it was built and ended with a statement that it was built and completed, so the account of the vessels is composed of passages bracketed by statements in the beginning that they were made (*wayya'aś* or *wayyaś mĕlā' ḵâ*) and statements at the end that they were completed (*klh, šlm, tmm mĕlā' ḵâ 'ăšer 'āśâ*.

A similar phenomenon is noticed in the description of the secular buildings which starts off with the sentence:

wĕ'et bêtô bānâ šĕlōmōh šĕlōš 'eśrēh šānâ waykal 'et kol bêtô (7.1).

A review of certain key sentences in chs. 6–7 shows that the words and expression *bānâ, 'āśâ (mĕlā' kâ)*, separately at the beginnings of passages, or at the ends of passages and in conjunction with *klh, šlm, tmm (mĕlākâ)*, are in fact structural markers throughout this section of the building story.

The picture will not be complete without some remark concerning two other passages in the account of Solomon's reign. In 3.1 we find concerning Solomon's marriage of Pharaoh's daughter:

> *waybî'ehā'el 'îr dāwiḏ 'aḏ kallōṯô liḇnôṯ 'eṯ bêṯô wĕ'eṯ bêṯ YHWH wĕ'eṯ ḥômaṯ yĕrûšāla(y)im sāḇîḇ.*

This passage alludes to all of Solomon's building projects by mentioning the two key words *bnh* and *klh*. Similarly, in 9.10, 25 we find:

> *wayhî miqṣēh 'eśrîm šānâ 'ăšer bānâ šĕlōmōh 'eṯ šĕnê habbāttîm . . . w ĕšillam 'eṯ habbāyiṯ.*

These two verses bracket certain appendices to the main building story and should be read together. It might be added that exegetes have had difficulty understanding the expression *wĕšillam 'eṯ habbāyiṯ*, but these words are merely synonymous with *wekillah 'eṯ habbāyiṯ*, and they are not to be considered separately from the expression *'ăšer bānâ šĕlōmōh 'eṯ šĕnê habbāttîm* earlier in the passage. They refer to no specific, additional activity of the king. The words *bānâ* and *killâ* or *šillēm* summarize the entire building project.

In addition, these two passages have structural significance in the account of Solomon's reign. The first passage marks the beginning of the second period in Solomon's career, the period climaxing with the building of the temple. The second passage is the end of this phase, and in fact, the pair marks the real end of the building account.

These and similar or synonymous expressions appear in other building stories as well, both in the Bible and in extra-biblical sources. Only a few examples will be cited, some from the stories included in Part I of this study, and others from texts not yet mentioned. In many texts, the expressions appear—as they do in 1 Kings 5–9, as structural markers—in 'refrains' which open or close the descriptions of the buildings (section 3 in the traditional outline of building accounts), and there are some texts where the entire building account is compressed into a short sentence containing 'built and finished (the work)': *banû, epēšu, raṣāpu // (šipram) šuklulu, quttû* and the like.

In the Bible itself, these expressions appear first in the Tabernacle account (Exod. 39.32, 42-43; 40.16, 33; cf. Num. 7.1). In the Aramaic accounts of rebuilding the walls of Jerusalem and the temple, the pair *bnh // škll* which is exactly equivalent to the Akkadian pair *banû//šuklulu*, appears seven times (Ezra 4.12, 13, 15; 5.3, 9, 11; 6.14). It also occurs in the memoirs of Nehemiah (Neh. 6.15-16:

wattišlam hahômâ. . . wayyēdĕ'û kî mē'ēt 'ĕlōhênû ne'ĕśtâ ham-melā'kâ hazzō't).[1] In the Tabernacle account and in Nehemiah's memoirs the expressions appear at the end of the descriptions of the buildings and implements, as a concluding refrain to section 3 of the pattern.

Similar expressions appear in Mesopotamian building accounts throughout history.[2]

1. In the famous brick foundation inscription of Yahdun-lim, king of Mari, which tells of the building of a temple for Shamash, the entire building account is compressed into two sentences. The first sentence is a 'dedicatory' statement announcing that the temple was built for Shamash for the life of the king. The following sentence reports seating the god in the temple, probably a reference to the dedication ceremony. In the 'dedicatory' statement we find (Dossin 1955: 15 IV 5-8):

ana balāṭīšu	For his life
bīt Šamaš bēlīšu	the temple of Šamaš his lord
bītam ša ipištam	a house which is complete in (its)
šuklulūma	construction
ummēnūtam quttû	and finished in (its) workmanship
simat ilūtīšu īpussumma	as befitting his divinity
	he constructed for him.

Note here the chiastic arrangement of the words:

ipištu -šuklulū // quttû- īpussumma

which enhances the refrain nature of the expression.

2. In the inscription of Tiglath-pileser I reporting the building of the Anu and Adad temple (*AKA*, 97-98 VII 90-97, see above) we find:

bīta ella. . .	The pure temple. . .
akpud ānah	I planned, I exerted myself,
ēpuš ušiklil	I built, I completed.

In the prayer which concludes the inscription, the king repeats his

---

1. For the pair *bnh // šlm* see Ezra 5.16 and perhaps Isa. 44. 26, 28.

2. Petitjean (1969: 228) suggested relating these Akkadian expressions to the pair of words *YSD // BṢ'* found in Zech. 4.9, and there he lists many references to the Akkadian material, and especially Neo-Babylonian texts. For Sumerian forerunners to this formula see Chapter 1, section 4 (Lugalannemundu), above.

240 *I Have Built You an Exalted House*

previous statement, although in somewhat different style (*AKA*, 101-102 VIII 17-21):

kīma anāku	Just as I
bīta ella. . .	the pure temple. . .
akpudma la apparkūma	planned and did not desist
ana epīši aḫī la addû	and was not negligent in building
ḫanṭiš ušaklilma	but speedily completed.

3. In three inscriptions of Sennacherib concerning the 'Palace Without a Rival' in Nineveh, the description of the dedication festivities begins (Luckenbill 1924: 98: 91; 116 VIII 65-68):

ultu šipri ekallīja uqattû	After I finished the work on my palace
Aššur bēlu rabû. . .	Assur the great lord. . .
ina qerbīšu aqrīma	I invited inside.

4. Esarhaddon, in an inscription reporting the construction of the armory (*ekal mašarti*), concludes the description of the edifice and its construction with a retrospective passage which mentions certain building rites and the joy of the builders at work. This passage is bracketed as follows (Borger 1956: 62 §27 Nin A-F 35ff.):

[ultu] ekallu šuātu	[After] that palace
ultu uššēša adi gabadibbīša[1]	from foundation to parapet
arṣipu ušaklilu	I built and completed
lullê umallû	and filled with abundance
. . . . . .	. . . . . .
šipirša . . . agmurma	and completed . . . its work.

5. Assurbanipal concludes his account of building the residence of the crown prince (*bīt ridûti*) (Streck 1916: 88-90, 103-106; cf. Aynard 1957: 62 V 52-60):

bīt ridûti šuāti . . .	That crown prince's palace. . .
ana siḫirtīšu ušaklil	I completed in its entirety
šipir epīštīšu agmurma	the work of its making I finished.

6. Nebuchadnezzar II, king of Babylon, in one of his surveys of his building projects, tells of seven temples to seven gods which he built

---

1. For this expression and the synonymous expressions *ultu uššēšu adi gabadibbīšu, ultu uššēšu adi naburrīšu, ultu uššēšu adi šaptīšu*, see Baumgartner 1925: 219-99. These expressions appear in dozens of Akkadian building inscriptions and may apparently be compared with the expression *mimmasad 'ad ṭepāḫôt* (1 Kgs 7.9), as suggested already by M. Weinfeld (*apud* Cohen 1978: 89 n. 222).

in seven cities of his realm. This enumeration opens as follows (Langdon 1912: 74, Nebuchadnezzar no. I col. II 26-27):

ana mār-bīti bēlīja . . .	To Mar-biti my lord . . .
bīssu ina Barsippa eššiš ēpuš	His temple in Borsippa I built anew.

The king concludes the list with the sentence (ll. 36-38):

ešrēti ilāni rabûti	The sanctuaries of the great gods
eššiš ēpušma	I built anew and
ušaklil šipiršin	I completed their work.

In the continuation of the same inscription, at the very end of the survey in a concluding summary pronouncement, it is written (ll. 54ff.):

epēšu māḫāzī ilāni u ištar	(Of) building the holy cities of the gods and goddesses
ša bēlu rabiu Marduk ušadkânni	to which the great lord Marduk had
libbam	aroused my heart
palḫiš la baṭṭilšu	fearfully and without interruption
ušallam šipiršu	I completed its work.

7. Finally, Nabonidus tells about the Sin temple, Eḫulḫul (Langdon 1912: 222 *Nabonidus* no. 1 col. II 7-9):

eli ša šarrāni abbēja	More than the kings my ancestors
epšetīšu udanninma	had strengthened its work
unakkilu šipiršu	and made its workmanship artistic,
ekur šuātim	that temple
ultu temenšu adi gabadibbīšu	from foundation to parapets
eššiš abnīma	I built anew and
ušaklil šipiršu	I completed its work.

Only a small selection of the many possible texts has been cited in order to illustrate some of the ways in which these expressions were employed. It should be pointed out that despite the wide distribution of these expressions in the Bible and in Akkadian texts, they do not seem to occur in the building inscriptions from the west.[1] If so, the wide use of such expressions in building stories may represent a linguistic point of contact specifically between the biblical tradition and the Mesopotamian literary tradition.

There is an interesting corollary to the use of these expressions in biblical and Mesopotamian building accounts. It was noticed long ago

---

1. See, perhaps, in the Baal epic (*UT* 51 IV 72): *bt arzm ykllnh // hm bt lbnt y'msnh*, and conceivably also *KAI* 18: *p'lt tklty*.

that these expressions appear both in the Priestly account of the building of the Tabernacle and in the Creation story in Gen. 1.1–2.4a, also a product of the Priestly school. The conclusion drawn from this coincidence has been that the Tabernacle story was formulated at these points in conscious imitation of the Creation story, the theological implication being that building the Tabernacle is portrayed as Israel's participation in putting the finishing touches on Creation.[1] This interpretation is attractive and may in fact not be devoid of truth. Nonetheless, it is not the whole truth. The numerous biblical and extra-biblical texts containing the very expressions which link the Tabernacle and Creation stories show clearly that the natural habitat of such expressions is the building story.[2] Their appearance in the Creation story, therefore, must be interpreted as an attempt to describe Creation in terms of building! By employing building terminology in the Creation story, the priestly author has done nothing new, but has joined other biblical writers who describe the world as a building, the Creation as an act of building, and the Creator as a wise, knowledgable and discerning architect.[3]

1.   See Fishbane 1979: 12-13.
2.   The background of *wayyar' mōšeh 'et kol hammĕlā'kâ* (Exod. 39.43), which parallels *wayyar' 'ĕlōhîm 'et kol 'ăšer 'āśâ* in Gen. 1.31 (see also 1.4, 9, 18 etc.), remains problematic, with the direction of imitation still in doubt. These terms may be from the realm of building, and possibly should be related to Akkadian *ṣubbû*, used of inspecting and building, and to *šutesbû,* meaning to execute according to plan (see Veenhof 1985a; note also *hâṭu* and *barû* in several accounts of searching for foundations, and especially the words *bītam ahīṭ alaktašu uštassiqma,* 'The temple I examined, its ordinances I had put in order', which are to be found in an inscription of Takil-ilissu of Malgium—Kutscher and Wilcke 1978: 115 ll. 48-49). If this is the case, the realm of building has once again influenced the language of the Creation account. However, there are no Mesopotamian building accounts, to the best of my knowledge, which report that the builder inspected the finished building. Furthermore, the words *amāru* and *ṣubbû* also occur in Akkadian creation myths, and note in particular the recently published myth about the creation of man, Mayer 1987 (see especially ll. 24', 25', 26', and 35'). It must also be pointed out that this myth uses the term *nabnīssu ušaklil* to describe the creation of mankind. This could mean that the 'building' language entered the biblical Creation story not in conscious imitation of the Tabernacle story (with all that that would imply) but under the influence of extra-biblical background material.
3.   See, for instance Isa. 40.12-13; Ps. 102: 2, 3, 5; Prov. 3.19-20 and in particular Job 38.4-11. Cassuto (1975b: 103-104) suggests that these passages (along with some others) represent an ancient Israelite creation tradition somewhat different

4. Length and Brevity in the Descriptions of the Buildings

In his commentary on Kings, John Gray (1970) remarks concerning the description of the secular buildings (p. 157):

> The most striking feature of this section is the contrast between the detail in which the Temple and its fittings are described (6.2-36; 7.13-51) and the vagueness of the description of the palace complex (7.1-12). This suggests that the writer was more familiar with, or more interested in, the Temple than the palace, and was probably a priest.[1]

Other scholars have pointed out identical discrepancies between the detailed descriptions of the decorative or symbolic bronze *objets d'art* made by Hiram and displayed in the Temple courtyard (7.13-47) and the telegraphically brief, inventory-like list of cultically vital gold implements manufactured by Solomon and installed within the Temple building itself.[2] These phenomena, are, however, not unusual at all, and anyone familiar with descriptions of buildings contained in Mesopotamian royal inscriptions might even come to expect them!

Most Mesopotamian building inscriptions were composed on the occasion of constructing one specific building or restoring a certain part of a particular building. It is natural that the building, or part of it, should stand center stage in the building account and be described in detail. The building stories analyzed in the first part of this study amply testify to this. But along with the building inscriptions which concentrate exclusively on the structures for which they were composed,

---

from the one in Genesis 1. He does not, however, point out that one of the common idioms is that of building. It is this particular idiom which finds expression in the concluding verses of this creation story. The use of these particular terms, which are on the one hand taken from building parlance but on the other hand are not explicit, may be somewhat polemical by virtue of being less anthropomorphic. Various midrashim also describe God and Creation in terms of an architect planning and constructing a building. They may have been inspired in their choice of metaphors by recognition of this motive in the biblical texts themselves. Building motives are found as well in *Enuma Elish*, both with regard to several 'cosmic' temples, and the world itself.

    1.   Liver (1971a: 94) already rejects the possibility that the descriptions of the temple in 1 Kgs 6–7 came from priestly circles and suggested that 'overall they are from royal archival sources'.

    2.   Cf. Waterman 1943, 1947; Fritz 1987 and most recently Hurowitz forthcoming 3.

there are a significant number of inscriptions which also mention additional buildings erected by the same king.[1] Even so, the scribes of Mesopotamia were accustomed to emphasize the building in honor of which the inscription was written. Emphasis was achieved by some sort of literary device such as brevity and concentration in the 'secondary' descriptions, or placing the 'secondary' descriptions in a less prominent place in the inscription than the 'primary' description. It is not impossible that by chance a scribe was not as familiar with the other buildings as he was with the one for which the inscription was written, but his familiarity or lack of familiarity cannot be determined on the basis of the relative lengths of the descriptions. The length of the description and its place within the building account or inscription indicate only the scribe's interests at the time and say nothing about the depth of his knowledge or his professional standing.

5. *The Nature of the Biblical Descriptions of Buildings as Compared with the Mesopotamian Descriptions*

The descriptions of the buildings and vessels in 1 Kings 6–7 are different in nature from descriptions of buildings or vessels found in extra-biblical building accounts. The Mesopotamian building accounts describe the structures and furnishings in poetic but very general language. The Mesopotamian scribes emphasized mainly the valuable and

---

1. Inventory-like lists of temples and cult objects built or fashioned by individual kings are found as early as the royal dedicatory and building inscriptions of Ur-Nanshe of Lagash (see Cooper 1986: 22ff.; Steible 1982). For later periods, see in particular the inscription of Tiglath-pileser I, which describes at length the Anu-Adad temple; in the middle of this description is found a relatively short account of the building of a *bīt ḫamri*. The same inscription also contains a summary list of other building projects in the city of Assur itself as well as in other cities. In the inscriptions of Nebuchadnezzar we find the 'main' building story at the end, while what might be called a 'historical introduction' contains accounts of all the other building projects which he undertook. The Sippar cylinder of Nabonidus (Langdon 1912: 218 *Nabonidus* no. 1), and Langdon 1915–16 are composed of later recensions of several independent building accounts. The Thompson Prism of Assurbanipal also includes several independent building accounts. The inscriptions of Sargon, Sennacherib and Esarhaddon contain building accounts which describe a certain building at length and mention other projects only briefly. Certain inscriptions of Assurnasirpal II, Sargon and Sennacherib describe at considerable length whole new cities, emphasizing the palaces, or one particular palace, but glossing over the temples.

rare materials—wood, precious stones and metal—that were used in the buildings. Similarly, they often mention the high artistic level of the craftsmanship, stating frequently that the buildings and vessels were beautiful, sophisticated, immense, overwhelmingly striking and superior in some way or another to their predecessors. Typical of these descriptions are Esarhaddon's nearly poetic words concerning Ešarra, the temple of Assur (Borger 1956: 5 Ass A, V 27–VI 27):

> When the second year came
> I raised to heaven the head of Ešarra, my lord Assur's dwelling.
> Above, heavenward, I raised high its head.
> Below, in the underworld I made firm its foundations.
> Ehursaggula, (meaning) House of the Great Mountain
> I made beautiful as the heavenly writing.
> I piled it up like a mountain.
> That temple,
> from foundation to top,
> I built and completed.
> I filled it with luxury astonishing to look at.
> Beams of cedars and cypress
> produce of Mount Sirara and Mount Lebanon,
> whose fragrance is sweet, I spread over it.
> I bound up cypress door with gold bands and set them in its portals.
> The disordered chapels, daises, stands and drawings,
> I restored and improved
> and made bright as the sun.
> Its lofty high head scraped the sky,
> below, its roots spread in the subterranean water.
> All the furnishings needed for Ešarra
> I made anew and placed therein.

Clearly, descriptions such as this are intent on glorifying the building and the accomplishment of the builder and have no clear desire to present an exact description which would enable the reader to visualize the edifice in any but the most general details.[1] All the characteristics

---

1.   This particular description displays certain similarities to the description of Solomon's Temple and its furnishings in 1 Kings 6–7. It begins with a chronological statement: *šanītum šattu ina kašādi*, 'when the second year arrived'. It contains the formulaic expressions *arṣip ušaklil*, 'I built and completed', and *ultu uššešu adi gabdibbīšu*, 'from foundations to top'. It seems to first describe the outside of the temple, telling of its height and how it looks like a mountain—something a viewer from without would appreciate. Afterwards it describes the roofing and then the inside, emphasizing the use of wood and gold and mentioning the doors and reliefs.

of these descriptions mentioned here are totally lacking in the biblical descriptions.[1]

In contrast, the descriptions of buildings found in Kings, and, for that matter, in Exodus and Ezekiel as well, are striking in the exact details given, and especially the fact that dimensions are provided. It is true that dimensions are not entirely absent in the Mesopotamian texts. As a matter of fact, certain Neo-Assyrian building accounts may even display a tendency towards providing them. Even so, the dimensions given are never sufficient to allow a reconstruction of the building. Dimensions of vessels or furnishings are never provided. In cases where the dimensions of buildings are stipulated, the information is limited to the external dimensions of the buildings (length, width and height).[2] Frequently (and especially when the king has added to the height of a building) the height of the building as well as that of the platform upon which it is built are given according to the number of brick courses (*tipku*; note 1 Kgs 6.36; 7.12; Ezra 6.3-4).

In contrast to this, the information provided by the biblical descriptions seems to be intent on enabling the reader actually to visualize the building or object described. It must be said that the language of the descriptions is technical, detailed, and at times enigmatic or even totally incomprehensible. In addition, the biblical text is not necessarily in the most desirable state of preservation.[3] Furthermore, the description is not always as complete as might be wished, and certain information which seems essential to the modern reader, such as the thickness of walls, is missing. There is no doubt that the scholar who desires to reconstruct the buildings with the information provided in the Bible faces every conceivable type of difficulty. Nonetheless, the mission is

It concludes with a statement that the furnishings were made and placed within. It therefore follows the same basic outline as the biblical description, all this despite its laudatory, poetic nature. For additional examples of temples described as filling the entire universe see W.G. Lambert 1975: 327.

1.   The Mesopotamian descriptions of buildings seem to continue a tradition found in the Sumerian 'Temple Hymns' in which a poet would describe and praise a temple and its divine resident. Words of praise to the temple or a city are rare in the Bible but they are not entirely lacking. See for example Pss. 15; 46; 48; 66.67; 87; 147.1, 12. For a relatively late Akkadian temple hymn and for references to additional compositions see Köcher 1959. Add to this list perhaps *LKA* 38 obv. 10– rev. 6.

2.   See Ezra 6.3.

3.   See Gooding 1965 and 1967, as well as Stade 1883.

not impossible, and proof is the fact that biblical exegetes and scholars throughout the ages have attempted to sketch, draw or even construct three-dimensional models of the temple[1] with no small degree of success! Any like attempt to reconstruct a Mesopotamian structure solely on the basis of textual evidence from the royal inscriptions would be simply inconceivable.[2] Therefore, even if the biblical and Mesopotamian descriptions share a tendency to mention the metals and wood used,[3] it is clear that they are vastly different in nature and intent. The biblical descriptions totally lack the laudatory aspect, tending instead towards precision, tangibility and concreteness.

6. *The Origin of the Biblical Style of Describing Buildings and Furnishings*

The descriptions of Solomon's Temple, the Tabernacle and the temple of the future envisioned by Ezekiel, which resemble each other in all the aspects specified above, indicate the development of an independent Israelite or Judaean tradition of describing buildings. This tradition even seems to have a continuation in the post-exilic Jewish literary tradition, especially in the Temple Scroll, as well as perhaps the

1.   For a survey of such attempts from the seventeenth century to the present, see Busink 1970: 44-60, 60-76; Ouellette 1976.

2.   The complaints of scholars such as Waterman, Gray and Fritz about the defective nature of the description of the temple are misguided. It is true that not every detail is described and it is certainly without question that a modern author might have described the temple in a somewhat different manner. Waterman claims that the biblical author was not interested in architecture for its own sake, and he may well be right. It is also reasonable to assume that the descriptions of the buildings have some ideological or religious purposes, something especially apparent in the emphasis placed on the temple at the cost of the palace and governmental compound. But statement of all these reservations and misgivings does little to further illuminate and help us appreciate the true literary nature of the descriptions available. The job of the modern scholar is to evaluate the ancient texts for what they are, rather than criticize them for what they are not! The biblical author is exceptional in his attempt to describe in words three-dimensional objects and concretize them for his readers. His Mesopotamian colleagues and counterparts make no such attempt. The degree to which the biblical author has achieved or missed his goal of concretization should not influence our appreciation of what the goal actually was. Reading a Mesopotamian description of a building will bring the complaining scholar to appreciate the relatively informative nature of the biblical descriptions.

3.   See Montgomery and Gehman 1971: 151.

'Vision of a New Jerusalem'[1] and the rabbinic mishnaic tractate *Middoth*.[2] The beginning of this tradition is most likely to be the Temple description in the book of Kings. The other biblical descriptions of buildings may imitate the description set forth here, not necessarily in detail, but in style. The style seems innovative in comparison with the style of building descriptions in the Mesopotamian royal inscriptions, but it is necessary to investigate the origin of the innovation. It is possible that this innovation is based on the adaptation of another literary genre and applying it at the appropriate place in the framework of the building account.

Several suggestions have been made about the literary origin of the description of the Temple and is appurtenances. O. Eissfeldt was of the opinion that the Temple description is based on documents from the Temple archives.[3] He may be correct as to where such descriptive documents were stored and from whence they were retrieved, but I must express my opinion that the term 'archival' is an inadequate term. It has no inherent literary or genre meaning, since, as a matter of fact, any type of document could have found its way into an archive, just so long as the archivist deemed it worthy of preservation. Montgomery, who mentions the statue of Gudea portraying him holding on his knees a sketch of a temple, suggests that the description of the temple in 1 Kgs 6.2-10 is based on an architect's plan. As for the lists of public buildings in 7.2-8 and 9.15-17, Montgomery proposes that they originate in public inscriptions published by Solomon. As basis for this proposal he cites the Mesha inscription.[4] Noth suggested that the description of the buildings ultimately derives from oral instructions given the builders.[5] Recently, J. Van Seters has taken a position diametrically opposed to that of his predecessors, all of whom tried to find ancient, 'original' documents behind the Temple description. In his opinion the descriptions date not to the time of Solomon when the Temple was said to have been built, but to the exilic period, when the Temple no longer existed, and may be attributed to

1.   See Licht 1979.
2.   Descriptions of buildings and cities are found in the writings of Josephus and in the apocryphal books. They are much more detailed than the biblical descriptions, and we will not deal with them here.
3.   Eissfeldt 1966: 289.
4.   Montgomery 1934; Montgomery–Gehman 1951: 48.
5.   Noth 1968: 105. Gray tends towards this suggestion.

Deuteronomic scribes seeking to preserve memory of the building's form.[1] He adduces as analogies descriptions found in Herodotus, Josephus or *Middoth*, all of which were far removed geographically or chronologically from the buildings which they depict. He adds that ancient Near Eastern dedicatory inscriptions never describe the buildings because the buildings are readily visible to the reader of the inscriptions.

No definitive solution to this problem can be offered here. Nonetheless, examination of various extra-biblical documents may be useful in evaluating the plausibility of the proposals raised so far. It may even suggest some new candidates for the source of literary inspiration which gave rise to the biblical descriptions. In any case, it seems that whatever conjectures are offered should call upon support from the literary realities of the ancient world and should be supplemented by an attempt to define the circumstances under which these ancient documents were composed.

I have already stated that the building accounts contained in the Mesopotamian building inscriptions do not include descriptions of buildings and vessels resembling those characteristic of the biblical building accounts in general and 1 Kings 6–7 in particular. There is, however, one exception to this generality. Certain neo-Assyrian inscriptions, and especially those of Sennacherib in which he describes his 'Palace without a Rival', display an inclination towards detail, precision and attempts at visualization in describing buildings, and are far less laudatory. The possibility arises, therefore, that the biblical authors continued and developed this particular tendency. This possibility should be weighed seriously, especially in light of other possible connections between the biblical building account and the neo-Assyrian ones. However, even if a genetic relationship between the biblical building descriptions and those of Sennacherib is rejected, the very existence of such descriptions in the Assyrian texts calls into question Van Seters's contention that buildings are described in detail only by or for the benefit of people who cannot see them.

But this possibility is not the only one. If the biblical building descriptions are compared only to descriptions contained in royal inscriptions, significant differences are to be noticed. However, descriptions of buildings more like those found in the Bible appear in other types of

---

1. Van Seters 1983: 109-10; cf. Zevit 1985.

documents, and these documents may provide us with alternate candidates for the literary prototype of 1 Kings 6–7.

A partial, not necessarily representative sampling of the numerous Mesopotamian documents available[1] brings to the fore about a dozen documents containing descriptions of buildings or vessels which might be of use in defining the literary type represented by the biblical description of the temple and its furnishings:

    a. *The Esagila Tablet* (Unger 1970: 237-49 = Wetzel and Weissbach 1938: 49-56).

    b. *A description of Babylon* (Unger 1970: 252-53).

    c. *A description of Esagil and Ezida found at Assur* (Unger 1970: 250-52 = Weidner 1963: 116 pls. VII–VIII).

    d. *A description of the Adad temple at Assur* (Weidner 1932–33: 43).

    e. *A description of the Resh Temple in Uruk* (Van Dijk 1962: 60).

    f. *Descriptions of three temples from Hall 115 of the Palace of Mari* (Charpin 1982 1983.

    g. *A description from Nineveh of buildings and doors* (Waterman, *RCAE*, 457).

    h. *A description of three doors of the Shamash temple in Sippar* (Röllig 1966: 298-301).[2]

    i. *A description of the bed of Marduk and Ṣarpanitu* (Barnett 1950: 40-42).

    j. *A description of pillars from Kar-Tukulti-Ninurta* (Weidner 1954–55; Grayson, *ARI*, I §§509-14; Freydank 1971: 533).

    k. *An inventory from Kar-Tukulti-Ninurta* (Köcher 1957–58: 300-13).

Each of these documents describes either a single building, a number of buildings, a part of a building, a piece of furniture or several pieces of furniture. They are all strictly factual in that they contain no words of praise for the object described. Each description states the dimensions of the object depicted. Since all the descriptions are of 'public' buildings or objects, it may be assumed that the texts are not private documents, and they may be conveniently isolated from numerous contracts, deeds and other such legal or administrative documents which also describe fields or structures in an exact, precise, objective style.

    1.   Most of these documents are listed in Borger 1967–75: III, 117-19 §106 as topographical texts. It was not possible to survey systematically all of the administrative and legal documents which may contain detailed and precise descriptions of fields, buildings and vessels of various types. Letters as well often contain descriptions of buildings, parts of buildings and furnishings.

    2.   For two texts containing measurements of doorposts and doors published in a collection of letters, see *ABL* 130 (= Parpola 1987 no. 202) and *ABL* 457 (= Parpola 1987 no. 203).

The scribes of Mesopotamia were obviously not concerned with making life easier for modern-day form critics, and they did not always indicate the purpose, practical function or *Sitz im Leben* of the documents they composed. Not only this, but several of the texts listed above contain no particular characteristics which might reveal the purpose for which the document was written.[1] So we find that items d, e and h on the list are of undeterminable literary type and their practical use is no less obscure than that of the biblical texts which we wish to illuminate. For this reason these texts cannot be taken into account in our discussion. The remaining documents, however, may provide certain, albeit meager, evidence enabling us to make 'educated guesses' as to their aim and function. In the remainder of this chapter each of these documents will be discussed independently. First an attempt will be made to illuminate the character of each text unto itself and the circumstances leading to its composition. Afterwards I will present the Mesopotamian document as an analogy or model for the biblical texts, and by doing so will try to clarify what the background of the biblical text might have been. I will deal first with the seven descriptions of complete buildings (a, b, c, e and f [three buildings]) and then with the three descriptions of furnishings (i, j and k).

Descriptions of Buildings

1. *The Esagila Tablet* (a) describes in detail two of the chambers of the Esagila temple in Babylon. It is known from a copy written in year 83 of the Seleucid era (229 BCE). According to Unger,[2] this tablet is the sixth in a long series describing the city of Babylon (*Stadtbeschreibung*) with all its streets and temples. There are, to be sure, certain difficulties with this suggestion,[3] and it is possible that the tablet originally led an independent existence. But even if Unger's position that the tablet belongs to the *Stadtbeschreibung* is accepted, this will not detract from the tablet's special character, for whereas the other tablets in the series contain lists of temples, chambers and streets, the Esagila Tablet describes the parts of one particular building with

1. See Wiseman 1972 and 1983: 71 for an attempt to determine the 'literary' type and the function of a picture of a ziqqurat. See also IM 44036,1 (Schmid 1975).
2. Unger 1970: 245 n. 7.
3. See Gurney 1974: 40. Unger (1927: 145) suggested that the Esagila tablet is based on a description composed at the time of Esarhaddon in connection with the king's restoration of Babylon.

exact, mathematical precision. Not only this, but the description resembles in style the mathematical school texts described by Neugebauer as 'problem texts'.[1] The expressions *aššum/ kî . . . la tīdi* ('since you do not know') and *. . . ana amāri* ('in order to calculate') are expressions borrowed from school texts. The Esagila Tablet, therefore, may be characterized probably as a school exercise or problem in geometry, surveying or some related discipline.[2]

If the description of Solomon's Temple is assumed to be based on some type of school text, one can explain more readily certain problems in the description, such as the missing information concerning the thickness of the walls or the mathematical error in the dimensions of the bronze 'Sea' (1 Kgs 7.23). The information provided cannot have originated from measuring the objects, but rather than explaining it as 'rounding off', it can be attributed to calculation based on a mistaken notion that $\pi = 3$ and schematization.[3] The absence of the walls' thickness may also be attributed to schematization. Drawing an analogy between the Esagila Tablet (which bears signs of being a school tablet) and the biblical description of the Temple may lead to the conclusion that the author of the biblical description was influenced in his work by exercises which he would have done while learning the scribal art. Describing the Temple and its furnishings may even have been part of the scribal or priestly curriculum in some Jerusalem Temple school. We might add here, that this would somewhat correspond with a novel theory proposed by S.E. McEvenue: that P's description of the Tabernacle has a 'didactic style' and was meant for educating the children of priestly families.[4]

2. *The description of the Resh Temple in Uruk* (e) gives the spatial dimensions of the temple both according to length and width and according to area (the amount of seed which can be sown in the

1.   Neugebauer 1945: 1.
2.   Wiseman (1987: 71) suggests that 'the tablet appears to be a copy of an older original, perhaps made to aid the restoration by some successor of Alexander'. This evaluation resembles the evaluations of other descriptions of buildings suggested by various scholars. Nonetheless, it ignores the specific peculiarities of the Esagila tablet pointed out here.
3.   On the 'Sea', see Bagnani 1964 and more recently Zuidhof 1972. For descriptions as school exercises, see Wiseman 1972.
4.   McEvenue 1974.

space—a way of area measure familiar also from Lev. 27.16 and rabbinic sources, using the term *bêṭ sē'â*). This text too may possibly have been a school exercise, but it may equally have been a surveyor's report. It seems that this text is not to be dissociated from the maps of fields and buildings which were drawn up for administrative purposes. On the reverse sides of such maps there is at times a repetition or sum-total of the words which were written along the lines of the drawing on the obverse.[1]

3. *The description of Babylon* (b) was written on the reverse of a drawing, and it seems to be an attempt to describe verbally the structures which were drawn on the obverse.[2]

If the Temple description in the book of Kings is taken to be analogous to these two documents, the conclusion will be that the biblical description is based on the report of a surveyor prepared for some administrative purpose. But it must readily be admitted that these two descriptions are somewhat far removed from the biblical ones. Furthermore, even if we agree that descriptions of buildings were prepared for administrative purposes, such an evaluation would be valid only for descriptions of private houses. It would still be difficult to conclude that descriptions of public buildings were also meant for administrative purposes. This being the case, the function of these two documents must remain a subject of further inquiry and speculation.

4. *The description of Esagila and Ezida found at Assur* (c) leads us in another direction. Weidner suggested that this tablet describes an existing temple which is to be either restored or imitated, and that it is

1. See Nemat-Nejat 1982 for a discussion of these documents. For city maps and drawings of buildings, see Nemat-Nejat 1982: 11-13. In connection with the document being discussed, it is possible to mention the list of temples from Nippur published by Bernhardt and Kramer (1975) which gives the area measurement of all the temples both according to regular dimensions (*IKU*, *SAR*) as well as according to seeding capacity (*gin*). The three descriptions of temples found at Mari to be discussed below mention the thickness of the temples' walls as well as the areas of the various rooms of the temples.

2. Donald (1962: 188 n. 1) suggested that this text has a military function ('There is a military text on the reverse') but he did not offer any support or explanation of his opinion. He may have based his view on the word *EN.NUN* (*maṣṣartu* = watch) in ll. 5 and 6 as well as the possibility that the maps themselves had military functions. On this text, see also the remarks of Wiseman (1972: 145 n. 18).

therefore a type of written blueprint for the builder.[1]

Taking this text and its proposed function as models for explaining the biblical temple descriptions may lead to the conclusion that the biblical author was influenced by written instructions given to the builders.[2] This conclusion corresponds with the proposal of Montgomery and Noth that the biblical description of the Temple originated in the instructions given the builders. On the other hand, it somewhat weakens Noth's contention that these instructions were given orally.[3] We might even find in this document and Weidner's

---

1. 'Schwer zu beantworten ist die Frage, warum man gerade diesem Text in Assyrian kopierte; der rechteckige Anstaz und der oberen Schmalseite lehrt zudem, dass er ein in offiziellem Auftrage abgefasstes Dokument darstellt. . . Sollten die Masse von Esagil und Ezida beim Bau assyrischer Tempel als massgebend gelten oder hat man sich eine Abschrift des Textes aus Babylonien besorgt, als es gegen Ende der Regierung Sanheribs galt, Babylon und damit auch Esagil in den alten geheiligten Massen wieder aufzubauen?' (Weidner 1963: 116).

2. Since the builders of Solomon's Temple were Tyrians, it is not impossible that the instructions given them reflect somehow the architecture of some Tyrian temple, and that this temple served as a prototype for Solomon's Temple.

3. This is not to imply that oral instructions were never given to builders. The Tabernacle story states that Moses gathered the congregation and told them the list of structures and cultic vessels which the skillful among them were commanded to fashion (Exod. 35.10-19). The Baal epic contains an account of a conversation between Baal and the craftsgod KotharwaHasis concerning the form of the palace and Baal even informs him what the area of the buildings is to be (*UT* 51 V 106–VI 17; for the area measure see V 118-19—is this related to the Mesopotamian texts from Nippur, Mari and Uruk which describe the area of buildings?). A fragmentary text about Adad-šuma-uṣur (a king of Babylon during the Kassite period) relates that the contributors to the restoration of Esagila gathered all the artisans and described to them the work they were to perform. Afterwards, the text states that the king gathered them and added additional detail to the work to be done (Grayson 1975: 72). It is important to note that in all these cases the instructions given are very brief and general and do not resemble in content or style the descriptions of the buildings in 1 Kings 6–7 or the text from Assyria being discussed here. The writing down of building instructions is mentioned in Ezek. 43.11 and in 1 Chron. 28.11-19. Ezekiel's instructions, at least, resemble in style and content the building descriptions in Kings. It should, however, be mentioned that committing the instructions to writing in both these cases is done so as to enable the instructions to be handed down to a future generation. In both cases, the writer of the instructions has merited a divine revelation and a divine command, although the execution of the instructions is not imposed on him but on someone else. The command is to be fulfilled sometime in the future and not by the man to whom it was delivered. For this reason, the

reconstruction of its function support for Van Seters's proposal that the Temple description is exilic, for the biblical description may reflect a document meant to be used by potential rebuilders of the Temple who will want to replicate exactly the old one. A biblical analogy for such a scenario might be Ezek. 40.1–43.12. The prophet describes the Temple which is to be built, but probably has in his mind the image of the Temple which was just destroyed.

5. *Three descriptions of temples found at Mari* (f). These three short texts were all found in Hall 115 at Mari, and all were apparently written by the same scribe. They give the dimensions (length, width and area) of the room, dividing walls and doorways of the Teshub (?) temple at Kahat, the Bēlet-apim temple at Shubat-Enlil and an unknown temple (text mutilated). D. Charpin mooted the idea that the text about the Kahat temple may have been composed for an architect envisaging the temple's reconstruction after it had been damaged by the armies of Zimri-Lim. He rejected the idea, however, because this text ends by giving the Akkadian and Sumerian names of the temple in question, a piece of information which he feels would be unnecessary for the builder to whom the text was addressed. He suggests then that the text may be a sort of descriptive inventory.

We might add to Charpin's reservations about the 'architect's plan' explanation of the texts the fact that the area is stated. As mentioned before, this is something one describing an existing structure might include, but one which an architect building a new edifice would find unnecessary. In addition, the existence of three similar texts seriously calls into question the possibility that they were composed to facilitate reconstruction. Were all three temples damaged, and were they all simultaneously slated for restoration? As Charpin pointed out, these texts resemble the text from Uruk describing the Resh temple. If so, the same hesitations expressed above about assigning that text an 'administrative' function may be expressed in this case as well. Although an 'administrative' role cannot be dismissed as a possibility, the exact nature of that function must await further investigation.

All the descriptions mentioned so far were of complete buildings.

---

writing down of the temple plan in these two cases is to be seen as an example of the wider phenomenon of writing down prophecies and divine words which are to be fulfilled only at a future date (Deut. 31.19-30; Isa. 30.8; Hab. 2.2-23; Dan. 12.4 and see on this phenomenon Loewenstamm 1962b).

Each document suggested one or more possibilities as background for the description of the temple building in 1 Kings 6. Obviously, the existence of a document constitutes no proof for a suggestion which it engenders. Nonetheless, these documents supply at the least actual examples for what would otherwise be purely speculative. The documents presented also suggest possibilities not previously entertained by biblical scholars.

Descriptions of Furnishings

1. *The description of the bed of Marduk and Ṣarpanitu* (i)[1] appears as part of two different inscriptions. One text (K 8664) includes a dedication of Sennacherib to Assur, a description of the bed, and a colophon describing an inscription on the bed. The second text (K 2411) contains a dedication of Assurbanipal to Marduk, a dedication of Sennacherib to Assur, a description of the bed, and a colophon describing both the inscription on the bed and an inscription which had already been erased from the bed.

Despite the paragraphs of dedication and prayer found in these two texts, the inscriptions themselves *are not* dedicatory inscriptions. The two inscriptions are in fact descriptions of the bed. The words of dedication which are included in these two inscriptions are *copies* of true dedicatory inscriptions which were inscribed on the bed itself, where a dedicatory inscription should be written! It turns out that the words of dedication included in these two texts are really a part of the description of the bed. It was part and parcel of a depiction of the bed in its entirety for the scribe to copy out the inscription written on the bed.

For what purpose were these descriptions written? The longer of the inscriptions (K 2411) is dated to 27 Kislimu in the *līmu* of Awianu, which is the thirteenth year of Shamash-shum-ukin. Since the bed of Marduk was returned to Babylon only in Shamash-shum-ukin's fourteenth year, and since the inscription contains a citation from an inscription which had been erased together with a citation from the newly written inscription, it seems that the writing of the description is connected somehow with the preparation of the bed for its rededication. The inscription may be a report of the work supervisor overseeing the exchange of inscriptions. It is also possible that this report

---

1.   For the part of the inscription describing the bed, and for literature on the text, see Barnett 1950: 40-42. For the history of the bed and the inscription, see Landsberger 1965: 25-26 and n. 40, as well as Millard 1964: 19-23.

was prepared in the workroom in Assur before the bed was sent on to Babylon. We cannot know with certainty what the circumstances of the tablet's composition actually were, but the data available enable us to conjecture that the tablet was prepared for some administrative purpose, and that it is connected with the transfer of the bed from one temple to the other. The shorter inscription (K 8664) contains no date formula and Assurbanipal is not mentioned, but it is hard to imagine that its composition was not connected with the same circumstances for which the longer text was written.

2. *The description of pillars from Kar-Tukulti-Ninurta* (j)[1] is a most promising document in the quest after a literary model for the description of the vessels in 1 Kings 7. The text, written on a small tablet discovered at Assur, was composed, so it seems, on the occasion of dedicating several wooden columns to a temple in the city Kar-Tukulti-Ninurta (Grayson, *ARI*, I §509-14 = Weidner 1954–55: 145-46). The text contains two parts. The first part describes the columns (ll. 1-11) and their capitals (ll. 12-15), specifying their length and thickness as well as the quality of the workmanship (2). The second part of the text (ll. 19-35) states that the columns bore royal dedicatory inscriptions (ll. 21-25) and that they were brought from Assur to Kar-Tukulti-Ninurta and set up in the temple (*bīt papāhi*) on the fifth day (of the month Qararatu?) when the king made an offering. The transfer of the columns from one place to the other was done upon order of the king. This document, then, describes the pillars, their capitals, their lengths and thicknesses, the places where they stood and the inscriptions inscribed upon them. It is reminiscent not only of the two previously discussed texts, but also of the detailed description of the pillars Jachin and Boaz which also specifies the length of the columns (1 Kgs 7.15), their girth (v. 15b), the place where they were set up (v. 21) and their names (v. 21).[2]

1. See Postgate 1973 no. 212 concerning pillars described in a 'library' text.
2. It has been suggested that the names Jachin and Boaz are connected somehow with inscriptions which were inscribed on the pillars themselves. See Scott 1939. On the symbolism of the pillars, see most recently Meyers 1983. She does not discuss the names. According to Scott, the appellations *yākîn* and *bō'az* are the first words in sentence-long inscriptions which were dynastic oracles or prayers. In support of the feasibility of this suggestion, we might mention the fact that in various Mesopotamian inscriptions, doors or gates of cities and palaces are given festive

Both the literary form and the function of this tablet are more or
less clear. It seems to be an administrative record, a type of receipt,
which records a gift given by the king on the occasion of his participation in a certain cultic celebration.

On the basis of this document, it may be suggested that the description of the temple furnishings in 1 Kings 7 is based, ultimately, on
administrative records written when the vessels were given over to or
installed in the temple. The priests who were in charge of the temple
property both accepted the vessels (from the king) and entered a written record of the donation in the temple's account books. Alternatively, palace scribes made records of the bronze objects when they
were given over to the temple by the king.

3. *The inventory from Kar-Tukulti-Ninurta* (k)[1] is a detailed list describing various decorations and furnishings found in the palace in the
city. According to the suggestion of the text's editor, this text is an
inventory and description of objects which were brought from the city
Assur. They were contributed and placed in a temple in the new capital city, Kar-Tukulti-Ninurta. The end of the text, which is only partially preserved, mentions the *qîpu* (temple administrator) named Bel-
Assur who seems to have been the official who received all the income
of the temple and who registered the incoming items, with detailed
and exact descriptions.

These three descriptions (i, j and k) derive, as we have seen, from
administrative circles and were written, apparently, on different occasions when the king would dedicate some cultic object to the temples.
The biblical description of the temple furnishings also contains certain
administrative features, as well as a reference to the dedication of
certain vessels to the temple. Within the description of the vessels

names (*Prunknamen*) which are in fact blessings or wishes for the king. See, for
instance, concerning the name of a gate in Dur-Sharrukin, *Enlil-mukīn-išdī-ālīja
Ninlil-mudeššat-ḫiṣbi zikri abullī Enlil u Ninlil. . . ambi*, 'I named the Gates of
Enlil and Ninlil Enlil-Keeps-the-Foundations-of-My-City-Secure (and) Ninlil-
Creates-Abundance' and other references found in *CAD* N I, p. 34 *s.v. nabû*
A1a3′c′. Sennacherib gives names to all fifteen gates of Nineveh, one of them being
Enlil mukīn palêja, 'Enlil (is the) establisher of my reign' (Luckenbill 1924: 112 VII
77. See also Gelb 1956). In the Bible as well, names are given to cultic objects.
Jacob sets up an altar (pillar?) and calls it *'ēl 'ĕlōhê yiśrā'ēl* (Gen. 33.20). Moses
builds an altar which he calls *YHWH nissî* (Exod. 17.15).
    1. See Köcher 1957–58: 100-13, and most recently Barrelet 1977.

themselves, there are 'summary' statements giving the total number of vessels manufactured as well as the quantities of the materials expended in their production (1 Kgs 7.40-47; cf. also 1 Kgs 6.9-12). The entire account concludes with the statement that '. . . Solomon brought in the sacred donations of his father David—the silver, the gold, and the vessels—and deposited them in the treasury of the House of the Lord'. We might add that the Tabernacle account contains a passage which can only be called a 'balance sheet', registering income, expenditures, the names of the clerks and accountants, and also reflecting an 'administrative' background (Exod. 38.21–39.1).[1]

There is room to conjecture that at least the description of the temple appurtenances was influenced in content and style by official administrative documents composed by the priests or royal scribes who tended to the temple income. Now, one might be inclined to follow M. Noth and expect that 'receipts', 'inventories' or similar administrative documents would merely list the objects and not contain verbs noting the fact that the objects had been made. If this assumption is valid, such verbs as do appear in these descriptions could be considered the words of the biblical narrator who has reformulated administrative diction into narrative style suited to the wider context of a building account. As for the description of the temple building itself (1 Kgs 6), it is not impossible that the author has imitated in his description the style of exercises which he had done in school, but it is more likely that he was influenced by the style of written instructions which would have been given to a builder. Here too, it should be added, the verbs in the description might be construed as the contribution of a scribe turning the prescriptive document into narrative.

The comparison of the biblical descriptions of building and vessels to the Mesopotamian texts has not, it is true, enabled us to determine with absolute certainty—and still less constitutes no 'proof' of—the origin and the literary form of the descriptions. Nevertheless, the fact that precise descriptions are on the one hand absent in royal building accounts, and on the other hand well attested outside this limited corpus, reinforces the possibility that the biblical author was influenced from some already existing literary form, and did not invent his style of description *ex nihilo*.

---

1.   See also Ezra 1.7-11 and 8.23-34a for 'ledgers' with many of the same features found in the 'Tabernacle Ledger'.

Chapter 11

The Dedication of the Temple (1 Kings 8.1-11, 62-66)

The festivities, rituals, speeches and prayers marking the dedication (*ḥănukkâ*) of Solomon's temple are described at length in 1 Kings 8. A revised version of this account is found in the parallel description in 2 Chronicles 5–7. Other dedication ceremonies are described in Numbers 7 (dedication of the Tabernacle altar); Ezra 6.16-22 (the restored Temple), Neh. 12.27-44 (the repaired walls of Jerusalem) and Daniel 3 (an idol).[1] Although not designated *ḥănukkâ*, there are also related 'sanctification' (*qiddûš*) rituals described for the Tabernacle in Exodus 40 (cf. also Exod. 30.22-33) and Leviticus 8–9;

---

1.   Certain scholars would associate Ps. 24.1-7 and Ps. 68 with the dedication of the temple or with an annually recurring festival commemorating the event. See, for instance, Schreiner 1963: 174-90. The only Psalm specifically associated with the dedication of some 'House'(?) is Psalm 30, but the title and the reference remain enigmatic. Rabbinic and mediaeval Jewish exegesis connects this Psalm with the dedication of the first temple. Rashi suggests that David composed it to be used by the Levites when the temple would be built and dedicated. Radaq, however, countered with the proposal that the 'House' dedicated was David's cedar palace. Modern scholars tend to treat the title separately from the Psalm to which it is appended, claiming that the body of the chapter is a psalm of an individual, and that only after the purification of the temple under the Maccabees and institution of the Jewish Hanukkah festival was the Psalm given a nationalistic interpretation by affixing the title (see, for example, Mowinckel 1967: I, 3, 5; II, 19; Weiser 1962: 119). The most likely candidate for a Psalm associated with temple building in general and the dedication of the temple in particular is Psalm 132. It deals with the search for a resting place for the Ark, and contains various temple-building motifs. The divine promises with which it concludes (vv. 15-17) are comparable to the blessings or requests included in the ancient Near Eastern building inscriptions, and associated with prayers uttered at dedication festivities. The Chronicler is the first to associate this Psalm with the dedication of the Temple, paraphrasing parts of it (vv. 1, 8 10) as part of his revised version of Solomon's dedication prayer (2 Chron. 5.41-42). For modern opinions, see the commentaries on Psalms (especially Kraus 1958 on Ps. 132) and Chronicles, and Hillers 1968.

initiation ceremonies for the priests (*millûy yādayim*) prescribed and described in Exodus 29 and Leviticus 8 (note also Num. 8.5-22 which reports the purification and dedication—*tĕnûpâ*—of the Levites); and sanctification (*qiddûš*) rites for the altar prescribed at the end of Exodus 29, and carried out (perhaps) in Leviticus 8. Ezek. 43.18-27 contains instructions for the purification and 'hand filling' of the altar in the temple of the future. Each of these accounts has its own character and internal problems, and a separate study of each is required, which is well beyond the scope of the present work.[1] In this chapter the discussion will be restricted to four aspects of 1 Kings 8: (a) certain higher critical problems of 1 Kgs 8.1-11 and in particular the extent and purposes of the 'Priestly' insertions; (b) the essence of the dedication ceremonies and the relationship between the dedication of Solomon's temple and the dedications of other biblical temples; (c) the account of the dedication of Solomon's Temple and its relationship to 2 Samuel 6; (d) the relationship of 1 Kings 8 (and 2 Sam. 6) to parallel accounts from Mesopotamia. In this context some aspects of the Mesopotamian dedication ceremonies which appear to have been ignored by Assyriologists and not fully appreciated by biblical scholars will be examined and elucidated.[2]

1.   I dealt extensively with these ceremonies in my Hebrew University Master's thesis, *Temple Dedication Ceremonies in the Bible (in Light of Extra-biblical Material)* (in Hebrew) (Jerusalem, 1974), and I hope to return again to this subject. The consecration of the Tabernacle and the initiation of the priests has been treated again by Milgrom (1991) and Levine (1989) in their commentaries on Leviticus and Numbers. For dedication of the Tabernacle altar in Num. 7, see Levine 1965 and Milgrom 1985a.

2.   For public festivals in general, dedication ceremonies included, see Renger 1970. Renger emphasizes the public and social aspects of these occasions. Ellis (1968) restricts his discussion of building rituals to those which left archaeologically recoverable remains, and for this reason he passes over dedication festivities in silence. It is possible, however, that certain Sumerian texts such as Gudea Cylinder B, the Kesh Temple building hymn and the Lugalannemundu inscription make brief references to objects placed in the temple upon its completion. The Bible may contain references to rites of completing certain buildings (Zech. 4.7; Ps. 118.22; Job 38.6-7), although the enigmatic terms *'eben hāro'šāh, rō'š pinnâ* and *'eben pinnâ* may refer to foundation stones (see Isa. 28.16). McCarter (1983) claims that 2 Sam. 6 describes the dedication of Jerusalem as David's new capital, comparing it with ancient Near Eastern material. It should be noted, however, that not all the evidence he adduces is equally relevant. For rites accompanying the installation of gods into temporary dwellings, see Appendix 4.

1. *The 'Priestly' Expansions in 1 Kings 8.1-11*

All the 'Priestly' elements in the account of the Temple dedication are concentrated in the opening part of the account which describes bringing the Ark to the new Temple, placing it inside, and the entry of the *kābôd*, the visible manifestation of YHWH's presence. The starting point in the higher critical study of this chapter, and especially the question of the Priestly contribution, has customarily been the version which appears in the Greek translation. This version is somewhat shorter than the Masoretic Text, particularly in the first five verses, and attempts have been made to discover a correlation between the minuses in the Greek version and a later 'Priestly' editing. Understandably, these attempts are based on the common assumption of the late date of the P source. Wellhausen spoke of Priestly expressions and later expressions,[1] while Burney assigned the siglum R^P to everything missing in the Greek translation.[2] When a problem arose and it was noticed that 'Priestly' elements were found also in parts of the MT which are not missing in the Greek,[3] Wellhausen was forced to explain them by speaking about knowledge of the Tabernacle, while Burney just invented another sign—SS^P—to describe such elements. Some more recent scholars explain them all as 'Priestly' without superscripts and what is implied therein. Others take none of them to be 'Priestly'.[4] It seems that examination of all the evidence together will show that there is no systematic correlation between minuses in the Greek and the Priestly expressions, and that the Greek version can be explained as the result of the intentional shortening of a somewhat confused text. The following table shows the divergent elements and their distribution. The places where a Priestly element found in MT

---

1. Wellhausen 1963: 265-68.
2. Burney 1903: 107.
3. Burney attributes to R^P 1 Kgs 6.11-13 as well, but there is no justification for this. The expression *wešākantî bĕtôk bĕnê yiśrā'ēl* is Priestly, but the rest of the passage is not. An expression such as *wĕlō' 'e'ezōb 'et 'ammî yiśrā'ēl* is not only not Priestly, but seems to be Deuteronomic. The entire passage is most likely a very late addition to the story, made by an author who is equally 'fluent' in Priestly and Deuteronomic style, namely, one who already is familiar with the entire Pentateuch.
4. Haran (1978: 141 n. 11) regards the entire group of 'Priestly' glosses as emanating from the same hand, while Friedman (1961: 48) would have none of the expressions attributed to P.

(+) corresponds to an element missing in the Greek (–) are marked by a zero (0).

Verse	Expression	Priestly	Correlation	Greek
1	*'eṯ kol-rā' šê hammaṭṭôt*	+	0	–
	nĕśî'ê hā'āḇōṯ liḇnê yiśrā'ēl			
	'el-hammelek šĕlōmōh	–		–
2	*wayyiqqāhălû 'el-hammelek šĕlōmōh*	–		–
	kol-'îš yiśrā'ēl			
	behāg	–		–
	hû' hahōḏeš haššĕbî'î	?	0?	–
3	*wayyāḇō'û kōl ziqnê yiśrā'ēl*	–		–
4	*wayya'ălû 'eṯ-'ărôn YHWH*	–		–
	wĕ'eṯ-'ōhel mô'ēḏ	+		+
	wĕ'eṯ-kol-kĕlê haqqōḏeš 'ăšer bā'ōhel	+		+
	wayya'ălû 'ōṯām hakkohănîm wĕhalwiyyim	+	0	–
5	*šĕlōmōh*	–		–
	'ăḏaṯ	+	0	–
	hannô'āḏîm 'ālâw ittô	+	0	–
6	*'el-qōḏeš haqqŏḏāšîm*	+		–

Only in the four (or five) cases marked by 0 is there a correlation between an element identifiable as 'Priestly' and a minus in the Greek (+ –). In six cases, the Greek deletes words or expressions which are not Priestly (– –), and in three cases characteristically Priestly language is not missing in the Greek (+ +). Examination of three more expressions enhances to an even greater degree the likelihood that the Greek has intentionally revised the Hebrew:

5	MT	*'ăšer lō' yissāpĕrû wĕlō' yimmānû mērōḇ*	Gk	ηναράθμητα
6	MT	*'ărôn bĕrîṯ YHWH*	Gk	τlν κιβωτὰν
10	MT	*bêṯ YHWH*	Gk	τὰν ϲἶκον

In each of these three cases there is not a full minus but an abbreviation of the Hebrew idiom. The second case, *'ărôn berîṯ YHWH*, is a Deuteronomistic expression while the other two are not characteristic of the style of any particular school. The third case is the exchange of a term with a synonymous one.

Just as the last three instances are cases of abbreviation on the part of the Greek translator, it seems that in the other cases as well he has shortened the text, and especially in places where MT is repetitive. For example, Gk retains *'āz yaqhēl Šĕlōmōh 'et ziqnê yiśrā'ēl* but deletes two non-priestly expressions which add no new information and seem superfluous: *wayyiqqāhălû 'el hammelek šĕlōmōh kol 'îš yiśrā'ēl*, and *wayyābō'û kol ziqnê yiśrā'ēl*. Gk retains *beyeraḥ hā'ētānîm* but deletes *behāg hû' haḥōdeš haššĕbî'î*, which is obviously a gloss, but not necessarily a Priestly one. Gk retains *leha'ălôt 'et 'ărôn bĕrît YHWH* with a certain revision, but deletes *wayya'ălû 'et 'ărôn YHWH*. While retaining *wayyābî'û hakkōhănîm 'et hā'ărôn*, Gk deletes *wayya'ălû 'ōtām hakkōhănîm wĕhalwiyyim*. The Hebrew text is admittedly full and verbose, and perhaps a bit clumsy. For this reason the Greek translator 'cleaned it up', and by chance he removed certain Priestly elements which were to begin with some of the causes of the text's inflated nature. But, as we have seen, there is no full correlation between the elements removed and the Priestly elements in the MT, so it cannot be claimed (as has been done) that the Greek text indicates a pre-MT stage in the literary development of the pericope.

Although efforts have been made to identify the Priestly elements in the chapter, not much attention has been given to accounting for their presence. This is most surprising, for it is the only place in the entire book of Kings that this school has contributed anything. (1 Kgs 6.11-13, especially v. 13, sounds Priestly but is not. It is an insertion by a late author who is already equally familiar and comfortable with the styles of D and P, and uses them freely and simultaneously.)[1] This intrusion is even more surprising if Priestly contributions are limited to those passages missing in the Greek, for the deleted words do not actually contribute any significance to the account and may as well have been left out in the first place. The only verse that adds some vital new information is v. 4 which speaks of bringing the tent and the sacred vessels which were in the tent, and this verse is found in the Greek as well as in MT. It is most likely that it was this essential piece of information that led to the Priestly intrusion and brought along with it the remaining Priestly expansions. There is no reason to follow Wellhausen and attribute this verse to some early, unidentified source and the rest to a later Priestly scribe. All the Priestly language was contributed by the same pen at the same time.[2] It seems that this description of a crucial event in the history of the Jerusalem Temple became the object of a unique, one-time Priestly revision, the purpose of which was to mention the Tabernacle and its sacred vessels,

---

1.   Paran (1989) notes Priestly-like diction in 2 Kgs 12 and 14, but explains that this is proto-P, namely the Temple jargon and style from which P's distinctive language derived.

2.   See Haran 1978; Friedman 1961.

thereby informing the reader that the Jerusalem Temple built and dedicated by Solomon is the legitimate heir of the ancient Tabernacle and cult of the desert period. What we have here is what P.R. Ackroyd has called a 'continuity motif'.[1] The idea of linking a new temple with an old one may be expressed in the Mesopotamian rite of the *libittu mahrītu*, 'the former brick', by which a brick from a temple being restored is ritually removed and then placed in the foundations of the new temple.[2] In the Bible it is known to us from the account in Ezra of the restoration of the Temple. One of the actions taken by Cyrus is to return to Sheshbazar the vessels removed from the Temple destroyed by Nebuchadnezzar (Ezra 1.7-11). The Priestly reviser has introduced the 'continuity motif' into the account of the Temple dedication. While so doing, he also takes the opportunity to equate the dedication of the Temple with the dedication of the Tabernacle by mentioning *kol rāšê hammaṭṭôt nĕśî'ê hā'ābôt libnê*

---

1. Ackroyd: 161-81. I totally reject the odd proposal made in at least three scholarly and popular publications by Friedman (1980, 1981, 1987) to the effect that the Tabernacle was placed in the Holy of Holies of the Solomonic Temple, under the wings of the Cherubim. F.M. Cross, quoted in a review article of Friedman's book in the *Wall Street Journal* from mid-September, 1987, says, 'It's a thoroughly defendable position even though I don't agree with it'. Weinfeld (1983b: 104) even went as far as to adduce a Hittite parallel for the proposed practice. Support could also imaginably be adduced for this theory from a frequent refrain found in the Anzu myth, *ina kibrat erbetti šitakkana māḥāzīka, māḥāzūka līrubū ana ekur*, 'Place your shrines across the world, Even into the Ekur your shrines shall reach' (Hallo and Moran 1979, *passim*). Nonetheless, as I pointed out in my review of Friedman's book (Hurowitz 1984b: 67-69), the revolutionary reconstruction of the Tabernacle necessitated by the proposal is not only far from 'thoroughly defendable', but it is quite impossible. It depends ultimately on a totally unjustifiable emendation of an intelligible, crucial 'keystone' passage (Exod. 26.33) into virtual nonsense. Friedman's proposal shows a lack of appreciation for the precise and economical style of the Priestly description, and he errs by finding and filling in gaps which are actually not there. There is no basis whatever in the text for the overlapping *qĕrāšîm*—an architectural refurbishing of the Tabernacle proposed as well by Aharoni (1973: 82) as part of an unsuccessful attempt to make the Tabernacle identical in structure to the Arad temple. The poetic passages from Psalms and Lamentations, supposedly referring to the Tabernacle, are simply archaic metaphors for the Temple. The passages from Chronicles which refer to the Temple as a Tabernacle reflect the Chronicler's view that the Temple is the legitimate heir of the desert tent-shrine, and are not to be separated from passages in the description of the Temple which describe parts of the temple as if they were parts of the Tabernacle.
2. Ellis 1968.

yiśrā'ēl. The dignitaries mentioned here are the same ones mentioned in Num 7.1-2 as participating in the dedication of the Tabernacle altar.

2. *The Essence of the Dedication Ceremonies*

Houses were dedicated in ancient Israel by taking up residence in them, probably amid certain festivities, rituals and prayers. Although there are no sources describing the dedication of a house, the nature of such events may be indicated by a comparison of two passages from the book of Deuteronomy.[1] In the charge to the army officials going out to battle, they are told to proclaim (Deut. 20.5-7):

> Is there anyone who has built a new house *but has not 'dedicated' it* (*hănākô*)? Let him go back to his home, lest he die in battle and another *'dedicate' it* (*yahnĕkennû*). Is there anyone who has planted a vineyard and has never harvested its first fruits? Let him go back to his home, lest he die in battle and another harvest its first fruits. Is there anyone who has paid the bride-price for a wife, but who has not yet married her? Let him go back to his home, lest he die in battle and another marry her.

In a somewhat parallel passage in the great list of covenant maledictions, we find (Deut. 28.30):

> If you pay a bride price for a wife, another man shall lie with her.
> If you build a house, *you shall not live in it* (*lō' tēšēb bô*).
> If you plant a vineyard, you shall not harvest its first fruits.

The parallel nature of these two passages shows that 'dedicating' (*hnk*) a house is done by 'living in it' for the first time, just as 'taking a

---

1.   See Reif 1972. Reif accepts the opinion of Rankin (1930) that the word *HNK* means to initiate, i.e. to start to use something. Although, for the sake of convenience, I have used the term 'dedicate' to refer to ceremonies performed when a building or other object is initially put in use, I accept the interpretation offered (which is, as Reif indicates, already found among mediaeval commentators). In the Mesopotamian inscriptions the verbs *nadānum, qiāšum, šarākum* and *karābum* (all of which mean to give or to dedicate) are almost never used with a temple as the object. For an exception, see Langdon 1915–16: 104: 6 and 21 (// Langdon 1912: 242 Nabonidus no. 4:15), and perhaps Grayson 1987: 32 Irišum I A. O. 33.10 Col. II 1-3. It must be remembered, nonetheless, that in Mesopotamia, even though not stated explicitly, the temple was considered a royal gift to the god, and the dedication ceremonies may indeed have had certain overtones of 'dedication' or 'presentation', and not merely 'initiation'. In the next chapter we will see that Solomon, in the Deuteronomic prayer attributed to him, wrestles with this very concept.

wife' is equivalent to consummating the marriage by lying with her for the first time.

If the dedication of a house is accomplished by its builder taking up residence in it, so a temple, which is primarily conceived of as a divine dwelling place, is dedicated by its divine resident taking up residence within it. Now the Jerusalem Temple was originally conceived of as God's residence, even though throughout the biblical period there were greater or lesser revisions in this conception. Accordingly, the dedicatory rites involve bringing into the Temple symbols of the divine presence. Thus the major event in the original, pre-Deuteronomic and pre-Priestly form of 1 Kings 8 is the introduction into the Temple of the Ark of YHWH, which in the pre-monarchic and early monarchic period had been the major symbol of YHWH's presence. The Ark was YHWH's footstool or pedestal upon which or beside which he could be expected to be present. The priests place it in the inner sanctum, the *debîr* under the outstretched wings of the Cherubim, which represented YHWH's throne, but which were another symbol of his presence. All this is obviously on the mundane, tangible level of artistic objects. On the 'supernatural' level we are told that when the priests had finished their task of installing the Ark and had vacated the Temple, the Cloud of YHWH entered, and along with the *Kābôd* which it enveloped, filled the Temple (vv. 10-11).

Other biblical authors did not share the 'divine residence' concept of the Temple. Accordingly, they made revisions in this account and in accounts of other dedication ceremonies. The Deuteronomist, who saw the Temple as a place where God's name resided but not where God himself could be found, stresses that the Ark is not a symbol of God's presence, but only a receptacle containing the Tablets of the Covenant. He places in Solomon's mouth this description of the event (1 Kgs 8.20-21):

> . . . I have built the House for the Name of the Lord, the God of Israel; and I have set a place there for the Ark, containing the covenant which the Lord made with our fathers when he brought them out from the Land of Egypt (see also 8.9).

The Temple houses the Ark, but rather than symbolizing God's nearness to the Ark, it is a sign of the covenant relationship between him and his people.

The Priestly author views the Tabernacle as a place of YHWH's presence, so for him, the Tabernacle dedication is a time when God's *kābôd* fills the Tabernacle (Exod. 40.34-38) and may be witnessed by the people (Lev. 9.6, 23). This author associates with the dedication of the Tabernacle other important cultic events. Aaron and his sons are initiated into the priesthood (Exod. 29; Lev. 8), the altar is dedicated by sumptuous offering by the heads of the twelve tribes (Num. 7) and by the miraculous consumption of special sacrifices by a fire from God (Lev. 9.24). The first regular offerings are also made on this occasion (Lev. 9.17b).

Ezekiel shares the Priestly view and prophesies that God's *kābôd* will enter and fill the future temple (Ezek. 43.1-7) just as it had before it departed (Ezek. 1, 8–12). The Chronicler, describing the dedication of the Solomonic Temple, is quite content with the notion that the *kābôd* entered the Temple, and mentions the event twice (2 Chron. 5.14; 7.2). He also replaces Solomon's second benediction with a revised version of Num. 10.35-36 and Psalm 132, identifying the presence of the Ark with the presence of the Lord. Finally, he borrows from the Tabernacle dedication ceremony the information that the entire people witnessed the miraculous heavenly fire and the *kābôd* over the Temple (2 Chron. 7.1-3 // Lev. 9.23-24).

Nonetheless, this view is not shared by other exilic and post-exilic prophets. It seems to be explicitly opposed in Isa. 66.1 (rejecting specifically Ps. 132.8 and 14 which refer to the Temple as God's eternal resting place, *mĕnûḥâ*). It is reinterpreted in Hag. 2.7-9, where the prophet admits that *kābôd* will fill the Temple, but sees the *kābôd* as wealth and plenty, which symbolize God's blessing (see also Hag. 1.8). It is not the conception of the temple expressed by the author who (apparently many years after the fact and certainly not as an eyewitness) actually described the dedication ceremony of the restored temple. Ezra 6.17-22 reports the dedication of the rebuilt temple, but contains no reference to the crucial event of God's entry into the temple, or to the installation in the temple of any symbol of divine presence. The main events are sacrifices which include twelve purification offerings for the twelve tribes (perhaps reminiscent of the sacrifices of the twelve *nĕśî'îm* mentioned in Num. 7) and initiation of the priests and Levites recalling the initiation of priests marking the Tabernacle dedication (Lev. 8; Num. 8). Just as the Tabernacle had been dedicated in the first month, so is the rebuilt Temple, and the Passover celebrations seem to be part of the dedication ceremonies in the same way that the dedication of Solomon's Temple coincided with the Tabernacles Festival. Another element common to all the dedication ceremonies is the 'Happiness' (1 Kgs 8.66; Ezra 6.16, 22, 22; Lev. 9.24; note as well the happiness at the dedication of the walls of Jerusalem mentioned over and over again, five times in Neh. 12.43). In summary, the descriptions of temple dedication ceremonies of various authors are barometers reflecting the ongoing reassessment in Israelite thought of the function and meaning of the Temple itself.

3. *The Account of the Temple Dedication Ceremonies and 2 Samuel 6*

The closest parallel to the ceremonies and festivities described in 1 Kgs 8.1-11, 62-66 is the description in 2 Samuel 6 of how David brought the Ark from Kiryath-Jearim to Jerusalem. Comparison of these two passages will help clarify certain problems which have arisen and elucidate certain aspects of each.

	2 Samuel 6		*1 Kings 8*
1	*wayyōsep ʿôd dawid*	1	*ʾāz yaqhēl šĕlōmōh*
	ʾet-kol-bāḥûr bĕyiśrāʾēl		*ʾet-ziqnê yiśrāʾēl*
2	*lĕhaʿălôt*		*lĕhaʿălôt*
	miššām		
	ʾēt ʾărôn hāʾĕlōhîm		*ʾet-ʾărôn bĕrît YHWH*
			mēʿîr dawid
3-4	*wayyiśśăʾuhû. . . wayyiśśăʾuhû*	3	*wayyiśʾû hakkōhănîm ʾet hāʾārôn*
	[5-11 The Uzza Incident]		------------------
13	*wayhî kî ṣăʿădû nōśeʾê*	5	*wĕhammelek wĕkol-ʿădat yiśrāʾēl*
	ʾărôn-YHWH šiššâ ṣĕʿādîm		*ittô lipnê hāʾārôn*
	wayyizbaḥ šôr ûmrîʾ		*mĕzabbeḥîm ṣōʾn ûbāqār*
			ʾăšer lōʾ-yissāpĕrû
			wĕlōʾ yimmānû mērōb
17	*wayyābiʾû*	6	*wayyabiʾû hakkōhănîm*
	ʾet-ʾărôn YHWH		*ʾet-ʾărôn bĕrît-YHWH*
	wayyaṣṣigû ʾōtô bimqômô		*ʾel-mĕqômô*
	bĕtôk hāʾōhel		*ʾel-dĕbîr habbayit*
	--------------------		[10-11 The Cloud and Kābôd]
	--------------------		[12-61 Prayers and Speeches]
17	*wayyaʿal dawid ʿōlôt*	62	*wayyizbaḥ šĕlōmōh ʾet*
	lipnê YHWH ûšlāmîm		*zebaḥ haššĕlāmîm*
18	*waykal dawid mēhaʿălôt*	64	*kî ʿāśâ šām ʾet-hāʾōlâ*
	hāʿōlâ wĕhaššĕlāmîm		*weʾet-hamminḥāh wĕʾēt*
			ḥelbê haššĕlāmîm
	waybārek ʾet-hāʿām	66	*bayyôm haššĕmînî šillâḥ ʾet-hāʿām*
			waybārĕkēhû (so Gk!)

```
        běšēm YHWH ṣěbā'ôt
19      wayhallēq lěkol-hā'ām              -------------------
        lěkol-hămôn yiśrā'ēl              -------------------
        ḥallaṭ leḥem 'aḥaṭ'
        wě'ešpār 'eḥād wa'ăšišāh 'eḥāt    -------------------
        wayyēlek kol-hā'ām               wayyēlěkû
        'îš lěbêtô                       le'ohŏlêhem śěmēḥîm wěṭôbê lēb.
```

The similarities are so many and so pervasive that we must regard both texts as either deriving from the same author, being mutually dependent, or reflecting a common pattern. P.K. McCarter recently compared 2 Samuel 6 with accounts of temple and city dedication ceremonies from extra-biblical sources, suggesting as a result that the event described is the dedication of the new capital.[1] More of this evidence will be discussed below, emphasizing its importance for 1 Kings 8. Since the two biblical passages are so similar, and since they have equally strong extra-biblical parallels, it seems that they should be seen as representatives of a common Near Eastern pattern rather than as mutually dependent.

The similarities between the two accounts impart to them, to a certain extent, the status of 'parallel texts', and as such, there are certain minor textual implications. The parallel between 2 Sam. 6.18 and 1 Kgs 8.66 lends significant support to the Greek translation's reading *waybārěkēhû*, 'and he blessed them', as opposed to MT *waybārěkû 'et hammelek*, 'and they (the people) blessed the king'. Furthermore, although no evidence can be mustered from the versions, the first word in 2 Samuel 6.1, *wayyōsep*, should be explained as an ellided form of *wayye'ěsōp*, 'and he gathered' (see Radaq), because of the parallel with the word *yaqhēl*, 'he congregated', in 1 Kings 8. The similarities between the two passages should also demonstrate that 1 Kgs 8.1-11 really belongs together with vv. 61-66, and that their separation is secondary. This soundly refutes B. Stade's suggestion[2] that the account of the transfer of the Ark to Jerusalem was originally a separate event from the Temple dedication.

1.   See McCarter 1983.
2.   Stade 1883.

4. *The Dedication of the Temple and Mesopotamian Parallels*

Investigation into some Mesopotamian accounts of dedication ceremonies shows that the events described in both these biblical passages derive from a common ancient Near Eastern pattern.

a. *The Mesopotamian Sources*

Mesopotamian sources describe mostly two types of dedication ceremonies. Descriptions (some brief, some detailed) of dedication ceremonies for temples are found in Sumerian, Babylonian and Assyrian documents. A number of Assyrian inscriptions depict the dedications of royal palaces. There are a few inscriptions which refer to the dedication of a city in a manner reminiscent of the temple dedications. The dedication of divinely built temples is described in some myths. There is also certain artistic evidence concerning dedication ceremonies. Some individual inscriptions portray the dedication of a boat, an armory or a canal.

The Sources for Dedication of Temples. The longest existing description of a temple dedication ceremony is the one found in Cylinder B of Gudea. This account was discussed at length in the first part of the present study. We saw there that the major event was the introduction of Ningirsu and his spouse Bau into the new temple. The celebration of the dedication during the first month of the year, the presentation of gifts to the gods and the union of the two gods in sacred marriage were all intended to assure a good destiny for the temple, for the king who built it, and for the city in which it stood. All the citizens of Lagash celebrated the dedication of the temple for seven days, and there was reportedly a parallel celebration among the gods themselves.

Although no other dedication ceremony has been described at such length and in such detail, numerous inscriptions refer to similar celebrations and ceremonies, by recalling some of the main elements, and in particular bringing the god into the temple and seating him in his place in joy. Descriptions of or allusions to these ceremonies are found in the inscriptions listed in detail in the appendix at the end of this chapter. The sources for palace dedications and city dedications will also be listed there.

b. *The Differences between Temple and Palace Dedication Ceremonies*
When comparing these two types of dedication ceremonies, one is
liable to become falsely impressed by the similarities, and this is on
account of the fact that at both types of ceremonies huge amounts of
sacrifices and gifts were said to have been offered to the gods. But this
similarity is superficial, and relates to only a small number of inscriptions (see especially the dedication of Esharra and Enirgalanna by
Esarhaddon, the dedication of the Nabu and Tashmetum temple by
Sin-shar-ishkun and the dedication of Ehulhul by Nabonidus). The
similarity does not extend to the essence of the ceremonies. Careful
examination of all the sources reveals a clear, consistent and significant difference between the two types. All of the sources relating to
the dedication of a temple say either that the king brought the god into
the temple and seated him in his place in happiness, or that the god
entered the temple. Some sources even state that the king held the
(statue of the) god by the hand and led him in a procession to the
temple (see the inscriptions of Esarhaddon, Assurbanipal and
Nabonidus). In addition to this, the annals of Tiglath-pileser I tell us
that the dedication ceremony is called *terubat bītim*, 'the entry into the
house' (King, *AKA* 87 VI 90-93). This crucial element of the god
entering and sitting in his temple is entirely absent from the inscriptions relating to the building and dedication of palaces. Instead, all the
accounts of palace dedications, with no exception, state that the king
'invited' or 'called' (*qarû*) the gods of the city and the land into the
new palace. This invitation was so that the gods might join the party
and celebrate along with the people, the princes and the king. The
gods were invited to participate in the celebrations, but not to stay!
Sargon's account of the dedication of Dur-Sharrukin even says that the
gods returned to their own cities following the dedication of the
palace. This central idea of inviting the gods to the popular, mass
celebrations is, for its part, totally absent from the descriptions of
temple dedication ceremonies. In addition, the Akkadian verb *šurrû*
and the derived noun *tašrītu*, which mean 'to commence, initiate, start
off', are found in those inscriptions of Assurnasirpal, Sennacherib and
Assurbanipal which tell of the dedication of palaces in the cities Tiluli,
Tushata, Kalhu and Nineveh. Yet these words do not occur at all in
the descriptions of temple dedication ceremonies.[1] The difference in

1.   According to Streck 1916: 172 l. 62), the word *šurrû* occurs in connection
with the dedication of Ehulhul, and he reads *u-šar[ri?]*, but this text is broken and

the nature of the dedication ceremonies and the role of the gods in them derives, naturally, from the different functions of the buildings. In a temple dedication ceremony, the god takes up residence in his own new house, while in a palace dedication ceremony the god is only an honored guest in the house of the king. In his account of the rebuilding and rededicating of the Crown Prince's Palace (*bīt ridûti*), Assurbanipal relates that he entered his new palace accompanied by songs of praise.[1]

c. *The Dedication of Solomon's Temple in Comparison with the Dedication of Temples and Palaces in Mesopotamia*
The biblical account of the Temple dedication in Jerusalem resembles in many ways the Mesopotamian dedication ceremonies of both types. The similarities lie in the essence of the ceremonies, the structure of the descriptions and numerous details.

The essence. As we have already stated, the most important event in the dedication of the Temple is the introduction of the Ark and the entry of the *kābôd*, respectively the natural and 'supernatural' symbols of YHWH's presence. This parallels the Mesopotamian accounts of the introduction of divine statues into the temples and, in the cases of Nabonidus dedicating Eḫulḫul, the radiance lighting up the land when the god enters the temple.

The structure of the description. The biblical account is divided clearly into three parts: (1) entry of the Ark and YHWH into the Temple to the accompaniment of countless sacrifices (vv. 1-11); (2) the king's prayers (vv. 12-61); (3) the popular celebrations in the Temple courtyard (vv. 61-66). This three-stage celebration has parallels in the inscriptions of Sargon and Esarhaddon. It should be compared

Luckenbill (*ARAB*, II §915) translates, 'and caused him to take up his abode', obviously restoring the text *ušarmīšu šubassu*. In a collection of proverbs, Ebeling (*MAOG*, IV, 21-23 l. 10) reads *[u]-sa-ri-e bita-ma la-am il-pu-su*, and translates, 'Er hat das Haus [ge]weiht, bevor er es angefangen hat'. R. Pfeiffer (*ANET*, 425a) accepts this and translates, 'He consecrated the temple before he started it'. However, W.G. Lambert (1967: 278) leaves the line incomplete and untranslated, indicating thereby his rejection of Ebeling's reading.

1. *CAD* Z, p. 66, reads *za-rat*, 'canopy', but see von Soden, *AHw*, 1344 *s.v. taknûm* 2, who reads *zamar*, and likewise Berger 1970: 130-33.

especially to the account of the dedication of Dur-Sharrukin found at the end of Sargon's annals.[1] The king reports that in a good month and on a propitious day (see 1 Kgs 8.2) he invited the gods to the new city and offered before them countless gifts and sacrifices (cf. 8.5). Afterwards the king is said to prostrate himself and pray (Lie 1929: 80 ll. 12-13; compare 1 Kgs 8.14-16). Finally, the gods returned to their cities and Sargon celebrated along with the dignitaries of his empire who brought him tribute (cf. 8.61-66). Similar events are recorded in Esarhaddon's inscription describing the dedication of his armory (*ekal māšarti*).[2] The king reports that he invited the gods of Assur and offered sacrifices. Afterwards he claims that the gods blessed the kingdom. Finally there is a description of a great feast for the notables and commoners. Lastly we may compare the biblical account with the dedication of the Assur temple described by Esarhaddon.[3] There we read that the king seated Assur in his eternal dais (*parak dārāte*), placed around him gods and goddesses, and offered countless sacrifices. The gods saw his deeds and blessed him. Afterwards, together with his dignitaries and the people of his land, he celebrated for three days in the temple courtyard.

The Details of the Celebrations
a. *The participants in the festivities.* According to the pre-Priestly substratum of 1 Kings 8, the participants in the dedication of the Temple were the king, the priests (8.3), the elders (8.1, 3) and 'a great assemblage, [coming] from Lebo-hamath to the Wadi of Egypt' (v. 65). The Priestly hand has added to these 'all the heads of the tribes and the ancestral chieftains of the Israelites' (8.1) and the Levites (8.4). The Mesopotamian monarchs also boast that they celebrated along with their dignitaries and people from all lands of their dominion. Esarhaddon mentions *anāku adi rabûtīja nišē mātīja*, 'I, together with the notables and the people of my land'[4] as participants in the dedication of both the Assur temple and the armory.[5] Assurnasirpal II, in his famous 'Banquet Stele', relates that the dedication of Kalhu was attended by

1. Lie 1929: 78-83.
2. Borger 1956: 63 epis. 23.
3. Borger 1956: 5 ll. 28–6 l. 34.
4. Borger 1956: 6 ll. 26-27.
5. Borger 1956: 63 l. 49.

47,074 men, women, invited guests from all parts of my land, 5,000 notables representing the lands of Shuah, Hindanu, Hatiku, Hatti, Tyre, Sidon, Gurgum, Malik. . . (as well as) 16,000 residents of Kalhu (who were) palace officials, altogether 69,574 celebrants from all my lands as well as the people of Kalhu.[1]

Sargon dedicated Dur-Sharrukin along with

the kings of the four quarters of the earth, his provincial governors, princes, eunuchs and elders of the land of Assyria.[2]

In another version he expands the list somewhat, speaking of

the kings of the lands, the provincial governors of my land, supervisors, officers, princes, eunuchs and the elders of the land of Assyria.[3]

b. *The site of the festivities.* According to the biblical account, 'That day the king consecrated the center of the court that was in front of the House of the Lord. For it was there that he presented the burnt offerings, the meal offering (etc.)'. This remark may be compared with Esarhaddon's description of the dedication of the Assur temple (Borger 1956: 6 ll. 26-30):

I, along with my notables
(and) the people of my land
for three days in the courtyard of Esharra
I made a festival.

c. *The duration of the celebration.* Solomon celebrated the dedication of the Temple 'seven days and again seven days, fourteen days in all' (8.65). Multiple-day dedication rites are known as well from other biblical passages. The Tabernacle altar was dedicated in twelve days (Num. 7). The initiation of the priests which preceded the consecration of the Tabernacle lasted seven days (Lev. 8). The consecration of the altar in the Tabernacle was also to last seven days (Exod. 29.37),

1. Wiseman 1952.
2. Weissbach 1918: 184.
3. Lie 1929: 80 ll. 14-15. The description of 'Nebuchadnezzar's Court', found at the conclusion of a building inscription telling of construction of the royal palace in Babylon (Unger 1970: 282-93, esp. 284ff. = A.L. Oppenheim, *ANET*, 307-308), may actually be a register of the guests at the dedication celebration (I thank Professor M. Elat for this suggestion). Wiseman (1987: 74-75) also raises the possibility, only to reject it and propose that the celebration is not a dedication ceremony, but rather 'a procession to commemorate a special occasion'. He does not specify what type of a special occasion he has in mind.

as was the consecration of the future altar prescribed by Ezekiel (Ezek. 43.18-27, especially v. 26). The dedication of the Second Temple may have lasted at least seven days if it coincided or was joined with the Passover celebrations (Ezra 6.22). Purification of the defiled Temple at the time of Hezekiah lasted, according to the account in 2 Chronicles 29, seven (eight?) days whereas the consecration rites which followed immediately lasted eight days (2 Chron. 29.17; according to S. Zeitlin, it was this sequence of events that served as the paradigm for the purification and rededication of the Second Temple at the time of the Maccabees, celebrated by the eight-day Hanukkah festival).[1] Dedication ceremonies in Mesopotamia were also multi-day events. Gudea celebrated the dedication of Eninnu for seven days. Assurnasirpal spent ten days dedicating Kalhu, while Esarhaddon gave three days to dedicating Esharra.

d. *Countless offerings.* According to 1 Kgs 8.5:

> Meanwhile, King Solomon and the whole community of Israel, who were assembled with him before the Ark, were sacrificing sheep and oxen in such abundance that they could not be numbered or counted.

Similar statements appear in the inscriptions of Sargon (Lie 1929: 78 . 10) and Esarhaddon (Borger 1956: 5 V 37–VI 1). Yet despite this statement, the end of the description tells us (8.62-63):

> The king and all Israel with him offered sacrifices before the LORD. Solomon offered 22,000 oxen and 120,000 sheep as sacrifices of well being to the LORD.

Among the Mesopotamian inscriptions is a unique document, the so-called 'Banquet Stele' of Assurnasirpal II (Wiseman 1952), which itemizes literally 'from soup to nuts', down to the very last detail, the grand fare which was served up to the more than 60,000 celebrants at the dedication of the new palace in Kalhu. This detailed inscription is also interestingly comparable to the note in 2 Sam. 6.19:

> And he (David) distributed among all the people—the entire multitude of Israel, man and woman alike—to each a loaf of bread, a cake made in a pan, and a raisin cake.

---

1.   Zeitlin 1938–39. See Petersen 1977: 77-85, for an analysis of 2 Chron. 29 and Hezekiah's purification of the temple. Note also Milgrom 1985b.

e. *Sending the people home*. The account of the Temple dedication concludes with the statement (8.66):

> On the eighth day he let the people go. They blessed the king [Gk. reads, probably correctly, 'he blessed them'] and went to their tents, joyful and glad of heart. . .

This parallels 2 Sam. 6.19: 'Then all the people left for their homes'. These two passages are to be compared with the 'Banquet Stele' in which Assurnasirpal states:[1]

> In well being and happiness
> I returned them to their lands.

5. *Conclusions*

The biblical account of the dedication of the Temple in Jerusalem has numerous parallels in the Mesopotamian building inscriptions. The essence of dedicating the Jerusalem Temple is identical to the essence of dedicating a Mesopotamian temple. As for the structures of the ceremonies and various details of the description of the events, there are numerous and important parallels in the Mesopotamian temple and palace dedication ceremonies and the texts describing them. Yet at the same time, the Mesopotamian evidence is somewhat circumscribed as to its historical background. The building stories from the neo-Babylonian period do not contain descriptions of dedication ceremonies similar to those found in the Assyrian royal inscriptions from the time of Assurnasirpal II until Assurbanipal and Sin-shar-ishkun. At most there are references (in 'secondary' building stories) to the god sitting in his temple in joy.[2]

The most obvious parallels to the biblical account are found in the Assyrian royal inscriptions, and in a few of Nabonidus' inscriptions which are known for being subject to Assyrian influence.[3] For this reason it may be conjectured that the account of dedicating the Jerusalem Temple either grew out of the literary background of the Neo-Assyrian period, or out of the religious and cultural circumstances of that age.

---

1. The similarity between the two texts was pointed out by Mallowan (1967: 62). He suggests that the two celebrations, which occurred within about a century of one another, represent a common ancient Near Eastern custom.
2. See my remarks on this matter in Part I.
3. See Tadmor 1965.

EXCURSUS: OIL, SCENTS AND DOORS IN DEDICATION RITES

In Nabonidus's description of the dedication of Shamash's temple Ebabbar, we read (Langdon 1912: 258 *Nabonidus* no. 6 col. II 13-15):

> The door posts, locks, bolts and door leaves
> I drenched with oil
> and for the entry of their exalted divinity
> I made the contents of the temple full of sweet fragrance.
> The Temple, for the entry of Shamash my lord,
> its gates were wide open
> and it was full of joy.

The anointing of the bolts in order to bring a god into his temple is mentioned in the Nabû-apla-iddinna inscription (King 1912: 124 col. V 33-34) and in an Esarhaddon text (Borger 1956: 76 §48 ll. 14-15) and note also W.G. Lambert 1959–60: 59 ll. 163-64. Esarhaddon's inscription reports the introduction of Ishtar of Uruk in a procession into her temple Enirgalanna. The Nabû-apla-iddinna text, like the Nabonidus inscription, reports bringing a new statue of Shamash into his temple Ebabbar in Sippar. This calls to mind immediately the anointing of the Tabernacle and all its cultic equipment at the time of its dedication (Exod. 40.9-16; Lev. 8.10-11 and cf. Exod. 30.22-33 for the fragrant components of the anointing oil), although the exact functions emphasized by the texts may not be identical (the anointing oil imparts special contagious sanctity to the anointed object, while the oils used in the Mesopotamian texts fill the anointed objects with their fragrance). The use of oil, although with a totally different function, is mentioned in the Weld–Blundell Prism of Nabonidus, also describing the building of Ebabbar in Sippar (Langdon 1923: 36 ll. 21-30):

> So as not to cause within it
> anger, curse and sin
> and not to place in the mouth
> of the workers doing its work—
> (but instead) to place in
> their mouths good blessings—
> loaves, beer, meat and wine
> abundantly I heaped on them,
> and salves of pure oil
> I (rubbed) abundantly on their bodies.
> With perfume and sweet (smelling) oil
> I drenched their heads.

(Compare the 'sweet smelling oil', literally 'good oil', Ì.GIŠ DÙG.GA with the *šemen ṭôb* running from Aaron's head down onto his beard and underwear in Ps. 133.2.) Filling the temple with fragrant odors was apparently meant to attract the god to it. In connection with this rite we may mention the famous passage in the flood story (*Gilgamesh*, Tablet XI 155-61) in which the gods are attracted to Utnapishtim like flies when they smell the aroma of his sacrifices which were offered along with incense, fragrant reed, cedar and myrtle. The use of incense with the specific purpose of attracting gods is mentioned in an Old Babylonian Diviner's Prayer (Goetze 1968: 28 l. 15), as well as in a related text published by Starr 1983: 30 l. 5. But Nabonidus's use of aromatics should be compared especially to an instruction appearing in an Assyrian building ritual for opening a new gate in a building. First the new gate is to be purified, and afterwards we read (Borger 1973a: 51 l. 16):

> A censer with myrhh, sweet reed and flour
> in the new gate
> for Ea, Asalluhi (Marduk) and the building's protective genius
> you shall set up!

For the importance of gates in dedication ceremonies in general and in association with the entry of the god into the temple in particular, there is an echo in Ezek. 43.1-9 (see also Ezek. 44.1-4 and perhaps Ps. 24). On this, see Levine and Hallo 1967: 48-50. The importance of the gate as a place of the god's entry into the temple is expressed as well in Anatolian and Syrian iconography as discussed by Barnett 1981. See also Meyers 1983, who explains the pillars Jachin and Boaz as monuments to God's entry into the new Temple in Jerusalem. Takil-ilissu (Wilcke and Kutscher 1978: 115 ll. 42-47, p. 120 n.) mentions the lion gods Dān-bītum and Rašab-bītum as being seated in the temple. The place in the inscription where this is mentioned is where one would expect a dedication ceremony to be described, indicating that the entry of the god may be indicated by installing the two 'Tor-Löwen'.

Appendix: Sources for Mesopotamian Dedication Ceremonies

1. *Temple Dedications*

The Builder	The Temple	Source
Lugalannemundu	Enamzu in Adab	Güterbock 1934: 42 l. 24–p. 43.
King of Kesh (?)	Nintu temple in Kesh	Gragg 1969: p. 173 l. 103–p. 175 l. 132; Biggs 1971: p. 202 l. 105–p. 203 l. 120.
Gudea	Eninnu in Lagash	Gudea, Cylinder B
Ur-Nammu	Ekur in Nippur	Castellino 1959: 107 ll. 31-35.
Naram-Sin	Laz temple	Lambert 1973.
Samsuiluna	Ebabbara in Sippar	Sollberger 1967b: 42 ll. 88-92.
Yaḫdun-Lim	Egirzalanki in Mari	Dossin 1955, IV 9-10.
Takililissu	Emaš in Malgium	Kutscher and Wilcke 1978: 115 ll. 42-47 (49?).
Agum-kakrime		Unger 1970: 279 V.
Kurigalzu	Anu Temple (?)	Ungnad 1923:19 i 16-18 (cf. *CAD* K, 533 *s.v. kummu* Aa).
Tukulti-Ninurta I	Anunitum Temple	Weidner 1959: 22 no. 13 ll. 25-28.
Tiglath-pileser I	various temples	King, *AKA*, 87 l. 91–p. 88 l. 93.
	Anu-Adad temple in Assur	*AKA*, 99 ll. 109-14.
	bīt-ḫamri of Adad	*AKA*, 101 ll. 9-10.
Assurnasirpal II	Ishtar-Kidmuri temple	*AKA*, 164 l. 26–165 l. 2.
	Mahir temple	*AKA*, 171 ll. 9-10 (cf. 171 ll. 1-2).

Appendix

281

	Ishtar temple in Nineveh	Thompson 1932: 110 no. 272 l. 37.
	Shamash temple in Assur	Michel 1954: 320 l. 9.
Sargon II	Temple in Dūr-šarrukīn (?)	ABL 841 = Parpola 1987: 106 no. 132 ll. 5-6, 9.
Esarhaddon	Esharra in Assur	Borger 1956: 5 VI 28-34.
	Esagila in Babylon	Borger 1956: 23 epis. 32 ll. 16-17.
	Enirgalanna in Uruk	Borger 1956: 76 epis. 48 ll. 14-15.
	[New idols brought from Assur to Esagila in Babylon]	Borger 1956: 88-89 epis. 57 ll. 8-24; p. 91 epis. 60 (and see pp. 89-90 epis. 58-59).
Assurbanipal	bīt-akītu	Thompson 1931: 36.
	Ehursaggalkurkurra	Thompson 1931: 29 ll. 19-20 (Streck 1916: 146 ll. 15-16).
	Emašmaš	Thompson 1931: 31 ll. 21-22.
	Ehulhul	Thompson 1931: 32 ll. 31-34.
	Sin temple, Uruk	Thompson 1931: 33 ll. 33-35.
	Ehilianna/Eanna	Thompson 1931: 35 ll. 27-32; Streck 1916: 58 ll. 119-24; p. 220 ll. 29-35; Thompson 1933: 85 ll. 103-104; Bauer 1933: 35 K 2664 III 30; p. 43 K 2628 vs. 9–rvs. 1ff.
	Emelamanna	Streck 1916: 152 ll. 78-79.
	Ehulhul in Sippar	Streck 1916: 172 l. 62.
	Sin temple et al. in Nineveh	Thompson 1933: 84 l. 69.
	Sarpanitu temple (?)	Thompson, 1933: 84 l. 69.
	Edimgalkalama	Thompson, 1933 xxx l. 70
Sin-sharra-ishkun	Nabû-Tašmetum temple	Böhl 1936: 35 ll. 31-34.
	Erragal temple in Sirara	Borger 1961: 101 l. 13-14 (cf. Grayson, ARI, I, 143 §933 n. 273).
Nebuchadnezzar II	Ezida in Borsippa	Langdon 1912: 92 no. 9 ll. 23-25 = p. 158 no. 19 ll. 54-57; Unger 1970: 272 ll. 2-4.
	Various temples in Babylon	Langdon 1912: 106 no. 13 ll. 52-53.

	Temples in various cities	Langdon 1912: 108 no. 13 ll. 68-71 = p. 182 no. 20 ll. 19-22.
	Ebabarra in Sippar	Langdon 1912: 142 no. 16 ll. 31-32.
Nabonidus	Eḫulḫul in Harran	Langdon 1912: 222 ll. 18-25; p. 290 no. 9 II 12-17; Gadd 1958: 48 no. 1 col. II 17-21; p. 64 no. 2 ll. 22-28.
	Ebabbara in Sippar	Langdon 1912: 226 ll. 6-7; p. 258 no. 6 ll. 13-15; see perhaps Langdon 1923: 36 ll. 21ff.
	Unnamed temple (*kissu*) to Nana in U-BA-UG-SI	Dhorme, 1914: 111 col. III 5-7.
	Eulmaš in Akkad	Langdon 1912: 228 no. 1 col. III ll. 34-38.
Anu-uballit	Resh temple in Uruk	Clay 1915: 83 no. 52 ll. 16-19

Naram-Sin, before building a temple for Laz and Erra (Lambert 1973: 357-63 obv. 26-27) prays *lūpuškum bītam ša tašilātu libbi taššab iqqiribīšu rimi parak šarrūtim*, 'May I build you a temple of the heart's rejoicing, dwell in it and set up a kingly dais', referring to the eventful dedication of the temple. The entry of gods into their new temples is also mentioned as the occasion for granting the requests made in prayers concluding a number of building inscriptions of Nabopolassar, Nebuchadnezzar and Nabonidus. An inscription of Nabonidus (Langdon 1912: 236 no. 3 I 49; p. 238 II 30-31) mentions that gods were put in their places by Nebuchadnezzar I and Burnaburiash, and this information is probably based on the inscriptions of these two kings found by Nabonidus while restoring the temples. Dedication ceremonies are also mentioned in various mythological texts. Babylon is dedicated by the gods in *Enuma Elish* VI 70-76. Apsu seems to be dedicated in *Enuma Elish* I 78 by the act of Ea and Damkina taking up residence there. A divine banquet in honor of Eengurra at Eridu is mentioned in *Enki's Journey to Nippur*. Numerous references in Sumerian temple, divine and royal hymns to the god sitting on his dais, in his temple or in his *muš*[1] may be connected with the act of dedicating a temple. References to such events in the so-called Akkadian 'Prophetic' texts[2] may also be based on the regular experience of dedicating temples.

Temple dedication ceremonies may be depicted in Sumerian art. A votive plaque of Ur-Nanshe (*ANEP*, no. 427; Kramer 1963: 3; Boese 1971: 197-98; Tafel XXXIX 1) displays both foundation and dedication ceremonies. The upper register depicts the king carrying a brick basket, while the lower register shows him sitting with his five sons seated around him. He is holding a cup in his hand. This picture is reminiscent

1.   Gragg 1969 for *Muš*; cf. Weinfeld 1980: 285.
2.   Weinfeld 1979.

and illustrative of the dedication rites described in particular in the Lugalannemundu inscription, *Enuma Elish* tablet VI, the Baal epic, *Enki's Journey to Nippur* and Esarhaddon's dedication of Esharra in Assur.

The Ur-Nammu stele from the University of Pennsylvania Museum shows on one side various stages in the building of Ekur (?), while the reverse contains some broken scenes from the dedication ceremonies. According to Frankfort (1954: 51), 'Men pour blood from the carcass of a decapitated lamb—a rite known in the later New Year festival to have served as the ritual purification of the building. An ox is cut up; huge drums are sounded.'

An Early Dynastic cylinder seal, which shows in the upper register a building scene, contains in the lower part a picture of a sacrifice. According to van Buren (1952: 73), 'It is as if the seal engraver wished to relate the whole story in as few words as possible: under the supervision of the goddess the temple-tower was constructed in accordance with the divinely appointed ground-plan as here set forth; it was consecrated amidst the rejoicings of the worshippers with a sacrifice'.

2. Dedications of Palaces and Cities

The Builder	Location	Source
Assurnasirpal II	Kalhu	Wiseman 1952: 24-44 (cf. Postgate 1973 for collations).
	Tiluli	King, *AKA*, 226 ll. 35-36; 326 l. 87.
	Tushata	*AKA*, 231 l. 18
Sargon	Dur-Sharrukin	Lie 1929: 78 ll. 7–80: 1; Weissbach 1918: 184 ll. 54-69; Lyon 1883: 46 ll. 97-100; Borger 1973b: 57 ll. 123–58: 130; Winckler 1889: 130 ll. 167–132 l. 175; 144 ll. 34-45.
	Cypress Palace in Kalhu	Winckler 1889: 172 ll. 19-20.
Sīn-aha-uṣur	Dur-Sharrukin	Loud and Altmann 1938: II, 104 no. 2.
Sennacherib	'Palace without a Rival', Nineveh	Luckenbill 1924: 98 ll. 91-92; p. 116 ll. 65-76; p. 125 ll. 48-52.
Esarhaddon	Esgalsidadudua (Armory, Nineveh)	Borger 1956: 62 ll. 35-43, p. 63 epis. 23 ll. 44-53.
	'Small Palace' in Nineveh	Borger 1956: p. 69 epis. 30.
	Palace for Assurbanipal in Tarbis	Borger 1956: 72 ll. 32-33.
Zakutu-Naqija	Nineveh	Borger 1956: 116 III 12-20; IV 1-18.

Assurbanipal	*bīt-ridûti* in Nineveh	Streck 1916: 90 ll. 106-108; Aynard 1957: 62 ll. 60-61.
Bel-ḫarran-bēl-uṣur		Unger 1917.
Šamaš-rēš-uṣur		Weissbach 1903: 10 no. 4 col. III 3-4 (cf. Dalley 1984).

Šulgi R describes the dedication of a divine boat. The dedication of a canal is described by Sennacherib (Luckenbill 1924: 81: 27-34). A West Semitic reference to the dedication of a city is found in the Azittiwada inscription.

Chapter 12

THE DEDICATION PRAYER (1 KINGS 8.12-61)

In the middle of the account of the Temple dedication stands a long
passage recording the words—addresses, blessings and prayers—said
to be uttered by Solomon in honor of the momentous occasion (1 Kgs
8.12-61). The first two verses in this 'liturgical' tractate are regarded
by most scholars as very ancient because of their poetic form, and
because the Greek translation ascribes them to a certain *Biblio tes
Odes*, 'The Book of Songs' or in Hebrew *sēper haššîr*, which is considered to be a simple corruption through metathesis of the well-
known *sēper hayyāšār*.[1] Despite the antiquity of these initial two
verses, all modern scholars, with the exception of Y. Kaufmann, are

1.   For the many suggestions as to the original form, meaning and background
of these verses, see the commentaries on Kings and the critical introductions to the
Old Testament and their bibliographies. Note especially (for textual issues)
Wellhausen 1963: 269; Burkitt 1909; Thackeray 1910; Gooding 1969: 7; Albright
1968: 231. For suggestions concerning possible ancient Near Eastern roots of these
two verses, see Born 1965; Görg 1974; Loretz 1974. Gevaryahu (1985) recently
made the interesting and not impossible suggestion that Solomon's words in these
verses are the incipit of a royal inscription, one of many, which stood in the temple
courtyard, and which were copied out by some later scribe with an antiquarian bent.
This proposal is potentially fruitful, but developing it would require a more careful
investigation of the Greek versions and the supposed Hebrew *Vorlage* as well as
examination of possible ancient Near Eastern parallels. For the expression *bêt zĕbûl*,
see Held 1968: 90-91. The description of the Jerusalem temple as a *bêt zĕbûl* may be
parallel to the frequent Akkadian designation of temples as *atmanu ṣīru, bītu ṣīru,
gigunû ṣīru, kisallu ṣīru, kummu ṣīru, parakku ṣīru* and *šubtu ṣīru* (cf. *CAD* Ṣ: 211-
12 *s.v. ṣīru*; note especially the lexical equation *ṣīru = rubû*). For the expression
māḳôn lĕšibtĕkā 'ôlāmîm and its Akkadian parallels *parak dārāti* and *šubat dārāti*, see
Albright 1950: 16; Weinfeld 1972: 35, 195. Weinfeld (p. 35) suggests that this passage, which may be considered an invitation to YHWH to take up residence in his new
Temple, is parallel to Gudea's invitation to Ningirsu and Bau to come and reside in
Eninnu in Gudea Cylinder B cols. II–III.

in agreement that the remaining verses, which constitute Solomon's 'Oration' and make up the lion's share of the tractate, are the product of the Deuteronomic school which edited and compiled the book of Kings.

I readily admit that this pericope is full of unmistakable Deuteronomic expressions and ideas, and is in fact programmatic of the designs for theological reform and cult centralization of this school. It goes without saying that any attempt to deny the Deuteronomic pedigree of this passage and date it to the age of Solomon will appear highly questionable,[1] and no attempt will be made here to deny the Deuteronomic nature of the passage as it now stands. Nonetheless, the Deuteronomic composition before us is not to be seen as a literary creation wholly without roots in literary types and ideas independent of the Deuteronomic school. Despite the near unanimous verdict of lateness, there is, at least theoretically, still room for finding early, original elements beneath the Deuteronomic rhetoric. Burney, for example, writes:[2]

> The final portion (vv. 62-66) may perhaps exhibit an older narrative into which Deuteronomic additions have been incorporated, *but the remainder, and especially the central prayer of dedication, has been so thoroughly amplified by the editor that it is impossible to discover any older kernel upon which he may have based his work* [my italics].

Although the 'kernel' is undiscernible, Burney implicitly acknowledges the possibility that such a kernel nonetheless existed. In this chapter I will address the problem of whether the Deuteronomic 'Oration of Solomon' is a totally new creation, which sprang full-grown from the mind of the Deuteronomic compiler(s) of the book of Kings, reflecting only his (their) own theological and programmatic purposes, or whether it stems ultimately from external prototypes—in

---

1.   See Kaufmann 1967: 106-208, 367-68. In addition to proposing the prayer's silence on cult centralization, Kaufmann claims that the prayer contains evidence of primitive universalism, reflecting what he sees as the religion of the early monarchy. Kaufmann's position on this matter has not been received and is rejected even by his students and disciples. It arguably reflects his own growing conservatism, and ignores the fact that one of the main purposes of the prayer is to prepare Israelite worship for a one-temple system (see below on this point). For the date of this prayer and the question of its unity or growth, see Levenson 1981. For a detailed philological analysis see Wheeler 1977.

2.   Burney 1903: 112.

other words, is there a kernel? By 'external prototypes', I mean both pre-existing, defined literary compositions and well-known literary patterns recognized and used by ancient authors, including Israelite and Judaean scribes. The date of such documents or patterns is not an issue here. What is at issue is whether the Deuteronomist worked in a literary vacuum, or whether, when composing Solomon's prayer, he had at his disposal specific material or literary patterns—sources and paradigms such as those which served the author of the book of Deuteronomy itself, who avails himself both of previous literary works (such as J, E) and well-known literary forms (such as treaty forms, etc.). I will also address the question of the implications of such prototypes for the meaning of Solomon's words.

Before searching for possible parallels and prototypes[1] to Solomon's oration, its literary structure and some of its central ideas are to be clarified.

1. *The Literary Structure and Some Central Ideas of Solomon's Oration*

Solomon's words may be divided into three parts, both according to their form and according to specific statements in the text.

vv. 14-21	First blessing of the congregation of Israel
vv. 22-53	A prayer
vv. 54-61	Second blessing of the congregation of Israel

The author separates these three sections by designating the (changing) postures of Solomon (vv. 14, 22, 54-55).[2] The three sections also

---

1.   The similarity between the Mesopotamian prayers and Solomon's prayer was already alluded to by Jirku (1923: 155) and more recently (although not independently) by Corvin (1972: 225-28). Corvin's suggestion that the Mesopotamian prayers be viewed as a precedent for Solomon's prayer was rejected by Wheeler (1977: 34-35), who remarks: 'The composition does not reflect the concerns typical of ancient Near Eastern royalty in their building inscriptions but those of the Deuteronomistic Historians, as that [sic] the comparisons with other ancient Near Eastern texts shed little light on the present text'.

2.   There is a certain inconsistency in the description of Solomon's shifting posture. In v. 14 he is standing in front of the congregation (who are also standing), turning his face. In v. 22 he is once again said to be standing. Verses 54-55, however, report that when finishing his prayer he arose from kneeling on his knees and stood once again to bless the people. But there is no statement that he ever bowed down. The missing information is supplied, apparently, by 2 Chron. 6.13, where we

differ from each other in their form. The two 'Blessings' start with
the formula *bārûk YHWH 'ăšer* . . . (vv. 15, 56). The 'Prayer' itself
begins and ends by invoking the name of God (v. 23. . .*YHWH 'ĕlōhê
yiśrā'ēl*; v. 53 *'ădōnâ 'ĕlōhîm*). Moreover, the 'blessings' are phrased
in the second person with the Lord referred to in the third person,
while the 'prayer' addresses the Lord in the second person, referring
to the people in the third. Thus Solomon's oration has a concentric
structure A/B/A, at least with regard to formal criteria, both internal
and external. If we now look at the content of the middle section
alone, we find that the 'prayer' itself (vv. 23-53) has a chiastic structure. It begins with an enumeration of God's acts of kindness to David
(vv. 23-24) and concludes with reference to his kindness to the entire
people of Israel (vv. 51-53). In the middle are, first, requests on
behalf of the king (vv. 25-29) and afterwards seven requests for the
people (vv. 29-50).[1] The requests for the people are enveloped by a

read: 'Solomon had made a bronze platform and placed it in the midst of the Great
Court; . . . He stood on it; then, kneeling in front of the whole congregation of
Israel, he spread forth his hands to heavens and said, . . . ' The words *neged kol
qĕhal yiśrā' ēl wayyiprōś kappâw hāššāmāyim* are identical to the end of the previous
verse (v. 12), and this leads one to suspect that the verse was deleted by the book of
Kings because of homoeoteleuton. There is no need to assume that the Chronicler
tried to repair the inconsistency on his own. We may also reject the suggestion made
by, among others, Gray (1970: 219): 'This parallel passage in 2 Chron. 6.13
significantly omits any mention of the altar and depicts Solomon as officiating on a
bronze scaffold some seven feet high in the temple court. This reflects the increased
status and cultic monopoly of the priestly caste in the post-exilic period'. Gray seems
to forget that the tendentious Chronicler has preserved the previous verse which
states explicitly that Solomon stood before the altar! In delivering his Oration, it may
be assumed that he faced the people in order to bless them, turning his face from side
to side, looking them over, and while he prayed, he turned his back to the people,
faced the Temple, raised his hands and then kneeled down, keeping his hands out-
streched. Upon concluding his prayer, he retracted his hands, resumed a standing
position, turned around to again face the onlookers and blessed them as he had previously. Solomon's movements may be compared with those of Moses and Aaron at
the consecration of the Tabernacle. According to Lev. 9.22-23, Aaron lifts up his
hands to bless the people, then descends the altar and enters the Tabernacle along
with Moses—presumably to pray. Afterwards, they both come out and this time they
both bless the people. Both temple dedication ceremonies thus have a sequence of
blessing of the people, prayer to God, blessing of the people.

1.   See Avishur 1973: 38-40; Levenson 1982. Note also the seven blessings
requested in Shalmaneser's Kurba'il Inscription (see Kinier-Wilson 1962 and
Lackenbacher 1982: 199), in the Tell-Fekherye Inscription of Adad-it'i, governor of

transitional verse which mentions together the prayer of the king and the prayers of the people (v. 30), and a similar verse occurs at the conclusion of the requests for the people (v. 52). From this we see that the 'Prayer' has an AB//BA structure. Furthermore, the first part of the 'Prayer' revolves about the king while the second part focuses on the people. As a result, the first part of the prayer continues the subject of the first 'Blessing', while the subject of the second part of the 'Prayer' leads into the subject of the second 'Blessing'. If we combine what we have seen about the structure of the entire Oration with the structure of the 'Prayer' at its heart, the complete Oration will then have a chiastic arrangement of ABC//C′B′A′.

Solomon's words have historiographic and theological as well as programmatic significance. The author of the blessings and prayer has placed in Solomon's mouth his own views, which happen to be those of the Deuteronomic school, concerning the place and importance of the construction of the Temple in the history of the nation. In addition, he attributes to Solomon the determination of the role the Temple is to play in the future relationships between God and his people. Building the Temple is presented as a critical juncture in two developments in the relationships between YHWH and Israel. The first blessings (vv. 15-21) and the first half of the prayer (vv. 22-27) recall how God kept his promise to David with regard to the building of the Temple and the establishment of a firm royal dynasty—two promises made to David in Nathan's famous oracle in 2 Samuel 7. The second part of the prayer (vv. 28-53) and the second blessing (vv. 54-61) which follow it mention the fulfillment of God's promise to the entire people by giving rest to the people who came out of Egypt.[1] Together with surveying God's past kindnesses to Israel, Solomon's prayer also lays down conditions for the continuation of such favorable relationships between God and the Royal house on the one hand, and God and the whole nation on the other.

Solomon's prayer also defines the function of the Temple in three

---

Gozan (Abou-Assaf 1982), Akkadian version ll. 10-14; in Streck 1916: 366 ll. 9-12, and in Ebeling 1935: 72 ll. 12-14 (Assur-etil-ilani). Gudea Cylinder A XX 24–XXI 13 lists seven blessings Gudea gave to Eninnu when laying the foundations, but these are not to be associated with the types of requests mentioned in the votive inscriptions mentioned here.

1. See von Rad 1966: 94-102.

I Have Built You an Exalted House

ways: in the negative, *e silentio* and through positive statements.[1] The Temple will not be and cannot be a place on earth where God will dwell (v. 27). Furthermore, no special role for sacrifice in the Temple is stipulated. Even the altar is described not as a place of sacrifice but, as regards its function, as a place of adjuration in certain judicial proceedings (vv. 31-32)! In place of this function, the Temple is to be a place where the Ark of YHWH's covenant will rest—and *not* the place of the Ark which is God's footstool (v. 21). In other words, the Ark standing in the Temple represents the special legal bond uniting God and Israel and does not represent God's tangible presence. Furthermore, the Temple will be a place where God's 'Name' is found. The Temple is also to be a focal point for prayers. On the one hand, every prayer uttered in the city, in the Land of Israel or even outside the Land will be directed towards the Temple. On the other hand, God's eyes will be directed there constantly. As is well known, cult centralization was foremost in the mind of the Deuteronomist. The lack of explicit mention of this major tenet, mentioned so vociferously in the book of Deuteronomy itself, was perhaps the primary factor behind Y. Kaufmann's remarkable denial of the Deuteronomic character of the Oration. Nonetheless, cult centralization is implied in the prayer, and lies behind the structure of the seven requests which Solomon makes concerning prayers offered by the people. Solomon surveys the prayers by their location—prayers said inside the Temple, in the city, in the countryside outside the city and outside the Land. All these prayers are to be directed towards the Temple in Jerusalem, and they will from there ascend to heaven where they will be accepted by God, thus obviating the need for local temples. Farmers or soldiers need not resort in time of trouble to a local temple or high place since they can simply offer their prayers in the direction of the Temple to have them attended to. The reference to judicial oaths being made at the altar in the Jerusalem Temple (vv. 31-32) is meant to compensate for the judicial functions of the defunct local temples.[2]

1. Weinfeld 1962.
2. Temples were places of judgment throughout the ancient Near East. According to rabbinic sources, the Sanhedrin sat in the Chamber of Hewn Stone in the Temple. Much earlier and far away, we find that in the temple of Assur in Assur judgment was carried out in the *mušlalu*, 'step gate' (see *CAD* M II: 277 and the bibliography listed there, especially Larsen 1976: 58). The Ekur, temple of Enlil in Nippur, seems to have had a prison in it, as indicated by a hymn to the goddess

2. *The Background of Solomon's Prayer*

It is unimportant whether the Deuteronomist was the first compiler of the story of the building of the Temple or whether he created the present story by reworking or replacing pieces of pre-existing historical and literary sources. In either case, in the very act of composing a prayer for Solomon to have been recited at the dedication festivities, he is following the example of a traditional literary topos.

The building prayers found in the Mesopotamian building accounts[1] are couched sometimes in the third person, but often in the first person. This is especially true in the Assyrian and neo-Babylonian building prayers. Solomon's prayer is also phrased in the first person. Not only this, but the prayers are sometimes prefaced by narrative statements describing the king's attitude of prayer. So we find that Sargon, on dedicating his new palace in Dur-Sharrukin, says (Lie 1929: 80 ll. 12-13):

> In order that he (Assur) grant me a happy life (and) length of days and make my reign endure. I reverently bowed down and prayed before him.

Nebuchadnezzar, on building his palace in Babylon, states (Langdon 1912: 94 *Nebuchadnezzar* no. 9 col. III 43-44):

> I lifted up my hands,
> I prayed to the lord of lords.
> To merciful Marduk
> went my supplications.

Nungal (see Sjöberg 1973b; Frymer-Kensky 1967; Kramer 1988: 10-11). For temple-cities as places from which justice should emanate and where injustice cannot be found, see Weinfeld 1985: 57ff. It is this judicial function of the temple which underlies the famous End of Days prophecy in Isa. 2.1-5 and Mic. 4.1-5 which envisions the Temple as an international court of justice to which all nations will be able to appeal, thus alleviating the need for war. The judicial functions of the local temples in Israel are also done away with by the Deuteronomic legislation, for which see Weinfeld 1972: 23ff.

1. All the prayers discussed here are from building inscriptions. Mayer (1976: 378) lists several house-building prayers found in ritual texts and not in the royal inscriptions. For several short, fragmentary temple-building incantations from Ebla, see Krebernik 1984: 92-93 no. 16 and 17 and pp. 146-49 no. 27. Von Soden (*RLA*, III, 165 *s.v.* 'Gebete' II §70) distinguishes between 'blessing formulae' and true royal prayers. According to him, prayers *per se* occur only from the Sargonids onwards.

In another inscription, also relating to the building of his palace, he prefaces the concluding prayer (Langdon 1912: 120 *Nebuchadnezzar* no. 14 col. III 35; and see also p. 140 no. 15 IV 45):

> To Marduk my lord I prayed
> and lifted up my hands.

These formulae obviously resemble the formulae introducing and concluding the second part of Solomon's Oration—the 'Prayer' proper (vv. 22, 54):

> Then Solomon stood before the altar of the LORD in the presence of the whole community of Israel; he spread the palms of his hands towards heaven and said:. . .

> When Solomon finished offering to the LORD all this prayer and supplication, he rose from where he had been kneeling, in front of the altar of the LORD, his hands spread out towards heaven.

Let me state at this point that, in my opinion, the fact that a king prays for himself and his people on the public occasion of dedicating a building is not to be seen as an indication that he does so in the capacity of a priest, as has been suggested by certain scholars.[1] Although the Assyrian king was in fact considered the high priest (*šangu*) of the god Assur,[2] this is not the case for the Babylonian kings. As for evidence adduced in favor of a priestly role for the king of Israel, it is to be noted that nearly all the occasions when such 'priestly' activity is explicitly evidenced are dedicatory festivals of some sort—David bringing the Ark to Jerusalem (and perhaps 'dedicating' his new capital city, as P.K. McCarter suggested),[3] David sacrificing at the new altar in the threshing floor of Araunah, Solomon dedicating the Temple, Jeroboam initiating the (re)new(ed?) form of worship at Bethel, Ahaz dedicating the new altar, and Moses dedicating the Tabernacle and installing the priests. On several of these occasions, proper priests are appointed for the continuation of the cult (Lev. 8; 2 Sam. 8.18; 2 Kgs 16.15ff.; 1 Kgs 12.31; cf. Ezra 6.18) and this is the case in certain Mesopotamian dedication festivals as well.[4]

1. See for instance Montgomery and Gehman 1951 and Soggin 1977: 369.
2. On the priestly status of the king of Assyria, see Driel 1969: 170ff. and Menzel 1981: 130ff.
3. See McCarter 1983.
4. For appointing priests in conjunction with building temples, see especially Nabonidus's inscriptions which tell how he consecrated his daughter as an *entu*

Returning to the prayer itself, most important is whether its content, language or form are dependent on external prototypes or whether all that is attributed to Solomon is in fact a completely new creation.

Before turning to such possible external prototypes, Solomon's words themselves must be examined in order to determine what their thrust actually is. It was found above that Solomon's prayer contained first requests concerning the king (vv. 23-30a) and then requests concerning the people (vv. 30b-53). Looking for a moment only at the requests concerning the king, we find that they are two—a request that God keep his promise to David concerning the conditions for dynastic continuity, and a request that the king's prayers in the future be answered. The prayer concerning the people is actually a continuation of the second request concerning the king. If Solomon's prayer on behalf of himself is reduced to its bare essentials what remains is the following:

25	*wĕ'attâ YHWH 'ĕlōhê yiśrā'ēl*
	šĕmōr lĕ'abdĕkā dāwid 'ābî 'ēt 'ăšer dibbartā lô lē'mōr
	lō' yikkārēt lĕkā 'îš millĕpānāy yōšēb 'al kissē'
	yiśrā'ēl...
28	*ûpānîtā 'el tĕpillat 'abdĕkā...*
	lišmōa' 'el-hārinnâ wĕ'el hattĕpillâ
	'ăšer 'abdĕkā mitpallel lĕpānêkā hayyôm
29	*lihyôt 'ênekā pĕtuhōt 'el habbayit hazzeh laylâ wāyôm...*
	lišmōa' 'el hattĕpillâ 'ăšer yitpallēl 'abdĕkā
	'el hammaqôm hazzeh...

| 25 | And now, O Lord God of Israel, keep the further promise that you made to your servant, my father David: 'Your line on the throne of Israel shall never end...' |
| 28 | Yet turn, O Lord my God, to the prayer and supplication of your servant...and hear the cry and prayer which your servant offers before you this day (29) that your eyes be open day and night toward this house...to hear the supplications which your servant will offer toward this place... |

Everything else, including the famous v. 27, which will be discussed in more detail below, is secondary and explanatory of these two basic requests. The same can be said about the bulk of the prayer in

priestess (Böhl 1939 = Reiner 1985: 4, 166; Dhorme 1914: 111 ll. 13-15). In connection with Ezra 6:18 *wahaqîmû kāhanayyā' bipluggātehôn* note Borger 1956: 24 epis. 33 ll. 20ff.: *ramkī pāšiši angubbê amēl bārûte nāṣir pirište maḥaršun ušzīz išibbē āšipē kalê nārē...ušzīz maḥaršun*. See also Winckler 1889: 128 ll. 157-58 (Sargon).

vv. 31ff. The prayers to be said in seven different situations (and received by God if they are directed towards the Temple) are actually elaborations, itemizing and explaining the basic, single request that prayers towards the Temple be accepted.

If this is the essence of the prayer, are there prototypes? One possible prototype may be related to vv. 12-13. If these verses are remnants of an authentic, Solomonic dedication prayer, then it is not impossible that the Deuteronomist knew of the full version and was influenced by it. This possibility is enhanced by the fact that v. 27 relates polemically to the idea presented in the part of the prayer which has been spared. The rest of Solomon's prayer as well may reflect parts of the original prayer which no longer exist. However, since we do not have access to the full version, anything which might be said about what it originally contained is purely speculative.

Another candidate as a possible prototype is Ps. 132.11-18. The psalm as a whole contains various ideas relating to temple building and resembling both biblical and extra-biblical temple building accounts. The immutable divine vow with which it concludes contains promises resembling the blessings requested in certain extra-biblical temple building prayers, including those discussed immediately below. This Psalm certainly is worthy of comparative treatment in the broader discussion of temple building in the ancient Near East. However, since its date, background and exact nature are questionable, and since it may even be dependent in places on 1 Kings 8, it is best to put it aside in a discussion of possible prototypes for Solomon's Prayer.[1]

We come at last to extra-biblical sources. I have chosen several texts for examination. The first is a passage of Tiglath-pileser I which comes from the prism analysed in the first part of this study (King, *AKA*, 101-103 VIII 17-38).

> Just as I planned
> a pure house, a lofty shrine
> for the dwelling of Anu and Adad
> the great gods, my lords,
> and was not negligent and
> was not slack in building (it)

---

1. I was graciously reminded by Professor Shemaryahu Talmon that Ps. 72 contains numerous motifs and requests common to the ancient Near Eastern royal prayers.

but completed it quickly[1]
and made the heart of their
great divinity happy—
so may Anu and Adad faithfully turn to me.
May they love the uplifting of my hands,
may they hear my fervent prayer.
Plentiful rain, years of abundance and plenty,
may they grant my reign.
In warfare and battle
may they always lead me in safety.
All the lands of my enemies,
the difficult mountain regions
and the kings hostile to me,
may they cause to submit at my feet.
Me and my priestly progeny
may they bless with a good blessing and
my priesthood before Assur and their great divinities
until the distant future may they found firmly like a mountain.

This passage begins by summarizing the building account which precedes it. It therefore parallels in content Solomon's first 'Blessing' in which he surveys the history of the building of the temple (vv. 15-21). There is then a request that the gods will turn again to the king and heed his prayers. This parallels Solomon's request that God turn to the prayers which he and the people of Israel will pray towards the Temple. Tiglath-pileser's prayer concludes with a request that the gods bless the king's reign, which is called his 'priesthood' (*šangûtu*) and make the dynasty firm for ever. This parallels Solomon's dynastic request. The Assyrian king's remaining requests, namely for plenty, for safe guidance in war, and for dominion, may have somewhat distant

---

1.   Speed is desirable in doing the will of the gods (see *CAD* Ḥ, p. 63b *s.v.* ḥamātu A 4c for examples of the speedy bringing of offerings and sacrifices). Hag. 1.9 chides the people, saying, 'You have been expecting much and getting little; and when you brought it home I would blow on it! Because of what?—says the Lord of Hosts. Because of my house which lies in ruins, while you all *run* to your own houses!' The prophet is blaming the people for seeing to their own business with the speed which should be devoted to building God's temple. I am grateful to Professor Yohanan Muffs for bringing this aspect of worship to my attention.

parallels in Solomon's discussion of prayers to be offered in time of
war and famine, and the prayer of the gentile.[1] Whatever may be the

1. Tiglath-pileser's request for plentiful rain and years of abundance corresponds to 1 Kgs 8.35-40, which speak about prayers to be offered in times of
drought and famine. His request for guidance on the battlefield corresponds to
Solomon's request concerning prayers to be offered at times of defeat (vv. 33-34,
46-51) and during a war which God sent the people to fight (vv. 44-45). Requests
for dynastic stability, victory in battle, long life and answering prayers, such as those
mentioned in these prayers, are found frequently in other prayers as well. The
request for rain and abundance is relatively rare, but even so, there are other examples. In the Bible itself we should mention Ps. 132.11-18, especially v. 15, as well
as Hag. 2.15-19. From extra-biblical sources, first to be mentioned is the Azitiwadda
inscription (*KAI* 28 III 17–IV 12). In the Mesopotamian building prayers, this type
of request appears in inscriptions of Yahdun-lim (Dossin 1955: 16 IV 14-23 esp. 21
u šanāt ḥegalli rīšāti. . .); Marduk-nadin-ahi (Ebeling 1926: 40 l. 16; *adi ṭuḥdi u
ḥegalli*); Sargon (prayer mainly for rain to Adad from Dur-Sharrukin; Meissner 1944:
32); Esarhaddon (Borger 1956: 27—a request for rain and abundance in ll. 14-20);
Šagaraktašuriaš (prayer quoted in inscription of Nabonidus—Langdon 1915–16: 109
l. 61, *šanāti ḥegalli ana širikti lišrukūnu*); Agum-kakrime (in an inscription from the
library of Assurbanipal which tells how Agum-kakrime restored the statue of Marduk
to Babylon—Unger 1970: 279); and note the inscription of Arik-dīn-ili which reports
that the king planned and built a temple 'in order that the produce of my land will
prosper' (Ebeling 1926: 48 l. 15). The reference to 'locusts or caterpillars' ('*arbeh
ḥāsîl*) which will plague the land and bring the people to prayer (v. 37) may be compared to a prayer concerning a locust plague in the time of Sargon (Craig, *BA* 5 629
no. 4 IV 26 = *ABRI* 1 l. 54). The reference to 'any plague, any disease' (*kol negaʻ
kol maḥălāh*) in the same verse may be compared with the request of Adad-itʼi in the
Tell-Fekherye statue and of Shalmaneser III in his Kurbaʼil monument about removing disease (Abou-Assaf 1982, ll. 12-13; Kinier-Wilson 1962: 95 ll. 40-41). Cf. also
the inscription of Bēl-tarṣi-iluma, Schrader, *KB*, I, 192 l. 11. Finally, Solomon's
request made in his second 'blessing' and not in the prayer (vv. 57-58), 'May the
Lord our God be with us. . . May he incline our hearts to him, that we may walk in
all his ways and keep the commandments, the laws and the rules, which he enjoined
upon our fathers', may be compared with a request which Nabonidus made to his
god (Langdon 1912: 252 *Nabonidus* no. 5 II 13-16):

> The awe of your great divinity
> place in his people's heart so
> they will not sin to your great divinity. . .
> As for me, Nabonidus, king of Babylon,
> save me from sinning to your great divinity!

As in the case of the 'core requests', so it is in the case of these requests for material
advantages: the motive for granting the request is different in Solomon's prayer from
that seen in the extra-biblical sources. In the Mesopotamian prayers, the divine bles-

case of the last-mentioned requests, we find that the two major concerns expressed by Solomon, which determine the form of his prayer, are two of the major concerns informing the prayer of Tiglath-pileser, and it may be significant that they appear first and last, thus forming an 'envelope' to this prayer.

A second prayer to be considered is one of Shalmaneser I. This prayer stands at the end of his inscription reporting the restoration of Ehursagkurkurra, the temple of Assur in the city Assur. There we read (Ebeling, *IAK*, 124: 27ff. = Grayson, *ARI*, I, §536):

> When the lord Assur enters into that house
> and his lofty dais sets up happily—
> My dazzling work, that house,
> may he see and rejoice.
> May he accept my supplications,
> May he hear my prayer.
> May a destiny for the well-being of my priesthood
> and of my priestly progeny,
> (and) abundance during my reign
> from his honored mouth
> until far off days, greatly be declared.

This prayer as well contains a request that Assur hear and accept the king's prayers and supplications. There is also a request for eternal (*ana ūm ṣâti*) well-being for the monarchy. As such, Shalmaneser's prayer presents a brief forerunner to Tiglath-pileser's prayer, as well as an additional parallel to Solomon's. Similar and somewhat longer prayers can be found in the later Assyrian as well as Neo-Babylonian royal building inscriptions such as those of Esarhaddon, Nebuchadnezzar and Nabonidus. I quote here two more such prayers.

Langdon 1912: 226 *Nabonidus* no. 1 III 11-21 (Sippar Cylinder, second building account describing building of Ebabarra in Sippar):

> O Shamash, great lord
> of heaven and earth!
> When you enter Ebabarra, your beloved house,
> when you set up your eternal dais,

sings are, again, remuneration for the king's good deeds. Solomon's prayer, however, assumes that the state of divine blessing is the normal one, which only need be restored if upset. It therefore speaks of ways in which the normal, good situation is liable to be disturbed (by sin) and provides for rectification (through repentance and prayer).

> For me, Nabonidus, king of Babylon,
> the prince who sustains you and gladdens you,
> and who builds your exalted cella—
> Look happily on my good works.
> Daily, when rising and setting,
> In heaven and on earth
> make my portents good.
> Take my supplications,
> accept my prayer.
> The staff and scepter of justice
> which you placed in my hand,
> may I carry forever.

Langdon 1912: 190 *Nebuchadnezzar* no. 23 Col. I 10ff. is also from an account of restoring Ebabarra:

> O Shamash, great lord!
> Upon my good works
> look joyfully!
> Life, long days,
> ripe old age,
> stability of throne and
> longevity of reign
> grant me as a gift.
> Truly accept the uplifting of my hands!
> By your exalted command,
> the work done by my hands
> may I cause to become eternally ancient.
> May my descendants flourish constantly in kingship,
> May it (my kingship) be stable in the land.
> Whenever I lift up my hands,
> may you, O Lord Shamash,
> be the one who opens my path
> to slaying the enemies.

In both these prayers, the themes of dynastic stability and the answering of prayers are prominent. Of particular interest, however, are the beginnings of Shalmaneser's and Nabonidus's prayers. They both contain temporal clauses making the granting of the king's requests dependent upon the god entering the temple. Before the gods will hear the kings' prayers and bless them and their reigns, they must first enter the temple and rejoice. It is precisely this idea that is rejected by the Deuteronomist in 1 Kgs 8.27.

There is possibly a corollary to the rejection of the idea that the

Temple is God's earthly habitation. In the inscriptions we have just examined, the building of a temple is a favor the king does for his god and for which he expects a reward. The god, by entering the temple, benefits from the king's good works, and is therefore indebted and beholden to him. By rejecting the concept that a temple is a divine habitation, the Deuteronomist implicitly also rejects the idea that God benefits from the Temple. In turn, rejecting the idea that God benefits from the Temple renders inoperative the 'votive' element in the act of building the temple and in the building prayer. By building the Temple, the king of Israel has in fact done nothing beneficial for God, and he cannot therefore expect to be rewarded—in marked contrast to his Mesopotamian colleagues. The only way in which he can enjoy those blessings which his foreign counterparts expect as a matter of course, is through reliance on other historical promises and on covenants, and on God's own good will—two factors summarized as *habbĕrît wĕhaḥesed*. This explains Solomon's seemingly superfluous request in v. 26, 'And now, may your word to David my father be reliable (*yē'āmen*)'. Unlike Tiglath-pileser or Shalmaneser who can rely on their own gift to their gods as a guarantee of their own dynastic continuity, Solomon must depend on God's promise to David. He therefore asks that it be kept. The reason he makes this seemingly superfluous request seems to be given immediately: 'For will God really (*ha'umnām*) dwell upon the earth? Behold the heaven and the highest heaven cannot hold you, let alone this house which I have built you' (note the word play between *yē'āmen* and *ha'umnām* linking these two verses and inviting the reader to interpret one in light of the other). Unlike the Assyrian and Babylonian kings who can expect their prayers to be answered when Assur, Anu and Adad, or Shamash enter their new abodes, Solomon must rely on God's promise that his name will be in his temple 'to the place which *you said* "My name will be there"' (v. 29). In both the dynastic request and the request concerning prayer, the operative motive is God's promise. The votive dimension in the extra-biblical prayers has been cancelled and replaced by reliance on the word of God.

In conclusion, the above discussion indicates that the Deuteronomist did not have to create Solomon's prayer *ex nihilo*. The prayer which he produced stands where it should in the framework of the building story and reflects the custom of ancient Near Eastern kings praying upon such occasions. Moreover, it reflects at its core certain of the major concerns which occupied the minds of Mesopotamian kings and their scribes. It is also aware of, criticizes, rejects and duly compensates for the operative votive dimension of the Mesopotamian building prayers. The Deuteronomic prayer of Solomon is undoubtedly programmatic, aimed at introducing and inculcating the revolutionary idea of a single temple devoid of a divine resident. It also is imbued with an awareness of Israelite history, theology and ideology. Nonetheless, when reduced to its bare essentials, it is not far removed from the prayers uttered by the kings of Israel's neighbors. It has been transformed, metamorphosed and mutated almost beyond recognition, yet it remains a member of the species of ancient Near Eastern building prayers. It is not impossible that the Deuteronomist did in fact have access to a prayer offered by Solomon, but this possibility can neither be proven nor refuted. Whatever the case may be, it seems that the kernel or prototype which lies behind 'Solomon's' great dedicatory Oration is a long, well-attested ancient Near Eastern literary tradition of building prayers.

Chapter 13

GOD'S REPLY TO SOLOMON'S PRAYER (1 KINGS 9.1-9):
BLESSINGS AND CURSES

The account of building the Temple concludes with a report of God's reply to Solomon's prayer.[1] This reply consists of three parts. (1) God announces to Solomon that he has heard his prayer and that he himself has consecrated the Temple as a place where he will cause his Name to reside and a place towards which he will direct his eyes and heart. This promise is essential to the Deuteronomist, serving as a necessary replacement for the entrance of God, his *kābôd* and symbols of his presence found in 1 Kgs 8.10-11. Without an explicit divine proclamation, the new building would remain, to all intents and purposes, lacking in importance and devoid of any real divine content. God's reply to a prayer which was offered in the Temple serves as a tangible sign that the new Temple, with its newly defined role, actually does fulfill its function as a House of Prayer—just as the entry of YHWH and his symbols had served witness to the pre-Deuteronomic writers (contra Noth 1968: 197) that the Temple is God's residence on earth. (2) God promises that if Solomon goes before Him as has his father David, his reign over Israel will remain secure. (3) God threatens that if Israel goes after other gods, they will be exiled and the Temple will be destroyed.

Just like Solomon's Oration, discussed in the previous chapter, God's answer to the Prayer is stamped with the unmistakable mark of the Deuteronomic school. The whole paragraph is full of Deuteronomic expressions and ideas. Even vv. 8-9, which are amazingly similar to sentences found in extra-biblical treaties and royal inscriptions describing the abrogation of treaties, have connections in the Deuteronomic literature as well. Nonetheless, examination of the Mesopotamian

---

1. On 1 Kgs 9.6-9, see Friedman 1981: 12-13.

building inscriptions compels us to weigh the possibility that in this passage too the Deuteronomic writer did not work in a literary vacuum, but actually introduced his own ideological message into a pre-existing literary vessel. J. Gray remarks (1970: 235-36):[1]

> This passage, modelled on 3, 4-15, is a typical exhortation and admoni-tion such as the Deuteronomist liked to insert at a critical point in the his-tory of Israel, e.g. on the eve of the invasion of Palestine (Deuteronomy and Josh. 1), and on the completion of Joshua's conquests (Josh. 23f.).

Gray's evaluation is acceptable as far it concerns the routine Deuteronomic features in the passage, but the overall content (blessings and curses) and the positioning in this particular place—at the conclusion of the building story, following the account of dedi-cating the Temple and the dedication prayer—call for further investi-gation. Is this merely a 'critical point in the history of Israel', or are the composition and content of this passage dictated and required by a literary convention of the topos of contemporary building accounts?

What is the component in other building stories which parallels God's reply to Solomon? There are several candidates. According to the Priestly account of the building of the Tabernacle, God appeared at the end of the consecration rites of the Tabernacle and altar (Lev. 9.4, 23, 24; Num. 7.89). Both stories speak about a visual revelation (Lev. 9 // 1 Kgs 9.1) as well as an audible one (Num. 7.89 // 1 Kgs 9.2ff.). This parallel is interesting in and of itself, and we may assume some sort of genetic link between the two accounts. But there is no clear parallel in any other account, so that the revelation should not be considered one of the fixed components in the building story pattern. Moreover, the Tabernacle account contains no hint of blessings and curses. In addition, the possibility is not to be ruled out that the Tabernacle building account has imitated the Temple building story on this point and cannot, therefore, be seen as 'background' for it.

Several building stories do, to be sure, conclude with a divine reve-lation to the builder, even though these stories make no specific men-tion of a revelatory experience. Psalm 132, which is related to the topos of building stories, concludes with God's oath to David expressed in the first person (vv. 11-17). At the end of Gudea Cylinder B,

---

1.   But see Weinfeld 1972: 10-58, who has not included this passage in his dis-cussion of the Deuteronomic Orations.

Ningirsu blesses Gudea in direct speech (cols. xx-xxiv). In the Ur-Nammu Hymn as well, which contains an account of the building of Ekur, Enlil addresses Ur-Nammu and blesses him for what he has done. The Sumerian myth *Enki's Journey to Nippur* tells how Enki journeys to report to the divine assembly in Nippur that he has built a temple in Eridu. The story relates that Enlil blesses Enki, and Enlil's words are reported in the first person (ll. 117-29). Other building accounts state that the gods have blessed the king, but the blessing is mentioned in the third person, and is not presented as a divine message delivered directly to the king. So, Samsuiluna A claims that the great gods looked upon the king with their radiant countenances and blessed him. Esarhaddon, in his account of the building of the temple of Assur, announces that the god Assur blessed him and called him 'builder of my house' (Borger 1956: 5-6 ll. 17-25).

Nonetheless, all the passages just cited do not easily offer the sought-after background for the biblical passage under discussion. It is likely that the divine blessings, addresses and promises to the builders mentioned in all these inscriptions are in fact nothing more than substitutes for the standard, more common concluding prayers (*Schlussgebete*). Rather than recording the king's wish that the gods bless him, the authors of these compositions incorporate the requested blessings into divine promises, as if the requests were already granted and assured. To the best of my knowledge, only one inscription mentions both a royal prayer and a divine blessing of the king (Esarhaddon, Borger 1956: 63-64), and even in this text the divine blessing is mentioned with utmost brevity. It seems that these two elements—a prayer to the gods asking them to bless the king, and a statement that the gods have in fact blessed the king—are interchangeable and that if one is mentioned it is considered unnecessary to mention the other. Furthermore, God's reply to Solomon is not a promise of unqualified blessing, rewarding Solomon for what he has already accomplished, but contains qualifications for further blessings as well as the threat of curses. It goes without saying that both the element of qualification and the element of malediction are totally absent from the divine blessings in the Mesopotamian texts.

I wish to propose that the qualified blessings and curses which conclude the account of Solomon's temple building, and which are incorporated into the framework of a divine revelation to the king, are reflexes of, or inspired ultimately by, the benediction and malediction component which conclude many of the Mesopotamian building inscriptions. In order to assure that a dilapidated or ruined building will be restored by a king in the future, and in order to guarantee that the present monarch's own building inscriptions will be treated with proper respect, the Mesopotamian rulers would conclude their inscriptions with a plea to their future heirs. The king to come would be asked to restore the building and place within it the ancient building inscriptions which he would encounter in the course of his restoration work. Divine blessing was asked for kings who would do so, while kings who would not respect their predecessors' inscriptions were threatened with terrible maledictions.

One may naturally object to this proposition with the claim that the blessings and curses mentioned in God's reply to Solomon are dependent on the religious and moral behavior of the future kings and people, and that there is not the slightest hint of care and respect or negligence and disrespect for buildings, monuments, inscriptions or anything similar. This objection is not without merit, but may be overcome. The biblical account has adapted the literary pattern to its own literary and theological idiosyncrasies. We have seen time and again in this study that the biblical story of building the temple does not represent the contemporary building story topos in its pristine form. In the case of the blessings and curses as well, intentional revision has occurred. The element of blessing and cursing in the Mesopotamian inscriptions is meant to preserve both the inscription and building against the ravages of time and future neglect, and to preserve memory of the king and his accomplishments. This has been adapted by the biblical author, and now serves to assure future allegiance to God and His commandments, and by so doing serves to preserve the existence of the Temple and the royal dynasty.

The literary transformation proposed here is not merely one of expedience, fabricated to serve the purpose of the present claim. In fact, examples of the very same type of transformation appear in several Mesopotamian texts:

1. There are certain texts which have been designated '*narû* literature' since their study by H. Güterbock, and which are now designated by some scholars (A.K. Grayson, W.G. Lambert, T. Longman) 'pseudo-autobiographies'. These inscriptions, which tell of great kings of the distant past, are similar in structure to the standard royal

inscriptions.[1] Since they follow the structure of royal inscriptions, they end in a section which contains blessings (and curses) for future generations. But, these concluding sections, rather than being concerned about preserving the inscription (for the *narû* texts are literary compositions to be read, learned and copied, and not building inscriptions meant to be placed inside a building) are of didactic or hortatory character, and relate to the behavior of the king. The biblical passage too is didactic or hortatory in nature. The difference between the two is only that in the pseudo-autobiography the king speaks to the future generation, while in 1 Kings 9 God speaks to Solomon (and the future generations). In any case, the biblical passage resembles the concluding passages in the *narû* texts in that a structural component meant to preserve the physical existence of an inscription or a building has been incorporated into the building account itself, and has been transformed into something aimed at preaching proper behavior to future generations.

2. A similar example of the utilization for alternative literary purposes of the pattern of a royal inscriptions, *blessing and curse section included*, is found in a prayer of Assurbanipal to Shamash.[2] The prayer is composed of praise to the god (ll. 1-13); praise of the king's deeds on behalf of the god (in the first person, ll. 14-16); a prayer for the king (ll. 17-21); wishes of blessings for anyone who will sing this hymn and mention the name of the king (ll. 22-25); curses for anyone who will silence the song (ll. 26-28). Here too, the blessings and curses are not meant to preserve the inscription itself, and seem to be included in the inscription simply out of imitation of a stereotyped literary pattern.

3. The Tukulti-Ninurta Epic is an historical poem structured along the literary pattern of the Mesopotamian building inscriptions. P. Machinist, who is in the advanced stages of preparing this text for definitive publication, has remarked concerning the end of the composition:[3]

1. On this literary genre see Lewis 1980: 87-93 and Longman 1991.
2. See Stephen's translation in *ANET*, 386-87, and note in particular his introductory remarks.
3. Machinist 1976: 459.

When the Epic goes on with praise between Tukulti–Ninurta and the
gods, and with curses on any who would harm the king, it may reflect the
conclusion of the inscriptions which curse those who would destroy the
work of the king, i.e. the building and steles just described.

4. The statue dedicated to Nabu by Bēl-tarṣi-ilumma, governor of
Kalhu under Adad-nerari III, ends not with the expected blessings and
curses for protecting the object, but with an admonition (I R 35.2 =
Schrader 1889: 192 l. 12):

> O man of the future,
> trust in Nabu!
> Trust not in another god!

5. But the most significant example of the transformation of the
blessing–curse section is found in an actual building inscription. In a
text of Nabopolassar (Langdon 1912: 68 *Nabopolassar* no. 4 ll. 31-41;
see also Al-Rawi 1985) discussed in the first part of this study, the
blessing section (there are no curses) has a clearly moral or religious
message. Before the future king is called upon to restore Nabopolassar's
building or to respect his inscriptions, he is asked to imitate those
qualities which brought Nabopolassar to the throne. He is called upon
to reject the use of force and resort rather to piety and good thoughts:

> Whatever king at any time,
> be he a son or grandson following me,
> whom Marduk, for mastery of the Land
> will call his name—
> Strength and might bring not into your heart,
> Seek out the sanctuaries of Nabu and Marduk,
> may they kill your enemies.
> Marduk my lord examines the mouth (exterior)
> (and) looks into the heart.
> Whoever is firm with Bel,
> his foundations are firm.
> Whoever is firm with Bel's son
> will grow old for ever.

Such a future king is promised a stable reign. Literarily, this inscription resembles the *narû* texts in that the address to the future king is
related in content and language to the historical passage describing the
king's personal experience (see the selection of the king described in
Langdon 1912: 66 *Nabopolassar* no. 4 4-10). Even so, the text is a

building inscription with a building account similar in structure to the standard pattern. The request to the future king to emulate Nabopolassar's piety as a condition for enjoying a long rule resembles God's words to Solomon admonishing him to imitate David's piety so that his dynasty may endure (1 Kgs 9.4-5).

The three literary texts mentioned have a structure influenced by that of the royal inscriptions. They are all poetic, literary compositions with no particular importance to the clay tablet upon which they were inscribed. Blessings and curses to help preserve them and their authors are unnecessary. Even so, the authors have adhered faithfully to a certain literary form *in its entirety*. But they have adapted the 'extraneous' appendage by filling it with new content. The scribes of Bēl-tarṣi-ilumma and Nabopolassar have done likewise with their inscriptions. They decided, for some reason that is not entirely clear, that it was just as important to teach a lesson of history than to burden a future king with an exercise in building conservation or tablet-preservation. The Deuteronomic composer of 1 Kgs 9.1-9 has allowed himself the same literary license as these Mesopotamian colleagues. He has composed (or reworked) a building account according to a fixed, traditional, well-known pattern. The final element in the pattern which informed his writing was found to be a set of blessings and curses for some future king who would find the building in ruins and the inscriptions buried within its foundations or inscribed on its walls. This element, in its traditional form would, for obvious reasons, not suit the story he was composing, but rather than deleting it and deviating from the pattern he was following, he did something which his Mesopotamian counterparts were accustomed to doing in similar situations. He simply introduced into the available slot a more relevant message, but one in keeping with the general, if not the specific, demands of that slot.

Identifying the blessings and curses in God's reply to Solomon with the benedictions and maledictions found at the ends of Mesopotamian building inscriptions may have certain historical ramifications. A survey of all the Mesopotamian building inscriptions reveals that this element is nearly entirely missing from the corpus of Neo-Babylonian inscriptions, and can be found mostly in places where Assyrian influence may be expected. This fact alone may suggest that there is some specific relationship between the form of the biblical building account and the form of the Assyrian building accounts. On the other hand, there are no indications of a specific connection between the biblical account and the Babylonian ones. (The Nabopolassar text just discussed may still bear the marks of Assyrian influence, since it is an 'apology' and tells of how the Assyrians were routed). One may claim, of course, that blessings and curses are regular components concluding inscriptions of all sorts, from all times and from all geographical regions. This is certainly true in regard to curses. It is well known that curses were meant to protect inscriptions, objects, buildings, privileges and other things found not only at the ends of building inscriptions, such as memorial-tombstone inscriptions, 'boundary'-stones (actually real estate documents) and treaties. But this is almost never the case with the blessing formulae![1]

Blessing formulae meant to protect and preserve a building, or anything else, appear at the end of law codes, treaties,[2] building inscriptions, burial inscriptions,[3] and documents of grant from Assyria. Dozens of Assyrian building inscriptions, from the time of Aššur-bēl-nišēše until the time of Assurbanipal and Sin-Shar-ishkun, contain the short formula referring to the king who will honor the inscriptions: *DN ikrībīšu išemme*, 'DN will listen to his prayers!' This formula, which is characteristic of Assyrian inscriptions, is found neither in Babylonian inscriptions nor in inscriptions from the west. Furthermore, the inscriptions of Tiglath-pileser I, Assurnasirpal II, Esarhaddon and Assurbanipal have expanded forms of the blessing. Tiglath-pileser I wishes his successors (King, *AKA*, 106 VIII 60):

> Just like me, may Anu and Adad, the great gods, constantly lead him well in happiness and achieving triumph.

1.   For some rare exceptions, see Hallo 1962: 22 nn. 195-96, who states that curse formulae are more common than blessings; Ur-Nammu no. 28 = *IRSA* III A1g; Amar-Suen *UET* I 71 = *IRSA*, 147 III A3c and the Hammurabi legal monument have both blessing and curse formulae.

2.   For blessings and curses in these compositions, see Noth 1966b. Note the fact that in extra-biblical treaties the blessings appear after the curses (this is not the case, however, in Lev. 26 and Deut. 28, where blessing precedes curse). For the curses concluding the legal monuments, see Paul 1970: 11-26. Since 1 Kgs 9 is not the conclusion of a treaty, covenant or law corpus, there is no reason to view these types as the source of the blessings and curses in the chapter.

3.   For a blessing formula in an Assyrian burial inscription, see Clay 1915: 61 no. 43 ll. 7-10.

Esarhaddon wished the king who comes after him (Borger 1956: 75
l. 39: Goetze 1963: 130 l. 19):

> The gods will heed his prayers,
> He will have long days and a large family!

Assurbanipal writes (Piepkorn 1933: 88 ll. 87-90):

> May the great gods . . .
> constantly bless his reign
> May they grant in his place strength and might!

In other places we find (Streck 1916: 90 ll. 114-15; Aynard 1957: 64
l. 69):

> May the great gods . . .
> as unto me, (also)
> give him strength and might![1]

More than anyone else, Assurnasirpal II wishes his successors mainly
victory in battle, but sometimes even abundance and wealth (Grayson,
ARI, II §§620-21, 666, 672, 690, 695, 708, 719, 731, 771). But one
particular inscription contains a somewhat unusual blessing (King,
AKA, 172 ll. 15-17; Grayson, *ARI*, II §§695):

> May Assur the great lord
> and Mamu who dwells in that temple
> look steadily upon him
> with their glance.
> May his memory and progeny
> be established in their land!

This wish of Assurnasirpal may be compared, of course to God's
reply to Solomon in 1 Kgs 9.3-5:

> I consecrate this House which you have built and I set my name there for-
> ever. My eyes and my heart shall ever be there. . . then I will establish
> your throne of kingship over Israel for ever . . .

The frequent request that the gods listen to the prayers of the future

---

1. See also in Nabonidus's Sippar inscription (Langdon 1912: 228 *Nabonidus*
no. 1 III 43-50; and see also the Harran stele). He opens with the expression *mannu
atta*, 'Whoever you are', known from western inscriptions, and goes on to list maledictions known to us from the Assyrian inscriptions, and adds to the request his own
particular Sin-oriented theology!

kings may perhaps be compared with God's announcement to Solomon, 'I have heard the prayer and the supplication which you have offered me' (v. 3).

Taking all this into consideration, there is room to suggest that the passage concluding the building account, containing conditional blessings and curses for future generations, is rooted in a pattern known specifically only from Assyrian inscriptions. In tabular form this is the distribution of blessings and curses.

	1 Kings 9	*Western and OB inscriptions*	*Assyrian*	*NB*
Blessings	+	– (rare)	+	–
Curses	+	+	+	–

Conclusion

It may be conjectured that the biblical author was familiar with a literary pattern (known to us almost exclusively from Assyrian inscriptions) according to which a building story was concluded with conditional blessings and curses addressed to a future king who would find the current building in ruins. These blessings and curses were irrelevant to the Israelite author, who, after all, was not writing a building inscription to be placed in the Temple, but a historiographic survey with theological and didactic bent. Nonetheless, in order to remain faithful to the full literary pattern which he had chosen to follow, he resorted to a practice used by contemporary scribes writing under analogous conditions. He placed the blessings and curses into God's own mouth and turned the conditions for activating the blessings and curses into conditions suiting his own ideological and religious purposes. By using such a literary adaptation, the biblical writer followed the example of his Mesopotamian counterparts, making some idiosyncratic changes. Both in the Bible and in the contemporary Mesopotamian writings, the 'monumental' literary topos has been adapted and made to fit the needs and purposes of 'non-monumental' literary works.

SUMMARY AND CONCLUSIONS

1. *The Biblical Accounts of Temple Building are Written according to a Well-Known Ancient Near Eastern Pattern*

In the first part of this study, more than twenty extra-biblical building accounts were analyzed and found to possess similar or nearly identical thematic structures. Despite certain flexibility and variability in the structure, all the stories examined preserved the same basic sequence of topics and central events, including: (1) a reason to build or restore a building along with the command or consent of the gods to the proposed project; (2) preparations for the project including enlisting workers, gathering and manufacturing building materials and laying the foundations of the building; (3) a description of the building process and of the edifice under construction; (4) dedication of the building by populating it, along with celebrations and rituals; (5) a prayer or a blessing meant to assure a good future for the building and the builder. Some of the stories included an additional element: (6) conditional blessings and curses addressed to a future king who will repair the building when it falls into ruin. An analysis of 1 Kgs 5.15–9.25 showed that this building account as well is strikingly similar in its structure to the extra-biblical stories. The same can be said about other biblical building accounts—the building of the Tabernacle, the restoration of the Temple by the returnees from Exile, and the repair of the walls of Jerusalem carried out and reported by Nehemiah. Even Josephus's account of the rebuilding of the Temple by Herod seems to have adhered to this structure. These stories share not only the same thematic structure, but display many common motifs, expressions and ideas as well.

In the subsequent chapters the individual components of the building stories were examined, concentrating on 1 Kings 5–9. It was seen that, as far as ideas and linguistic usage are concerned, these components have parallels in many other extra-biblical building stories, in addition to the ones discussed in Part I because of their characteristic structure. These analyses were not only comparative, but were contrastive as well, and due note was taken of significant differences between the biblical account on the one hand and the Mesopotamian ones on the other. Significant affinities with other types of writings were also discovered (see below).

As a result of our discussions, and on the basis of numerous points of similarity both in overall structure and individual points of language and ideas, the 'building account' may safely be added to the list of traditional literary types or forms recognizable as common to Israelite and neighboring literatures of the ancient Near East in general and of Mesopotamia in particular. The similarities between the biblical 'building account' and the traditional Mesopotamian 'building account' are no less and no different in nature than the recognized, well known similarities between other types of biblical and ancient Near Eastern literary forms, such as treaties and covenants, law corpora, proverb collections and wisdom instructions, letters and the like. The 'building account' was an important, prominent and even formative element in the historical writings of the kings of Mesopotamia, and the prominence it has achieved in biblical writings as well can be taken as a sign of connections between historical writing in Israel and historical writing in neighboring cultures.

2. *The Ancient Near Eastern Building Account Probably Originated in Mesopotamia*

Despite the prevalence of building inscriptions among all the peoples of the ancient Near East, there is no evidence known to me that 'building accounts' of the form discussed in this study were customary and firmly rooted in the literary tradition anywhere outside of Mesopotamia. The 'building account' not only served the Mesopotamian scribes as an independent literary form, but was also the common literary skeleton or vehicle for types of historical writings (royal inscriptions in particular), and was also a literary topos in hymns, myths and epics. The entrenchment of the building account and its intrusion into Mesopotamian writings of various genres may be accredited not only to literary and religious conservatism and affection for traditional patterns, but to the special place which building undoubtedly occupied in Mesopotamian daily life in general,[1] and to the vast royal building works which occupied the Mesopotamian people and monarchs throughout the entire history of Mesopotamian civilization.

The building account served primarily and above all as a literary topos suitable for glorifying kings, and, by analogy, divine kings as well. The application of the building story to gods is facilitated by the fact that, according to widespread Mesopotamian beliefs, it was the gods who founded many of the major cities and temples, and it was the gods who suffered under oppressive construction labor before the creation of humanity. It is reasonable to surmise that the 'building account', as a recognized, fixed and well-defined literary form, passed from one culture to another along with and through the same channels as other elements of royal ideology. Just as a building project would be considered meritorious of a Mesopotamian monarch or a Mesopotamian god, it could just as well be considered to the glory of a Canaanite, Israelite or Egyptian king or deity. To speak of an avenue by which royal ideology and the image of an ideal king could pass from one culture to another, is immediately to speak of an avenue potentially suitable for the migration of the building account from one culture to the other.

3. *1 Kings 5.15–9.25 is Particularly Similar to Assyrian Building Accounts*

Despite the overall similarity in structure and ideas, there seem to have been no two individual building accounts which were equivalent in all their details,[2] and the differences between various stories may in

1.   For the importance of building in Mesopotamian consciousness, see the allusions to the building of temples and cities, digging canals, work and building tools in several myths such as those translated by Heidel (1951: 61-75). See also the so-called 'Eridu Genesis' (Miller 1985) for the building of primordial cities.

2.   I refer here to independent inscriptions. Inscriptions which (before being inscribed in the buildings for which they were intended) were written in 'draft' form are not included. Nor is reference made to royal inscriptions which were occasionally recopied for either didactic or archival purposes. There are also instances in which a king has his own inscriptions copied for secondary use in other inscriptions. So we find in the case of Nabonidus's Sippar inscription, Harran stele and Langdon 1915–16 or Nebuchadnezzar's Wadi Brissa inscription. Sargon, king of Assyria plagiarized and put to his own use and aggrandizement a building inscription written by

fact be quite large at times. In addition, the extent of similarity or difference between one story and another varies significantly. As one might expect, the Mesopotamian building accounts resemble each other more than any individual Mesopotamian building story resembles any biblical building account. But it seems to me that, of all the Mesopotamian building stories, the ones that most resemble 1 Kings 5–9 are those of the Assyrian kings (as opposed to those of the Chaldaean kings of Babylon). This particular closeness was revealed in the following components:

1. The dedication of the Temple described in 1 Kings 8 resembles in essence, structure and numerous details the dedication ceremonies described in the Assyrian royal inscriptions. The Neo-Babylonian inscriptions do not, as a rule, mention such celebrations with the exception of some inscriptions which may have been written under the influence of Assyrian inscriptions.
2. Only the Assyrian building inscriptions conclude with conditional blessings and curses for future kings. The Babylonian building inscriptions have no trace of this element. There is reason to believe that this element underlies the blessings and curses in God's reply to Solomon's prayer (1 Kgs 9.1-9).
3. The individual Mesopotamian inscriptions closest in total structure and particular details to the biblical account are building stories of the Assyrian kings Tiglath-pileser I and Esarhaddon.
4. Numerous Assyrian building stories begin by praising the great wisdom of the king (see, for one example out of many, the Cylinder inscription of Sargon). It is possible that this characteristic is to be connected with the praise of Solomon's wisdom found in the passage immediately preceding the biblical building account (1 Kgs 5.9-15).

It seems to me that all of these considerations, individually and together, constitute evidence that the building account found in 1 Kings 5–9 reflects the literary environment of the Assyrian period. This

Merodach-baladan (Gadd 1953). Nabonidus is guilty of 'lifting' some events from inscriptions of Nebuchadnezzar, using them in his own inscriptions and applying them to his building ventures.

evidence is, to be sure, very fragile and new finds or reinvestigation of the texts discussed here may throw new light on it. Nonetheless, it is now possible to suggest that there was some influence of Assyrian literary practices on this account, even if the influence may have been indirect. The other biblical accounts may be for the most part imitative of this 'original' story in both structure and detail, but there seems to be, nonetheless, continued contact with and dependence on extra-biblical literary traditions and beliefs.

If, as I suggest, there is some sort of genetic relationship between the building account in 1 Kings 5–9 and those specifically of the Assyrian period, there are possible implications for the higher-critical literary-historical questions of the process and date of the biblical story's composition. The building story in its present, canonical form includes certain Deuteronomic elements—various glosses in the beginning of the story (5.16-19), Solomon's dedicatory oration (8.15-61) and God's reply with its blessings and curses (9.2-9). In all of these elements we found signs of Assyrian affinities. These signs of Assyrian influence may be explained in a number of ways. If they are the personal contributions of the Deuteronomist, we must conclude that the Deuteronomic form of the story dates to a time when Assyrian literature still had an impact on Israelite literature. This possibility would somewhat strengthen the theory propounded by F.M. Cross and his disciples[1] of a pre-exilic Deuteronomic redaction of the book of Kings, perhaps from the time of Josiah. But no less likely is the possibility that Assyrian literary influence did not die out in the west with the fall of Assyria. It is possible that certain specifically Assyrian literary practices took root in the west and lived on in the periphery, even after their extinction in the Mesopotamian homeland. If direct Assyrian influence on the Deuteronomist is deemed improbable, then another conclusion may be reached, namely, that the Deuteronomist re-worked an existing building story and *replaced* or rewrote certain passages which had originally taken form under direct Assyrian influence. He maintained some of the original content, but rewrote them according to his own beliefs and purposes. Certain factors point towards this conclusion: (a) the account of the dedication ceremonies, which has strong similarity to Assyrian texts, is on the whole pre-Deuteronomic; (b) Solomon's Prayer (which

---

1. See Cross 1973: 274-89; Friedman 1981; Peckham 1985.

resembles Tiglath-pileser's prayer more than any other) and the concluding blessings and curses do not appear in the Bible exactly as they would in an Assyrian text. Solomon's Prayer polemicizes against the basic premises of the Mesopotamian building prayers, while the blessings and curses have been adapted to fit the needs of Deuteronomic historical thinking. For these reasons we may conjecture that there was a pre-Deuteronomic building account corresponding in all its structural details to the Assyrian building accounts and written under their (indirect?) influence, and that, at a later date, the Deuteronomic redactor (or redactors) added their glosses to certain parts of the story and rewrote others, so as to reflect their own views about the nature of the Temple and about the place its building occupied in their view of Israelite history.

We cannot answer all the questions which stem from the possibility that the building account received its form under the influence of Assyrian literary conventions, and it was not our intention to suggest all possible explanations. Nor did we deal with the obviously important question of how Assyrian building accounts could have been known by and influenced the biblical writers. Whatever the case may be, however, it is a question which should be further pursued by all scholars interested in the literary history of the building story in particular and the historical growth of the book of Kings in general (see below).

4. *1 Kings 5.15–9.25 has Incorporated Material of Various Genres and Backgrounds*

Everything said so far about the similarity of the biblical building account to Mesopotamian building accounts in general and to the Assyrian ones in particular relates to the biblical story *in its overall form*. But a structural and comparative analysis can be misleading and engender a false impression about the degree and depth of the similarity. When the story was examined in greater detail, penetrating below the surface structure, significant differences between the biblical account and its Mesopotamian parallels were revealed, and it was even seen that at several points the biblical author was writing according to the conventions of other literary types. Affinities were also found with the writings of other cultures, specifically non-Mesopotamian ones.

1. The description of the return of the Ark to the Temple in 8.1-11 parallels in function the descriptions in Assyrian royal inscriptions of the god being brought into the temple. But in its details, this story has its closest parallel in 2 Samuel 6. Both of these accounts have extra-biblical prototypes in Mesopotamian texts (not necessarily from building accounts)[1] that describe processions of divine statues.

2. The long, detailed descriptions of the buildings and vessels have few stylistic or formal parallels in the Mesopotamian building accounts, but they do have counterparts in Mesopotamian writings of other types, such as instructions to builders, administrative documents such as receipts, and perhaps didactic texts.

3. The negotiations for purchasing cedars were described in epistolary style and form. The commercial acquisition of building materials, as well as the description of the event through letters, are without parallel in the extra-biblical building accounts, but they reflect known practices attested in other types of writings. It is not impossible that the biblical writer was influenced at this point by certain trade letters which were actually available to him.

4. The date formulae in 1 Kings 6 and 7 have no parallel in the Mesopotamian building accounts. Nonetheless, they have close parallels in Phoenician (and Aramaic) building and dedicatory inscriptions, as well as Mesopotamian chronicles.

5. The description of the corvée in 5.27-32 (not discussed above) has numerous parallels in the Mesopotamian building accounts which report the massive call-up of workers for the projects. But in all the reports, the narrator never specifies the number of workers actually employed, and certainly makes no reference to the work shifts or to the foreman. Montgomery has suggested that this passage contains 'archival' information.[2] It is indeed possible that the scribe was privy to some

1. For Mesopotamian accounts of the return of divine statues to their cities and temples, see Miller and Roberts 1977 (Nebuchadnezzar I); Streck 1916: 262-69 (Assurbanipal); Borger 1956: 88-89 (Esarhaddon).

2. See Montgomery and Gehman 1951: 137. This opinion was challenged by Noth 1968: 13, citing as proof the round numbers. But even the admission that the

administrative document related to the work procedures, or that he was at least influenced by the style of administrative documents.

6. *The Master Craftsman.* The biblical building story mentions by name the Tyrian master artisan who forged the bronze furnishings for the Temple. The description of Hiram resembles that of Bezalel and of Oholiab son of Ahisamak who made the Tabernacle. It must be pointed out that, in all the Mesopotamian building accounts known to me, there is not a single example of an artisan mentioned by name. Admittedly, groups of artisans or experts of various sorts are mentioned, but never is there reference to any specific person who either worked individually or stood at the head of a guild of craftsmen.[1] In distinction from what was encountered in the Mesopotamian building stories, we find in the Baal epic that the building of Baal's (and other gods') palace(s) is attributed to Kothar waHasis, called at times Hayin. In a broken passage in *Enuma elish* V, Ea is mentioned as the architect who would build Esagila for Marduk. Artisans are also mentioned by name in grant documents such as the Agum-kakrime inscription (Unger 1970: 279 col. IV), and the 'boundary stone' of Merodach-baladan I (King 1912: V col. II 11-18; see *CAD* Ṣ, p. 227 *s.v. ṣubbû* 4.1 and see also Streck 1916: 290 l. 19). It is possible that the mention of the builder or artisan by name is a characteristic of either Western or mythic literature which is different in nature from the main stream of the building account tradition. (We should note on this matter that the Greek tradition as well attributes the

---

numbers themselves are round says nothing about the literary inspiration for this passage. The Mesopotamian inscriptions contain no information of this type. As for Montgomery's term 'archival', I repeat my reservations about it as a genre designation (see above), and suggest speaking about 'administrative' documents instead. For the terms and institution *mas 'ôḇēḏ,* and *nōśē' sabbāl,* see Birm 1952 and Held 1968. Held has gathered from the Mesopotamian building accounts the references to the parallel Akkadian terms. For the equation of *mas* with Akkadian *ilku,* see Weinfeld 1983, esp. 90-91.

1. For wandering artisans in the ancient world, see Zaccagnini 1983 with reference to the biblical sources on his p. 259.

building of divine palaces to Hephaistos, and the parallel between this god and Kothar waHasis has already been noted by T. Gaster, C.H. Gordon and others.)[1]

5. *The Growth and Emergence of 1 Kings 5.15–9.25*

Analysis of the overall structure of the biblical building account has revealed that it resembles many extra-biblical building accounts in general and Assyrian building accounts in particular. On the other hand, investigation of the form, content and style of the individual components of the story shows adherence to various other literary forms, not related to or resembling the building accounts. On the basis of these two diverging indications, the work of the biblical author may be characterized as that of an editor who combined (and revised or adapted as necessary) independent original documents into a story which does not have a smooth literary texture, but which follows, nonetheless, a predetermined and coherent outline. Where the outline dictated that he disclose how the building materials were prepared and how workers were drafted, our author incorporated into his work in more or less their original form the relevant letters or administrative decrees. In the place where he was called upon to provide dates, our author quoted the appropriate chronographic or monumental sources. And where he had to describe the buildings, he turned to his archive and retrieved for his own use the descriptions which had been prepared for or by the architect. In order to describe the temple vessels, he cited the descriptive records of receipt which had been prepared at the time the vessels had originally been dedicated.

This analysis enables us to suggest several possible scenarios for the actual growth and emergence of the building account. According to one scenario, the account may have developed over four or five stages:

1. The original documents—the letters, administrative records, chronographic records, dedicatory inscriptions, building plans, and prayers—came into existence as part of the building process and were contemporary with it. A 'building account' describing the project in the traditional fashion does not yet exist.

---

1. Gaster 1946; Gordon 1965: 236-37.

2.   The 'original' documents were combined according to a pre-conceived pattern, making the necessary adjustments for incorporation into a narrative. The stage is pre-Deuteronomic. The author was familiar with literary conventions and practices typical of Assyrian writings. The scribe himself composed the description of the dedication ceremony. At this stage, a full building account comes into existence.

3.   A Deuteronomic scribe revised the original building account, making no structural changes, but adding glosses and replacing entire sections with substitutes which he himself composed. The new, replacement parts are Deuteronomic in language and ideology, but reflect the theme of the building account components which they supplanted.

4.   Later additions were made. A divine revelation to Solomon (6.11-13) was placed somewhere near the beginning of the building story, perhaps by a scribe who was not happy with the fact that the story which reached him had mentioned no explicit divine sanction of the project directly to Solomon. The archaic month names Ziv, Eithanim and Bul were glossed for the benefit of readers not familiar with the ancient calendar.

5.   Possible changes in the temple architecture may have occasioned changes in the description at any time in the process of the account's development. The Priestly revision of the dedication ceremony, intent on legitimizing the Solomonic Temple as the final destination and resting place of the Mosaic Tabernacle, may have been entered at any stage in the development. (There are no Deuteronomic glosses of Priestly elements or Priestly glosses of Deuteronomic elements which might indicate the sequence.)

An alternative possibility is that stage two did not exist, or that it was combined with stage three. In such a scenario the Deuteronomic editor would have been the original composer of a connected building story, and he would have been the one who combined the original documents. A third possibility is that the original building story was written without resorting to documents of any sort, and that over the course of time parts of the original story were replaced or revised under the influence of external, independent documents. One last alternative is that a single biblical author—certainly of the Deuteronomic school—who did not have access to any original documents, composed a building story from scratch in such a way that it would look like a collage of sources. He might have wished to achieve a semblance of authenticity by writing such a pseudepigraphic hotch-potch.

I do not pretend to have alighted unquestionably upon the authoritative and exclusive explanation of how 1 Kgs 5.15–9.25 grew into its present form. I hope, however, to have come reasonably close! It is clear, all the same, that comparison and contrast with extra-biblical sources has greatly enhanced the proper identification of certain elements composing this narrative. Any new attempt to further our understanding of the form, growth, content and message of the several biblical building accounts discussed in this work will do well to be informed by this method.

Appendix 1

TEMPLE BUILDING AND FERTILITY

In Hag. 2.15-19 we read:

> And now take thought, from this day backward:
> As long as no stone had been laid on another in the House of the Lord,
> if one came to a heap of twenty measures, it would yield only ten;
> and if one came to a wine vat to skim off fifty measures, the press would yield
> only twenty.
> I struck you—all the works of your hands—with blight and mildew and hail,
> but you did not return to Me—declares the Lord.
> Take note, from this day forward—from the twenty-fourth day of the ninth
> month, from the day when the foundation was laid for the Lord's Temple—take
> note while the seed is still in the granary, and the vine, fig tree, pomegranate,
> and olive tree have not yet borne fruit.
> For from this day on I will send blessings.

Ideological parallels between the prophecies of Haggai and Mesopotamian literature
in general and Gudea Cylinder A in particular were suggested over sixty years ago by
Bewer (1919). However, his specific comparison of the situation of the Tigris
described in Cylinder A col. I and the drought in the time of Haggai are no longer
tenable because Bewer based the parallel on the mistaken translation of Thureau-
Dangin, according to which the river did not rise. Note, however, that the parallel
between Haggai's promise of agricultural abundance (2.15-19) and Ningirsu's
promise in the second dream may still be maintained. There we read (Cylinder A XI;
Jacobsen's translation; see also Kramer 1988: 2-3):

> When to my house . . .
> you put effectively the hand for me,
> I shall call up a humid wind
> that from above it bring you abundance;
> and the people may spread hands for you
> on the abundance.
> May with the laying of the foundations
> of my house
> abundance come!
> All the great fields shall raise their hands (in appeal) to you,
> dike and canal will crane their necks at you, and hills
>   to which waters rise not,

> waters will rise for you.
> Summer will be able to pour surplus cream,
> able to weigh out surplus wool.

On these parallels, see most recently Meyers and Meyers 1987: 65 on 2.19. Andersen (1987: 91-126) discusses the relationship between fertility and temple building especially as concerns Haggai's prophecy, but has overlooked the Gudea passage. An additional text ignored by all studies of this motif is the inscription of Arik-din-ili I (*RIMA* I 121 ll. 14-18), where the king says that he built the Shamash temple to insure the fertility of the land's produce:

> I planned to rebuild that temple
> in order that the harvest of my land might prosper.

The relationship between temple building and agricultural productivity is also a major motif in the Sumerian epic *Enmerkar and the Lord of Aratta*.

Appendix 2

THE UNTIRING TEMPLE BUILDER

In Psalm 132, a text certainly associated with the traditions about building the Temple in Jerusalem, we read (vv. 3-5):

> I will not enter the tent of my dwelling, nor will I mount my bed and mattress. I will not give sleep to my eyes or slumber to my eyelids, until I find a place for the Lord, an abode for the Mighty One of Jacob.

Weinfeld (1972: 48) has compared this verse with a depiction of Gudea who, while building Eninnu, is described as follows (Cylinder A XVII 7–9): 'For the sake of building the house for his master, he slept not nights, nor rested the head at noon'. This motif is in fact much more widespread. These two passages can be compared with l. 24 in *The Curse of Agade*, where Inanna goes without sleep in order to do good things for Agade, and when she is outfitting the temple and city which she has built for herself (see A. Falkenstein's discussion, 1965, pp. 82-83 and S.N. Kramer's translation in *ANET*, 647 b 1.24 and Cooper 1983). In Šulgi R (Klein 1990), ll. 5-6, we read: 'He of the intelligence wide took great counsel about you [Enlil's ceremonial barge], The shepherd, day and night sleeps not...' These passages may also be compared with IV R 20.1 (see Miller and Roberts 1977: 79 ll. 7-8) where Nebuchadnezzar I describes his efforts in returning the statue of Marduk to Babylon from Elamite exile ('Until I had seen his exalted form, every day my...was unceasing, bowing down did not depart from my body, and in the sweet embrace of night I did not finish out my sleep'). Cf. also the words of Nabonidus in the Weld-Blundell Cylinder (Langdon 1923: 34 col. II l. 20: 'upon the bed at night I could not get my fill of sweet sleep' (*CAD* Q, p. 182 col. a *s.v. qatû* 5b). Note as well, W.G. Lambert 1988: 161 l. 9: 'He did not sleep during the night, until the maker of the decisions, the lord of lords Šamaš, shone' describing Esarhaddon's attempt to return Marduk's statue (see also Lambert 1988: 163 l. 5). These statements from Sumerian and Babylonian texts have their counterparts in assertions of various Assyrian kings that they exerted themselves or became exhausted (*anāhu*) while building temples (Shalmaneser I in *IAK*, 122 l. 9; Tiglath-pileser I *AKA*, 98 col. VII l. 96), and that they were not negligent (*aham ul iddi*). See the passages in *CAD* N I, p. 92 *ahu (nadû)*. Returning to the Bible, we find that Haggai admonishes the returnees from Exile for neglecting the building of the Temple: 'Is it a time for you to dwell in your paneled houses, while this House is in ruins?' (Hag. 1.4), and 'You have been expecting much and getting little. . . Because of what?. . . Because of my House which lies in ruins, while you all hurry to your own houses!' (Hag. 1.9). The prophet may be making a veiled allusion here to what we read about David, who became aware of the need to build God a Temple when he noticed that he himself was dwelling in a cedar palace while the Ark of the Lord was in a mere tent (2 Sam. 7.3). All the passages mentioned here express the expectation that the person called upon to build a temple for his god will place the needs of the deity above his own personal comfort, and will spare no effort until the construction of the divine residence is completed.

Appendix 3

SURVEYING THE BUILDING SITE

Ezekiel is conducted on his visionary tour of the future temple by 'a man who shone like copper' and who carried 'in his hand a cord of linen and a measuring rod' (Ezek. 40.3). A similar man, holding a measuring line, going 'to measure Jerusalem to see how long and wide it is to be' is beheld by the prophet Zechariah (2.5-9). This character, unheard of in the biblical building accounts *per se* and only mentioned in the words of these two prophets, in fact possesses roots deep in ancient Near Eastern iconography and texts.

The Ur-Nammu Stele from Ur pictures the various stages of the building project, beginning with the divine command and the granting of the measuring rope and rod (symbols of divine revelation of the plan) and ending with the dedication ceremonies. For this stele, see *ANEP*, no. 306 and Perkins 1959. The presentation of the measuring rod and measuring rope to the king in preparation for his building a temple is the ultimate origin of the motif of the linen-clad angel who carries a measuring rod and line and surveys the eschatological temple and the restored Jerusalem (cf. Ezek. 40.3 and Zech. 2.5). Note also the descriptions of Nabu and Inanna as carriers of the measuring rod (cf. *CAD* G: 79 *s.c. ginindanakku*). In Langdon 1912: 254 *Nabonidus* no. 6 col. I ll. 30-38 (discussed below), surveyors are instrumental in uncovering the old foundations of Ebabarra laid by Naram-Sin—and the 'discovery' may possibly be thought of as divine revelation. In Langdon 1912: 62, *Nabopolassar* no. 1 ll. 14-32, regarding the construction of Etemenanki, experts and wise men survey the building site, after which the measurements are confirmed by Shamash, Adad and Marduk. A text describing Amar-Su'ena's attempts for seven years to restore a temple for Enki (Michalowski 1977) says that at first the surveyors were unable to reveal the temple's form with their rods. Surveying the building site for a temple is mentioned as well in the Pap-ulle-garra Hymn (Pinches 1924: 73 VI 18-19; Seux 1976: 49) where we read: 'May he pull the boundary rope, may he make the (border) paths, may he lay out the temple, may he put the (boundary) pegs in place.'

Surveying seems to be mentioned as well in the Assyrian royal inscriptions, although in these texts it is not associated with attempts to reveal a plan. In Tiglath-pileser I's account of building the Anu-Adad temple *qaqqaršu umessi* and *ašaršu umessi* in VIII 5 are translated by King as 'I cleared the ground', taking *mussû*, as a D form of *mesû*, to clean, purify, wash. Grayson renders these phrases (perhaps idiomatically) 'I delineated its area'. We must follow, however, *CAD* M II: 236 *s.v.*

mussû 1c and A, p. 1497 *s.v. wussûm* in translating 'I identified'. In addition to the material adduced by Muffs (1969: 200), note the equation ZU: *mussû* in a commentary to *Enuma Elish* VII 40, as well as the parallelism with *lamādu* in Lyon 1883: 7 l. 46. The physical activity designated by this expression remains obscure.

In Egypt, the surveying of the temple site was done ritually and with royal participation. According to a building inscription of Sesostris I (Erman 1960: 52; Lichtheim 1973: 118), 'The king appeared in the plumed crown, with all the people following him. The chief lector-priest and scribe of the divine books stretched the cord. The rope was released, laid in the ground, made to be this temple'.

The surveying of a building site has been borrowed in the Mesopotamian and biblical traditions as a motif in creation stories. *Enuma Elish* IV 141-46 states that Marduk 'examined (*ibri!*) the heavens and investigated the building site; He measured off an area equal to that of Apsu. Nudimmud's dwelling; the Lord measured the shape of Apsu, and founded Ešarra, a splendid abode in its image.' In this passage, the cosmic temples Ešarra and Apsu are referred to, thus combining temple building and creation. In Job 38.4-7, God asks Job 'Where were you when I laid the earth's foundations?. . .Do you know who fixed its dimensions, or who measured it with a line? Onto what were its bases sunk? Who set its cornerstone? When the morning stars sang together, and all the divine beings shouted for joy'. This passage makes no mention of any cosmic temple, and the surveying is of the earth itself.

Appendix 4

TEMPORARY DWELLINGS FOR DEITIES

According to 1 Sam. 7.1:

> The men of Kiriath-Jearim came and took up the Ark of the Lord and brought it into the house of Abinadab on the hill; and they consecrated his son Eleazar to have charge of the Ark of the Lord.

2 Sam. 6.7 relates that the Ark of the Lord was housed in a tent which David pitched for it to accommodate it after it was removed from Shiloh. Shiloh was perhaps destroyed, and the Ark was now awaiting new, more appropriate accommodations. Professor Moshe Eilat suggests (in conversation) that the problematic word *wayyinnahû* in 1 Sam. 7.2 should be taken to mean 'and they moaned mournfully' (cf. Hebrew *nehî*, Akkadian *na'û* [*CAD* N II, p. 134), referring to cultic mourning performed for the displaced Ark.

The use of temporary housing, institution of cultic dues and performance of mourning rites for gods who were for some reason or other displaced from their own sanctuaries are practices known also from several Mesopotamian texts. Nabonidus (Langdon 1912: 254 no. 6 col. I 30-31) claims to have placed Shamash in a temporary dwelling while restoring Ebabbar. For a parallel account, see Langdon 1912: 224 *Nabonidus* no. 1 col. II 54-55 and Nabonidus's Weld–Blundell Cylinder, Langdon 1923: 34 col. II 4-7, and see Borger 1978 no. 156. In Langdon 1912: 276, *Nabonidus* no. 8 col. IV 14-33 (= A.L. Oppenheim, *ANET*, 309) Nabonidus reports that his predecessor Nergalsarezer had placed Anunitum of Sippar in a chapel in Sippar-Amnanu because her own temple was destroyed, and that he provided her there with regular offerings. Similar events are described in the pseudepigraphic inscription of Agum-kakrime (Unger 1970: 279 = Jensen 1892: 142 col. IV 2-8, for which see *CAD* A II, *s.v. aširtu*, p. 439):

> I placed (the holy artifacts) on cedar daises
> until I provided for them 'temples' (befitting)
> their august divinities.

In a letter from Ištar-šumu-ēreš to the king of Assyria (Parpola 1970: 14-15 n. 19 = *ABL* 1378), ll. 9-13, we read that when the temple of the god Amurru fell into ruins, the god was moved into the temple of Anu, and that when his own temple was completely restored, the king was asked for advice as to what to do. According to an inscription of Sin-šar-iškun (Böhl 1936: 35 1. 25), Nabu and Tashmetum were temporarily quartered in the temple of Ishtar-Assuritu while the king rebuilt their temple. In the *Curse of Agade* (*ANET*, 650 = Falkenstein 1965b = J. Cooper 1983) ll. 195-211, Enlil is said to have taken up residence in a small temple after Ekur was demolished and the Guti ravished the land. This may actually reflect a part of Naram-Sin's preparations to rebuild Ekur. Much mourning accompanies his move.[1]

1.　For an extended discussion of temporary divine dwellings, see Hurowitz forthcoming 4.

Appendix 5

TEMPLES, TEMPLE BUILDING AND DIVINE REST

M. Weinfeld (1983) discusses in detail the relationship between temple building and divine rest in the Bible in light of select ancient Near Eastern sources. G. von Rad had earlier (1966) called attention to the related motif of (national) rest in Deuteronomy and the Deuteronomic historiography. The motif of rest and building is developed in the writings of the Chronicler as well. For instance, in 2 Chron. 14.5 we read concerning the reign of Asa: 'He built fortified towns in Judah, since the land was untroubled (*šāqĕṭāh hā'āreṣ*) and he was not engaged in warfare during those years, for the Lord had granted him respite (*kî hēniaḥ YHWH lô*). P. Machinist (1983) discusses the motif of divine rest in the Akkadian epic of Erra. Note also Loewenstamm 1982. The most recent study is Batto 1987. Divine 'rest' is mentioned in several royal building inscriptions. Enlil-bani, king of Isin, builds a temple to ^{d}*Nintin-ug$_5$ -ga* called *é-ní-dúb-bú*, 'house of relaxation'. Temples at Ur built by Warad-Sin and Rim-Sin are called *ki-tuš ní-dúb-(bu)-(da-ni)*, '(his) dwelling place which will provide rest'. These titles go back as early as the time of Entemena (cf. Hallo: 54). Nabonidus, in a prayer to Shamash calls Ebabbar (Langdon 1912: 258 *Nabonidus* no. 6 II 15-16) *šubat tapšuhtīka*, 'the residence of your rest', and prays (ll. 18-19): *ilāni ālīka u bītīka lišapšihu kabtatka*, 'may the gods of your city and your temple cause your heart to "rest"'. Nabopolassar calls Eedinna, the temple of Belet-Sippar, *bīt tapšiḥtīšu* (Langdon 1912: 66 *Nabopolassar* no. 3 II 8). A creation myth recited in the course of a rite for manufacturing Ninšubur figurines (figurines places in foundations of buildings) says that Enlil and Ea *parak tanīḥta šubta ella irammû,* 'they will dwell on a "restful" dais in a pure dwelling' (Borger 1973: 180 ll. 68-69). In the Baal Epic, we read about Hayin (Kothar waHasis) who made for Il a *ḥym wtbtḥ* (*UT* 51 I 30). There are those who interpret this as a 'tent and resting place', namely a tent for resting (see Dietrich and Loretz 1978, esp.: 58-60). The same passage mentions also (1. 34) *kḥt il nḥt bzr* = a gold resting chair for Il. As in the Bible, so in Akkadian, the expression *šubat nēḥtim* (resting place) is used in relationship to human beings in their lands as well as to gods in their temples (see *CAD* N II: 150-51). Note especially the prayer recited thrice by the prince (*rubû*) in a building foundation ceremony, *napḫar matilja šubtu neḥta lišbā*, 'May my entire land dwell in a restful dwelling' (Borger 1971a: 78 ll. 56-57) and see also in connection with divine rest the prayer of the *kalû* priests recited during a building ritual, *inu Anum. . .parak nūḥ libbīšunu ina mātim īpuš*, 'when Anu built in the land a dais for the rest of their heart' (Mayer 1978: 438 ll. 1-7). It should be emphasized that the Hebrew terms *měnûḥâ, nûaḥ* and *hinnāpēš* and the Akkadian terms *nâḫu, nēḫtu, nêḫu, pašāḫu, tapšaḫtu, tanīḫtu* and the like are *not* completely synonymous (they have connotations of 'rest' from physical exertion, 'calm' from anger and 'peace' from warfare, etc., and the exact nuance in each case is not always unambiguous). There is still plenty of room to ask whether all the passages mentioned above actually express the same idea, and which of the various nuances is appropriate in each case (it is not to be excluded that several meanings are intended in certain contexts). Note in this direction the welcome comments of Loewenstamm in his article mentioned above.

Appendix 6

GODS AS BUILDERS OF TEMPLES AND CITIES

In what is widely considered to be one of the oldest pieces of biblical poetry, we read (Exod. 15.17):

> *tĕḇī'ēmô wĕt ittā'ēmô bĕhar naḥălāẽkā*
> *mākôn lĕšiḇtĕkāp ā'altā YHWH*
> *miqqĕdāš 'ădōnâ kônnănû yādêkā.*

The proper translation of this passage, and in particular the tense of the verbs, is still in question, as can be seen readily by comparing the translations and commentaries. It also remains problematic what mountain is referred to as the site of YHWH's sacred dais of habitation. The latter problem was discussed recently by D.N. Freedman (1981), who opted for Sinai/Horeb as opposed to Jerusalem/Zion. There is no question, however, that it is YHWH who has built the temple. The idea that YHWH is a temple builder occurs again in Ps. 78.69, where we read:

> He built his Sanctuary like the heavens,
> like the earth that he established forever.

The notion that God builds temples lives on past the biblical period and appears in a well-known passage in the *Temple Scroll*, in which God declares (col. XXIX 7-10):

> I will accept them, and they will be my people and I will be theirs forever, and I will be present among them forever after and I will sanctify my temple with my Majesty by causing my Majesty to be present over it until the day of blessing *when I myself will create my temple so that it be established for me all the days*, according to the covenant which I made with Jacob in Bethel.

In all these passages it is YHWH who will build a temple for himself. A somewhat different motif is found in Ps. 127.1, 'Unless the Lord builds the house, its builders labor in vain on it; unless the Lord watches over the city, the watchman keeps vigil in vain'. In this passage the Lord is depicted as a necessary partner for the successful accomplishment of a venture. According to Ps. 147.2, God is the builder of Jerusalem, and in v. 13 of the same chapter he strengthens its gates.

Divine temple and city building is a well-attested motif in Canaanite and Mesopotamian literature as well, although the ways in which it appears are even more varied than those found in the Bible.

According to the Baal epic from Ugarit, Kothar waHasis builds palaces for various gods, including Baal. The earthly counterpart of Baal's palace may be Mt Casius or some earthly temple for Baal. In this myth, the craftsgod is performing his expected function as builder and architect, and it is not the gods for whom the temples are built who are doing the construction.

Enuma Elish relates how Ea built Apsu—his own (cosmic) temple (I 71-78), how Marduk built Ešarra (IV 141-146), and how all the gods built Babylon and Esagila for Marduk (V 113–VI 75). The temples referred to in these passages are simultaneously earthly temples and cosmic regions associated with various gods. In the first case, the god builds his own temple, while in the remaining two, gods are involved in constructing temples for other gods, either as artisans or as simple laborers. The beginning of the Etana epic tells how certain gods (Sebitti, Igigi) planned, founded and built Kish (see Kinnier-Wilson 1985: 82, Late Version I 1-5). According to the Harab myth (Jacobsen 1984: 6 l. 6), the city of Dunnu was built jointly by the deities [Harab] and Sumuqan.

The large brick inscription of Yahdun-lim, king of Mari, refers to the founding of the city by 'the god' (Dossin 1955 col. I l. 34-35: *ša ištu ūma ṣât ālam Mari ilum ibnû*). S. Dalley (1979) takes this to refer to Itur-Mer, the first king of Mari, who was subsequently deified. A. Malamat (1987: 186 n. 11 and 1992: 213 n. 2) suggests, however, that the god in question is actually the West-Semitic or Canaanite deity Il.

The figure of the divine builder is especially prominent in Sumerian literature, where it takes on various guises.

Å. Sjöberg (1960: 39) lists numerous references to An, the senior god in the pantheon, as builder of cities and temples for subordinate deities including Uruk-Kulaba, Zabalam, Isin, Enamtila, Eanna, Eninnu, Etarsirsir, the temple in Tirash, and the temple of Kesh.

Several gods are said to have built their own temples. The great hymn to Enlil (S.N. Kramer, *ANET*, 574) attributes the building of Nippur to Enlil himself, although a *Hymn to Nippur* from Ur (UET V 118; see Oberhuber 1967) describes the work as being done by a band of gods, reminiscent of *Enuma Elish* and Etana. *Enki's Journey to Nippur* refers to the building of E-engurra in Eridu by Enki. The same event is described somewhat more briefly in *Enki and the World Order* (Benito 1969, ll. 94-106, 285-99; cf. Kramer 1963: 171-83 esp. 176, 180). *The Curse of Agade* tells that Inanna built Agade (Cooper 1983: 80 ll. 7-9). In the Nungal hymn (Sjöberg 1973b, ll. 68, 83, 84 and 104), the goddess boasts of having founded her own shrine.

There are also various references to the participation of certain 'crafts-gods' in building projects. In Ishbi-Erra's hymn to the scribe goddess Nisaba (Reisman 1976), who is probably the patroness of surveying as well, the goddess is said to rebuild wastelands and cities (ll. 7, 33), and without her no cities or palaces can be established (ll. 22-24). In a hymn to the beer goddess Ninkaši (Civil 1974), we read: 'Having founded your town on wax, she lavished its great walls for you, Ninkaši, having founded your town on wax, she finished its great walls for you'. This passage may refer to Ninhursag building a city for Ninkaši. A passage later on in the hymn says (ll. 64-65): 'You poured a libation over the brick of destiny, you placed the foundations in peace (and) prosperity'. These verses may be addressed to the beer goddess herself describing the role of the goddess in the foundation ceremonies. Lastly, the Gudea cylinders make numerous references to the gods as participating in various aspects of building Eninnu.

Appendix 7

THE COSMIC DIMENSIONS OF CITIES AND TEMPLES

In Ps. 78.69, we read:

> He built his Sanctuary like the heavens,
> like the earth that he established forever.

Not only does this passage reflect the traditional idea that temples are built by deities (see Appendix 6), but the language is strikingly similar to stereotypic Mesopotamian descriptions of temples or cities. (For some parallels, see Weinfeld 1972: 196 n. 1.) The epilogue to the Hammurabi law monument says that the stele was erected (CH xl 63-69):

> In Babylon
> the city which Anum and Ellil
> raised up its head,
> in Esagila
> the temple which like heaven and earth
> its foundations are firm.

In a Neo-Assyrian 'city-hymn' the city of Arba-ilu is depicted (Ebeling 1951–53):

> 1.2   Arba-ilu is the unrivaled heaven,
> 1.14   Arba-ilu lies like the heavens.
> 1.15   Its foundations are firm like those [of the earth].
> 1.16   The head of Arba-ilu is lofty
>   it rivals the heavens.

In the biblical passage, the permanence of the temple is the focus of interest, as is indicated by the word *lĕ'ôlām*, 'forever', whereas, in the Hammurabi passage and the Arba-ilu hymn, both the size of the temple and its stability are lauded. These three texts may be variations on a stereotyped description stressing only the size of the temple, as illustrated by the following texts.

In the Papulegara hymn (Pinches 1924; see W.G. Lambert 1967: 327), Kesh is described:

> The head of the temple is lofty
> Below its roots touch the netherworld
> The head of the Kesh temple is lofty

> Below its roots touch the netherworld
> Above may its. . . rival heaven
> Below its roots touch the netherworld

In a temple hymn to Ezida in Barsippa (Köcher 1959) we read:

> 1 Barsippa resembles heaven.
> 2 Rivaling Ešarra, is lofty Ezida.
> 5 Its foliage reaches the clouds,
> 6 Its roots are founded piercing the netherworld.

In an inscription of Esarhaddon discussed above, the temple of Assur is described (Borger 1956: 5 Ass. A V 27–VI 27):

> I raised the top of Esharra to heaven,
> Above, to heaven I elevated its top.
> Below in the netherworld
> I made firm its foundations.

Nabopolassar says he was commanded by Marduk to rebuild Etemenanki and (Langdon 1912: 60, *Nabopolassar* no. 1 col. I ll. 36-39):

> to found its foundations
> in the bosom of the netherworld
> and cause its head
> to rival heaven.

Nebuchadrezzar II reports how he built the walls of Babylon (Langdon 1912: 72, *Nebukadnezzar* no. 1 col. 1 ll. 31-32; Al-Rawi 1991: 3 Text 4 col. i l. 30–col. ii l. 3):

> Its foundations in the bosom of the
> netherworld I founded,
> Its head
> I made high as a mountain.

In another text he says (Langdon 1912: 180, *Nebukadnezzar* no. 20 col. I ll. 68):

> Its foundations I founded in the subterranean waters
> Its head I made lofty like a mountain range

Sumerian prototypes of these passages may be found regularly in the temple hymns, as well as in the passages from Gudea Cylinder B and other texts discussed above in the Excursus to Chapter 1 (see also Weinfeld 1972: 196 n. 1).

The possible Akkadian and Sumerian parallels may indicate a better reading for the Hebrew text of Ps. 78.69. It may cautiously be suggested that the verse be emended as follows:

wayyiben kĕmô rāmîm miqdāšô	He built his temple like the heaven
bā'āreṣ yĕsādô mē'ôlām	In the earth he established it in days of yore.

These textual cosmetics are slight and some have certain support in ancient manu-scripts and versions (see *BHK*³). The fact that the resulting verse is identical in intent to the majority of Akkadian passages cited here is admittedly not conclusive proof of the suggested reading, but it does speak in favor of at least considering it. On the other hand, the passages cited from Hammurabi and the Arba-ilu hymn are close enough to the idea expressed in MT as to justify retaining the current Hebrew text as is.

These passages present two topoi. According to one topos the temple fills the universe. According to the other the temple exists forever. In both, the temple or the city is of cosmic dimensions, only some authors choose to emphasize the spatial aspects, others the temporal aspects and yet others do service to both.

BIBLIOGRAPHY

Abou-Assaf, A., P. Bourdreuil and A.R. Millard
1982   *La Statue de Tell Fekherye et son inscription bilingue assyro-araméenne*
        (Etudes assyriologiques, 7; Paris: Editions recherche sur les civilisations).

Abramsky, S.
1982   'The Chronicler's View of King Solomon' (in Hebrew), in *H.M. Orlinsky
        Volume* (ed. B.A. Levine and A. Malamat; Eretz Israel, 16; n.p.): 3-14.

Ackroyd, P.R.
1972   'The Temple Vessels—A Continuity Theme', in *idem, Studies in the
        Religion of Ancient Israel* (VTSup, 23; Leiden: Brill): 166-81.

Adler, H.P.
1976   *Das Akkadische des Königs Tušratta von Mitanni* (AOAT, 201;
        Neukirchen–Vluyn: Neukirchener Verlag).

Aharoni, Y.
1962   '*Lĕḇānôn*' (in Hebrew), *EM*, IV, cols. 425-30.
1962b   'The Districts of Israel and Judah' (in Hebrew), in *Bimey Bayit Rishon:
        Malkhuyot Yisrael Vi-Yhudah* (ed. A. Malamat; Jerusalem: Israel
        Exploration Society): 110-31.
1973   'The Solomonic Temple, The Tabernacle and the Arad Sanctuary' (in
        Hebrew), *Beer Sheva* 1: 79-86.
1975   *Arad Inscriptions* (in Hebrew) (Judean Desert Series; Jerusalem: The Bialik
        Institute and the Israel Exploration Society).

Ahituv, S.
1970   'Aspects of Trade in Canaan in the Late Canaanite Period' (in Hebrew), in
        *Sefer Shemuel Yevin: Mehqarim be-Miqra, Arkhiologiyah, Lashon we-
        Toledot Yisra'el Muggashim Lo be-Haggi'o le-Seva* (ed. S. Abramsky
        et al.; Jerusalem: Kiryath Sefer): 318-30.
1977   'Two Ammonite Inscriptions' (in Hebrew), *Cathedra* 4: 178-89.

Ahl, S.W.
1973   *Epistolary Texts from Ugarit: Structural and Lexical Correspondence in
        Epistles in Akkadian and Ugaritic* (PhD dissertation, Brandeis University;
        Ann Arbor, MI: University Microfilms).

Ahlström, G.W.
1982   *Royal Administration and National Religion in Ancient Palestine* (ed.
        M.H.E. Weippert; Studies in the History of the Ancient Near East, 1;
        Leiden: Brill).

Albright, W.F.

1934 'The North-Canaanite Poems of Al'eyan Ba'al and the "Gracious Gods"',
   JPOS 14: 101-40.

1950 'The Psalm of Habakkuk', in *Studies in Old Testament Prophecy
   Presented to Professor Theodore H. Robinson LittD, DD, DTh by the
   Society for Old Testament Study on his Sixty-Fifth Birthday, August 9th
   1946* (ed. H.H. Rowley; Edinburgh: T. & T. Clark): 1-18.

1958 'Was the Age of Solomon without Monumental Art?', in *Eretz Israel*, V
   (dedicated to Professor Benjamin Mazar on his Fiftieth Birthday; n.p.): 1*-
   9*.

1968 *Yahweh and the Gods of Canaan: A Historical Analysis of Two
   Contrasting Faiths* (The Jordan Lectures 1965, delivered at the School of
   Oriental and African Studies, University of London; Garden City, NY:
   Doubleday).

1969 *Archaeology and the Religion of Israel* (The Ayer Lectures of the Colgate–
   Rochester Divinity School, 1941; Garden City, NY: Doubleday).

Ali, F.A.

1964 *Sumerian Letters: Two Collections from the Old Babylonian Schools* (PhD
   dissertation, University of Pennsylvania; Ann Arbor, MI: University
   Microfilms).

Alkim, U. Bahadir

1968 *Anatolia I: From the Beginnings to the End of the 2nd Millennium BC*
   (Archaeologia Mundi; Geneva: Nagel).

Alster, B.

1970 'On The Earliest Sumerian Literary Tradition', *JCS* 28: 109-26.

1976 'Early Patterns in Mesopotamian Literature', in *Kramer Anniversary
   Volume: Cuneiform Studies in Honor of Samuel Noah Kramer* (ed.
   B.L. Eichler, J.S. Heimerdinger and Å.W. Sjöberg; AOAT, 25;
   Neukirchen–Vluyn: Neukirchener Verlag).

Amadasi, M.G.G. and V. Karageorghis

1977 *Fouilles de Kition*. III. *Inscriptions phéniciennes* (Nicosia: Department of
   Antiquities).

Andersen, G.A.

1987 *Sacrifices and Offerings in Ancient Israel: Studies in their Social and
   Political Importance* (HSM, 41; Atlanta: Scholars Press).

Aptowitzer, V.

1931 'The Heavenly Temple in the Agada' (in Hebrew), *Tarbiz* 2: 137-53, 257-
   87.

Avishur, Y.

1973 'The Forms of Repetition of Numbers Indicating Wholeness (3, 7, 10)—In
   the Bible and in Ancient Semitic Literature' (in Hebrew), *Beer-Sheva* 1:
   1-55.

1979 *Phoenician Inscriptions and the Bible—Studies in Stylistic and Literary
   Devices and Selected Inscriptions* (in Hebrew) (Jerusalem: E. Rubenstein).

1981 '*RWM (RMM)-BNY* in Ugaritic and in the Bible (and *lᵉhaprîaḥ* "to build"
   in the Bible and Tosephtha' (in Hebrew), *Leš* 45: 270-79.

1988   'Treaty Terminology in the Moses–Jethro Story (Exodus 18.1-12)', *Aula Orientalis* 6: 139-47.

Ayish, A.H.
1976   'Bassetki Statue with an Old Akkadian Royal Inscription of Narām-Sin of Agade (BC 2291–2255)', *Sumer* 32: 63-75 + 2 plates.

Aynard, J.M.
1957   *Le prisme du Louvre AO 19.939* (Paris: Honoré Champion).

Baer, A.
1971   'Goudéa, cylindre B, colonnes XVIII à XXIV, essai de restauration', *RA* 65: 1-14.

Bagnani, G.
1964   'The Molten Sea of Solomon's Temple', in *The Seed of Wisdom, Essays in Honour of T.J. Meek* (ed. W.S. McCullough; Toronto: University of Toronto Press): 114-17.

Barnett, R.D.
1950   'The Excavations of the British Museum at Toprak Kale near Van', *Iraq* 12: 1-43.
1981   'Bringing the God into the Temple', in *Temples and High Places in Biblical Times: Proceedings of the Colloquium in Honor of the Centennial of Hebrew Union College–Jewish Institute of Religion, Jerusalem 14–16 March, 1977* (Jerusalem: The Nelson Glueck School of Biblical Archaeology of Hebrew Union College–Jewish Institute of Religion): 10-20.

Barrelet, M.T.
1977   'Un inventaire de Kar-Tukulti-Ninurta: textiles décorés assyriens et autres', *RA* 71: 51-72.

Batto, B.F.
1987   'The Sleeping God: An Ancient Near Eastern Motif of Divine Sovereignty', *Bib* 68: 153-77.

Bauer, T.
1933   *Die Inschriftenwerk Assurbanipals, vervollständigt und neu bearbeitet*, I, II (Assyriologische Bibliothek, ns 1, 2; ed. B. Landsberger; Leipzig: Hinrichs).

Baumgartner, W.
1925   'Untersuchungen zu den akkadischen Bauausdrücken', *ZA* 36: 29-40, 123-38, 219-53.

Beaulieu, P.-A.
1985   *The Reign of Nabonidus, King of Babylon (556–539 B.C.)* (PhD dissertation, Yale University; Ann Arbor, MI: University Microfilms International).

Beit-Arieh, I., and B. Cresson
1985   'An Edomite Ostracon from Horvat 'Uza', *Tel Aviv* 12: 96-101.

Behrens, H.
1978   *Enlil und Ninlil, ein sumerischer Mythos aus Nippur* (Studia Pohl, Series Maior, 8; Rome: Biblical Institute Press).

Benito, C.A.
1969   *'Enki and Ninmaḫ' and 'Enki and the World Order'* (PhD dissertation, University of Pennsylvania; Ann Arbor, MI: University Microfilms).
Bentzen, A.
1948   *Introduction to the Old Testament,* I, II (Copenhagen: Gad, 6th edn).
Berger, P.R.
1970   'Zur Nabonid-Inschrift Nr. 3 und ihren Duplikaten', *ZA* 60: 128-33.
1973   *Die neubabylonischen Königsinschriften, Königsinschriften des ausgehenden babylonischen Reiches (626–539 a. Chr.)* (AOAT, 4.1; Neukirchen–Vluyn: Neukirchener Verlag).
Berlin, A.
1979   *Enmerkar and Ensuḫkešdanna, A Sumerian Narrative Poem* (Occasional Publications of the Babylonian Fund, 2; Philadelphia, PA: University Museum).
Bernhardt, I., and S.N. Kramer
1975   'Die Tempel und Götterschreine von Nippur (Tab. VII–VIII)', *Or* 44: 96-102.
Bewer, J.A.
1919   'Ancient Babylonian Parallels to the Prophecies of Haggai', *AJSL* 35: 126-33.
Beyerlin, W.
1978   *Near Eastern Religious Texts Relating to the Old Testament* (trans. J. Bowden; Philadelphia: Westminster Press).
Bickerman, E.
1946   'The Edict of Cyrus in Ezra 1', *JBL* 65: 247-75.
Biggs, R.D.
1971   'An Archaic Sumerian Version of the Kesh Temple Hymn from Tell Abu Salabikh', *ZA* 61: 193-207.
1974   *Inscriptions from Abu Salabikh* (Oriental Institute Press, 99; Chicago: University of Chicago Press).
Bimson, J.J., and D. Livingston
1987   'Redating the Exodus', *BARev* 13: 40-53, 66-68.
Birm, A.
1952   ' "*Mas 'ôbed*" ' (in Hebrew), *Tarbiz* 23: 137-42.
Blenkinsopp, J.
1987   'The Mission of Udjahorresnet and those of Ezra and Nehemiah', *JBL* 106: 409-21.
Boese, J.
1971   *Altmesopotamische Weihplatten, eine sumerische Denkmalsgattung des 3. Jahrtausends v. Chr.* (Untersuchungen zur Assyriologie und vorderasiatischen Archäologie, Ergänzungsband zur Zeitschrift für Assyriologie und Vorderasiatische Archäologie, ns 6; Berlin: de Gruyter).
Böhl, F.M.T. Liagre
1936   *Mededeelingen uit de Leidsche Verzameling van Spijkerschrift—Inscripties. III. Assyrische en Nieuw-Babylonische Oorkonden (1100–91 v. Chr.)* (Mededeelingen der Koninklijke Akademie van Wetenschappen,

Afdeeling Letterkunde, Deel 82, Serie B, 2; Amsterdam: N.V. Noord-hollandsche Uitgevers-Maatschappij).

1939   'Die Tochter des Königs Nabonid', in *Symbolae ad iura orientis antiqui pertinentes Paulo Koschaker dedicatae* (ed. J. Friedrich, J.G. Lautner and J. Miles; Studia et documenta ad iura orientis antiqui pertinentia, 2; Leiden: Brill): 151-78.

1947   *Akkadian Chrestomathy*. I. *Selected Cuneiform Texts* (Leiden: Nederlandisch Archaeologisch-Philologisch Instituut voor het Nabije Oosten).

Borger, R.

1956   *Die Inschriften Asarhaddons, Königs von Assyrien* (AfOB, 9; Graz: E. Weidner).

1957-58   'Die Inschriften Asarhaddons (AfOB, 9); Nachträge und Verbesserungen', *AfO* 18: 113-18.

1961   *Einleitung in die assyrischen Königsinschriften, Erster Teil: Das zweite Jahrtausend v. Chr.* (Handbuch der Orientalistik; ed. B. Spuler; Leiden: Brill).

1965-75   *Handbuch der Keilschriftliteratur*, I, II, III (Berlin: de Gruyter).

1971a   'Das Tempelbau-Ritual K 48+', *ZA* 61: 72-80.

1971b   'Gott Marduk und Gott-König Šulgi als Propheten—Zwei prophetische Texte', *BO* 28: 3-24.

1973a   'Keilschriftentexte verschiedenen Inhalts', in *Symbolae Biblicae et Mesopotamicae Francisco Mario Theodoro de Liagre Böhl Dedicatae* (ed. M.A. Beek *et al.*; Nederlands Instituut voor het Nabije Oosten, Studia Francisci Scolten Memoriae Dicata, 4; Leiden: Brill): 38-53.

1973b   'Tonmännchen und Puppen', *BO* 30: 176-83.

1973c   *Babylonische-assyrische Lesestücke*, II (Rome: Pontifical Biblical Institute).

1978   *Assyrisch-babylonische Zeichenliste* (AOAT, 33; Neukirchen–Vluyn: Neukirchener Verlag).

Born, A. van den

1965   'Zum Tempelweihspruch (I Kg VIII, 12f)', *OTS*: 4: 235-44.

Bottéro, J.

1965   'The First Semitic Empire', in *The Near East: The Early Civilizations* (ed. J. Bottéro, E. Cassin, J. Vercoutter; trans. R.F. Tennenbaum; London: Weidenfeld & Nicolson): 91-132.

Braun, R.L.

1973   'Solomonic Apologetic in Chronicles', *JBL* 92: 503-11.

1976   'Solomon the Chosen Temple Builder: The Significance of I Chron 22, 28, 29 for the Theology of Chronicles', *JBL*: 95: 581-90.

Breasted, J.H.

1906   *Ancient Records of Egypt: Historical Documents from the Earliest Times to the Persian Conquest, Collected, Edited and Translated with Commentary*, I–V (Chicago: University of Chicago Press).

Brekelmans, C.H.W.

1982   'Solomon at Gibeon', in *Von Kanaan bis Kerala: Festschrift für Prof. Mag. Dr. Dr. J.P.M. van der Ploeg O.P. zur Vollendung des siebzigsten*

Lebensjahres am 4. Juli 1979. Überreicht von Kollegen, Freunden und Schülern (ed. W.C. Delsman *et al.*; AOAT, 211; Neukirchen–Vluyn: Neukirchener Verlag): 53-59.

Brinkman, J.A.
1968   *A Political History of Post-Kassite Babylonia: 1158–722 BC* (AnOr, 43; Rome: Pontifical Biblical Institute).

Brongers, H.A.
1965   'Bemerkungen zum Gebrauch des adverbialen We'ATT ĀH im alten Testament; ein lexicologischer Beitrag', *VT* 15: 289-99.

Brown, J.P.
1969   *The Lebanon and Phoenicia, Ancient Texts Illustrating their Physical Geography and Native Industries. I. The Physical Setting and the Forest* (Beirut: American University of Beirut, Centennial Publications).

Buren, E.D. van
1944   'The Sacred Marriage in Early Times in Mesopotamia', *Or* ns 13: 1-72.
1952a   'Foundation Rites for a New Temple', *Or* ns 21: 293-306.
1952b   'The Building of a Temple Tower', *RA* 46: 65-74.

Burkitt, F.C.
1909   'The Lucianic Text of 1 Kings viii 53b', *JTS* 10: 439-46.

Burney, C.F.
1903   *Notes on the Hebrew Text of the Book of Kings, with an Introduction and Appendix* (Oxford: Clarendon Press).

Busink, T.A.
1970   *Der Tempel von Jerusalem von Salomo bis Herodes; eine archäologisch-historische Studie unter Berücksichtigung des westsemitischen Tempelbaus. I. Der Tempel Salomos* (Nederlands Instituut voor het Nabije Oosten, Studia Francisci Scholten Memoriae Dicata, 3; ed. A.A. Kampen; Leiden: Brill).

Cassuto, U.
1975a   'The Israelite Epic', in *Biblical and Oriental Studies. II. Bible and Ancient Oriental Texts* (trans. I. Abrahams; Jerusalem: Magnes Press): 69-109.
1975b   'The Palace of Baal in Tablet II AB of Ras Shamra', in *Biblical and Oriental Studies. II. Bible and Ancient Oriental Texts* (trans. I. Abrahams; Jerusalem: Magnes Press): 113-39.

Castellino, G.R.
1959   'Urnammu, Three Religious Texts (continued)', *ZA* 53: 106-32.
1977   *Testi Sumerici e Accadici* (Classici delle Religioni, 1; ed. O. Botto; Torino: Unione Tipografico–Editrice Torinese).

Charpin, D.
1982   'Le temple de Kahat d'après un document inédit de Mari', *MARI* 1: 137-47.
1983   'Temples à découvrir en Syrie du nord d'après des documents inédits de Mari', *Iraq* 45: 56-63.

Civil, M.
1968   'Išme-Dagan and Enlil's Chariot', *JAOS* 8: 3-14.

Clements, R.E.
1965   *God and Temple: The Idea of the Divine Presence in Ancient Israel* (Oxford: Basil Blackwell).

Clifford, R.
1979   'The Temple in the Ugaritic Myth of Baal', in *Symposia Celebrating the Seventy-fifth Anniversary of the Founding of the American Schools of Oriental Research [1900–1975]* (ed. F.M. Cross; Zion Research Foundation Occasional Publications; Cambridge, MA: American Schools of Oriental Research): 137-45.

Cogan, M.
1978   'A New Join to Ashurbanipal Prism T(hompson)', *JCS* 30: 176.
1980   'Tendentious Chronological Data in the Book of Chronicles' (in Hebrew), *Zion* 45: 165-72.
1983   'Omens and Ideology in the Babylonian Inscriptions of Esarhaddon', in *History, Historiography and Interpretation—Studies in Biblical and Cuneiform Literatures* (ed. H. Tadmor and M. Weinfeld; Jerusalem: Magnes Press): 76-87.
1984   'New Additions to the Corpus of Esarhaddon's Historical Inscriptions', *AfO* 31: 72-75.
1985   'The Chronicler's Use of Chronology as Illuminated by Neo-Assyrian Royal Inscriptions', in *Empirical Models for Biblical Criticism* (ed. J. Tigay; Philadelphia, PA: University of Pennsylvania): 197-209.

Cogan, M., and H. Tadmor
1981   'Ashurbanipal's Conquest of Babylon: The First Official Report—Prism K', *Or* ns 50: 229-40.

Cohen, H.R.
1978   *Biblical Hapax Legomena in the Light of Akkadian and Ugaritic* (SBLDS, 37; Missoula, MT: Scholars Press).

Cohen, M.E.
1981   *Sumerian Hymnology: The Eršemma* (*HUCA* Supplements, 2; Cincinnati, OH: Hebrew Union College).

Cohen, S.
1973   *Enmerkar and the Lord of Aratta* (PhD dissertation, University of Pennsylvania; Ann Arbor, MI: University Microfilms).

Cooper, J.S.
1978   *The Return of Ninurta to Nippur, an-gim-dim-ma* (AnOr, 5; Rome: Pontifical Biblical Institute).
1983   *The Curse of Agade* (The Johns Hopkins Near Eastern Studies; Baltimore: Johns Hopkins University Press).
1986   *Sumerian and Akkadian Royal Inscriptions*. I. *Pre-Sargonic Inscriptions* (AOS Translation Series; New Haven: American Oriental Society).

Corvin, J.W.
1972   *A Stylistic and Functional Study of the Prose Prayers in the Historical Narratives of the Old Testament* (PhD dissertation, Emory University; Ann Arbor, MI: University Microfilms).

Cross, F.M.
1947   'The Priestly Tabernacle', *BA* 10: 45-68.

1973   *Canaanite Myth and Hebrew Epic, Essays in the History of the Religion of Israel* (Cambridge, MA: Harvard University Press).

Dalley, S.

1979   'ARMT X reviewed, with a discussion of ^{d}Šar Mātim and ŠiTrum', *BO* 36: 289-92.

1984   *Mari and Karana, Two Old Babylonian Cities* (London: Longman).

Deller, K.

1987   'Sanheribs Zababa-Tempel in Aššur', *Baghdader Mitteilungen* 18: 21-28.

Demsky, A.

1976   *Literacy in Ancient Israel and her Neighbors during the Biblical Period* (unpublished PhD dissertation; Jerusalem: The Hebrew University Press).

Dever, W.G.

1990   'Of Myths and Methods', *BASOR* 277/278: 5-22.

Dhorme, P.

1914   'La fille de Nabonide', *RA* 11: 105-17.

Dietrich, M., and O. Loretz

1978   'Die sieben Kuntswerke des Schmiedegottes in KTU 1, 4I 23-43', *UF* 10: 57-63.

Dijk, J. van

1962   'Die Inschriftenfunde', in *Vorläufiger Bericht über die von dem deutschen archäologischen Institut und der deutschen Orient-Gesellschaft aus Mitteln der deutschen Forschungsgemeinschaft unternommenen Ausgrabung in Uruk-Warka*, XVIII (ed. H.J. Lenzen *et al.*; Berlin: Gebr. Mann): 39-62.

1983   *LUGAL UD ME-LÁM-BI NIR-ĜÁL- Le récit épique et didactique des travaux de Ninurta, du déluge et de la nouvelle création, texte, traduction et introduction*, I, II (Leiden: Brill).

Dommershausen, W.

1982   '*ḥānak*',*ThWAT*, III, cols. 20-22.

Donald, T.

1962   'A Sumerian Plan in the John Ryland Library', *JSS* 7: 184-90.

Dossin, G.

1955   'L'inscription de fondation de Iaḫdun-Lim, roi de Mari', *Syria* 3: 1-28.

Driel, G. van

1969   *The Cult of Aššur* (Studia Semitica Neerlandica, 13; Assen: van Gorcum).

Driver, G.R.

1956   *Canaanite Myths and Legends* (Old Testament Studies, 3; Edinburgh: T. & T. Clark).

Driver, S.R.

1965   *A Critical and Exegetical Commentary on Deuteronomy* (ICC; Edinburgh: T. & T. Clark).

Dunham, S.

1982   'Bricks for the Temples of Šara and Ninurra', *RA* 76, pp. 27-41.

1986   'Sumerian Words for Foundation', *RA* 80, pp. 31-64.

Dupret, M.-A.

1974   'Hymne au dieu Numušda avec prière en faveur de Sîniqīšam de Larsa', *Or* ns 43: 327-43.

Ebeling, E.

1930–34   *Neubabylonische Briefe aus Uruk* (Beiträge zur Keilschriftforschung und Religionsgeschichte des Vorderen Orients, 1-4; Berlin: E. Ebeling).

1935   'Eine Weihinschrift Aššuretililânis für Marduk', in *Miscellanea Orientalia dedicata Antonio Deimel Annos LXX Complenti* (AnOr, 12; Rome: Pontifical Biblical Institute): 71-73.

1942   *Altbabylonische Briefe der Louvre-Sammlung aus Larsa*, (MAOG, 15.1–2; Leipzig: Otto Harrassowitz).

1951–53   'Ein Preislied auf die Kultstadt Arba-ilu aus neuassyrischer Zeit', *Jahrbuch für Kleinasiatische Forschung*, 2: 274-82.

1954   *Stiftungen und Vorschriften für assyrische Tempel* (Deutsche Akademie der Wissenschaften zu Berlin, Institut für Orientforschung Veröfentlichung, 23; Berlin: Akademie Verlag)

Ebeling, E., B. Meissner, and E.F. Weidner,

1926   *Die Inschriften der altassyrischen Könige* (Altorientalische Bibliothek, 1; Leipzig: Quelle & Meyer).

Edzard, D.O.

1960   'Die Beziehungen Babyloniens und Ägyptens in den mittelbabylonischen Zeit und das Gold', *JESHO* 3: 47-55.

Edzard, D.O., W. Farber, and W.R. Mayer

1978   *Ergänzungsheft zu A. Falkenstein, Grammatik der Sprache Gudeas von Lagaš (AnOr, 28 und 29)* (AnOr, 29a; Rome: Pontifical Biblical Institute).

Eissfeldt, O.

1966   *The Old Testament, an Introduction including the Apocrypha and Pseudepigrapha, and also the Works of Similar Type from Qumran: The History of the Formations of the Old Testament* (trans. P.R. Ackroyd from 3rd German edn; Oxford: Basil Blackwell).

Elat, M.

1977   *Economic Relations in the Lands of the Bible, c. 1000–539 BC* (in Hebrew) (Jerusalem: Mosad Bialik).

Ellis, R.S.

1968   *Foundation Deposits in Ancient Mesopotamia* (YNER, 2; New Haven, CT: Yale University Press).

Erman, A.

1966   *The Ancient Egyptians: A Sourcebook of their Writings* (trans. A.M. Blackman; New York: Harper Torchbooks).

Eskenazi, T.C.

1988   'The Structure of Ezra–Nehemiah and the Integrity of the Book', *JBL* 107: 641-56.

Fales, F.M.

1984   'Assyro-Aramaica: Three Notes', *Or* ns 53: 66-71.

1987   'Aramaic Letters and Neo-Assyrian Letters', *JAOS* 107: 451-69.

Falkenstein, A.

           'Gudea', in *RLA*, III, 676-79.

1941   'Untersuchungen zur sumerischen Grammatik (Fortsetzung)', *ZA* 47: 191-223.

| 1949–50 | *Grammatik der Sprache Gudeas von Lagaš*, I, II (AnOr, 28, 29; Rome: Pontifical Biblical Institute). |

1949–50   *Grammatik der Sprache Gudeas von Lagaš*, I, II (AnOr, 28, 29; Rome: Pontifical Biblical Institute).

1951   'Die Eridu-Hymne', *Sumer* 7: 119-25.

1964   'Eine Inschrift Waradsîns aus Babylon', *Baghdader Mitteilungen* 3: 25-40.

1965a   ' "Wahrsagung" in der sumerischen Überlieferung', in *La divination en mésopotamie ancienne et dans les régions voisines* (XIVe Rencontre Assyriologique Internationale, Strasbourg, 2–6 juillet 1965; Paris: Presses Universitaires de France): 45-68.

1965b   'Fluch über Akkade', *ZA* 57: 43-124.

1966a   'Sumerische Bauausdrücke', *Or* ns 35: 229-46.

1966b   *Die Inschriften Gudeas von Lagaš*. I. *Einleitung* (AnOr, 30; Rome: Pontifical Biblical Institute).

Falkenstein, A., and W. von Soden

1953   *Sumerische und akkadische Hymnen und Gebete* (Zürich: Artemis).

Farber, A.

1986   'On the Structural Unity of the Eshmunazar Inscription', *JAOS* 106: 425-32.

Fensham, F.C.

1969   'The Treaty between the Israelites and Tyrians', in *Congress Volume, Rome, 1968* (VTsup, 17; Leiden: Brill): 71-87.

Ferrara, A.J.

1973   *Nanna-Suen's Journey to Nippur* (Studia Pohl, Series Maior, 2; Rome: Biblical Institute Press).

Ferrara, A.J., and S.B. Parker

1972   'Seating Arrangements at Divine Banquets', *UF* 4: 37-39.

Finkelstein, J.J.

1979   'Early Mesopotamia, 2500–1000 BC', in *Propaganda and Communication in World History*. I. *The Symbolic Instrument in Early Times* (ed. H.D. Lasswell *et al.*; Honolulu, HA: University Press of Hawaii): 50-110.

Fishbane, M.

1979   *Text and Texture: Close Readings of Selected Biblical Texts* (New York: Schocken Books).

Fisher, L.R.

1963   'The Temple Quarter', *JSS* 8: 34-41.

1965   'Creation at Ugarit and in the Old Testament', *VT* 15: 313-24.

Fitzmeyer, J.A.

1974   'Some Notes on Aramaic Epistolography', *JBL* 93: 201-45.

Fohrer, G.

1970   *Introduction to the Old Testament* (trans. D. Green; London: SPCK, 10th edn).

Al-Fouadi, A.A.

1969   *Enki's Journey to Nippur: The Journeys of the Gods* (PhD dissertation, University of Pennsylvania; Ann Arbor, MI: University Microfilms).

Frankfort, H.

1948   *Kingship and the Gods: A Study of Ancient Near Eastern Religion as the Integration of Society and Nature* (Chicago: University of Chicago Press).

1954   *Art and Architecture of the Ancient Orient* (London: Penguin Books).

Frayne, D.R.

1982   'New Light on the Reign of Išbi-Erra', in *Vorträge gehalten auf der 28. Rencontre Assyriologique Internationale in Wien 6–10 Juli 1981* (AfOB, 19: Horn: Ferdinand Berger & Söhne): 25-32.

1984   'Notes on a New Inscription of Šar-kali-šarrī', *ARRIM* 2: 23-27.

1990   *Old Babylonian Period (2003–1595 BC)* (The Royal Inscriptions of Mesopotamia, Early Periods, 4; Toronto: University of Toronto).

Frayne, D.R., and V. Donbaz

1984   'Hammurapi and the Wall of the Cloister', *ARRIM* 2: 28-30.

Freedman, D.N.

1981   'Temple without Hands', in *Temples and High Places in Biblical Times: Proceedings of the Colloquium in Honor of the Centennial of Hebrew Union College–Jewish Institute of Religion, Jerusalem, 14–16 March, 1977* (Jerusalem: The Nelson Glueck School of Biblical Archaeology of Hebrew Union College–Jewish Institute of Religion): 21-30.

Freydank, H.

1971   'Anmerkungen zu mittelassyrischen Texten', *OLZ* 66: 533-35.

Friedman, R.E.

1980   'The Tabernacle in the Temple', *BA* 43: 241-48.

1981   *The Exile and Biblical Narrative: The Formation of the Deuteronomistic and Priestly Works* (HSM, 22; Chico, CA: Scholars Press).

1987   *Who Wrote the Bible?* (New York: Summit).

Fritz, V.

1987   'Temple Architecture—What Can Archaeology Tell us about Solomon's Temple?', *BARev* 13: 38-49.

Frymer-Kensky, T.

1967   'The Nungal Hymn and the Ekur Prison', *JESHO* 20: 78-81.

1985   'Inclusio in Sumerian', *RA* 79: 93-94.

Gadd, C.J.

1948   *Ideas of Divine Rule in the Ancient Near East* (Schweich Lectures 1945; London: The British Academy).

1951   'En-an-e-du', *Iraq* 13: 27-39.

1953   'Inscribed Barrel Cylinder of Marduk-apla-iddina II', *Iraq* 15: 123-34.

1954   'Inscribed prisms of Sargon II from Nimrud', *Iraq* 16: 173-201.

1958   'The Harran Inscriptions of Nabonidus', *AnSt* 8: 35-92.

Galling, K.

1961   'Serubbabel und der Hohepriester beim Wiederaufbau des Tempels in Jerusalem', in *Verbannung und Heimkehr: Beiträge zur Geschichte und Theologie Israels im 6. und 5. Jahrhundert v. Chr. Wilhelm Rudolph zum 70. Geburtstage dargebracht von Kollegen, Freunden und Schülern* (ed. A. Kuschke; Tübingen: Mohr): 67-96.

Galter, H.D.

1984   'Der Tempel des Gottes Zababa in Assur', *ARRIM* 2: 1-2.

Gardiner, A.

1961   *Egypt of the Pharaohs: An Introduction* (Oxford: Oxford University Press).

Gaster, T.H.
1946a   'Psalm 29', *JQR* 37: 55-65.
1946b   'A King without a Castle—Baal's Appeal to Asherat', *BASOR* 10: 21-30.
1966   *Thespis: Ritual, Myth and Drama in the Ancient Near East* (New York: Harper Torchbook).

Gelb, I.J.
1948   'A New Clay-Nail of Ḫammurabi', *JNES*: 267-71.
1949   'The Date of the Cruciform Monument of Maništušu', *JNES* 8: 346-48.
1956   'The Names of Ex-voto Objects in Ancient Mesopotamia', *NAMES* 4: 65-69.

Gelb, I.J., and B. Kienast
1990   *Die Altakkadischen Königsinschriften des Dritten Jahrtausend v. Chr.* (Freiburger Altorientalische Studien, 7; Stuttgart: Franz Steiner).

George, L.C., and W. de Filippi
1985   'The Inscription on the Reverse of the Šarrat-nipḫi Lion: An Ashurnasirpal Text from Calaḫ', *ARRIM* 3: 18-20.

Gevaryahu, H.M.
1985   'A Temple in Jerusalem for a God without Form or Image, "The Lord Hath Said He Will Dwell in Thick Darkness" (I Kings 8.12-13)' (in Hebrew), *Beth Mikra* 30: 142-55.

Ghirshman, R.
1961   *Iran from the Earliest Times to the Islamic Conquest* (London: Penguin Books).

Gibson, J.C.L.
1978   *Canaanite Myths and Legends* (Edinburgh: T. & T. Clark).

Ginsberg, H.L.
1936   *Kitbey Ugarit* (in Hebrew) (Linguistic Studies; ed. N.H. Torczyner; Jerusalem: Mosad Bialik).

Goedicke, H.
1975   *The Report of Wenamun* (The Johns Hopkins Near Eastern Studies; Baltimore: Johns Hopkins University Press).

Goetze, A.
1952   'The Texts Ni 615 and Ni 641 of the Istanbul Museum', *JCS* 6: 142-45.
1963   'Esarhaddon's Inscription from the Inanna Temple in Nippur', *JCS* 17: 119-131.
1965   'An Inscription of Simbar-Šīḫu', *JCS* 19: 171-35.
1968   'An Old Babylonian Prayer of the Divination Priest', *JCS* 22: 25-29.

Gooding, D.W.
1965   'An Impossible Shrine', *VT* 15: 405-20.
1967   'Temple Specifications: A Dispute in Logical Arrangement between the MT and LXX', *VT* 17: 143-72.
1969   'Problems of Text and Midrash in the Third Book of Reigns', *Textus, Annual of the Hebrew University Bible Project* 7: 1-29.

Goosens, G.
1948   'Les recherches historiques à l'époque néo-babylonienne', *RA* 42: 149-59.

Goppelt, L.
1969   'τύπος', *TDNT*, VIII, 246-59.

Gordis, R.
 1978   *The Book of Job: Commentary, New Translation and Special Studies* (Moreshet, 2; New York: Jewish Theological Seminary of America).

Gordon, C.H.
 1965   *The Common Background of Greek and Hebrew Civilizations* (New York: Norton).
 1977   'Poetic Legends and Myths from Ugarit', *Berytus* 25: 5-133.

Görg, M.
 1974   'Die Gattung der sogenannten Tempelweihsprüche (I Kg 8.12)', *UF* 6: 55-63.

Gragg, G.B.
 1969   'The Keš Temple Hymn', in Å.W. Sjöberg and E. Bergmann, *The Collection of the Sumerian Temple Hymns* (TCS, 3; Locust Valley, NY: J.J. Augustin): 155-88.

Gray, J.
 1970   *I & II Kings: A Commentary* (OTL; London: SCM Press, 2nd edn).

Grayson, A.K.
 1972–1976   *Assyrian Royal Inscriptions. I. From the Beginning to Ashur-resha-ishi I. II. From Tiglath-pileser I to Ashur-nasir-apli II* (Wiesbaden: Otto Harrassowitz).
 1975a   *Babylonian Historical Texts* (Toronto Semitic Texts and Studies) 3; Toronto: University of Toronto Press).
 1975b   *Assyrian and Babylonian Chronicles* (TCS, 5; Locust Valley, NY: J.J. Augustin).
 1980   'Assyria and Babylonia', *Or* ns 49: 140-94.
 1985   'Rivalry over Rulership at Aššur: The Puzur-Sîn Inscription', *ARRIM* 3: 9-14.
 1987   *Assyrian Rulers of the Third and Second Millennia BC (To 1115 BC)* (The Royal Inscriptions of Mesopotamia. Assyrian Period, 1; Toronto: University of Toronto Press).
 1991a   *Assyrian Rulers of the Early first Millennium BC I (1114–859 BC)*. (The Royal Inscriptions of Mesopotamia, Assyrian Periods, 2; Toronto: University of Toronto Press).
 1991b   'A Text of Shalmaneser III on an Amulet Stone', *ARRIM* 9: 19-25.

Green, A.R.
 1983   'David's Relations with Hiram: Biblical and Josephan Evidence for Tyrian Chronology', in *The Word of the Lord Shall Go Forth: Essays in Honor of David Noel Freedman in Celebration of his Sixtieth Birthday* (ed. C.L. Meyers and M. O'Connor; Winona Lake, IN: Eisenbrauns): 373-97.

Green, M.W.
 1975   'Eridu in Sumerian Literature' (Unpublished PhD dissertation, University of Chicago).

Greenberg, M.
 1983   *Ezekiel 1–20: A New Translation with Introduction and Commentary* (AB, 22; Garden City, NY: Doubleday).

Greenfield, J.
 1978   'Notes on the Asitawada (Karatepe) Inscription' (in Hebrew), in

H.L. Ginsberg Volume (ed. Menahem Haran; Eretz Israel, 14; n.p.): 74-
77.

Greenstein, E.L., and D. Marcus
1976   'The Akkadian Inscription of Idrimi', *JANESCU* 8: 59-96.

Grintz, Y.M.
1975   *From the Ancient Egyptian Literature* (in Hebrew) (Jerusalem: Bialik
        Institute).

Gruber, M.I.
1980   *Aspects of Nonverbal Comunication in the Ancient Near East* (Studia Pohl,
        Dissertations Scientificae de Rebus Orientis Antiqui, 12.1, 12.2; Rome:
        Biblical Institute Press).

Gurney, O.R.
1957   'The Sultantepe Tablets (continued), VI. A Letter of Gilgamesh', *AnSt* 7:
        127-36.
1974   'The Fifth Tablet of "The Topography of Babylon"', *Iraq* 36: 39-52.

Güterbock, H. G.
1934, 1938   'Die historische Tradition und ihre literarische Gestaltung bei Babyloniern
            und Hethitern bis 1200', *ZA* 42: 1-91; *ZA* 4: 45-149.

Hallo, W.W.
1955   'Oriental Institute Museum Notes, No. 10: The Last Years of the Kings of
        Isin', *JNES* 18: 54-72.
1961   'Royal Inscriptions of the Early Old Babylonian Period: A Bibliography',
        BO 18: 4-14.
1962   'The Royal Inscriptions of Ur: A Typology', *HUCA* 33: 1-43.
1966   'The Coronation of Ur-Nammu', *JCS* 20: 133-41.
1970   'The Cultic Setting of Sumerian Poetry', in *Actes de la XVIIe Rencontre
        Assyriologique Internationale, Bruxelles, Université Libre de Bruxelles 30
        juin–4 juillet 1969* (ed. A. Finet; Ham-sur-Heure: Comité belge de
        recherches en Mésopotamie): 116-34.
1977   'New Moons and Sabbaths: A Case Study in the Contrastive Approach',
        HUCA 48: 1-18.
1980   Biblical History in its Near Eastern Setting: The Contextual Approach', in
        Scripture in Context: Essays on the Comparative Method (ed. C. D. Evans,
        W.W. Hallo and J.P. White; PTMS, 34; Pittsburgh: Pickwick Press):
        1-26.
1981   Review of J.S. Cooper, *The Return of Ninurta to Nippur, JAOS* 101: 253-
        57.
1984-85 'The Concept of Eras from Nabonassar to Seleucus' *JANESCU* 16–17:
        143-51.

Hallo, W.W., and W.L. Moran
1979   'The First Tablet of the SB Recension of the Anzu-Myth', *JCS* 31: 65-115.

Halpern, B.
1978   'The Ritual Background of Zechariah's Temple Song', *CBQ* 40: 167-90.
1990   'A Historiographic Comentary on Ezra 1–6: Achronological Narrative and
        Dual Chronology in Israelite Historiography', in *The Hebrew Bible and Its
        Interpreters* (ed. W.H. Propp *et al.*, Winona Lake: Eisenbrauns): 81-142.

Hansman, J.
 1976   'Gilgamesh, Humbaba and the Land of the *Erin*-Trees', *Iraq* 3: 23-35.
Haran, M.
 1978   *Temples and Temple-Service in Ancient Israel: An Inquiry into the Character of Cult Phenomena and the Historical Setting of the Priestly School* (Oxford: Clarendon Press).
 1985   'Catch Lines in Ancient Paleography and in the Biblical Canon' (in Hebrew), in *Nahman Avigad Volume* (ed. B. Mazar and Y. Yadin; Eretz Israel, 18; n.p.): 124-29.
Hawkins, D., and A. M. Davies
 1978   'On the Problems of Karatepe: The Hieroglyphic Text', *AnSt* 28: 103–14.
Hecker, K.
 1974   *Untersuchungen zur akkadischen Epik* (AOAT, 8; Neukirchen–Vluyn: Neukirchener Verlag).
Heidel, A.
 1951   *The Babylonian Genesis: The Story of the Creation* (Chicago: University of Chicago Press, 2nd edn).
 1953   'The Octagonal Sennacherib Prism in the Iraq Museum', *Sumer* 9: 117-88.
 1956   'A New Hexagonal Prism of Esarhaddon (676 BC)', *Sumer* 12: 9-37.
Heimpel, W.
 1968   *Tierbilder in der sumerischen Literatur* (Studia Pohl, 2; Rome: Päpstliches Bibelinstitut).
 1987   'Gudea's Fated Brick', *JNES* 46: 205.
Heinrich, E.
 1982   *Die Tempel und Heiligtümer im alten Mesopotamien: Typologie, Morphologie und Geschichte* (2 vols.; Deutsches archäologisches Institut, Denkmäler antiker Architektur, 14; Berlin: de Gruyter).
Held, M.
 1965   'The Action Result (Factitive–Passive) Sequence of Identical Verbs in Biblical Hebrew and Ugaritic', *JBL* 84: 272-82.
 1968   'The Root *ZBL/SBL* in Akkadian, Ugaritic and Biblical Hebrew', *JAOS* 88: 90-96.
 1969   'Rhetorical Questions in Ugaritic and Biblical Hebrew', in *W.F. Albright Volume* (ed. A. Malamat; Eretz Israel, 9; n.p.): 71-79.
Hermann, A.
 1938   *Die ägyptische Königsnovelle* (Leipziger ägyptologische Studien, 10; ed. W. Wolf; Glückstadt: J.J. Augustin).
Hermann, G.
 1968   'Lapis Lazuli: The Early Phases of its Trade', *Iraq* 30: 12-57.
Herrmann, S.
 1953–54 'Die Königsnovelle in Ägypten und in Israel: Ein Beitrag zur Gattungsgeschichte des Alten Testaments', *Wissenschaftliche Zeitschrift der Karl Marx Universität Leipzig* 3: 33-44.
 1985   '2 Samuel VII in the Light of the Egyptian Königsnovelle—Reconsidered', in *Pharaonic Egypt, The Bible and Christianity* (ed. S. Israelit-Groll; Jerusalem: Magnes Press): 119-28.

Hillers, D.
1968   'Ritual Procession of the Ark and Ps 132', *CBQ* 30: 48-55.
Hirsch, H.
1963   'Die Inschriften der Könige von Agade', *AfO* 20: 1-82.
Hölscher, G.
1923   'Das Buch der Könige, seine Quellen und seine Redaktion', in
        *Eucharistērion: Studien zur Religion und Literatur des alten und neuen
        Testaments Hermann Gunkel zum 60. Geburtstage dem 23. Mai 1922
        dargebracht von seinen Schülern und Freunden. I. Zur Religion und
        Literatur des Alten Testaments* (FRLANT, 36; Göttingen: Vandenhoeck &
        Ruprecht): 158-213.
Horowitz, W.
1991   'Antiochus I, Esagil and a Celebration of the Ritual for Renovations of
        Temples', *RA* 85: 75-77.
Horn, S.H.
1969   'The Amman Citadel Inscription', *BASOR* 193: 2-19.
Huffman, H.B.
1966   'The Treaty Background of Hebrew *yāda"* *BASOR* 181: 31-37.
Hunger, H. and S.A. Kaufman
1975   'A New Akkadian Prophecy Text', *JAOS* 95: 371-75.
Hurowitz, V. (A.)
1983–1984 'The Golden Calf and the Tabernacle' (in Hebrew), *Shnaton* 7: 51-59
        (English Abstract: 9-10).
1984a   'Literary Structures in Samsuiluna A', *JCS* 36: 191-205.
1984b   Review of *The Exile and Biblical Narrative*, by R.E. Friedman, *IEJ* 34:
        67-69.
1985   'The Priestly Account of Building the Tabernacle', *JAOS* 105: 21-30.
forthcoming 1 'I Kings 5.15–9.25' (in Hebrew), *Encyclopaedia Olam Ha-Tanakh*. VIIIa.
        Melakhim I (Jerusalem: Revivim).
forthcoming 2 'Solomon's Temple', in *Sefer Yerushalyim*, I (ed. S. Ahituv and
        A. Mazar; Jerusalem: Yad Yitzhak ben Tzvi).
forthcoming 3 'Solomon's Golden Vessels (I Kings 7: 48-51) and the Cult of the first
        Temple', in *Jacob Milgrom Festschrift* (ed. D. Wright; Winona Lake:
        Eisenbrauns).
forthcoming 4 'Temporary Temples', *Raphael Kutscher Memorial Volume* (ed. A.
        Kempinski), *Tel Aviv*.
Ishida, T.
1977   *The Royal Dynasties in Ancient Israel: A Study on the Formation and
        Development of Royal Dynastic Ideology* (BZAW, 142; Berlin: de
        Gruyter).
Jacobsen, T.
1937–39 'The Inscription of Takil-ili-su of Malgium', *AfO* 12: 363-66.
1941   Review of *Lamentation over the Destruction of Ur* by S.N. Kramer, *AJSL*
        58: 219-24.
1957   'Early Political Development in Mesopotamia', *ZA* 52: 91-140.
1970   *Toward the Image of Tammuz and other Essays on Mesopotamian History*

and Culture (ed. W.L. Moran; Harvard Semitic Series, 21: Cambridge, MA: Harvard University Press).

1970a   'Formative Tendencies in Sumerian Religion', in Jacobsen 1970: 1-15, 319.

1970b   'Ancient Mesopotamian Religion: The Central Concerns' in Jacobsen 1970: 39-46, 319-34.

1976   *The Treasures of Darkness: A History of Mesopotamian Religion* (New Haven, CT: Yale University Press).

1978-79 'Ipḫur-Kīshi and his Times', *AfO* 26: 1-14.

1984   *The Harab Myth* (Sources from the Ancient Near East, 2.3; Malibu, CA: Undena).

1985   'Ur-Nanshe's Diorite Plaque', *Or* ns 54: 65-72.

1987a   'The Graven Image', in *Ancient Israelite Religion: Essays in Honor of Frank Moore Cross* (ed. P.D. Hanson et al.; Philadelphia: Fortress Press): 15-32.

1987b   *The Harps That Once... : Sumerian Poetry in Translation* (New Haven, CT: Yale University Press).

Japhet, S.

1968   'The Supposed Common Authorship of Chronicles and Ezra–Nehemiah Investigated Anew', *VT* 18: 330-72.

1982-83 'Sheshbazzar and Zerubbabel—Against the Background of the Historical and Religious Tendencies of Ezra–Nehemiah', *ZAW* 94: 66-98; 95: 218-29.

Jelinkova-Reymond, E.A.E.

1969   *The Mythical Origin of the Egyptian Temple* (Manchester: Barnes & Noble).

Jensen, P.

1892   'Inschrift Agum-Kakrimis d.i. Agums des Jüngeren', in E. Schrader, *Sammlung von assyrischen und babylonischen Texten* (KB, 3.1; Berlin: H. Reuther): 134-52.

Jepsen, A.

1956   *Die Quellen des Königsbuches*, II (Halle: Niemeyer).

Jirku, A.

1923   *Altorientalischer Kommentar zum Alten Testament* (Leipzig: Deichert).

Kalugila, L.

1980   *The Wise King: Studies in Royal Wisdom as Divine Revelation in the Old Testament and its Environment* (ConBOT, 15; Lund: Gleerup).

Kapelrud, A.

1963   'Temple Building: A Task for Gods and Kings', *Or* ns 32: 56-62.

Kärki, I.

1968   *Die sumerischen Königsinschriften der frühaltbabylonischen Zeit im Umschrift und Übersetzung* (StudOr, 35; Helsinki: Societas Orientalis Fennica).

1983   *Die sumerischen und akkadischen Königsinschriften der altbabylonischen Zeit* (StudOr, 55.1: Helsinki: Societas Orientalis Fennica).

Katzenstein, H.J.

1973   *The History of Tyre: From the beginning of the Second Millennium BCE* until the Fall of the Neo-Babylonian Empire in 538 BCE (Jerusalem: Shocken).

Kaufmann, S.
1977   'An Assyro-Aramaic *egirtu ša šulmu'*, in *Essays on the Ancient Near East in Memory of Jacob Joel Finkelstein* (ed. M. de Jong Ellis; Memoirs of the Connecticut Academy of Arts & Sciences, 19; Hamden, CT: Archon Books): 119-27.

Kaufmann, Y.
1967   *The History of Israelite Religion: From Antiquity until the End of the Second Temple Period* (in Hebrew) (Jerusalem and Tel Aviv: Mosad Bialik, Dvir).

Kellerman, G.
1980   'Recherche sur les Rituels de Fondation Hittite' (unpublished dissertation, University of Paris).

Kenik, H.A.
1983   *Design for Kingship: The Deuteronomic Narrative Technique in 1 Kings 3.4-15* (SBLDS, 69; Chico, CA: Scholars Press).

Kent, R.G.
1950   *Old Persian Grammar, Texts, Lexicon* (AOS, 33; New Haven, CT: American Oriental Society).

King, L.W.
1912   *Babylonian Boundary Stones and Memorial-Tablets in the British Museum* (London: British Museum).

Kingsbury, E.C.
1963   'A Seven Day Ritual in the Old Babylonian Cult at Larsa', *HUCA* 34: 1-34.

Kinnier-Wilson, J.V.
1962   'The Kurba'il Statue of Shalmaneser III', *Iraq* 24: 90-115.
1979   *The Rebel Lands: An Investigation into the Origins of Early Mesopotamian Mythology* (Cambridge: Cambridge University Press).
1985   *The Legend of Etana: A New Edition* (Warminster: Aris L. Phillips).

Klein, J.
1976   Šulgi and Gilgameš: Two Brother-Peers Šulgi O)', in *Kramer Anniversary Volume: Cuneiform Studies in Honor of Samuel Noah Kramer* (ed. B.L. Eichler, J. W. Heimerdinger and Å.W. Sjöberg; AOAT, 25; Neukirchen–Vluyn: Neukirchener Verlag): 271-92.

Klein J.
1989   'Building and Dedication Hymns in Sumerian Literature', *Acta Sumerologica* 11: 27-67.
1989a   'From Gudea to Šulgi: Continuity and Change in Sumerian Literary Tradition', in *DUMU-E₂-DUB-BA-A. Studies in Honor of Åke W. Sjöberg* (ed. H. Behrens et al.; Occasional Publications of the Samuel Noah Kramer Fund, 11; Philadelphia): 289-301.
1990   'Šulgi and Išmedagan: Originality and Dependence in Sumerian Royal Hymnology', in *Bar-Ilan Studies in Assyriology dedicated to Pinhas Artzi* (ed. J. Klein and A. Skaist; Ramat Gan: Bar-Ilan University Press): 65-136.

Knudtzon, J.A.
1915   *Die El-Amarna-Tafeln, mit Einleitung und Erläuterungen*, I, II (VAB, 2; Leipzig: Hinrichs).
Köcher, F.
1957–58   'Ein Inventartext aus Kār-Tukulti-Ninurta', *AfO* 18: 300-13.
1959   'Ein spätbabylonischer Hymnus auf den Tempel Ezida in Borsippa', *ZA* 53: 236-40.
Komoroczy, G.
1978   'Die Königshymnen der III. Dynastie von Ur', *Acta Orientalia Acadamiae Scientiarum Hungaricae* 32: 33-66.
König, F.W.
1930   *Der Burgbau zu Susa nach dem Bauberichte des Königs Dareios I* (MVAG, 35; Leipzig: Hinrichs).
Kramer, S.N.
1961   'Sumerian Literature: A General Survey', in *The Bible and the Ancient Near East: Essays in Honour of William Foxwell Albright* (ed. G.E. Wright; Garden City, NY: Doubleday): 249-66.
1963   *The Sumerians: Their History, Culture and Character* (Chicago: University of Chicago Press).
1969   *The Sacred Marriage Rite: Aspects of Faith, Myth, and Ritual in Ancient Sumer* (Bloomington, IN: Indiana University Press).
1971   'Aspects of Mesopotamian Society, Evidence from the Sumerian Literary Sources', in *Beiträge zur sozialen Struktur des alten Vorderasien* (ed. H. Klengel; Schriften zur Geschichte und Kultur des alten Orients, 1; Deutsche Akademie der Wissenschaften zu Berlin, Zentralinstitut für alte Geschichte und Archäologie; Berlin: Akademie Verlag): 1-13.
1972   *Sumerian Mythology: A study of Spiritual and Literary Achievement in the Third Millennium BC* (rev. edn; Philadelphia: University of Pennsylvania Press).
1977   'Commerce and Trade: Gleanings from Sumerian Literature', *Iraq* 39: 59-66.
1988   'The Temple in Sumerian Literature', in *Temple in Society* (ed. M.V. Fox; Winona Lake, IN: Eisenbrauns): 1-16.
Kraus, F.R.
1980   'Der Brief des Gilgameš', *AnSt* 30: 109-121.
Kraus, H.J.
1960   *Psalmen 60–150* (BKAT, 15.2; Neukirchen–Vluyn: Neukirchener Verlag).
Kraus, P.
1932   *Altbabylonische Briefe aus der vorderasiatischen Abteilung der preussischen Staatsmuseen zu Berlin*, II (MVAG, 36.1; Leipzig: Hinrichs).
Krebernik, M.
1984   *Die Beschwörungen aus Fara und Ebla: Untersuchungen zurältesten keilschriftlichen Beschwörungsliteratur* (Texte und Studien zur Orientalistik, 2; Hildesheim: Georg Olms).
Kumaki, F.K.
1981   'The Deuteronomistic Theology of the Temple as Crystallized in 2 Sam 7, I Kgs 8', *Annual of the Japanese Biblical Institute* 7: 16-52.

Kutscher, R.
1975   *Oh Angry Sea (a-ab-ba ḫu-luḫ-ḫa): The History of a Sumerian Congregational Lament* (YNER, 6; New Haven, CT: Yale University Press).

Kutscher R., and C. Wilcke
1978   'Eine Ziegel-Inschrift des Königs Takil-ili ššu von Malgium, gefunden in Isin und Yale', *ŽA* 68: 95-128.

Labat, R.
1939   *La caractère religieux de la royauté assyro-babylonienne* (Etudes d'assyriologie, 2; Paris: Adrien-Maisonneuve).
1939b   *Hémérologies et ménologies d'Assur* (Etudes d'assyriologie, 1; Paris: Adrien-Maisonneuve).
1965   *Un calendrier babylonien des travaux, des signes et des mois (séries iqqur-îpuš)* (Bibliothèque de l'Ecole des Hautes Etudes ive section [sciences historiques et philologiques], 321; Paris: Honoré Champion).

Lackenbacher, S.
1982   *Le roi bâtisseur: Les récits de construction assyriens des origines à Teglatphalasar III* (Etudes assyriologiques, 11; Paris: Editions recherche sur les civilisations).
1983   'A propos de ADD 780', *Syria* 60: 47-51.

Lambert, M.
1955   'De quelques thèmes littéraires en sumérien et dans la Bible (Congres d'archéologique et d'orientalisme bibliques, Saint Cloud, 23–25 Avril, 1954)', *RHPR* 35: 4-15.
1959-60 'Three Literary Prayers of the Babylonians', *AfO* 19: 47-66.

Lambert, M., and R. Tournay
1948   'Le Cylindre A de Gudéa (nouvelle traduction)', *RB* 55: 403-37; 'Le cylindre B de Gudéa', *RB* 5: 520-43.
1951   'La Statue B de Gudéa', *RA* 45: 49-66.

Lambert, W.G.
1954–56 'An Address of Marduk to the Demons', *AfO* 17: 310-21.
1966   *Enūma Eliš: The Babylonian Epic of Creation: The Cuneiform Text* (Oxford: Clarendon Press).
1967   *Babylonian Wisdom Literature* (Oxford: Clarendon Press).
1968   'Literary Style in First Millennium Mesopotamia', *JAOS* 88: 123-32.
1968–69 'A New Source for the Reign of Nabonidus', *AfO* 22: 1-8.
1973   'Studies in Nergal', *BO* 30: 355-63.
1986   'Narām-sîn of Ešnunna or Akkad?' *JAOS* 106: 793-95.
1987   'The Sumero-Babylonian Brick God Kulla', *JNES* 46: 203-204.
1988   'Esarhaddon's Attempt to Return Marduk to Babylon', in *Ad bene et fideliter seminandum: Festgabe für Karlheinz Deller zum 21. Februar 1987* (ed. G. Mauer and U. Magen; AOAT, 220; Neukirchen–Vluyn: Neukirchener Verlag): 157-74.

Lambert, W.G., and A.R. Millard
1969   *Atra-ḫasīs: The Babylonian Story of the Flood* (Oxford: Clarendon Press).

Landsberger, B.
1954   'Assyrische Königsliste und Dunkles Zeitalter', *JCS* 8: 31-45.

1965   *Brief des Bischofs von Esagila an König Asarhaddon* (Mededelingen der Koninklijke Nederlandse Akademie van Wetenschappen. Afd. Letterkunde, ns 28.6; Amsterdam: N.V. Noord-Hollandsche Uitgevers-Maatschappj).

Landsberger, B., and K. Balkan
1950   'Die Inschrift des assyrischen Königs Irisum, gefunden in Kültepe 1948', *Belleten* 1: 219-68.

Landsberger, B., and J.V. Kinnier-Wilson
1961   'The Fifth Tablet of Enūma Eliš', *JNES* 20: 154-79.

Langdon, S.
1912   *Die neubabylonischen Königsinschriften* (trans. R. Zehnpfund; VAB, 4; Leipzig: Hinrichs).
1915-16   'New Inscriptions of Nabuna'id', *AJSL* 32: 102-17.
1923   *The H. Weld–Blundell Collection in the Ashmolean Museum*. I. *Sumerian and Semitic Religious and Historical Texts* (Oxford Editions of Cuneiform Texts, 1; London: Oxford University Press).
1935   *Babylonian Menologies and the Semitic Calendars* (The Schweich Lectures of the British Academy, 1933; London: The British Academy).

Larsen, M.T.
1976   *The Old Assyrian City-State and its Colonies* (Mesopotamia; Copenhagen Studies in Assyriology, 4; Copenhagen: Akademisk Forlag).

Leemans, W.F.
1960   *Foreign Trade in the Old Babylonian Period, as Revealed by Texts from Southern Mesopotamia* (Studia et Documenta ad iura orientis antiqui pertinentia, 6; Leiden: Brill).

Levenson, J.D.
1981   'From Temple to Synagogue: I Kings 8', in *Traditions in Transformation: Turning Points in Biblical Faith* (ed. B. Halpern and J.D. Levenson; Winona Lake, IN: Eisenbrauns): 143-66.
1982   'The Paronomasia of Solomon's Seventh Petition', *HAR* 6: 135-38.

Levine, B.A.
1965   'The Descriptive Tabernacle Texts of the Pentateuch', *JAOS* 85: 307-18.
1978-79   Review of *Ketobot Arad* (in Hebrew), by Y. Aharoni, *Shnaton* 3: 283-94.
1989   *Leviticus/Va-yikra* (The JPS Torah Commentary; Philadelphia: The Jewish Publishing Society).

Levine, B.A., and W.W. Hallo
1967   'Offerings to the Temple Gates at Ur', *HUCA* 38: 17-58.

Lewis, B.
1980   *The Sargon Legend: A Study of the Akkadian Text and the Tale of the Hero who was Exposed at Birth* (American Schools of Oriental Research, dissertation Series, 4; Cambridge, MA: American Schools of Oriental Research).

Licht, J.
1979   'An Ideal Town Plan from Qumran: The Description of the New Jerusalem', *IEJ* 29: 45-59.
1980   'The Biblical Claim of Establishment' (in Hebrew), *Shnaton* 4: 98-128.

Lichtheim, M.
1973   *Ancient Egyptian Literature: A Book of Readings*. I. *The Old and Middle*
1976, 1980   *Kingdoms*. II. *The New Kingdom*. III. *The Late Period* (Berkeley:
            University of California Press).

Lie, A.G.
1929   *The Inscriptions of Sargon II King of Assyria*. I. *The Annals: Tansliterated*
            and Translated with Notes (Paris: Paul Geuthner).

Limet, H.
1971   'Le poème épique "Innina et Ebiḫ", une version des lignes 123 à 182', *Or*
            ns 40: 11-28.

Lindblom, J.
1961   'Theophanies in Holy Places in Hebrew Religion', *HUCA* 32: 91-106.

Linder, E.
1986   'The Khorsabad Wall Relief: A Mediterranean Seascape or River Transport
            of Timbers?', *JAOS* 106: 273-81.

Lipiński, E.
1973   'Garden of Abundance, Image of Lebanon', *ZAW* 85: 358-59.

Liver, J.
1971a   'The Book of the Acts of Solomon' (in Hebrew), in *Studies in Bible and*
            Judean Desert Scrolls (Jerusalem: Bialik Institute): 83-105.
1971b   'The Problem of the Chronology of Hiram, King of Tyre' (in Hebrew), in
            Studies in Bible and Judean Desert Scrolls (Jerusalem: Bialik Institute):
            189-97.

Liverani, M.
1973   'Memorandum on the Approach to Historiographic Texts', *Or* ns 42:
            178-94.

Loewenstamm, S.E.
1962   'Miktaḇ' (in Hebrew), *EM*, IV, cols. 966-74.
1962b   'Y āpĕah, Yāpiaḥ, Yāpiah', *Leš* 26: 205-208.
1982   'Some Remarks on Biblical Passages in the Light of Their Akkadian
            Parallels' (in Hebrew), in *Bible Studies Y.M. Grintz in Memoriam* (ed.
            B. Uffenheimer; Te'udah, Tel Aviv: Hakibbutz Hame'uchad): 187-96
            (English Abstract).

Long, B.
1984   'I Kings with an Introduction to Historical Literature' in *The Forms of the*
            Old Testament Literature, IX (ed. R. Knierim and G.M. Tucker; Grand
            Rapids: Eerdmans).

Longman III T.
1991   *Fictional Akkadian Autobiography: A Generic and Comparative Study*
            (Winona Lake: Eisenbrauns).

Loretz, O.
1974   'Der Torso eines kanaanäisch-israelitischen Tempelweihspruches in I Kg
            8, 12-13', *UF* 6: 478-80.

Loud, G., and C.B. Altman
1938   *Khorsabad*. II. *The Citadel and the Town* (OIP, 40; Chicago: University of
            Chicago Press).

Luckenbill, D.D.
1924   *The Annals of Sennacherib* (OIP, 2; Chicago: University of Chicago Press).
1926–27   *Ancient Record of Assyria and Babylonia*, I, II (Chicago: University of Chicago Press).

Lyon, D.G.
1883   *Keilschrifttexte Sargon's Königs von Assyrien (722–705 v. Chr.)* (Leipzig: Hinrichs).

McCarter, P.K.
1983   'The Ritual Dedication of the City of David in 2 Samuel 6', in *The Word of the Lord Shall Go Forth: Essays in Honor of David Noel Freedman in Celebration of his Sixtieth Birthday* (ed. C.L. Meyers and M.O'Connor; Winona Lake, IN: Eisenbrauns): 273-77.

McEvenue, S.
1974   'The Style of Building Instruction', *Semitics* 4: 1-9.

McNeile, A.H.
1931   *The Book of Exodus, with Introduction and Notes* (Westminster Commentaries; London: Methuen).

Machinist, P.
1976   'Literature as Politics: The Tukulti-Ninurta Epic and the Bible', *CBQ* 455-82.
1983a   'Rest and Violence in the Poem of Erra', *JAOS* 103: 221-26.
1983b   'Assyria and its Image in the First Isaiah', *JAOS* 103: 719-37.

Malamat, A.
1965   'Campaigns to the Mediterranean by Iahdunlim and Other Early Mesopotamian Rulers', in *Studies. . . Landsberger* (AS, 16; Chicago: University of Chicago Press): 365-73.
1967   'Prophetic Revelations in New Documents from Mari and the Bible', in *E.L. Sukenik Memorial Volume* (ed. N. Avigad *et al.*; Eretz Israel, 8): 74-84.
1977   *Sources for Early Biblical History: The Second Millennium BC in Hebrew Translation* (Jerusalem: Academon, 3rd edn).
1980   'A Mari Prophecy and Nathan's Dynastic Oracle', in *Prophecy: Essays Presented to G. Fohrer on His Sixty-Fifth Birthday 6 September 1980* (ed. J.A. Emerton; BZAW, 150; Berlin: de Gruyter): 62-82.
1982   'Longevity: Biblical Concepts and Some Ancient Near Eastern Parallels', in *Vorträge gehalten auf der 28. Rencontre Assyriologique Internationale in Wien, 6.–10. Juli 1981* (AfOB, 19; Horn: Ferdinand Berger & Söhne): 215-24.
1982b   'Longevity in the Bible and in the ancient Near East' (in Hebrew), in *H. Orlinsky Volume* (ed. B.A. Levine and A. Malamat; Eretz Israel, 16): 146-51.
1987   'The Divinity of the Mediterranean in a pre-Ugaritic Text' (in Hebrew), in *Studies in Bible Dedicated to the Memory of U. Cassuto on the 100th Anniversary of his Birth* (ed. S.E. Loewenstamm; Jerusalem: Magnes Press): 184-88.
1988   'The Amorite Background of Psalm 29', *ZAW* 100: 156-60.

1992   'The Divine Nature of the Mediterranean Sea in the Foundation Inscription of Yahdunlim', in *Mari in Retrospect: fifty Years of Mari and Mari Studies* (ed. G.D. Young Winona Lake: Eisenbrauns): 211-215.

Mallowan, M.E.L.
1967   'Nimrud', *Archaeology and the Old Testament Study: Jubilee Volume of the Society for Old Testament Study, 1917-1967* (ed. D.W. Thomas; Oxford: Clarendon Press): 57-72.

Mann, T.W.
1977   *Divine Presence and Guidance in Israelite Traditions: The Typology of Exaltation* (The Johns Hopkins Near Eastern Studies; Baltimore: Johns Hopkins University Press).

Mayer, W.R.
1976   *Untersuchungen zur Formensprache der babylonischen 'Gebetsbeschwörungen'* (Studia Pohl; Series Maior, 5; Rome: Biblical Institute Press).
1978   'Seleukidische Rituale aus Warka mit Emesal-Gebeten', *Or* ns 47: 431-58.
1987   'Ein Mythos von der Erschaffung des Menschen und des Königs', *Or* ns 56: 55-68.

Meissner, B.
1944   'Die französischen und amerikanischen Ausgrabungen in Khorsabad', *ZDMG* 98: 28-43.

Melamed, E.Z.
1984   'The Purchase of the Cave of Machpelah (Genesis Ch. 23)' (in Hebrew), in *Biblical Studies in Texts, Translations and Commentators* (Jerusalem: Magnes Press): 33-41.

Menzel, B.
1981   *Assyrische Tempel*, I, II (Studia Pohl; Series Maior, 10.1, 2; Rome: Biblical Institute Press).

Meyers, C.
1983   'Jachin and Boaz in Religious and Political Perspective', *CBQ* 45: 167-78.
1987   'David as Temple Builder', in *Ancient Israelite Religion: Essays in Honor of Frank Moore Cross* (ed. J. Hanson *et al.*; Philadelphia: Fortress Press): 357-76.

Meyers, C.L., and E.M. Meyers
1987   *Haggai, Zechariah 1-8: A New Translation with Introduction and Commentary* (AB, 25B; Garden City, NY: Doubleday).

Michalowski, P.
1977   'Amar-Su'ena and the Historical Tradition', in *Essays on the Ancient Near East in Memory of Jacob Joel Finkelstein* (ed. M. da Jong Ellis; Memoirs of the Connecticut Academy of Arts & Sciences, 19; Hamden: Archon Books): 155-57.

Michel, E.
1947-67   'Die Assur-Texte Salmanassars III (858-824)', *WO* 1 (1947-52): 5-20, 57-71, 205-22, 255-71, 385-96; *WO* 2 (1954-59): 27-43, 137-57, 221-33, 408-15; *WO* 3 (1964-66): 146-55; *WO* 4 (1967): 29-37.
1952   'Ein neuentdeckter Annalen-Text Salmanassars III', *WO* 1: 454-75.
1954   'Die Texte Aššur-nāṣir-aplis II (88-859)', *WO* 2: 213-21, 404-407.

Milgrom, J.

1970   *Studies in Levitical Terminology: The Encroacher and the Levite, the Term 'Aboda* (University of California Publications Near Eastern Studies, 14; Berkeley: University of California Press).

1985a   'The Chieftans' Gifts: Numbers, Chapter 7', *HAR* 9: 221-25.

1985b   'Hezekiah's Sacrifices at the Dedication Services of the Purified Temple (2 Chr. 29: 21-24)', in *Biblical and Related Studies Presented to Samuel Iwry* (ed. A. Kort and S. Morschauser; Winona Lake, IN: Eisenbrauns): 159-61.

1991   *Leviticus 1–16: A New Translation with Introduction and Commentary* (AB, New York: Doubleday).

Millard, A.

1964   'Another Babylonian Chronicle Text', *Iraq* 26: 14-35.

1970   'Fragments of Historiographical Texts from Nineveh: Middle Assyrian and Later Kings', *Iraq* 32: 167-76, and pls. XXXIII–XXXVII.

Miller, P.D.

1985   'Eridu, Dunnu and Babel: A Study in Comparative Mythology', *HAR* 9: 227-51.

Miller, P.D., and J.J.M. Roberts

1977   *The Hand of the Lord—A Reassessment of the 'Ark Narrative' of I Samuel* (The Johns Hopkins Near Eastern Studies; Baltimore: Johns Hopkins University Press).

Montgomery, J.A.

1927   *A Critical and Exegetical Commentary of the Book of Daniel* (ICC; Edinburgh: T. & T. Clark).

1934   'Archival Data in the Book of Kings', *JBL* 53: 46-52.

Montgomery, J.A., and H.S. Gehman

1951   *A Critical and Exegetical Commentary on the Book of Kings* (ICC; Edinburgh: T. & T. Clark).

Moran, W.L.

1959   'Notes on the New Nabonidus Inscriptions', *Or* 28: 130-40.

1959b   'A New Fragment of DIN.TIR.KI=*Bābilu* and *Enūma Eliš* VI 61-66', in *Studia Biblica et Orientalia*, III (Oriens Antiquus; AnBib, 12; Rome: Pontifico Istituto Biblico): 257-65.

1963a   'The Ancient Near Eastern Background of the Love of God in Deuteronomy', *CBQ* 25: 77-87.

1963b   'A Note on the Treaty Terminology of the Sefire Stelas', *JNES* 22: 173-76.

Mowinckel, S.

1923   'Die vorderasiatischen Königs- und Fürsteninschriften', in *Eukharistērion: Studien zur Religion und Literatur des alten und neuen Testaments Hermann Gunkel zum 60. Geburtstages dem 23. Mai 1922 dargebracht von seinen Schülern und Freunden. I. Religion und Literatur des Alten Testaments* (FRLANT, ns 19.1; Göttingen: Vandenhoeck & Ruprecht): 278-322.

1964   *Studien zu dem Büche Ezra–Nehemia. II. Die Nehemia-Denkschrift* (Oslo: Universitatsforlaget).

1967 *The Psalms in Israel's Worship*, I, II (trans. D.R. Ap-Thomas; Oxford: Blackwell).

Muffs, Y.
1969 *Studies in the Aramiac Legal Papyri from Elephantine* (Leiden: Brill).

Munn-Rankin, I.M.
1956 'Diplomacy in Western Asia in the Early Second Millenium BC', *Iraq* 18: 68-110.

Na'aman, N.
1984 'Statements of Time-spans by Babylonian and Assyrian Kings and Mesopotamian Chronology', *Iraq* 46: 115-23.

Nemat-Nejat, K.R.
1982 *Late Babylonian Field Plans in the British Museum* (Studia Pohl; Series Maior, 11; Rome: Biblical Institute Press).

Neugebauer, O., and A. Sachs
1945 *Mathematical Cuneiform Texts* (AOS, 29; New Haven, CT: American Oriental Society).

Noth, M.
1966a 'Old Testament Covenant-Making in the Light of a Text from Mari', *idem*, *The Laws in the Pentateuch and other Studies* (trans. D. Ap-Thomas; Edinburgh: Oliver & Boyd): 108-17.

1966b 'For All Who Rely on the Works of the Law are under a Curse', *idem*, *The Laws in the Pentateuch and other Studies* (trans. D. Ap-Thomas; Edinburgh: Oliver & Boyd),: 118-31.

1968 *Könige* (BKAT, 9.1; Neukirchen–Vluyn: Neukirchener Verlag).

Oberhuber, K.
1967 'Eine Hymne an Nippur (*UET* VI 118)', *ArOr* 35: 262-70.

Olmo Lete, G. del
1983 'Aṯirat's Entreaty and the Order of the Ugaritic Tablets, KTU 1. 3/4', *Aula Orientalis* 1: 67-71.

Olmstead, A.T.
1908 *Western Asia in the Days of Assyria, 722–705 BC: A Study in Oriental History* (Cornell Studies in History and Political Science, 2; New York: Henry Holt).

1923 *History of Assyria* (Chicago: University of Chicago Press).

Oppenheim, A.L.
1947 'Mesopotamian Mythology I', *Or* ns 16: 207-38.

1956 *The Interpretation of Dreams in the Ancient Near East with a Translation of an Assyrian Dream-Book* (Transactions of the American Philosophical Society, ns 46.3; Philadelphia: The American Philosophical Society).

1960 'The City of Assur in 714 BC', *JNES* 19: 133-47.

1967 *Letters from Mesopotamia—Official, Business, and Private Letters on Clay Tablets from Two Millennia* (Chicago: University of Chicago Press).

Orthman, W.
1975 *Der Alte Orient* (Propylaen Kunstgeschichte, 14; ed. K. Bittel *et al.*; Berlin: Propylaen-Verlag).

Ota, M.
1974 'A Note on 2 Sam 7', in *A Light unto My Path: Old Testament Studies in*

Honour of Jacob M. Myers (ed. H.N. Bream, R.D. Heim and C.A. Moore; Gettysburg Theological Studies, 4; Philadelphia: Temple University Press): 403-407.

Ouellette, J.

1966   *The Temple of Solomon: A Philological and Archaeological Study* (PhD dissertation; Hebrew Union College–Jewish Institute of Religion, Cincinnati; Ann Arbor, MI: University Microfilms).

1976   'The Basic Structure of Solomon's Temple and Archaeological Research', in *The Temple of Solomon, Archaeological Fact and Medieval Tradition in Christian, Islamic and Jewish Art* (ed. J. Gutmann; American Academy of Religion, Society of Biblical Literature, Religion and the Arts, 3; Missoula, MT: Scholars Press): 1-20.

Owen, D.I.

1981   'An Akkadian Letter from Ugarit at Tel Aphek', *Tel Aviv* 8: 1-17.

Page, S.

1968   'A Stele of Adad-Nirari III and Nergal-ereš from Tell al Rimah', *Iraq* 30: 139-43.

Pallis, S.A.

1926   *The Babylonian Akîtu Festival* (Det Kgl. Danske Videnskabernes Selskab Historik-filologiske Meddelelser, 12.1; Copenhagen: Bianco Lunos).

Paran, M.

1989   *Literary Features of the Priestly Code: Stylistic Patterns, Idioms and Structures* (in Hebrew) (Jerusalem: Magnes Press).

Pardee, D.

1976   'The Preposition in Ugaritic', *UF* 8: 215-322.

1978a   'Letters from Tel Arad', *UF* 10: 289-336.

1978b   'An Overview of Ancient Hebrew Epistolography', *JBL* 97: 321-46.

1982   *Handbook of Ancient Hebrew Letters: A Study Edition* (SBLSBS, 15: Chico, CA: Scholars Press).

Parpola, S.

1970   *Letters from Assyrian Scholars to the Kings Esarhaddon and Assurbanipal. I.Texts* (AOAT, 5.I; Neukirchen–Vluyn: Neukirchener Verlag).

1981   'Assyrian Royal Inscriptions and Neo–Assyrian Letters', in *Assyrian Royal Inscriptions, New Horizons in Literary, Ideological, and Historical Analysis: Papers of a Symposium held in Cetona (Siena) June 26–28. 1980* (ed. F.M. Fales; Orientis Antiqui Collectio, 17; Rome: Istituto per l'oriente).

1987   *The Correspondence of Sargon II. I. Letters from Assyria and the West* (State Archives of Assyria, 1; Helsinki: Neo-Assyrian Texts Corpus Project, University of Helsinki).

Paul, S.M.

1968   'Deutero-Isaiah and Cuneiform Royal Inscriptions', *JAOS* 88: 180-86.

1969   'Sargon's Administrative Diction in II Kings 17.27', *JBL* 88: 73-74.

1970   *Studies in the Book of the Covenant in the Light of Cuneiform and Biblical Law* (VTSup, 18; Leiden: Brill).

Peckham, B.

1976   'Israel and Phoenicia', in *Magnalia Dei: The Mighty Acts of God: Essays* on the Bible and Archaeology in Memory of G. Ernest Wright (ed. F.M. Cross et al.; Garden City, NY: Doubleday): 224-48.

1985   *The Composition of the Deuteronomistic History* (Atlanta: Scholars Press).

Perkins, A.
1957   'Narrative Art in Babylonia', *AJA* 61: 54-62, and pls. 17–20.

Petersen, D.L.
1977   *Late Israelite Prophecy: Studies in Deutero-Prophetic Literature and in Chronicles* (SBLMS, 23; Missoula, MT: Scholars Press).

Petitjean, A.
1969   *Les oracles du Proto-Zacharie. Un programme de restauration pour la communauté juive après l'Exil* (Etudes Bibliques; Paris: Gabalda).

Piepkorn, A.C.
1933   *Historical Prism Inscriptions of Ashurbanipal I, Editions E, B 1–5, D and K* (AS, 5; Chicago: University of Chicago Press).

Pinches, T.
1924   'Hymns to Pap-due-garra', *JRAS Centenary Supplement*: 63-86.

Poebel, A.
1947   '*Murnisqu* and *Nisqu* in Cylinder A of Gudea', in *Miscellaneous Studies* (AS, 14; Chicago: University of Chicago Press): 43-87.

Polak, F.
1985   'Literary Design in Ezra–Nehemiah' (in Hebrew), *Shnaton* 9: 127-43.

Pope, M.H.
1955   *El in the Ugaritic Texts* (VTSup, 2; Leiden: Brill).
1965   *Job* (AB, 15; Garden City, NY: Doubleday).

Porten, B.
1977   'The Return to Zion in Vision and Reality' (in Hebrew), *Cathedra* 4: 4-12.
1978   'The Archive of Jedaniah Son of Gemariah of Elephantine—The Structure and Style of the Letters (I)' (in Hebrew), in *H.L. Ginsberg Volume* (ed. M. Haran; Eretz Israel, 14; n.p.): 165-77.
1978–79   'The Documents in the Book of Ezra and the Mission of Ezra' (in Hebrew), *Shnaton* 3: 174-96, English Abstract pp. xix-xx.
1981   'The Identity of King Adon', *BA* 44: 36-42.
1986   *Vid.* Porten and Yardeni 1986

Porten, B., and A. Yardeni
1986   *Textbook of Aramaic Documents from Ancient Egypt, Newly Copied, Edited and Translated into Hebrew and English.* I. *Letters* (The Hebrew University Department of the History of the Jewish People, Texts and Studies for Students; Jerusalem: Hebrew University Press).

Postgate, N.
1969   *Neo-Assyrian Royal Grants and Deeds* (Studia Pohl; Series Maior, 1; Rome: Pontifical Biblical Institute).
1973   *The Governor's Palace Archive* (Cuneiform Texts from Nimrud, II; London: British School of Archaeology in Iraq).

1974   *Taxation and Conscription in the Assyrian Empire* (Studia Pohl; Series
                Maior, 3; Rome: Biblical Institute Press).
1983   Review of *Assyrische Tempeln*, by B. Menzel, *JSS* 28: 155-59.
Powell, M.A.
1991   'Naram-Sin, Son of Sargon: Ancient History, Famous Names, and a
                Famous Babylonian Forgery', *ZA* 81: 20-30.
Price, I.M.
1927   *The Great Cylinder Inscriptions A & B of Gudea (about 2450 BC) to which
                are Added his Statues as Part II, with Transliteration, Translation, Notes,
                Full Vocabulary and Sign-Lists* (Assyriologische Bibliothek, 26; Leipzig:
                Hinrichs).
Rad, G. von
1964   'Die Nehemia-Denkschrift', *ZAW* 76: 176-87.
1966   'There Remains Still a Rest for the People of God: An Investigation of a
                Biblical Conception', in *The Problem of the Hexateuch and other Essays*
                (trans. E.W. Trueman Dicken; Edinburgh, London: Oliver & Boyd): 94-
                102.
Rainey, A.F.
1967   'The Samaria Ostraca in the Light of Fresh Evidence', *PEQ* 9: 32-41.
1978   *El Amarna Tablets 359–379: Supplement to J.A. Knudtzon, Die El-
                Amarna-Tafeln* (AOAT, 8; Neukirchen–Vluyn: Neukirchener Verlag, 2nd
                edn, revised).
Rankin, O.S.
1930   *The Origins of the Festival of Hanukah: The Jewish New-Age Festival*
                (Edinburgh: T. &.T. Clark).
Al-Rawi, N.H.F.
1985   'Nabopolassar's Restoration Work on the Wall *Imgur-Enlil* at Babylon',
                Iraq 47: 1-13.
1991   'More Royal Inscriptions from Babylon', *ARRIM* 9: 1-10.
Reade, J.
1975   'Sources for Sennacherib', *JCS* 27: 189-96.
Reich, R.
1979   'Dur-Sharrukin (Khorsabad)' (in Hebrew), *Qadmoniot* 12: 2-11.
Reif, S.C.
1972   'Dedicated to *HNK*', *VT* 22: 495-501.
Reiner, E.
1985   *Your Thwarts in Pieces, Your Mooring Ropes Cut: Poetry from Babylonia
                and Assyria* (Michigan Studies in Humanities, 5; Ann Arbor, MI: Horace
                H. Rackham School of Graduate Studies at the University of Michigan).
Renger, J.
1970   '*isinnam epēšum*: Überlegungen zur Funktion des Festes in der
                Gesellschaft', in *Actes de la XVIIe Rencontre Assyriologique Inter-
                nationale, Université Libre de Bruxelles, 30 juin–4 juillet 1969* (ed. A.
                Finet; Ham-sur-Heure: Comité belge de recherches en Mésopotamie):
                75-80.
1972–75   'Heilige Hochzeit', *RLA*, IV, 251-59.

Roberts, J.J.M.
1987   'Yahweh's Foundation in Zion', *JBL* 106: 27-45.
Robinson, J.
1972   *The First Book of Kings* (The Cambridge Bible Commentary–New English Bible; Cambridge: Cambridge University Press).
Rofé, A.
1973   Review of *Deuteronomy and the Deuteronomic School* (in Hebrew), by M. Weinfeld, *Kiryat Sefer* 48: 83-89.
1979   *The Belief in Angels in the Bible* (in Hebrew) (Jerusalem: Makor).
Röllig, W.
1964   'Erwägungen zu neuen Stelen König Nabonids', *ZA* 56: 218-60.
1966   Review of *Die Türen des Alten Mesopotamien*, by A. Salonen, *Wiener Zeitschrift für die Kunde des Morgenlandes* 62: 298-301.
1987   'Literatur', *RLA*, VII, 35–66.
Rosengarten, Y., and A. Baer
1977   *Sumer et le sacré: le jeu des Prescriptions (me) des dieux, et des destins* (Paris: E. de Boccard).
Rowley, H.H.
1950   *From Joseph to Joshua: Biblical Traditions in the Light of Archaeology* (The Schweich Lectures of the British Academy, 1948; London: The British Academy).
Rummel, S.
1981   'Narrative Structures in the Ugaritic Texts', in *Ras Shamra Parallels: The Texts from Ugarit and the Hebrew Bible*, III (ed. S. Rummel; AnOr, 51; Rome: Pontifical Biblical Institute): 221-332.
Rupprecht, K.
1977   *Der Tempel von Jerusalem: Gründung Salomos oder jebusitisches Erbe?* (BZAW, 144; Berlin: de Gruyter).
Saggs, H.W.F.
1955   'The Nimrud Letters, 1952—Part II', *Iraq* 17: 126-54.
Salonen, A.
1972   *Die Ziegeleien im Alten Mesopotamien* (Suomalaisen Tiedeakatemian Toimituksia Annales Academiae Scientiarum Fennicae Sarja, ser. B, 171; Helsinki: Suomalainen Tiedakatemia).
Salonen, E.
1967   *Die Gruss- und Höflichkeitsformeln in babylonisch-assyrischen Briefen* (StudOr, 38; Helsinki: Societas Orientalis Fennica).
Samuel, A.E.
1972   *Greek and Roman Chronology Calendars and Years in Classical Antiquity* (Handbuch der Altertumswissenschaft, 1.7; Munich: Beck).
Šanda, A.
1911   *Die Bücher der Könige. I. Das erste Buch der Könige* (Exegetisches Handbuch zum Alten Testament, 9.1; Münster: Aschendorff).
Sasson, V.
1982–83   'The Siloam Tunnel Inscription', *PEQ* 114–15: 111-17.

Sauren, H.
          'Hymne an Numušda, Kritik und Versuch einer Interpretation', *ZDMG*
          Supp. 3: 76-99.
1969   'Besuchsfahrten der Götter in Sumer', *Or* ns 38: 214-36.
1971–72   'Beispiele sumerischer Poesie', *JEOL* 22: 255-305.
1975   'Die Einweihung des Eninnu', in *Le Temple et le Culte: Compte rendu de
          la vingtième Rencontre Assyriologique Internationale organisée à Leiden du
          3 au 7 juillet 1972 sous les auspices du Nederlands Instituut voor het
          Nabije Oosten* (Leiden: Nederlands Instituut voor het Nabije Oosten):
          95-103.
1977   'Der Handel zur Zeit Gudeas von Lagasch, Idealbild oder Realität', *Iraq*
          39: 71-72.

Scheil, V.
1939   *Mélanges épigraphiques* (Mémoires de la Mission Archéologique de Perse,
          28; Paris: Leroux).

Schmid, H.
1985   'Der Tempelplan IM 44036,1—Schema oder Bauplan', *Or* ns 54: 289-93.
Schmidt, M.
1948   *Prophet und Tempel, eine Studie zum Problem der Gottesnähe im Alten
          Testament* (Zollikon-Zürich: Evangelischer Verlag).

Schottroff, W.
1967   '*Gedenken*' *im alten Orient und im alten Testament—Die Wurzel* zakar *im
          semitischen Sprachkreis* (WMANT, 50; Neukirchen–Vluyn: Neukirchener
          Verlag, 2nd edn).

Schrader, E.
1889   *Sammlung von assyrischen und babylonischen Texten* (Keilinschriftliche
          Bibliothek, 1; Berlin: H. Reuther).

Schramm, W.
1973   *Einleitung in die assyrischen Königsinschriften, Zweiter Teil: 934–722 v.
          Chr.* (ed. B. Spuler; Handbuch der Orientalistik, 1. Abteilung: der nahe
          und der mittlere Osten; Ergänzungsband 5, Keilschrifturkunden; Leiden:
          Brill).
1956–76   'Assyrische Königsinschriften', *WO* 8: 37-48.
Schreiner, J.
1963   *Sion-Jerusalem: Jahwes Königsitz* (SANT, 7; München: Kösel).
Schroeder, O.
1917–18   'Aus den keilinschriftlichen Sammlungen des Berliner Museums', *ZA* 31:
          91-99.

Schwartz, J.
1985   'Jubilees, Bethel and the Temple of Jacob', *HUCA* 56: 63-85.
Scott, R.B.Y.
1939   'The Pillars of Jachin and Boaz', *JBL* 58: 143-49.
Seeligman, I.L.
1979–80   'The Beginnings of Midrash in the Book of Chronicles' (in Hebrew),
          Tarbiz 49: 14-32.

Segal, M.Z.
1968   *The Books of Samuel, Arranged and Explicated with a Detailed Introduction* (in Hebrew) (Jerusalem: Kiryath Sepher).
Selms, A. van
1975   'A Guest Room for Ilu and its Furniture: An Interpretation of CTA 4, I lines 30-44' (Gordon, 51 I 30-44)', *UF* 7: 469-76.
Seux, M.J.
1967   *Epithètes royales akkadienes et sumériennes* (Paris: Letouzey et Ane).
Shaffer, A.
1974   'Enlilbani and the "Dog House" in Isin', *JCS* 26: 251-55.
1981   ' "Up" and "down", "front" and "back": Gilgamesh XI, 78 and *Atrahasis* III 29-31', *RA* 75: 188-89.
Simpson, W.K.
1973   *The Literature of Ancient Egypt* (New Haven: Yale University Press).
Sjöberg, Å.W.
1960   *Der Mondgott Nanna Suen in der sumerischen Überlieferung* (Stockholm: Almquist & Wiksell).
1961   'Ein syllabisch geschriebener Urnammu Text', *Orientalia Suecana* 10: 3-11.
1967   'Zu einigen Verwandtschaftsbezeichnungen im Sumerischen', in *Heidelberger Studien zum alten Orient Adam Falkenstein zum 17. September 1966* (ed. D.O. Edzard; Wiesbaden: Otto Harassowitz): 201-31.
1973   'Hymn to Numušda with a Prayer for King Sîniqīšam of Larsa and a Hymn to Ninurta', *Orientalia Suecana* 22: 107-21.
1973b   'Nungal in the Ekur', *AfO* 24: 19-46.
1957–71   'Götterreisen Götterreisen', *RLA*, III, 480-83.
Sjöberg, Å., and E. Bergmann
1969   *The Collection of the Sumerian Temple Hymns* (TCS, 3; Locust Valley, NY: J.J. Augustin).
Smith, M.S.
1986   'Interpreting the Baal Cycle', *UF* 18: 313-39.
forthcoming *Kothar wa-Hasis—The Ugaritic Craftsman God* (YNER).
Smith, S.
1924   *Babylonian Historical Texts relating to the Capture and Downfall of Babylon* (London: Methuen)
Soden, W. von
1982   'Untersuchungen zur babylonischen Metrik, Teil I', *ZA* 7: 161-204.
1959–64   'Gebete II', *RLA* III, 160-70.
Soggin, J.A.
1977   'The Davidic–Solomonic Kingdom', in *Israelite and Judaean History* (ed. J.H. Hayes and J.M. Miller; London: SCM Press): 332-80.
Sollberger, E.
1967a   'The Rulers of Lagaš', *JCS* 21: 279-91.
1967b   'Samsu-iluna's Bilingual Inscription B, Text of the Akkadian Version', *RA* 61: 39-44.

Sollberger, E., and J.R. Kupper
1971   *Inscriptions royales sumériennes et akkadiennes* (Littératures anciennes du
           proche-orient; Paris: Cerf).
Speiser, E.A.
1967a   'The Idea of History in Ancient Mesopotamia', in *Oriental and Biblical
           Studies, Collected Writings of E.A. Speiser* (ed. J.J. Finkelstein and
           M. Greenberg; Philadelphia: University of Pennsylvania Press): 270-312.
1967b   'Word Plays on the Creation Epic's Version of the Founding of Babylon',
           in *Oriental and Biblical Studies: Collected Writings of E.A. Speiser* (ed.
           J.J. Finkelstein and M. Greenberg; Philadelphia: University of
           Pennsylvania Press): 53-61.
Stade, B.
1883   'Der Text des Berichtes über Salomos Bauten, I Kö. 5-7', *ZAW* 3:
           129-77.
Starr, I.
1983   *The Rituals of the Diviner* (Bibliotheca Mesopotamica, 12; Malibu, CA:
           Undena Publications).
Steible, H.
1982   *Die altsumerischen Bau- und Weihinschriften. I. Inschriften aus 'Lagaš'.
           II. Kommentar zu den Inschriften aus 'Lagaš'* (ed. B. Kienast; Freiburger
           altorientalische Studien, 6; Wiesbaden: Franz Steiner Verlag).
1991   *Die Neusumerischen Bau- und Weihinschriften. I. Inschriften der II.
           Dynastie von Lagaš. II. Kommentar zu den Gudea-Statuen, Inschriften der
           III. Dynastie von Ur, Inschriften der IV. und 'V.' Dynastie von Uruk,
           Varia* (Freiburger Altorientalische Studien 9.1, 9.2; Stuttgart: Franz
           Steiner).
Streck, M.
1916   *Assurbanipal und die letzten assyrischen Könige bis zum Untergang
           Niniveh's*, I, II, III (VAB, 7; Leipzig: Hinrichs).
Tadmor, H.
1958   'The Campaigns of Sargon II of Assur: A Chronological-Historical Study',
           JCS 12: 22-40, 77-100.
1964   'The Historical Background of Cyrus' Decree' (in Hebrew), in *Oz Le-
           David: Qovetz Mehqarim be-Tanakh Muggash le-David Ben Gurion bi-
           Mlot lo Shib'im wa-Sheba' Shanim* (Pirsumey Ha-Hevrah le-Heqer ha-
           Miqra be-Yisrael; ed. Y. Kaufmann *et al.*; Jerusalem: Kiryath Sepher).
1965   'The Inscriptions of Nabunaid: Historical Arrangement', in *Studies
           ...Landsberger* (AS, 16; Chicago: University of Chicago Press): 13-33.
1967   'Temple Cities and Royal Cities in Babylonia and Assyria' (in Hebrew), in
           *Holy War and Martyrology: Lectures Delivered at the Eleventh Convention
           of the Historical Society of Israel, March 1966; Town and Community,
           Lectures Delivered at the Twelfth Convention of the Historical Society of
           Israel–December 1966* (Jerusalem: The Historical Society of Israel): 79-
           205.
1970   'Chronology of the Ancient Near East in the Second Millennium BCE',
           Patriarchs. II. *The World History of the Jewish People* (ed. B. Mazar; Tel-
           Aviv: Massada): 63-101.

1973	'The Historical Inscriptions of Adad-Nirari III', *Iraq* 35: 141-50.

1977 'Observations on Assyrian Historiography', in *Essays on the Ancient Near East in Memory of Jacob Joel Finkelstein* (ed. M. de Jong Ellis; Memoirs of the Connecticut Academy of Arts and Sciences, 19; Hamden, CT: Archon Books): 209-13.

1981 'History and Ideology in the Assyrian Royal Inscriptions', in *Assyrian Royal Inscriptions: New Horizons in Literary, Ideological, and Historical Analysis. Papers of a Symposium Held in Cetona (Siena) June 26–28, 1980* (ed. F.M. Fales; Orientis Antiqui Collectio, 17; Rome: Istituto per l'Oriente, Centro per le Antichità e la Storia dell'Arte del Vicino Oriente): 13-33.

1984 'The Return to Zion' (in Hebrew), in *The History of Eretz Israel. II. Israel and Judah in the Biblical Period: The History* (ed. I. Eph'al; Jerusalem: Keter Publishing House): 251-83.

Talmon, S.

1975 'Ezra and Nehemiah', *IDBSup*, 317-28.

1977 'Return to Zion—Consequences for Our Future' (in Hebrew), *Cathedra* 4: 26-30.

Talshir, D.

1988 'A Reinvestigation of the Linguistic Relationship between Chronicles and Ezra–Nehemiah', *VT* 38: 165-93.

Talshir, Z.

1983 'The Description of the Founding of the Second Temple and its Development' (in Hebrew), in *Isac Leo Seeligmann Volume: Studies in Bible and the Ancient World* (ed. Y. Zakovitch and A. Rofé; Jerusalem: E. Rubinstein): 347-59.

Tawil, H.

1972 *Idioms in Old Aramaic Royal Inscriptions in the Light of Akkadian* (PhD dissertation, Columbia University; Ann Arbor, MI: University Microfilms).

1973 'The End of the Hadad Inscription in Light of Akkadian', *JNES* 32: 477-82.

1974 'Some Literary Elements in the Opening Sections of the Hadad, Zakir and the Nerab II Inscriptions in the Light of East and West Semitic Royal Inscriptions', *Or* ns 43: 40-65.

Thackeray, H.St.-J.

1909–10 'New Light on the book of Jashar', *JTS* 11: 518-32.

Thompson, R. Campbell

1931 *The Prisms of Esarhaddon and of Ashurbanipal: Found at Nineveh 1927–8* (London: British Museum).

Thompson, R. Campbell, and R.W. Hamilton

1932 'The British Museum Excavations on the Temple of Ishtar at Nineveh, 1930–31', *AAA* 19: 55-137.

Thompson, R. Campbell, and M.E.L. Mallowan

1933 'The British Museum Excavations at Nineveh, 1931–32', *AAA* 20: 71-186.

Thureau-Dangin, F.
1919   'Un acte de donation de Mardouk-zâkir-šumi', *RA* 16: 117-56.
1907   *Die sumerischen und akkadischen Königsinschriften* (VAB, 1.1; Leipzig:
            Hinrichs).
1921   *Rituels Accadiens* (Paris: Leroux).
1925   *Les cylinders de Goudéa découverts par Ernest de Sarzec à Tello* (TCL, 8;
            Paris: Musée du Louvre Département des Antiquitiés Orientales).
Tigay, J.H.
1982   *The Evolution of the Gilgamesh Epic* (Philadelphia: University of
            Pennsylvania Press).
Tsafrir, Y.
1977   'The Walls of Jerusalem in the Period of Nehemiah' (in Hebrew), *Cathedra*
            4: 31-42.
Tsevat, M.
1978   'A Window for Baal's House: The Maturing of a God', in *Studies in the
            Bible and the Ancient Near East: Presented to Samuel E. Loewenstamm on
            his Seventieth Birthday* (ed. Y. Avishur and J. Blau; Jerusalem:
            E. Rubenstein): 151-61.
Turner, G.
1970   'Tell Nebi Yūnus: The *ekal mašarti* of Nineveh', *Iraq* 32: 68-85.
Ulshoefer, H.K.
1977   *Nathan's Opposition to David's Intention to Build a Temple in Light of
            Selected Ancient Near Eastern Texts* (PhD dissertation, Boston University;
            Ann Arbor, MI: University Microfilms).
Unal, A.
1988   ' "You Should Build for Eternity": New Light on the Hittite Architects and
            their Works', *JCS* 40: 97-106.
Unger, E.
1938   'Dûr-Šarrukîn', *RLA*, II, 249-52.
1917   *Die Stele des Bel-Harran-Beli-Ussur, ein Denkmal der Zeit Salmanassars
            IV* (Publicationen der Kaiserlicher Osmanischen Museen, 3;
            Konstantinopel: Ahmed Ihsan).
1927   'Der Turm zu Babel', *ZAW* 45: 62-71.
1970   *Babylon—die heilige Stadt, nach der Beschreibung der Babylonier* (Berlin:
            de Gruyter, 2nd edn).
Ungnad, A.
1923   'Schenkungsurkunde des Kurigalzu mar Kadašman-Harbe', *Archiv für
            Keilschriftforschung* 1: 19-23.
1938a   'Datenlisten', *RLA*, II, 131-94.
1938b   'Eponymen', *RLA*, II, 412-57.
Van Seters, J.
1983   *In Search of History: Historiography in the Ancient World and the Origins
            of Biblical History* (New Haven, CT: Yale University Press).
Vanstiphout, H.L.J.
1989   'Enmerkar's Invention of Writing Reconsidered', in *DUMU-E2-DUB-BA-
            A: Studies in Honor of Åke W. Sjöberg* (ed. H. Behrens, *et al.*; Occasional
            Publications of the Samuel Noah Kramer Fund, 11; Philadelphia): 515-524.

Vaux, R. de
1945   'Notes sur le temple de Salomon' (in Hebrew), *Kedem, Studies in Jewish
                Archaeology 2: 48-58.
1971   'The Decrees of Cyrus and Darius on the Rebuilding of the Temple', in
                The Bible and the Ancient Near East (trans. D. McHugh; Garden City, NY:
                Doubleday): 63-96.
Veenhof, K.R.
1985a   'MARI 3 (1984): 42. A No. 1 Rev: 11'f...', *RA* 7: 190.
1985b   'VAS 1 No 32: 24...', *RA* 7: 190-91.
Vries, S.J. de
1988   'Moses and David as Cult Founders in Chronicles' *JBL* 107: 619-139.
Waldman, N.H.
1981   'The Wealth of the Mountain and the Sea: The Background of a Biblical
                Image', *JQR* 71: 176-80.
Walker, C.B.F.
1966   *Material for a Reconstruction of the mīs pî Ritual* (Unpublished thesis,
                Lincoln College, Oxford).
Walker, C.B.F., and S.N. Kramer
1982   'Cuneiform Tablets in the Collection of Lord Binning', *Iraq* 44: 71-86.
Ward, W.W.
1985   'Late Egyptian *'r.t*: The So-Called Upper Room', *JNES* 44: 329-35.
Waterman, L.
1943   'The Damaged "Blueprints" of the Temple of Solomon', *JNES* 2: 284-94.
1947   'The Treasuries of Solomon's Private Chapel', *JNES* 6: 161-63.
1948   'A Rebuttal', *JNES* 7: 54-55.
Weidner, E.
1923   *Politische Dokumente aus Kleinasien: Die Staatsverträge in akkadischer
                Sprache aus dem Archiv von Boghazköi* (Boghazköi-Studien, 8, 9;
                Leipzig: Hinrichs).
1932–33   'Assur 19763', in W. Schwenzen, 'Das Nationalheiligtum des assyrischen
                Reiches: Die Baugeschichte des Aššur-Tempels Ehursagkurkurra
                (Fortsetzung)', *AfO* 8: 34-45.
1954–55   'Säulen aus Nahur', *AfO* 17: 145-46.
1957–58   'Die Feldzüge und Bauten Tiglatpilesers I', *AfO* 18: 342-60.
1959   *Die Inschriften Tukulti-Ninurtas I. und seiner Nachfolger* (AfOB, 12;
                Graz: E. Weidner).
1963   'Die Masse von Esagil und Ezida', *AfO* 20: 116, Tafeln VII, VIII.
Weiher, E. von
1984   'Marduk-apla-uṣur und Nabû-šum-iškun in einem spätbabylonischen
                Fragment aus Uruk', *Baghdader Mitteilungen* 15: 197-224.
Weimar, P.
1988   'Sinai und Schöpfung, Komposition und Theologie der priesterschrift-
                lichen Sinaigeschichte', *RB* 93: 337-85.
Weinfeld, M.
1962   'The Change in the Concept of Divinity and Cult in the Book of
                Deuteronomy' (in Hebrew), *Tarbiz* 31: 1-17.

1970   'The Covenant of Grant in the Old Testament and in the Ancient Near East', *JAOS* 90: 184-203.

1972   *Deuteronomy and the Deuteronomic School* (Oxford: Clarendon Press).

1972b   '*Habbērȋ wĕhaḥeseḏ*—The Terms and their Development in Israel and in the Ancient World' (in Hebrew), *Lĕš* 3: 85-103.

1973   'Covenant Terminology in the Ancient Near East and its Influence on the West', *JAOS* 93: 190-99.

1976   'The Loyalty Oath in the Ancient Near East' (in Hebrew), *Shnaton*: 51-88.

1979   'Mesopotamian Eschatological Prophecies' (in Hebrew), *Shnaton* 3: 262-76.

1980   'Theology and Wisdom in Mesopotamian Tradition of the Third Millennium' (in Hebrew), *Shnaton* 4: 285-87.

1981   'Sabbath, Temple and the Enthronement of the Lord—The Problem of the Sitz im Leben of Genesis 1.1–2.3', *Festschrift Cazelles* (AOAT, 212; Neukirchen–Vluyn: Neukirchener Verlag): 501-12.

1982   'Instructions for Temple Visitors in the Bible and in Ancient Egypt', in *Egyptological Studies* (ed. S. Israelit-Groll; Scripta Hierosolymitana, 28; Jerusalem: Magnes Press): 224-50.

1982a   'The Counsel of the "Elders" to Rehoboam and its Implications', *Maarav* 3: 27-53.

1982b   'A Comparison of a Passage from the Šamaš Hymn (lines 65–78) with Psalm 107', in *Vorträge gehalten auf der 28. Rencontre Assyriologique Internationale in Wien. 6.–10. Juli 1981* (AfOB, 19; Horn: Ferdinand Berger & Söhne): 275-79.

1983a   'Zion and Jerusalem as Religious and Political Capital: Ideology and Utopia', in *The Poet and the Historian. Essays in Literary and Historical Biblical Criticism* (ed. R.E. Friedman; Chico, CA: Scholars Press): 75-115.

1983b   'Social and Cultic Institutions in the Priestly Source against their Ancient Near Eastern Background', in *Proceedings of the Eighth World Congress of Jewish Studies, Jerusalem, August 16–21, 1981: Panel Sessions, Bible Studies and Hebrew Language* (Jerusalem: World Union of Jewish Studies): 95-129.

1985   *Justice and Righteousness in Israel and the Nations—Equality and Freedom in Ancient Israel in Light of Social Justice in the Ancient Near East* (in Hebrew) (Jerusalem: Magnes Press).

1988   'Initiation of Political Friendship in Ebla and its Later Developments', in *Wirtschaft und Gesellschaft von Ebla: Akten der Internationalen Tagung Heidelburg 4.–7. November 1986* (ed. H. Hauptmann and H. Waetzold; Heidelberger Studien zum Alten Orient, 2; Heidelberg: Heidelberger Orientverlag): 345-348.

Weiser, A.
1962   *The Psalms: A Commentary* (trans. H. Hartwell; OTL; London: SCM Press).

Weissbach, F.H.
1903   *Babylonische Miscellen* (WVDOG, 4; Leipzig: Hinrichs).

1918	'Zu den Inschriften der Säle im Palaste Sargons II. von Assyrien', *ZDMG* 72: 161-87.

Wellhausen, J.
1963	*Die Composition des Hexateuchs und der historischen Bücher des Alten Testaments* (Berlin: de Gruyter, 4th edn).

Westenholz, A.
1979	'The Old Akkadian Empire in Contemporary Opinion', in *Power and Propaganda: A Symposium on Ancient Empires* (ed. M.T. Larsen; Mesopotamia, Copenhagen Studies in Assyriology, 7; Copenhagen: Akademisk Forlag): 107-24.

Wetzel, F., and F.H. Weissbach
1938	*Das Hauptheiligtum des Marduk in Babylon, Esagila und Etemenanki* (WVDOG, 59; Leipzig: Hinrichs).

Wheeler, S.B.
1977	*Prayer and Temple in the Dedication Speech of Solomon, 1 Kings 8.14-61* (PhD dissertation, Columbia University; Ann Arbor, MI: University Microfilms).

Whybray, R.N.
1968	*The Succession Narrative: A Study of II Samuel 9–20; I Kings 1 and 2* (SBT, 2.9; London: SCM Press).

Wightman, G.J.
1990	'The Myth of Solomon', *BASOR* 277/278: 5-22.

Wilcke, C.
1975	'Formale Gesichtspunkte in der Sumerischen Literatur', in *Sumerological Studies in Honor of Thorkild Jacobsen on his Seventieth Birthday, June 7, 1964* (ed. S.J. Lieberman; AS, 20; Chicago: University of Chicago Press): 205-316.

Williamson, H.G.M.
1976	'The Accession of Solomon in the Book of Chronicles', *VT* 26: 351-61.
1977	*Israel in the Books of Chronicles* (Cambridge: Cambridge University Press).
1982	*1 and 2 Chronicles* (NCB; Grand Rapids: Eerdmans).

Winckler, H.
1889	*Die Keilschrifttexte Sargons nach den Papierabklatschen und Originalen neu Herausgegeben*, I, II (Leipzig: Eduard Pfeiffer).

Wiseman, D.J.
1952	'A New Stela of Aššur-naṣir-pal', *Iraq* 14: 24-44.
1972	'A Babylonian Architect?', *AnSt* 22: 141-47.
1982	' "Is it peace"—Covenant and Diplomacy', *VT* 32: 311-26.
1983	*Nebuchadrezzar and Babylon* (The Schweich Lectures of the British Academy, 1983; Oxford: The British Academy, Oxford University Press).

Wright, G.E.
1948	'Dr Waterman's View concerning the Solomonic Temple', *JNES*: 53.

Würthwein, E.
1977	*Das erste Buch der Könige, Kapitel 1–16* (ATD, 11.1; Göttingen: Vandenhoeck & Ruprecht).

376 I Have Built You an Exalted House

Younger, K.L.
1986   'Panammuwa and Bar-Rakib: Two Structural Analyses', *JANESCU* 18: 99-103.
Zablocka, J., and P.R. Berger
1969   'Ein vollständigeres Duplikat zur Nebukadnezar II-Inschrift, *VAB* 4, Nr. 46'; *Or* ns 38: 122-25.
Zaccagnini, C.
1983   'Patterns of Mobility among Ancient Near Eastern Craftsmen', *JNES* 42: 245-64.
Zeitlin, S.
1938–39   'Hanukkah, its Origin and its Significance', *JQR* 39: 1-36.
Zelevsky, S.
1973   'YHWH's Revelation to Solomon at Gibeon', (in Hebrew), *Tarbiz* 42: 215-58.
Zevit, Z.
1985   'Clio, I Presume', *BASOR* 260: 71-81.
Zuidhof, A.
1972   'King Solomon's Molten Sea and π', *BA* 45: 179-84.

INDEXES

INDEX OF BIBLICAL REFERENCES

INDEX OF EXTRA-BIBLICAL SOURCES

SUMERIAN

SECOND TEMPLE AND RABBINIC JEWISH SOURCES

SECOND TEMPLE AND RABBINIC JEWISH SOURCES